CHILDREN AND YOUTH
Social Problems and Social Policy

THE LEGAL RIGHTS OF CHILDREN

Introduction by
Sanford N. Katz

ARNO PRESS
A New York Times Company
New York – 1974

Reprint Edition 1974 by Arno Press Inc.

Legal Rights of Children was reprinted from a copy in The University of Illinois Library

CHILDREN AND YOUTH
Social Problems and Social Policy
ISBN for complete set: 0-405-05940-X
See last pages of this volume for titles.

Manufactured in the United States of America

Library of Congress Cataloging in Publication Data
Main entry under title:

The legal rights of children.

(Children and youth: social problems and social policy)
CONTENTS: Wilcox, S. M. Legal rights of children, reprinted from U. S. Bureau of Education circulars of information, no. 3, 1880.--Kelley, F. On some changes in the legal status of the child since Blackstone, reprinted from the International review, v. 13, 1882.--Carrigan, T. C. The law & the American child, reprinted from the Pedagogical seminary, v. 18, 1911.--United States. Children's Bureau. The children's charter, 1930, reprinted from the Story of the White House Conferences on Children and Youth, 1967.--Foster, H. H. Children and the law, reprinted from Family law quarterly, v. 2, 1968.--Kleinfeld, A. J. The balance of power among infants, their parents and the state, pt. 1-3, reprinted from Family law quarterly, 1970-71.
1. Children--Law--United States. I. Series.
KF479.L43 346'.73'013 74-1692
ISBN 0-405-05968-X

CONTENTS

Introduction

The purpose of this volume is to preserve a collection of articles and to make them readily available. In addition it is to illustrate broadly by way of its chronological presentation the place of children in American law during the nineteenth and part of the twentieth centuries.

I shall refrain from describing the breadth of the book in terms of the "development" of children's rights, the "expansion" of those rights or their "widening." These words connote movement in the direction of growth and in the context of the subject matter this would have a further connotation of being desirable. The truth of the matter is that there has been no radical change in the child's situation in American law or indeed in the thinking about his condition for over a century.

The Bureau of Education piece that leads these selections begins:

> "Within the last few years associations have been formed in various localities having for their object the prevention of cruelty to children and the enforcement of their legal rights, and there appears to have been a disposition on the part of the several states in which such associations have been organized to aid them by appropriate legislation wherever the same appeared to be necessary.
>
> The operations of these associations seem to have awakened public interest in the subject, and frequent inquiries have been made as to the rights, liabilities, and disabilities of children, by what means they may be protected against any invasion of their rights, and who may act for those who are generally understood to be incapable of acting for themselves."

That this should have been written in 1880 should startle those crusading for children's rights almost a century later. Is the establishment of child advocacy centers, children's lobbies and children's defense funds new? One begins to get a feeling of déjà vu.

In 1974 we are still returning to the early Anglo-American law to show that what is now desired is a different approach. For this reason the early documents have value other than historical. They are useful for comparative purposes.

Laws are not made in a vacuum and laws relating to children are no different. They reflect social conditions and attitudes. If we are serious about providing meaningful protection for children in their homes, in schools, in courts and in the community as each of the selections proposes, we must do more than study this book or repeat in contemporary terms the messages being transmitted. Much of the contents of this book can be useful to those seeking to promote action for children's rights. Indeed, the blueprint for such action could be the statement of the White House Conference on Child Health and Protection in 1930.

April 17, 1974

Sanford N. Katz
Professor of Law
Boston College Law School

CIRCULARS OF INFORMATION

OF THE

BUREAU OF EDUCATION.

No. 3—1880.

LEGAL RIGHTS OF CHILDREN.

WASHINGTON:
GOVERNMENT PRINTING OFFICE.
1880.

141–142

CONTENTS.

144

LETTER.

DEPARTMENT OF THE INTERIOR,
BUREAU OF EDUCATION,
April 14, 1880.

SIR: The recent prolonged hard times have impressed educators anew with the great perils to public welfare arising from the neglect of the rights and privileges of children. Never before have those among us who are interested in education come to so lively an appreciation of the extent to which vice, pauperism, and crime in all their forms—with all their perils to the individual, family, State, and nation, or to labor and capital—are traceable to the misuse of the rights and privileges of childhood. The necessity of universal education is enforced by new arguments. A considerable number of States have sought to secure it by compulsory education, so called, but the manner in which it has been attempted has not always been cordially received, and the end sought has not always been attained. Important societies have been organized to prevent cruelty to children. Truant laws have been enacted and truant police employed with good results. Measures to prevent the employment in different industries of children that have not attended school a specified period of a given year have been found useful, and charitable visitation has increased the benefits of instruction among poor children by inquiries as to their school attendance and by providing food and clothing. More and more has agitation turned attention to the laws of the different States: this Office has been very much taxed in giving information of this character; teachers, parents, school officers, philanthropists, statesmen, have sought to find out what the laws now provide, to compare those of one State with another, and to ascertain what modifications are desirable. I have therefore had prepared, from the collection of school laws in this Office and from the unequalled collection of statutes and decisions of States in the law department of the Congressional Library, a summary of the legal rights of children. The difficult task has been executed by S. M. Wilcox, esq., a careful student of law, who has had the advantages of personal observation of these laws in New England, Pennsylvania, and this District. It will be observed how deeply embedded in the legal foundation of the several States is the child's right to education, and how the universal recognition of this right as obligatory would increase the efficiency of instruction in every State throughout the land. The papers are in two parts, the first treating of the rights of the children in general, including education, and the second giving a comparative view of the systems of education in the different States established to give force and effect to those rights, and thus assure the welfare of the individual and the State.

I have the honor to recommend these papers for publication, and am, sir, very respectfully, your obedient servant,

JOHN EATON,
Commissioner.

Hon. CARL SCHURZ,
Secretary of the Interior.

Approved, and publication ordered.

C. SCHURZ,
Secretary.

LEGAL RIGHTS OF CHILDREN.

Within the last few years associations have been formed in various localities having for their object the prevention of cruelty to children and the enforcement of their legal rights, and there appears to have been a disposition on the part of the several States in which such associations have been organized to aid them by appropriate legislation wherever the same appeared to be necessary.

The operations of these associations seem to have awakened public interest in the subject, and frequent inquiries have been made as to the rights, liabilities, and disabilities of children, by what means they may be protected against any invasion of their rights, and who may act for those who are generally understood to be incapable of acting for themselves.

The several legal text books which treat of this subject were prepared more for the lawyer than the general reader, and to meet the general purport of the inquiries made it has been thought best to prepare a statement of certain general rules, sanctioned by judicial decisions and approved by the best authors, with a reference to such of the State statutes as bear upon the subject, but omitting any extended discussion of the principles involved in the decisions, which, upon various points, are conflicting.

In doing this, free use has been made of the various text books. The latest revisions of the State statutes and many decisions have been examined, with the object of furnishing within a reasonable compass the general information sought for and with such reference to the authorities as might be of assistance to those who are desirous of making a more extended examination of the questions referred to.

THE CHILD FROM THE BEGINNING OF ITS BEING.

Mr. Tyler commences his elaborate treatise upon the Law of Infancy as follows:

> Man, upon his entrance into the world, is entirely incapable of protecting himself; and his natural powers and faculties, both physical and moral, require a number of years for their complete development. Probably there is no creature so helpless at birth as the human being. The law has, therefore, wisely imposed upon man, for a limited period, certain disabilities, and endued him with certain privileges, which are implied in the term infant.

But the law does not wait until the actual birth of the child before it extends its protection. Under the civil law an infant in ventre sa mere was, for the benefit of the child, reputed in the same condition as if born, and the common law is in this respect the same. Both in England and in this country, it is well settled that an infant in ventre sa mere is deemed to be in esse, or in being, for the purpose of taking a remainder, or any other estate or interest which is for his benefit, whether by descent, devise, or under the statute of distribution. Under the law of England a bill may be filed in its favor, a court of equity will grant an injunction to protect its rights, and the destruction of such a child is murder; and in most of our own States the destruction of such a child by any means is made a felony, unless where such act is necessary to preserve the life of the mother.

The common law doctrine as to such infants seems to have been recognized to its fullest extent in this country, although it is generally regulated by statute, but such statutes will, in most cases, be found to be reënactments of the common law, and where they vary from that it is in extending the common law rights of such infants.

The child, then, is to be considered in being from the time of conception, when it is for the benefit of the child that it should be so considered. As respects the rights of third persons, or those claiming through the infant, if the child should be born dead or in such an early stage of pregnancy as to be incapable of living, it is to be considered as never having been conceived or born. Children born within six months after conception are presumed to be incapable of living, and therefore cannot take and transmit property by descent unless they actually survive long enough to rebut that legal presumption.

When the mother dies before the birth of the child, and the latter is delivered by the cæsarean operation, it is considered in existence before its birth, for its own benefit to take the estate of the mother by descent, but not for the benefit of the father to enable him to hold as tenant by the curtesy. Tyler on Inf. §§ 151 to 158.

WHO ARE INFANTS.

By the common law no person acquires fully all his political and civil rights until he is 21 years of age, at which time his infancy terminates. This rule, however, does not prevail in all systems of jurisprudence, for in Spain and some other countries emancipation does not take place until the age of 25.

By the common law the period of emancipation is the same for both sexes. In the American States the common law rule prevails, except where it has been changed by statute. In Vermont, Ohio, Illinois, and Nebraska females are considered of full age at 18. In Maryland females of that age may dispose of their real estate by will, and in Texas a female under 21 who shall marry in accordance with the laws of the State is deemed of full age after such marriage. R. S. Vt. 1863, chap. 72, § 1; *Sparhawk* vs. *Buell's Adm.* 9 Vt. Rep. 41; *Stevenson* vs. *Westfall*, 18 Ill.

209; 1 R. S. Ohio, ch. 56, § 1; Md. Code, art. 93, § 300; R. S. Neb. ch. 22, § 1; Oldham & White's Digest, Texas, art. 1400.

DISPOSAL OF CHATTELS BY WILL.

While, as a general rule, an infant labors under certain disabilities, it is not our purpose to give a detailed account of these disabilities, but rather to give some idea of the privileges granted and guards thrown around him by the law. The adult may do many things in reference to which the infant is either forbidden to act, or, if not forbidden, can only act under certain well defined legal restrictions, but the tendency of the law in many respects has been to make the privilege the rule and the disability the exception.

While, as we have seen, an infant may take and hold property, real and personal, yet, by the common law, he cannot make a will of lands. But by the common law an infant may make a testament of chattels; if a male, at the age of 14, and if a female, at the age of 12 years. The civil law gave the infant the power to dispose of chattels by will at the age of 17.

In this country the matter has been very generally regulated by statute. The rule of the civil law has been adopted in Connecticut and Illinois. In Vermont, Massachusetts, New Hampshire, Ohio, Pennsylvania, Maine, Indiana, New Jersey, North Carolina, Mississippi, Nebraska, Texas, and Florida none under full age can devise either real or personal property. In Maryland, Rhode Island, Missouri, Oregon, and Virginia, wills of personal estate may be made after 18. In New York the period is 18 for males and 16 for females. In South Carolina an infant of 18 years may make a valid will of personalty by conforming to certain statute provisions.

VOID AND VOIDABLE ACTS.

In *Cecil* vs. *Salsbury*, 2 Vern. Ch. R. 224, Lord Mansfield is reported to have said:

> Miserable, indeed, must the condition of minors be; excluded from the society and commerce of the world; deprived of necessaries, education, employment, and many advantages; if they could do *no* binding acts. Great inconvenience must arise to *others* if they were *bound* by no act. The law, therefore, at the same time that it protects their imbecility from injury through their own imprudence, enables them to do binding acts for their own benefit and, without prejudice to themselves, for the benefit of others.

In an early case in Massachusetts Justice Wilde says:

> In all cases the benefit of the infant is the great point to be regarded; the object of the law being to protect his imbecility and indiscretion from injury, through his own imprudence, or by the craft of others. *Oliver* vs. *Houdlet*, 13 Mass. 237.

This protection is afforded by considering his acts as not binding in certain cases and allowing him to rescind his contracts with certain exceptions. There are two degrees in which his acts are not binding:

first, where they are held to be wholly void, and, second, where they are defeasible, at the election of the infant.

A void act never is or can be binding upon any one, and it is incapable of being confirmed. There is some uncertainty in the books as to the line of distinction between the void and voidable acts of an infant, with an apparent inclination in the courts to narrow the first and enlarge the latter. *Tucker* vs. *Moreland*, 10 Peters, 58.

The reason of this seems to be that, as the principle is the protection of the infant against his own weakness, if this protection can be secured to him without inflicting a detriment on innocent persons, such infliction must be unnecessary and unjust. To consider any acts of an infant absolutely void might operate to his own protection, but it would in many cases seriously affect the rights of third persons in no wise implicated in the infant's transactions, and might not unfrequently be prejudicial to the infant himself.

This is strongly enforced by Bingham, and his reasoning is in the main approved by Tyler. Bingham on Infancy, p. 14; Tyler on Infancy, § 10.

Any attempted enumeration of the acts which have been held void or voidable, or a discussion of the mode in which the infant may avoid or ratify and confirm his voidable acts, is not within the purview of the present inquiry. The precedents and decisions in these cases are numerous, easily accessible, and of sufficient variety to satisfy any reasonable inquirer.

The privilege conferred by law upon infancy is a personal one, and, as a general rule, no one but the infant himself or his legal representatives can avoid his voidable acts, deeds, and contracts, for while living he ought to be the exclusive judge of the propriety of the exercise of a personal privilege intended for his benefit, and when dead they alone should interfere who legally represent him. Tyler, § 19; *Hyer* vs. *Hyatt*, 3 Cranch C. C. 276.

The indulgence allowed by the law to infants, being for their own security, cannot be taken advantage of by persons of full age and legal capacity to contract. Hence, although the infant may avoid his contract, yet it is binding on a person of full age who contracts with him. "Every person deals with an infant at arm's-length, at his own risk, and with a party for whom the law has a jealous watchfulness." Story on Contracts, § 13.

All parties dealing with an infant, whether as co-contractors with him or as adverse parties, are liable upon such contracts, co-contractors in any event and adverse parties until the contract is disaffirmed by the infant.

As to the time when the voidable acts may be disaffirmed, the rule laid down is that all executory contracts and all contracts respecting personal property may be avoided by the infant either before or upon his coming of age, but conveyances of realty cannot be avoided until he attains full age. Tyler, § 30.

But an infant cannot retain the benefits of his contract and thus affirm it, and yet plead infancy to avoid the payment of the purchase money. *Henry* vs. *Root*, 33 N. Y. Rep. 526.

If the contract has been fully executed on both sides, and the infant disaffirm and reclaim what he has paid, he must restore the consideration received. *Bigelow* vs. *Kinney*, 3 Vt. 353; *Williams* vs. *Norris*, 2 Littell's R. 157; *Hill* vs. *Anderson*, Sme. & Mar. 216; *Grace* vs. *Hale*, 2 Humph. 27; *Smith* vs. *Evans*, 5 ib. 70; *Badger* vs. *Phinney*, 15 Mass. 359; *Edgerton* vs. *Wolf*, 6 Gray's [Mass.] Reps. 453.

WHEN INFANTS MAY BE WITNESSES.

An infant may be a witness if proved to have sufficient discretion and understanding of the obligation of an oath. The test universally is that the child feel the binding obligation of an oath from the general course of his religious education. The effect of an oath upon the conscience of a child should arise from religious feelings of a permanent nature, and not merely from instructions confined to the nature of an oath, recently communicated for the purpose of the trial. *Rex* vs. *Williams*, 32 E. C. L. 524. But in one case where a child 9 years old, though very intelligent, did not understand the nature of an oath nor the moral penalty of false swearing, the court instructed her on the spot and then allowed her to be sworn. *Jenner's case*, 2 City Hall R. (N. Y.) 147. And children of 10, 9, 7, and even 5 years of age have been held competent. *Regina* vs. *Perkins*, 38 E. C. L. 236; *Commonwealth* vs. *Hutchins*, 10 Mass. 225; *State* vs. *Whittier*, 21 Maine, 341.

But the question rests mainly in the discretion of the court. The adverse party may require that a witness of tender years shall be examined as to his understanding of the nature and obligation of an oath, and, before the child is admitted to testify, the judge must be satisfied that the child feels the binding obligation of an oath. *People* vs. *McNair*, 21 Wend. 608.

MARRIAGE.

The common law age of consent to marriage is 14 for males and 12 for females. Contracts of marriage, where both parties are of the age of consent, if executed, are as binding as if made by adults; but if either party is under that age, *both* have the privilege of avoiding, a principle not found in any other contracts of infants.

The common law rule is in force in New York and Texas and in most of the other States. In Maine, Vermont, Mississippi, and Missouri males under 21 and females under 18 are forbidden to marry without the consent of the parents. In Ohio the age is 18 for males and 14 for females. In Indiana and Illinois the age is 17 for males and 14 for females. In Wisconsin, Minnesota, and Oregon, males 18 and females 15. In Michigan and Nebraska, males 18, females 16. In Iowa and North Carolina, 16 and 14. Maryland imposes a fine for performing the marriage ceremony, where the parties are under 21 for males and 16 for females, without the consent of the parents.[1]

In most of the States the law requires publication of banns or a license, and as a general rule the consent of the parents is required where the parties, or either of them, are under full age.

In the absence of any specific provision declaring marriages not celebrated in the prescribed mode as between parties under certain ages absolutely void, it is held that all marriages regularly made according to the common law are valid and binding, although had in violation of specific statute regulations. 2 Kent's Com. 90, 91; 2 Greenl. Ev. § 460; *Londonderry* vs. *Chester*, 2 N. H. 268; *Hantz* vs. *Sealy*, 6 Binney (Pa.), 405; *Milford* vs. *Worcester*, 7 Mass. 48; *Parton* vs. *Hervey*, 1 Gray, 119

The punitive provisions of the statutes are treated as directory only upon ministers and magistrates, and to prevent, as far as possible, by penalties on them, the solemnization of marriages when the prescribed conditions and formalities have not been complied with. See on this subject Tyler, §§ 81 to 84, 91, 92.

THE STATUTE OF LIMITATIONS.

It is a maxim of the law that no laches or neglect is imputable to an infant during his minority, because he is not supposed to be cognizant

[1] The Lyon Médical gives the following as the legal marriageable ages for men and women in different countries of Europe:

Country.	For men.	For women.
	Years.	*Years.*
Austria	14	14
Belgium	18	15
France	18	15
Germany	18	14
Greece	14	12
Hungary (Orthodox and Catholic)	14	12
Hungary (Protestant)	18	15
Italy	18	15
Portugal	14	12
Roumania	18	16
Russia	18	16
Saxony	18	16
Spain	14	12
Switzerland	14 to 20	12 to 17

of his rights or capable of enforcing them. *Ware* vs. *Brush*, 1 McLean, 533. When, however, the matter is regulated by statute, and there is no exception or saving in favor of any incapacity, laches will bar an infant the same as an adult. *Rayner* vs. *Watford*, 2 Dev. (N. C.) Law R. 338.

By the common law the statute of limitations does not run against an infant, but this is now regulated by statute, and the statute will run against infants unless they are specially exempted. Angell on Lim. § 194.

By the English law the statute does not run against infants in personal actions; that is, the computation does not commence until the infancy terminates.

The same is true in Vermont, Massachusetts, Rhode Island, New Jersey, Pennsylvania, Maryland, District of Columbia, Virginia, North Carolina, South Carolina, Georgia, Florida, Mississippi, Louisiana, Kentucky, Missouri, Arkansas, Texas, Ohio, Indiana, Illinois, Michigan, California, Iowa, Nebraska, and Kansas.

In England real actions may be brought in ten years after the minority ceases, and the time is the same in Maine, Rhode Island, New York, Pennsylvania, Delaware, Virginia, South Carolina, Florida, Kentucky, Ohio, and Michigan.

The term is five years in New Hampshire, Massachusetts, Connecticut, New Jersey, Arkansas, Wisconsin, and California.

The term is three years in North Carolina, Alabama, Tennessee, and Missouri; and in Minnesota and Oregon one year.

In Maine personal actions must be brought in six months after arriving at full age; in New Hampshire, New York, Minnesota, and Oregon, in one year; in Delaware, Alabama, and Tennessee, in three years, and in Connecticut, in four years on bonds and specialties and in three years in other personal actions.

In the other States the statute does not begin to run until full age. Tyler, chap. 10.

The statute does not bar a trust estate, but the doctrine holds good only as between the trustee and cestui que trust, and not between them on the one side and third persons on the other. *Huntingdon* vs. *Huntingdon*, 3 P. Williams, 310; *Lyon* vs. *Marclay*, 1 Watts, 275; *White* vs. *White*, 1 Md. Ch. 53; *Thomas* vs. *Brinsfield*, 7 Geo. R. 154.

When the statute makes no exception in favor of infants, the court of chancery will make none. *Demarest* vs. *Wyncoop*, 3 Johns. Ch. 146.

LIABILITY OF INFANTS TO SUIT.

I.—Civil suits.

Whenever an infant may be intrusted with an office, it follows as a matter of course that he is liable to the consequences of his acts in the exercise of such office. Tyler, § 121.

Wherever the infant is allowed to make a binding contract or perform a valid act, he is liable to an action for non-performance or default, the same as an adult. *Railway* vs. *Coombe*, 3 Excheq. R. 569; *Railway* vs. *McMichael*, 5 ib. 126; *U. S.* vs. *Bainbridge*, 1 Mason, 71.

In all suits brought against infants, whom the law supposes to be incapable of understanding and managing their own affairs, the duty of watching over their interests devolves in a considerable degree upon the court. They defend by guardian appointed by the court, who is usually the nearest relative not concerned in point of interest in the matter in question. U. S. Supreme Ct. *Bank* vs. *Ritchie*, 8 Peters, 128.

Infants are liable for torts and injuries of a private nature and for all wrongs committed by them the same as adults. If the tort is committed with force, the infant is liable at any age. In such cases the intention is not regarded, and a lunatic is as liable to compensate in damages as a man in his right mind. Reeves' Dom. Rel. 256; *Baxter* vs. *Brush*, 29 Vt. 465; *Scott* vs. *Watson*, 46 Maine, 362; *Cutts* vs. *Phalen*, 2 Howard (U. S.), 376; *Vasse* vs. *Smith*, 6 Cranch, 226.

The general rule, however, is that the act must be wholly tortious in order to charge the infant. *Jennings* vs. *Rundell*, 8 Tenn. R. 337; *West* vs. *Moore*, 14 Vt. 447; *Merrill* vs. *Aden*, 19 Vt. 505; *People* vs. *Kendall*, 25 Wend. 399.

When the injury happened through unskilfulness, want of knowledge, discretion, or judgment, infancy will be a bar. *Campbell* vs. *Stokes*, 2 Wend. 137.

In New York it has been held that exploding fire crackers by an infant in the public streets of a city is unlawful, and if any damage to persons or property results therefrom the wrongdoer is liable to compensate the sufferer, and his infancy is no protection. *Conklin* vs. *Thompson*, 29 Barbour, 218.

In Massachusetts it has been held that an infant who hires a horse to go to a place agreed upon, but goes to another, is liable in tort for an unlawful conversion the same as an adult, but in Pennsylvania the reverse is held. *Homer* vs. *Thwing*, 3 Pick. 492; *Penrose* vs. *Curren*, 3 Rawle, 351; *Wilt* vs. *Walsh*, 6 Watts, 9; see also *Fish* vs. *Ferris*, 5 Duer, 49.

An infant who obtains property upon a representation that he is of full age is liable in an action of tort for damages or the recovery of the property. *Eckstein* vs. *Franks*, 1 Daily, 334; *Badger* vs. *Phinney*, 13 Mass. 345; *Cutts* vs. *Phalen*, 2 How. 376.

In cases of fraud, infancy is no defence in equity. Tyler, § 126.

An infant has been held liable in trespass for having procured another to commit an assault (*Sikes* vs. *Johnson*, 16 Mass. 389), but Chitty says an infant cannot be a trespasser by prior or subsequent consent, but only by his own act (1 Chitty's Pl. 7th Am. ed. 86), and an infant is not responsible for the negligence of one acting as his servant. *Robbins* vs. *Mount*, 33 How. Pr. Rep. 24.

II.—As to crimes.

Infants who have attained the years of discretion are regarded in law as capable of committing crimes the same as adults, and may be prosecuted and punished accordingly.

By the ancient Saxon law 12 years was established for the age of possible discretion. Between 12 and 14 one might or might not be guilty of a crime, according to his capacity or incapacity. Under 12 he could not be guilty in will; after 14 he could not be supposed innocent of any capital crime he had in fact committed.

In the absence of statutory provisions the court will look not so much to the age of the delinquent as to his strength of understanding and judgment. For, as has been said, "one lad at 10 years of age may have as much cunning as another of 14; and in these cases the maxim is Malitia supplet ætatem, "malice supplies the want of age." Tyler, § 129.

As a general rule, however, infants of less than 7 years cannot be punished as criminals. Before that age they are not in law considered as possessed of sufficient reason to be accountable or answerable for their acts, and it is only from 14 that the law holds them entirely responsible.

Under 7 the presumption of right is that one cannot have discretion, and no averment must be received against that presumption. Over 7 and under 14 he is prima facie not guilty; yet, if it appear by strong circumstances and pregnant evidence that he had discretion to judge between good and evil, judgment even of death may be given against him. *Rex* vs. *Owen*, 19 E. C. L. 493; *Commonwealth* vs. *McKeagy*, 1 Ashmead, 248; *State* vs. *Aaron*, 1 Southard, 231; *State* vs. *Doherty*, 2 Overton, 80; *Reniger* vs. *Fogossa*, Plowden, 19, note; see also Tyler, §§ 121–131.

This may be taken as the established rule where it has not been modified by statute, as it has been in some of the States. In Alabama, infants under 12 cannot be guilty of a crime or misdemeanor, and in California the age is fixed at 14.

All the books agree that where an act is denounced as a crime, even of felony or treason, by a general statute, it extends as well to infants if above 14 years, as to others. *People* vs. *Kendall*, 25 Wend. 399.

LIABILITY FOR NECESSARIES.

A husband is by law bound to support his wife, and if he refuse or neglect to provide her with necessaries suitable to his means and condition or so conduct himself towards her as to justify her in leaving him, or if, without reasonable cause, he drive her from his house, he thereby invests her with the right to pledge his credit for such necessaries.

By the common law parents are bound to maintain their children during their minority, and the same obligation is recognized in the civil law. They are entitled to the earnings of the infant, but it will be found that the rule of liability for necessaries in the case of parent and child is different from that enforced as between husband and wife.

There are cases in which it was held that the duty of a parent to maintain his offspring was a perfect common law duty; and that a stranger might furnish necessaries for the child and recover of the parent compensation therefor, when there was a clear and palpable omission of duty on the part of the parent in supplying his minor child with necessaries. *In re Rider*, 11 Paige, 188; *Van Valkenburgh* vs. *Watson*, 13 Johns. 480; *Edwards* vs. *Davies*, 16 Johns. 285; *Urmston* vs. *Newcombe*, 31 E. C. L. 393. But it may be noted that in several of these cases the parent was not charged.

Whether the fact that a father turns away his child from home, or neglects to provide for him, or so cruelly treats him that he cannot remain under the paternal roof, is sufficient to make the father responsible to any one supplying the child under such circumstances seems to be in doubt.

In a leading case in Connecticut the court says:

> Parents are bound by law to maintain, protect, and educate their legitimate children during their infancy. This duty rests in the father, but because the father has abandoned his duty and trust, by putting his child out of his protection, he cannot thereby exonerate himself from its maintenance, education, and support. The duty remains, and the law will enforce its performance, or there must be a failure of justice. The father having forced his child abroad to seek sustenance under such circumstances, sends a credit along with him, and shall not be permitted to say it was furnished without his consent or against his will. *Stanton* vs. *Wilson*, 3 Day, 37.

But in a subsequent case this decision was commented upon and the doctrine denied. *Finch* vs. *Finch*, 22 Conn. 411. And in New York the doctrine would seem to have been avowed, as against the earlier cases, that there is no legal obligation on a parent to maintain his child independent of the statutes. *Raymond* vs. *Loyle*, 10 Barbour, 483.

In *Gordon* vs. *Potter*, 17 Vt. 350, Redfield, J., says:

> I know there are some cases and dicta of judges, or of elementary writers, which seem to justify the conclusion that the parent may be made liable for necessaries for his child, even against his own will. But an examination of all the cases upon this subject will not justify any such conclusion.

In England the parent may by statute be compelled to support a minor child, and it is there held that the only remedy in case the child is abandoned to destitution is that pointed out by the statute. *Mortimer* vs. *Wright*, 6 Meeson & Welsby, 482. And the law is declared to be well settled that without some contract, express or implied, the father is not liable for necessaries. *Shelton* vs. *Springett*, 20 E. L. and Eq. 281; *Baker* vs. *Keene*, 3 E. C. L. 449.

In this country the laws of the several States impose the duty of support of minor children upon the parents, and they also make it the duty of the children to support their parents when they are of ability and the parent is in need. They provide the mode for enforcing the liability in either case, and the tendency of the decisions is in the same direction as the English. It may therefore be now taken as the rule that, in order to charge the father on his son's contract for necessaries, the same circumstances must be shown as would be sufficient to charge an uncle, brother, or any third person; that is, there must be an express or implied agency. Tyler, § 64.

But in order that an infant may not be forced into a position where, whatever his need, he might not be able to obtain food, shelter, or raiment, the law has adopted a rule, which is regarded and treated as an exception to the general rule, that an infant may make a valid contract for necessaries, and such contract is neither void nor voidable.

It is said that the obligations of infants to pay for necessaries arise, not so much by virtue of a contract so to do as on the ground of an implied legal liability, based upon the necessity of their situation, precisely in the same manner as with idiots and lunatics, who are absolutely incompetent to contract; yet in both cases, it being necessary for the parties to live, the law allows a reasonable compensation to any one supplying them. The infant's necessity, therefore, being the ground of his liability, it follows that when no such necessity exists all responsibility fails.

There are numerous cases in the books as to when and under what circumstances an infant may be bound for necessaries and what are to be considered necessaries, and the duty devolving upon the party furnishing, a review of which would require too much space for our present purpose. Upon these questions the inquirer is referred to the works of Bingham, Ewell, and Tyler.

RIGHTS OF CHILDREN AS TO PARENTS, MASTERS, OR GUARDIANS.

In treating of the subjects of guardianship, apprenticeship, adoption, and custody of children we are necessarily brought to consider more fully the respective rights, obligations, and powers of parent and child.

From the earliest times their respective rights and duties have been inculcated and enforced by law, and in modern times the state has assumed the power to control and regulate these relations. In a late case in New York Judge Westerbrook says: "The right of the state to care for its children has always, and with very great propriety, been exercised." In reference to the morals and education of children, the exercise of this power is worthy of especial notice, and this will be found to be a characteristic mark of the early colonial laws.

Perhaps the earliest of this character are to be found in the laws of the Massachusetts colony, afterwards adopted in Connecticut.

These early laws very clearly inculcate upon parents the duty of properly training and educating their children, and at the same time as clearly provide against any neglect of this duty. Inefficiency, negligence, and overindulgence on the part of parents were no more tolerated than a stubborn and rebellious spirit in the child. The inefficiency or want of control of the parents over the child would seem, in some instances, to have been visited heavily upon the child. But if in this respect they adopted the severity of the Levitical code, they added conditions in favor of the child not to be found in the original law. The general provisions, however, were such, and were so administered, as to have a marked effect upon their posterity, and established principles which may be traced through much of the modern legislation upon these and kindred subjects, and for this reason a brief sketch of these laws may not be inappropriate.

A law of 1642 denounces the penalty of death upon any child over 16 years of age who shall smite or curse his natural father or mother, "unless it can be sufficiently testified that the parents have been very unchristianly negligent in the education of such children, or so provoked them by extreme or cruel correction that they have been forced thereunto to preserve themselves from death or maiming." And the same penalty is imposed upon a stubborn and rebellious son of over 16, who persists in such conduct and refuses to obey the voice and chastisement of his parents, but lives in sundry and notorious crimes. Ancient Charters and Laws, p. 59, ch. 18, §§ 13, 14.

Their care for children is, however, better shown in a series of laws of the same year and later, chiefly relating to education and good morals, and asserting the right to limit and control parental authority.

In 1642 it was provided—

Forasmuch as the good education of children is of singular behoof and benefit to any commonwealth, and whereas many parents and masters are too indulgent and negligent of their duty in that kind: it is ordered that the selectmen of every town, in the several precincts and quarters where they dwell, shall have a vigilant eye over their brethren and neighbors to see, first, that none of them shall suffer so much barbarism in any of their families as not to endeavor to teach, by themselves or others, their children and apprentices so much learning as may enable them perfectly to read the English tongue, and knowledge of the capital laws, under penalty of twenty shillings for each neglect therein; also, that all masters of families do at least once a week catechise their children and servants on the grounds and principles of religion; and, if unable to do so much, that then at the least they procure such children and apprentices to learn some short orthodox catechism without book, that they may be able to answer unto the questions that shall be propounded to them out of such catechism by their parents or masters, or any of the selectmen when they shall call them to a trial of what they have learned of that kind; and farther, that all parents and masters do breed and bring up their children and apprentices in some honest lawful calling, labor, or employment, either in husbandry or some other trade profitable for themselves and the commonwealth, if they will not or cannot train them up in learning to fit them for higher employments.

And if any of the selectmen, after admonition by them given to such masters of families, shall find them still negligent of their duty in the particulars aforementioned, whereby children and servants become rude, stubborn, and unruly, the said selectmen, with the help of two magistrates, or the next county court for that shire, shall take such children or apprentices from them, and place them with some masters for years (boys till they come to 21 and girls 18 years of age complete) which will more strictly look unto and force them to submit unto government, according to the rules of this order, if by fair means and former instructions they will not be drawn unto it.

In the year before, it had been provided that—

If any person shall wilfully and unreasonably deny any child timely or convenient marriage, or shall exercise any unnatural cruelty towards them, such children shall have liberty to complain to authority for redress in such cases.

No orphan during their minority, which was not committed to tuition or service by their parents in their lifetime, shall afterwards be absolutely disposed of by any, without the consent of some court, wherein two assistants (at least) shall be present, except in case of marriage, in which the approbation of the major part of the selectmen of that town, or any one of the next assistants, shall be sufficient; and the minority of women in case of marriage shall be 16 years.

It was also provided that where children and servants behaved themselves disorderly and disobediently towards their parents or masters any one magistrate might by warrant summon such offender before him and, upon conviction, sentence him to such corporal punishment as the case might deserve, not exceeding ten stripes for one offence, or bind him over for appearance at court.

For the protection of young persons from evil disposed companions, who might draw them away from their callings, studies, and honest occupations, to the dishonor of God and the grief of their parents, &c., it was provided that whoever should in any way cause or suffer any young people or persons whatsoever, whether children, servants, apprentices, or scholars belonging to the college or any Latin school, to spend any of their time or estate, by night or by day, in his or their company, ship, shop, &c., and should not from time to time discharge and hasten all such youths to their several employments and places of abode or lodging, should forfeit 40 shillings.

Laws, 1651.—It was also provided that if any persons should give credit to any youths or other persons under 21 years of age without an order in writing from their parents, guardians, or friends, they should lose their debt, whatever it might be. And further, if any such youth or person incurred any penalty by such means, and had not the wherewithal to pay, such person or persons as were the occasion thereof should pay it as the delinquents in like manner should do.

Laws, 1647.—A similar provision as to credits given to students of the military school or of any incorporated college has been adopted in the State of Virginia (Code of 1849, chap. 143, § 1; West Virginia School Code, § 94), and also in New Jersey (Nixon's Dig. 4th edit. 388–9).

It is to be noted that these laws furnish the earliest example of that special legislation which is now known as the compulsory education laws, which will be hereafter referred to, to be found in American legislation.

APPRENTICESHIP.

As a general rule the contract for apprenticeship must be in writing. The infant cannot be bound in pais, nor unless he is a party to the writing or deed. The term of service for males is until 21, and for females until 18. This is the common law rule.

The subject, however, is now, both in England and this country, regulated by statute. The laws of the several States will be found very nearly uniform in their essential provisions, the differences being mainly in unimportant details.

The early New England law may be found in the general laws of New Hampshire, 1878, chap. 187, and nearly the same provisions in New York, 3 R. S. 173.

The provisions are in substance as follows:

Children under 14 may be bound as apprentices without their consent, until they arrive at that age, by the father; or, if the father is not living, by the mother or guardian; or, if they have no parents or guardian, they may bind themselves, with approval of selectmen or overseers of the poor.

Minors over 14 may be similarly bound with their consent; females, until 18, or to the time of their marriage within that age; and males, until 21.

The indentures must be in writing, in duplicate, signed, sealed, and delivered by both parties; and, whenever a consent or approval is required, such consent or approval must be in writing and indorsed upon both parts of the indenture. All indentures executed as provided by law are good and effectual against all parties thereto.

Such indentures cease to be binding upon the minor, his parents, or guardian, upon the death of the master, but in some States provision is made for assignment of the same.

Parents, guardians, and the selectmen or overseers of the poor are required to inquire into the treatment of persons so bound, and defend them from cruel treatment, and make complaint thereof to any magistrate, who may discharge such indenture.

If any apprentice is guilty of gross misbehavior, wilful neglect, or refusal of duty, or shall use personal violence towards his master, the master may make complaint thereof and the magistrate may give judgment for damages and costs, and discharge indentures.

Any apprentice leaving service without cause may be arrested and returned, and the master may recover his reasonable expenses and damages therefor. Enticing or carrying away an apprentice is forbidden.

Any master neglecting to teach or cause to be taught to any apprentice the art, trade, or profession he was bound to teach, or to fulfil any part of his contract, is liable to such apprentice after he comes of age for all damages therefor.

In most of the States the selectmen of the town, overseers of the poor, or other officers possessing similar powers may bind out poor and destitute children having no means of support.

The difficulty of the present day, however, is not in the want of wholesome statutory provisions regulating the relations of master and apprentice, but in the absence of the means and opportunity to apply them to practical use. Leaving out of the account all those children having independent property or parents who feel themselves responsible for their well being and aid them to the extent of their ability, what is to be done with that large class cast upon the world as waifs, either without parents or with parents or custodians whose highest ambition seems to be to sink them to the lowest level of vice and vagabondage? This is the problem which is becoming of great importance, especially in our large cities, the satisfactory solution of which is by no means free from difficulty.

GUARDIANSHIP.

Another mode in which the law provides for the protection of infants is by the provisions for the appointment of guardians.

The books classify guardianship as of two kinds, one by the common law and the other by statute. In this country, however, there is practically but one, inasmuch as the whole subject is regulated by statute provisions.

The father and, next to him, the mother are treated as the natural guardians, and have the preference in the appointment, but the courts having control of this relation may disregard this preference.

Judge Story says:

> Although in general parents are intrusted with the custody of the persons and the education of their children, yet this is done upon the natural presumption that the children will be properly cared for, and will be brought up with a due education in literature, morals, and religion, and that they will be treated with kindness and affection. But whenever this presumption is removed; whenever, for example, it is found that a father is guilty of gross ill treatment or cruelty towards his infant children, or that he is in constant habits of drunkenness and blasphemy, or low and gross debauchery, or that he possesses atheistical or irreligious principles, or that his domestic associations are such as to tend to the corruption and contamination of his children, or that he otherwise acts in a manner injurious to the morals or interests of his children, in every such case the court of chancery will interfere and deprive him of the custody of his children, and appoint a suitable person to act as guardian and to take care of them and superintend their education. (2 Story's Eq. § 1341.)

Guardians by statute are of four kinds: Testamentary guardians, who are appointed by the last will and testament of the father, and in some cases of the mother; guardians ad litem, who are appointed by the court to represent or defend an infant sued therein; special guardians, who are appointed by the court for a special purpose, to represent the infant in some special proceeding, or to perform some act which the infant might perform or would be required to perform if he were of full age, and whose duties are at an end when the transaction is accomplished; and, lastly, general guardians.

General guardians are appointed by certain courts upon which the jurisdiction is conferred by statute. In all the States, however, the court having chancery powers has a general jurisdiction over every guardian of an infant, and he is subject to the control and superintendence of such court. (2 Kent's Com. 227.)

As a general rule, an infant over 14 may by statute select his guardian, but such selection is subject to the approval of the court. It is the duty of the court to consult the best interests of the child, taking into consideration not only his temporary welfare but also his training, education, and morals.

It will be found that the statute provisions on this subject are framed with a jealous regard to the rights and property of the infant and the courts are equally scrupulous and guarded, and the person taking upon himself this relation will be held to a strict accountability by all legal tribunals. The decisions and established rules are numerous and easy of access, and reference must be had to them to show the mode and extent to which courts will go for the protection of infants against any breach of trust on the part of their guardians. Practically, general guardians are not appointed unless there is property to which the infant is, or may be, entitled. The others, and by no means a small proportion, are left to the charity of the various public or private orphan associations, and their welfare in a great measure depends upon the solution of the problem before referred to.

ADOPTION OF CHILDREN.

In very many of the States provision has been made by law for the adoption of children by third persons. This is usually done under the direction of some court, usually, too, upon petition of the person desiring to adopt, and when the petitioner is married both husband and wife must join.

The parents of the child, if living, or, if dead, the guardian, must consent in writing. In case of an illegitimate child, the consent of the mother is sufficient. If there are no parents or guardian, the next of kin, or, in the absence of next of kin, the court may appoint some person who may give or withhold such consent.

The court must be satisfied of the identity of the persons whose consent is required and of the ability of the petitioner to bring up the child and furnish suitable nurture and education, having reference to the degree and condition of his parents, and the decree must set forth the facts.

From the date of the decree the child is, to all legal intents and purposes, the child of the petitioner.

In some of the States the child so adopted becomes, for the purpose of inheritance and for all other legal consequences and incidents, the child of the parents by adoption, as if born to them in lawful wedlock, except that he cannot take property expressly limited to the heirs of the body or bodies of the parents by adoption, and the natural parents are deprived of all rights as respects the child.

The court may change the name of such adopted child to that of the parents by adoption, and either party may appeal from such decree.

The mode of proceeding in such cases must, of course, conform to the statute provisions in each State, which must be consulted in such cases.

LABOR OF CHILDREN.

There are certain provisions of statute law in some of the States having for their object the protection of children from excessive toil unsuitable to their tender years.

In England the hours of labor for apprentices and servants are limited to ten hours a day and fifty hours a week.

Maine prohibits the employment of any person under 16 over ten hours each day. And no child is to be employed or suffered to work in any cotton or woollen factory without having attended school, public or private, under competent teachers, if under 12, four months, and, if over 12 and under 15, three months out of the twelve next preceding such employment. R. S. 1871, 425–6.

In New Hampshire no child under 15 shall be employed in any manufacturing establishment unless he has attended some public or private school under competent teachers at least twelve weeks, and, if under 12, six months, during the year next preceding, and ten hours constitute a day's labor. Gen. Laws, 1878, chap. 91, §§ 11 and 12.

In Massachusetts children under 12 cannot be employed over ten hours in any one day. Children between 12 and 15 must have attended school at least eleven weeks during the twelve months next preceding, and they must attend school at least eleven weeks during each year so employed. Gen. Stat. 1860, ch. 42; Laws of 1866, ch. 283; 1878, ch. 217. See also New York, 2 Rev. S. 98, § 2; Laws of 1876, ch. 372; Penna. Brightly's Purden, 452, §§ 1–6; Conn. R. S. 1866, tit. 13, ch. 4, § 50; New Jersey Laws, 1851, 321; California Gen. Laws, § 8650; Wisconsin Laws of 1877, ch. 289, Laws of 1878, ch. 187; Minnesota R. S. 1866, 228; Rhode Island G. L. 1872, 343, §§ 21 to 26; Swan and Critchf., Ohio, 824.

CUSTODY OF CHILDREN.

The subject of the custody of infants — the defects of the law in relation thereto, and how the same should be remedied, the apparent uncertainty in the application of the law to the different cases as they have arisen — has been the cause of long and elaborate treatises. Cases of conflicting interests and claims and unfortunate family differences have frequently occurred, calling for the interference of judicial authority, and without some study of the circumstances and facts of each case there would seem to be a greater conflict of decision than there really is. In these cases much is of necessity left to the sound discretion of the judge who hears the case; but there are some general principles which have been settled by authoritative decisions, and the controlling principle is that the court must carefully investigate the circumstances of each case, and act according to sound discretion and for the welfare of the child.

The Roman law gave the father absolute power over the persons of his children, and according to some authorities over their lives and liberty, while the mother had no claim except for due reverence and respect.

The general rule of law in England was that the father had the legal power over his infant children, and during his life the mother had none. According to Blackstone, "a mother, as such, is entitled to no power, but only to reverence and respect." 1 Black. Com. 453.

And according to the common law the father had a right to the exclusive custody of his child, even at an age when it still required nourishment from its mother's breast. "It is the universal rule, with some exceptions, that the father is entitled to the custody of a young child even against the will of the mother" (*ex parte Gleve.* 4 Dowl. P. C. 293), and this even though they be within the age of nurture (*Rex* vs. *Greenhill*, 6 Nev. and Man. 244; 4 Adolph and Ellis, 624). However pure might be the conduct of the mother, however amiable and correct in all the relations of life, the father might, if he thought proper, exclude her from all access to her children, and do this from the most corrupt motives. This state of the law which took so little account of the feelings of the mother continued until 1839, when an act was passed authorizing the interference of the courts for the protection of the mother and child.

Chancellor Kent states the general doctrine in this country as follows:

> The father may obtain the custody of his children by the writ of habeas corpus when they are improperly detained from him; but the courts, both of law and equity, will investigate the circumstances, and act according to sound discretion, and will not always and of course take a child, though under 14 years of age, from a third person and deliver it over to the father against the will of the child. They will consult the inclination of an infant if it be of a sufficiently mature age to judge for itself, and even control the right of the father to the possession and education of his child when the nature of the case appears to warrant it. 2 Kent's Com. 194.

Again, he repeats:

> The father, and, on his death, the mother, is generally entitled to the custody of the infant children, inasmuch as they are their natural protectors, for maintenance and education. But the courts of justice may, in their sound discretion, and when the morals, or safety, or interests of the children strongly require it, withdraw the infants from the custody of the father and mother, and place the care and custody of them elsewhere. 2 Kent, 205.

It is sometimes said that the right of the father to the custody of the persons of his infant children is in consequence of his obligation to provide for their maintenance and education. But this obligation of support is in some degree mutual under our laws, and there are cases where the obligation is shifted, and the child is bound for the maintenance of his parent; but we doubt if in such case the custody of the person of the parent would belong as of right to the child. In this country the right is, as a general rule, derived from the statutory enactments.

In this country, too, there is a great uniformity in the laws of the several States upon this subject, and the spirit of the decisions is essentially the same.

Where the question is to be determined by a judicial tribunal the courts are not bound to deliver the child into the custody of any claimant, but, in the exercise of a sound discretion, will leave the child in such custody as may appear best for it. Where there is a controversy between parents for the custody of their child, the right of the father is preferred to that of the mother, but the welfare of the child will be the criterion by which the custody is awarded. If the child have arrived at the age of discretion, in ordinary cases, upon *habeas corpus*, the court will permit the child to elect in whose custody it will be placed, but the court will take care that the custody is not an improper one. If the child is not competent to form a judgment and to declare his election, the court, after examination, will exercise its judgment for him.

For authorities upon this question we may refer to the following among many: *Matter of Woolstoncraft*, 4 Johns. ch. 80; *Matter of Waldron*, 13 Johns. 18; *People* vs. *Chegaray*, 18 Wend. 637; *People* vs. *Kling*, 6 Barb. 366; *Foster* vs. *Alston*, 6 How. (Miss.) 406; *Com.* vs. *Addicks*, 5 Binney, 520; *Ex parte Crouse*, 4 Whart. 9; *U. S.* vs. *Green*, 3 Mason, 482; *State* vs. *Smith*, 6 Greenl. 262; *People* vs. *Mercier*, 3 Hill (N. Y.) 399; *People* vs. *Wilcox*, 22 Barb. 178; *Wilcox* vs. *Wilcox*, 14 N. Y. Rep 575; *Wellesby* vs. *Wellesby*, 2 Bligh (N. S.), 136; *Ex parte Skinner*, 9 Moore, 278; 2 Story's Eq. § 1341; Hurd on Hab. Corp. 528.

It sometimes happens that the father or, after his death, the mother may give the child to a third person, or may relinquish the custody of it until it arrives at full age, upon consideration that such party will adopt the child and care for it as his own, and that subsequently he or she, after a state of things has arisen which cannot be altered without risking the happiness of the child, may attempt to reclaim its custody.

Where this transfer is made under the laws relating to apprenticeship or the adoption of children, the parent would be barred from such a reclamation; but this is sometimes done without such statute laws or not in the mode prescribed by statute. It is easy to see that such an attempt at reclamation might be made under circumstances peculiarly unjust and aggravating, when the affections of both child and parents by adoption have become engaged, or where the father, by such an arrangement, while his child was of tender years and entirely dependent, might shift the burden of his care and support upon a third party, and when the child arrives at more mature years, and under the care and at the expense of his parents by adoption becomes capable of making some material return, the father by such recovery would secure to himself the benefit of the services and earnings of the child at the expense of those who had fitted him therefor.

There are, however, decisions, both in England and this country, to the effect that the father would not be bound by such a transaction, but may recover the custody of the child, even though the interests of the child had been promoted by the original transfer. Tyler (§ 187, p. 283) says that the better opinion is that the father in such case is not in a position to require the interference of the court in favor of his controlling legal right as against the rights, the feelings, and the interests of the other parties, and cites *Pool* vs. *Gott*, 14 Law Rep. 269; *State* vs. *Smith*, 6 Greenleaf, 462; *McDowle's case*, 8 Johns. 328; *Com.* vs. *Gilkeson*, Wallace (Philada.) R. 194; *State* vs. *Barrett*, 40 N. H. 15. See also *Matter of Murphy*, 12 How. Pr. R. 513; Hurd on Hab. Corp. 537. The only American cases which he cites as against this doctrine are *State* vs. *Oliver*, 1 Harr. (Del.) 419; *Mayne* vs. *Bredwin*, 1 Halstead, N. J. Ch. 454. Hurd, however, in a note, cites various other cases on both sides, but evidently agrees in opinion with Tyler.

In the case of illegitimate children the mother has the right to the custody. *Hulland* vs. *Malkin*, 2 Wilson, 126; *Rex* vs. *Soper*, 5 Term R. 278; *Rosalina* vs. *Armstrong*, 15 Barb. 247; *People* vs. *Mitchell*, 44 Barb. 245; *Wright* vs. *Wright*, 2 Mass. 109.

In many of the States these general principles of the law have been supplemented by specific statute provisions for the protection of children.

In many of the States the exposure of an infant under 6 years by the parents or other person having the custody of such child with intent to abandon it, and in some cases exposure such as endangers health or limb of infants, is punished by fine and imprisonment. R. S. Maine, 1871, 828; R. S. Conn. 1875, 500, § 15; Comp. Laws Mich. 1871, 2075; 3 Stat. Tenn. § 4620; R. S. Wisc. 1858, 974, § 8; 3 R. S. N. Y. 937, § 45; Code Ga. 1873, § 4373; Wagner Stat. Mo. 451, § 39; N. Y. Laws of 1876, chap. 122.

In New York, where parents abandon their children they forfeit all claim to their custody as against any person who has taken, adopted, or assumed the maintenance of such child. (3 R. S. 166, § 11.) And in Georgia parental power is lost by consent to adoption, by voluntary contract releasing custody to third person, by failure to provide necessaries, by abandonment of family, by consent to marriage, and by cruel treatment. (Code of 1873, § 1793.) The Minnesota law authorizes any incorporated orphan asylum to take charge of destitute and abandoned children. (R. S. 1866, §§ 65, 66.) And in New York and other States there are various societies having this power, many of them organized solely for this object.

Abducting, enticing, or conveying away minors is also prohibited under penalty. R. S. Me. 828; Mich. C. L. 2075; Tenn. 3 Stat. § 4621; Ga. Code, §§ 4367–8; Mo. Wag. Stat. 451, § 38; So. Car. R. S. 711, § 15; and others.

In many of the States the furnishing or sale of spirituous or intoxicating liquors, wines, or malt liquors is covered by a general prohibitory law, applicable to all; but in some States special provisions have been enacted as to minors. N. Y. 3 R. S. 937, § 21; Iowa Code, § 1539; Ill. 1878, 528; Ind. R. S. 872; Mich. C. L. 702; Tenn. 3 Stat. § 4863; Minn. R. S. 208, § 10; Mo. Wag. St. 552, § 20; Penna. Purden, 666, § 31.

Again, minors under a certain age are prohibited from being admitted to or remaining in any saloon or place of entertainment where spirituous or malt liquors are sold, exchanged, or given away, or at any place of amusement known as a dance house or concert saloon, unless accompanied by parents or guardians. N. H. G. L. 1878, ch. 269, § 23; Cal. Stat. 1877–8, p. 813; Mo. Wagner, 213, § 8; Penna. Purden, 49, § 9, 501, § 20; N. Y. 3 R. S. 982, § 91; Ohio, Sayler's Stat. 271, ch. 264.

Gambling or betting with minors, furnishing them with dangerous weapons, or selling poisons to them is prohibited. Ohio S. and C. 667; Tenn. 3 Stat. §§ 4864, 4887; Mo. Wagner, 662, § 5; N. Y. 2 R. S. 921, § 44.

Children found begging or soliciting charity may be arrested and committed. N. Y. 2 R. S. 837, § 4; Cal. Stat. 1877–8, 813, § 4. And the general laws against gaming, begging, and vagrancy apply to minors as well as to adults.

In some of the States there are provisions similar to those found in the Florida statutes, in which stubborn children, runaways, and those who misspend their time by frequenting gaming houses or tippling shops are classed with disorderly persons, rogues, and vagabonds, and made subject to the same punishment. See Bush's Digest, 249, § 24. As to *stubborn children*, there is the spirit of the old colony law of Massachusetts, but with a strong modification of the penalty.

But, perhaps, sufficient has been said to show the tendency of the legislation on this subject.

Within the last few years another matter has received attention at the hands of the State legislatures.

In the laws of New York for 1874, chap. 116, it is provided that any person, whether as parent, guardian, relative, employer, or otherwise, having in his care, custody, or control any child under the age of 16 years, who shall sell, apprentice, give away, let out, or otherwise dispose of any such child to any person, under any name, title, or pretence, for the vocation, use, occupation, calling, service, or purpose of singing, playing on musical instruments, rope-walking, dancing, begging, or peddling, in any public street or highway, or in any mendicant or wandering business whatever, and any person who shall take, receive, hire, employ, use, or have in custody any such child for such purposes, or either of them, shall be deemed to be guilty of a misdemeanor, &c. 3 R. S. 164, § 9.

Again, in 1876, it was enacted that any person having the custody, care, or control of any child under 16, who shall exhibit, use, or employ, or in any manner or under any pretence sell, apprentice, give away, let out, &c., any such child to any person in or for the vocation, occupation, service, or purpose of singing, playing on musical instruments, rope or wire walking, dancing, begging, or peddling, or as a gymnast, contortionist, rider, or acrobat, in any place whatsoever, or for and in any business, exhibition, or vocation injurious to health or dangerous to the life and limb, or who shall cause, procure, or encourage any such child to engage therein, shall be guilty of a misdemeanor. And upon conviction of such party the court or magistrate may, if he deem it desirable for the welfare of the child, deprive such person of its custody, and commit it to some orphan asylum, or make such other disposition of it as is or may be provided for by law. Laws of 1876, ch. 122.

Similar provisions of law are found in New Hampshire, Gen. Laws, 1878, ch. 269, § 24; California Laws of 1877–8, 813, act March 30, 1878; Pennsylvania, act of May 24, 1878; Illinois, Laws of 1876, chap. 122, revision of 1878, 496. And the same general provisions may perhaps be found in other States, whose later statutes we have been unable to examine.

In a case arising under the New York laws, Westbrook, J., says:

> The right of the State to care for its children has always, and with very great propriety, been exercised. Under its laws, whenever the welfare of the child has demanded, its courts have frequently interfered for the protection of children of tender years. It has again and again taken them from one parent and given them to the other, or has refused so to do, the good and welfare of the child being the object always in view. It has so acted without the intervention of a jury, and that power has never been supposed to have been improperly exercised because a jury was not allowed and due process of law not had. If the courts of the State may, by virtue of their general powers, interfere for the protection and care of children, it is not seen why the legislature may not prescribe the cases in which children shall be rescued from their custodians and a mode provided for their summary disposition. For example, if children should be placed to learn the business of stealing, could not the legislature provide a summary remedy for the evil? Has the law no power to rescue, summarily, female children held for the purposes of prostitution, or interfere in an expeditious manner in very many cases when children of tender years are exposed to peril or temptation? This will hardly be argued, or, if claimed, authority most abundant can be found to justify it. Precisely this ground the act of 1876 covers. In my judgment it is a most wise, salutary, and beneficent statute, born of Christian civilization and founded upon the teachings of Him to whom children were objects of tender love and care. It needs no evidence to demonstrate to our judgment that the life to which these children were subjected and from which they were rescued was perilous to their best interests. It was dangerous to them physically and morally. The contortions, evolutions, and performances of the acrobat are clearly physically dangerous, and the surroundings and companions of the circus ring are equally so morally. In the matter of *Donohue et al.* N. Y. Sept. term, 1876.

SPECIAL PROVISIONS IN REFERENCE TO EDUCATION.

Under this head it is not proposed to do more than to call attention to certain specific provisions of law enforcing the duty of parents, guardians, and others having the custody of children to provide for their education and intended to prevent truancy.

It is well settled that a proper education is included in the term "necessaries." Whether a "proper education" is to be construed to include more than a good common school education is a question upon which the decisions are not harmonious. In *The College* vs. *Chandler*, 20 Vt. 683, the supreme court say:

> A good common school education at least is now recognized as one of the "necessaries" for an infant. Without it he would lack an acquisition which would be com-

mon among his associates, and would ever be liable to suffer in his transaction of business. Such an education is moreover essential to the intelligent discharge of civil, political, and religious duties.

To this extent the courts are in accord, and the reason given in an English case was that it was for the benefit of the realm. *Manley* vs. *Scott*, 1 sec. R. 112.

In this country the education of children has been provided for by constitutional and statutory provisions for the organization of public schools, free to all within the scholastic age. Experience, however, has shown that the attendance upon the free public schools has never included all the children of school age. Parents have been found "so indulgent and negligent of duty in that respect," so regardless of the interests of their children, as to suffer them to grow up in ignorance and idleness, or so greedy for a little present gain that they are willing to sacrifice the future welfare of their children to obtain it, and especially in our large cities a class of children are found who prefer the unbridled license of the streets to the wholesome restraints of the school room.

To prevent this evil there have been added to the school systems of many of the States what are known as the provisions for compulsory education. The State, having provided a free gift for its children, has sometimes found it necessary to compel its acceptance.

These provisions are of two kinds, those that apply to parents or custodians of the children, the compulsory laws proper, and those that reach and apply to the children themselves, or the laws to prevent and punish truancy.

In many of the States there are some general provisions of law bearing upon this question. Vagrants and disorderly persons are placed under the ban of the law, and these are defined to include those who have no regular or lawful occupation, who misspend their time in idleness or frequent places of immoral tendencies, stubborn children, runaways, idle persons who go about begging, and the like. There are also laws providing for the arrest of vicious and unruly children, or of those suffered to run at large without proper restraint, and their commitment to some institution provided for such purpose, there to be employed at such suitable labor as they may be able to perform and to be educated and instructed so that they may make useful citizens.

The laws for the prevention of truancy reach all children of the prescribed age who do not attend school, and provide for their being placed in some proper institution to be educated and instructed until they are brought under proper restraint. These gather into the schools the street waifs who can be reached in no other way, and if they are not effective it is because they are not properly enforced.

In Maine, Massachusetts, and Rhode Island the truant question is referred to the towns, who are authorized to make by-laws respecting truants and children within a prescribed age not attending school, or who are without any regular or lawful occupation or growing up in ignorance. The towns may annex suitable penalties for the breach of these by-laws and appoint special officers to enforce the same—a plan which has not proved eminently successful. R. S. Me. 186, §§ 13 to 15; R. S. Mass. chap. 42, § 84; Gen. Stat. R. I. chap. 57.

The other branch is perhaps more effective and reaches the larger number of cases. It declares the duty of the parent or custodian, and enforces that duty by penalties for the breach thereof.

These compulsory provisions are not original in the Massachusetts law of 1642, but would seem to have been borrowed from the same source as the laws in reference to stubborn children or those who should smite or curse their natural parents.

In an article on "The criminal code of the Jews," in a recent number of the Pall Mall Gazette, the writer says:

> It must be remembered that education was well advanced among the Hebrews, especially after the first or Babylonian captivity. A system of compulsory instruction had been introduced by Joshua, the son of Gamala. There was a school board for each district. Every child more than 6 years of age was obliged to attend the communal schools. Such importance does the Talmud attach to the training of the young that it enters into the minutest details upon the subject.

The duty of preparing them to become good and useful citizens was not neglected. The Bible was their moral and legal code, and the study of this was enforced. A Jew could not but be well acquainted with the leading principles of his legal code and their general application.

And the same writer says:

> A man, who had not or had never had a fixed occupation, trade, or business, by which he earned a livelihood, was not allowed to act as judge. "He who neglects to teach his son a trade," say the rabbins, "is as though he taught him to steal."

The New Hampshire law requires parents, guardians, or other custodians of children between 8 and 14 years of age to send them to school at least twelve weeks in each year, six weeks of which at least must be continuous. With some variations as to age and time, the same law prevails in other States. Michigan, act 165, laws of 1871; California, act March 28, 1874; Conn. Gen. Statutes, revision of 1875, title xi, with amendments to 1879, § 1; Maine, act of 1875; Mass. laws of 1873, 279; 1874, 233; 1876, ch. 52; 1878, ch. 257; New York, laws of 1851, ch. 337, § 13; as amended, 1866, ch. 245; District of Columbia, R. S. D. C. ch. 12, § 1; Kansas, laws of 1876, ch. 92; Nevada, act Feb. 25, 1873; New Jersey, act April 9, 1875; Ohio, act of Sept. 1, 1877; Vermont, acts 1867, 1870, 1873; Wisconsin, laws of 1879; Arizona, act of Feb. 9, 1875; Wyoming, acts Dec. 12, 1873, and Dec. 15, 1877.

Washington Territory, by a law of 1877, applies a similar provision to all towns of 400 or more inhabitants. The constitutions of Colorado and North Carolina authorize such a law, but the legislatures do not appear to have acted upon it.

In Illinois the expense of the support and education of children are made a charge upon the property of both husband and wife, or either, in favor of the creditor therefor, who may sue either one or both. Stat. 1876, 693, § 15.

In Georgia a general provision makes it the duty of the father to provide for the maintenance and education of his children during minority. Code of 1873, § 1792.

And this is the general requirement of the law. Where there is sufficient property of either parent or belonging to the child, courts of equity under the general rules of the law are authorized to interfere, to secure to the child a proper education where the natural or legal custodian neglects that duty. But under the special compulsory provisions there is no question of property. The free public schools offer facilities for education without charge to parent or child, and it is made a penal offense for the parent or custodian to refuse the facilities so offered to the child.

If it be true that a good common school education is recognized as one of the necessaries for an infant, and essential to the discharge of civil and political duties, or, as generally stated, that a diffusion of knowledge among the people is essential to the preservation of free institutions, these so called compulsory or obligatory laws are founded upon the right and duty of self protection and preservation. They belong to the class of laws which are intended for the suppression of vice. They are intended to reach and bring within the influence of our schools a class who cannot be reached effectually in any other way. Wherever they have been properly enforced, the evidence is that great benefits have accrued therefrom; and in a somewhat extended examination of the various school codes but one instance has been found where these compulsory provisions once adopted have been abandoned, and that is in the Texas school code of 1879. Even there there was no direct repeal, but the clause was omitted in the revision, and it would seem that it was sought to do by implication what they hesitated to do by direct declaration. The same revision narrows the school age from 6 to 16 down to 8 to 14, and deprives all children under 8 or over 14 of the privilege of free education. Whatever may have been the cause of this retrograde movement, there will be found little disposition in other States to follow it. In the two adjoining States, Arkansas and Louisiana, the school age is from 6 to 21, which may be termed the general school age of the country, and it can hardly be supposed that Texas parents will persist in depriving their children of advantages which would be their right in every other State. The simple question is whether it is better to educate the children for our jails and workhouses or to become useful citizens. In the one direction or the other they will be sure to go, and if left to themselves, especially in our large cities, a large class will take the wrong direction and render the problem before referred to more difficult of solution.

GENERAL SCHOOL LAWS.

Among the rights and privileges of children, and by no means the least important, is the right to the education provided for them under the public school system. In a former paper one branch of this subject, known as the compulsory education system, was introduced. It is now proposed to treat of the public free school system of the various States, and to give an abstract of the various State school codes, as brief as is consistent with a fair understanding of the same.

It has been said that there is no American school system. If this means that there is no national system adopted and prescribed by the Federal Government the statement is true. The power to establish and enforce a public school system is one which the people have never delegated to the General Government. On the contrary, they watch with great jealousy any act which shows an intent on the part of the Government to interfere with this subject. It is true that a national Bureau of Education has been established, but it has no governing authority. It is simply an office of information, and its chief function is to collect and disseminate information upon educational subjects. It appeals through the history of experience to the reason and sound judgment of the people. It brings home to them a knowledge of all that is done for education.

The American school systems as they exist to-day are the result of the independent action of thirty-eight independent States and of nine Territories, each acting for itself. The various statutes of these States and Territories relating to common schools would fill volumes. The result sought to be attained has been the same in all. In some of the older States it is the growth of over two hundred years of practical experience, and this experience has inured to the benefit of the younger States. In many instances the new States have undoubtedly improved upon the old, and the old States have shown their appreciation by adopting the improvement. Hence, instead of such great diversities as might naturally be expected from the separate action of so many independent authorities, it will be found that upon the material points there is a remarkable unanimity.

As a general rule the people are slow to allow or assent to changes in constitutional provisions, even when it is freely admitted that some changes are desirable. In almost every legislative body there will be found a class of statesmen who seem to have no doubt of their ability to improve upon any existing law or system, and the people seem to expect and submit to a certain degree of instability in the statute law. But when the proposition is to change constitutional provisions they must be satisfied that some urgent necessity demands the change ere they will consent to remove the legal restrictions which bar any alteration of the fundamental law, and as a general rule the change when proposed must be approved by the popular vote before it can become effective.

Hence, when permanency is desired they secure it by incorporating the proposed ordinances in the constitution. This is not, as some foreign writers seem to understand, a compulsory power wielded by the State against the free action of its citizens, but a voluntary binding agreement entered into by the citizens themselves, which controls or compels State action. The people are bound by the constitution which they have adopted until it shall be legally changed or modified, but one of its most essential functions is to restrict the legislative power in certain directions, while it at the same time compels action in others.

The idea lying at the foundation of the American school system is found in the apothegm, "An ignorant people may be governed, but only an educated people can govern themselves." The doctrine which has been incorporated into many of the State constitutions, and is the governing principle in all, is that "knowledge and learning as well as virtue generally diffused throughout the community is essential to the preservation of a free government and of the rights and liberties of the people." Hence, for the protection and perpetuation of free government, they have inserted in their State constitutions provisions requiring the legislatures to establish and provide for the maintenance of an efficient and uniform system of public schools, free to all children of the State within the school age.

Many have gone further than this and provided for the setting apart of a special State school fund, the principal of which is not to be diminished, the interest on which is pledged for the support of schools and forbidden to be used for any other purpose, and in addition an annual State appropriation or the levy of a special State tax is usually made for the same purpose. In many States the provision is required to be sufficient to support a school or schools in every district for a certain specified time each year as a minimum limit.

In many of the State constitutions there are provisions for the appointment of supervisory officers, who are to have charge of the educational interests of the State, and in the constitution of Virginia the provisions substantially establish the system, leaving but little except details to be provided for by the legislature.

Another general principle, constitutional or statutory, is that the public schools shall be free from all sectarian or denominational influences. As enumerated in the constitution of Massachusetts, "humanity and general benevolence, public and private charity, industry and frugality honesty and punctuality in dealings, sincerity, good humor, and all social affections and generous sentiments" are to be inculcated, but sectarian or denominational teaching is rigidly excluded from the schools or school books. Perfect freedom of religious belief is the right of every citizen. He may adopt any form of religious belief which approves itself to him or he may reject all forms. He may bring up his children to believe in the teachings of any sect or creed, but he must provide for this outside of the public school. He cannot require others entertain ing different and frequently radically conflicting opinions to contribute to the inculcation of his own particular tenets. The public school is the neutral ground, free to all creeds and forms of belief, upon which the most discordant elements may meet and enjoy equal rights and privileges, a result which perhaps cannot be fully attained except by a secularization of the public schools.

In the matter of school statistics the provisions of the State codes are almost identical. At stated periods there is required from some school district officer a census of all persons residing in the district of the school age, some even requiring names, age, and sex. This is the school material. In every school a register is required to be kept by the teacher of the name of every pupil attending from day to day, and at stated periods reports are to be made showing the actual attendance of each, with the average attendance for the period, and unless these reports are made the teacher forfeits his pay. A comparison of these two shows the names of all who are denied or who neglect to avail themselves of the benefits of the school privileges. From each district must also come a statement of the number of schools, the length of time and by whom taught, their management and comparative condition, the wages of the teachers, with a complete statement of the financial condition of the district, the sources from which its funds were derived, and the cost per scholar. So specific are the details required that the reports furnish a complete annual history of the operations of each district.

Again it is made the duty of certain officers to visit the schools and examine into their condition and management and report upon the same. This is made peremptory upon the officers, beginning with the district and running up to the town or county and in some degree to the State supervisory officers. The theory of the law requires a careful study of the workings of the system, with a series of reports thereon which finally reach the legislature through the State superintendent or State board.

In all the States and all the Territories, except Alaska, which has no public school law, and New Mexico, where the provisions are extremely crude, the general supervision of educational interests is vested in a State or territorial superintendent, with or without a State board of education. In Connecticut, Massachusetts, and Texas the substantial duties of State superintendent are devolved upon the secretary of the State board, and in Maryland, upon the principal of the State Normal School, who is ex officio a member of the State board.

The State boards in some cases are merely the trustees of the school fund, and have the care and management of the school lands; in some their functions are simply advisory upon matters referred to them by the State superintendent, while in others they are charged with the general supervision of the school system, with power to make and enforce rules and regulations for the government of the same.

The State superintendents, with or without the direction of the State boards, are charged with the general supervision of the educational interests of the State and with the administration of the school laws. They are to advise with and instruct the county superintendents and other subordinate school officers, to prepare forms and blanks for reports and returns, examine into the workings of the system, collect statistics and information, devise plans for the improvement of the schools, and generally make themselves familiar with the wants and necessities of the system, and make full reports to the governor or legislature. They have also general supervision of the State normal schools and institutes for the education and instruction of teachers, and apportion the State school moneys to the counties or towns, in the mode provided by law.

In all the States outside of New England, except Michigan and Ohio, which seem to have adopted substantially the New England system, and Delaware, where there is no present provision in the law for any officers between the State superintendent and district boards, there are county superintendents or county boards or both, the parish boards of Louisiana corresponding to the county boards in other States.

These county boards or county superintendents generally occupy the same position with reference to the county schools as the State superintendent does to those of the State, but subject to the State superintendent. Under the New England system, the town school committees or supervisors perform the duties in their several towns which in the States which have adopted the county organization is performed by the county authority. Where the county is made the source of power, it is generally made the duty of the county authority to divide the territory into convenient subdistricts and establish in each a sufficient number of schools for the accommodation of all children of school age. In these States the duty of providing for the schools beyond the State provision is imposed by law upon the county, or the county and school district, while in New England and some of the other States the town or township is the head, and upon it is imposed the duty of providing for the support of the schools.

The school district is a territorial division of a county or town, which is recognized in all the States except Texas, where it simply includes families sending to a school. Under the laws of the New England States, while the towns were to a certain extent required to provide for the support of the schools, they were also to be divided into school districts, the extent and boundaries of which were to be determined by the town. The districts so formed were, for school purposes, independent municipal corporations. The town was required to levy a tax for the support of the schools, which was to be distributed to the several districts as provided by law or as it might direct. Aside from this the district might vote such additional tax as it saw fit for the same purpose. It provided its school-houses, fixed their location, determined the time when the schools should commence and close, whether they should be taught by male or female teachers, and managed its own affairs through its own officers. For a certain length of time it was bound to keep up its schools under competent teachers. The town school committee determined who were competent teachers and had the general supervision of the schools. If the district neglected or refused to perform its statutory duties the town or its committee might interfere, employ teachers, and establish and keep up the schools at the expense of the town or district. The present laws, however, in several States, authorize the towns to abolish the district system and assume control of the schools, and for that purpose it becomes the district; and in Massachusetts the town system has been substituted for the old district system in the larger part of the State. In many of the States outside of New England the law makes the city, borough, or township the school district; and in States where the county is to be divided, the formation of districts too small in means or population to be effective is sought to be avoided by forbidding the laying off of any district unless it contains a minimum number of children of school age.

The Texas school law of 1879 virtually abolishes school districts as territorial divisions and substitutes in their place what are called "school communities," which would seem to be associations of individuals, covering the same territory, like church or other associations, without other limitation than that in towns of less than 1,500 inhabitants but two such communities can be formed for whites and two for colored This is a new invention as applied to the school system, and what its effect may be remains to be seen.

Another point upon which all the school laws are in unison is the necessity of providing means to secure competent and qualified teachers. The early requirements were evidence of good morals and a satisfactory examination before some authorized board or officer as a condition precedent to employment. It was discovered, however, that the possession of knowledge and the faculty of communicating it to others did not always accompany each other; that teaching was of itself a science to be taught; and hence there have been added to the common school system State normal schools for the training of teachers, and State and county teachers' institutes, which the teachers are in most cases required to attend, the object of which is the improvement of the methods of teaching and to raise the standard of teachers' qualifications. In this way the States have not only undertaken the education of the children, but also provided for the instruction and education of the teachers.

Another universal requirement is that the schools shall be taught in the English language. The teaching of other modern or ancient languages is not prohibited, but on the contrary it is authorized under certain circumstances; but they are taught simply as a branch of study, and are not the language of the school. It has been said that one of the most remarkable features and the greatest work of the free school is its power of assimilation. It draws together the children of all races and stamps upon them the mark of nationality. It is described as a mill, into which go children of all nationalities and come out Americans. In the new constitution of Louisiana, however, while it is provided that the schools shall be taught in the English language, it is also provided that in parishes where the French language predominates they may also be taught in the French language.

If this is to be carried out, one manifest result must be the division of the school day between the two nationalities, which will of course shorten the school period for both, unless the school term is lengthened in proportion, which in city schools kept up for ten months would be impossible.

Mr. Francis Adams, in his work on the American school system, says:

The most conspicuous feature of the American school system is its representative character. The doctrine of the sovereignty of the people, pervading all American social and political organizations, is carried to its fullest limit in the schools of the country. The principle to which the people are most attached is thus fitly exhibited in the institution upon which they set the highest value.

Again he says:

The widespread popular regard which constitutes the propelling power appears to be chiefly due to two features: government by the people and ownership by the people. It is a vast proprietary scheme, in which every citizen has a share. For no reason is the principle of local government more dearly prized than because of the control which it gives the people over the schools. They would be as ready to surrender all municipal powers and privileges as to transfer their management to a sect or to any other private organization. This recognition of responsibility is the mainspring of the system and the cause of its best results. * * * The simple principle of the American school laws is that the people can be trusted to attend to their own business.

Bishop Fraser, another English writer, says:

Local self-government is the mainspring of the American school system.

Under the New England system the district was the chief source of power. The people had ordained that there must be each year a certain amount of school facilities furnished. Beyond that point the qualified voters of each district were free to act according to their discretion. The majority could extend their schools, divide them into different grades, add to the branches to be taught, build such houses as seemed best to them, the only limit being the amount for which they were willing to tax themselves. In Maine, if the majority proved to be too parsimonious, and refused to vote such sum as in the opinion of the minority it was necessary to raise, the minority were authorized to appeal to the town, and upon such appeal the town might overrule the majority and increase the amount.

This attachment to local control of the schools is undoubtedly one great reason why the people hold so tenaciously to the old district system in the New England States. This principle of local government, however, exists in a majority of the States to a greater or less extent, but in some there will be found school systems where it appears that this principle is not yet fully developed.

In Maryland the State board consists of certain persons who are ex officio members, but one of whom, the governor, is elective, and four others appointed by the governor from the presidents and examiners of the county boards. The county board is appointed by the circuit court, and the county examiner by the county board. The county board is a body corporate and holds all school property in the county. It determines the school districts and appoints for each a board of trustees, who appear to be merely subordinates of the board. The county board controls and manages all the schools. Not a school-house can be repaired unless the county board first fix the amount to be expended therefor.

In Georgia, North Carolina, South Carolina, Texas, and Virginia the system is substantially the same. In Louisiana the parish board, which is appointed by the State board, appears to have entire control. In the District of Columbia the trustees are appointed by the District commissioners, who are appointees of the President of the United States. In none of these localities do the people of the district, as such, have any voice, except in some cases where cities or towns have been vested with special powers as independent school districts.

In Florida and Mississippi the patrons of the school are allowed to recommend the trustees, but under the general school laws of the other States named these officers are selected by appointment. In some of the other States the doctrine that the people can be safely trusted to attend to their own business does not seem to prevail, for a limit has been prescribed to taxation, so that the people may not impose upon themselves too great a tax for the purpose of educating their children. It is not to be assumed, however, that the people of these States are of the class who may be governed but cannot govern themselves.

There is another matter which may with propriety be noticed before proceeding to the consideration of the State codes. While the institution of slavery existed in some of the States a public school system free to all was impossible. The two institutions were too antagonistic in their nature to exist harmoniously in the same community. The enfranchisement of the slaves left them, as the legacy of the institution, with a mass of ignorance to be provided for, and how to provide for it was a problem not easy of solution. Old customs and prejudices were to be adjusted to the new order of things. The war had left them impoverished and in no condition to impose upon themselves pecuniary burdens for any purpose. Their available means bore no proportion to the work to be done. To meet and overcome all the obstacles in the way of a free public school system was a work of no small difficulty. The difficulties which the Southern States were called upon to encounter were such as had never existed in any of the other States.

Whatever may have been the vices of some of the reconstruction governments of these States, their efforts to establish and provide for the free public school system were good and earnest, and must in the end be so acknowledged. The necessity for the work was admitted. The number of children of school age whose education was to be provided for was all at once doubled, and the addition was of a distinct race, and this race question was manfully met and solved. While as a general rule separate schools are required for white and colored children, they are all classed as children of the State, entitled to equal school privileges and facilities and to their pro rata share of the school moneys. If there are inequalities and discriminations, it would not seem to be the fault of the law, but of its administration, and that must depend for its correction upon the influence of enlightened public opinion.

Two States, however, Kentucky and Delaware, are exceptional. In the school systems of these States the color line is distinctly drawn. In Delaware the schools required by the constitution to be established are established exclusively for white children. The constitution acknowledges no obligation in respect to the education of the colored children. In both States the whites seem to disclaim any pecuniary responsibility in this matter, and no part of their money is allowed to be expended in that direction, except as it may be done in independent city districts, but the cost of the education of the colored children is imposed upon that race alone.

In Kentucky the regular school supervision is made to include the colored schools, while in Delaware the taxes collected from the colored people for the support of colored schools are by law turned over to a private association to be expended by them. In both States the fees for collection of the tax and other expenses are paid out of the colored fund.

ALABAMA.

The constitution requires the general assembly to establish, organize, and maintain a system of public schools throughout the State for the equal benefit of the children thereof between the ages of 7 and 21, separate schools to be provided for children of African descent.

It requires the levy of a poll tax, not exceeding $1.50 annually, to be applied to the support of schools in the counties where collected, and for an annual State appropriation of not less than $100,000 for the same purpose. Of the State moneys distributed not more than 4 per cent. can be applied to any purpose except the payment of teachers.

The school laws in force in 1878 provided for a State superintendent elected biennially, a county superintendent for each county, appointed by the State superintendent for two years, and three trustees, elected in each township or school district for the term of four years, these trustees, however, to be superseded in 1879 by a township superintendent in each township, appointed by the county superintendent, with the approval of the State superintendent.

The State superintendent has his office at the State capital and employs a clerk. He has the general supervision of the public schools of the State, is to devote his time to the care and improvement of the schools and the promotion of the general interests of education, prepare and distribute blanks for school returns, publish and circulate the laws and regulations concerning common schools, visit, if practicable, each county annually, and report to the governor the number of school districts, the number of schools taught, the number of scholars taught and number of children of school age, the amount of school funds received and expended, with a statement of the condition of the schools and with such suggestions and recommendations as he may deem proper. He is to apportion the school moneys to the counties, and keep special accounts with each county and township.

These may be termed the usual duties of the State superintendent.

The county superintendent has general charge and supervision of the schools of the county. In addition, he is to receive, disburse, and account for all county school moneys, apportion the same to the districts, and pay teachers. He is to report to the State superintendent annually, and oftener if required. In connection with two teachers of the county, appointed by himself, he is to examine teachers and conduct teachers' institutes.

In 1878 the district trustees had the immediate supervision of the schools in the district. They were to establish one or more schools for each race, as necessity might require. They were to contract with the teachers to pay a pro rata share of the school fund apportioned to the district according to the number of days' attendance shown in the teachers' report, payment to be made at the expiration of the year, but could not contract for less than three months nor for less than ten pupils of the scholastic age. They were forbidden to draw any warrant in favor of any teacher whose annual report showed an average attendance of less than ten scholars. They might remove teachers, but must allow a pro rata share of the fund at the time of the annual payment. Each two years they were to take enumeration of all children in the district between 7 and 21 years of age and report to county superintendent. These duties in 1879 were to be devolved on the township superintendents before mentioned, with some modifications.

The scholastic year begins October 1 and ends September 30 following. The school month is 23 days, the school day not less than 6 hours.

Districts.

Every township and fraction of a township divided by State or county lines, "or any other insuperable barrier, such as rivers, creeks, or mountains," and every incorporated city or town of 3,000 inhabitants, shall constitute a separate school district.

Every child between 7 and 21 years of age is entitled to admission into, and instruction in, any public school of his own race or color in the township of his residence, or in any public school of his race or color in the State.

In the apportionment of the State school fund the necessary amounts for contingent expenses and State normal schools are to be first set apart.

Each township is to receive the amount due from the sixteenth section or other trust fund held by the State. Townships having an income from trust funds are not to receive any part of the apportionment until other townships or districts having no trust funds shall have received such sum as will give them an equal share per capita with those having such trust funds.

Each county shall receive the poll tax collected in it, and each race is entitled to the poll tax paid by it.

For Mobile County a board of nine commissioners is provided, one-third to be elected biennially. This board is to elect a president, vice president, and superintendent and to have control and management of the schools. They have full power to continue in force, revise, modify, and improve, as to them may seem fit, the public school system existing in the county. They are made a body corporate, are to receive, assess, and collect all devises, revenues, and taxes for support of the schools, and purchase or lease all property necessary for school purposes and for the proper accommodation of pupils and teachers, the superintendent to have supervision of the schools.

The last general revision of the school law allowed the trustees to select teachers without reference to examination, but a subsequent amendment requires teachers to be examined by a county educational board. Under the restrictions imposed upon the payment of teachers no one can adopt teaching as a means of living unless possessed of sufficient funds to maintain himself for the first year. There is no pay until the expiration of the year, no matter how brief a time the teacher is employed, and even if the teacher has served the full year he may find himself entitled to no compensation if, upon the final summing up of his report, the average attendance is less than the minimum allowance. If this is to be continued the attendance should be made compulsory, under penalties sufficient to indemnify the teacher against any possible loss on account of non-attendance.

ARKANSAS.

Article XIV of the constitution requires the legislature to maintain a general, suitable, and efficient system of free schools whereby all persons in the State between 6 and 21 years of age may receive gratuitous instruction. It also requires that it shall provide by law for the support of schools by taxes, not to exceed two mills on the dollar in any one year and by an annual per capita tax of $1 on every male inhabitant over 21, and provides for a general law authorizing school districts by a vote of the qualified electors to levy taxes for school purposes not to exceed five mills in any one year.

The school code of 1875, as now in force, provides for the election of a State superintendent biennially, with the usual powers and duties. He is also to prepare and furnish to the county examiner suitable questions for the examination of teachers, hold teachers' institutes annually in each judicial district, prepare a list of text books for examiners and trustees, may grant State certificates to teachers and prepare three grades of certificates to be issued by county examiners, and is to apportion school moneys to counties semiannually upon the basis of scholastic population.

The county courts are to apportion school moneys to districts upon the same basis and at their first session after each general election to appoint a county examiner.

The duties of the county examiner are to examine and license teachers, encourage the inhabitants to form and organize school districts and establish public schools therein under competent teachers, furnish suitable text books, and send the children to school. He is to number the districts in his county in regular order and keep record of the same and report to State superintendent annually.

Each school district is to elect a board of three directors, with terms so arranged that one is to be elected each year to serve three years.

The directors have charge of school affairs, employ licensed teachers under written contracts, visit schools, submit estimates to district, and report to county examiner annually. Persons elected directors and refusing to serve forfeit $10, to be added to the school fund.

The revision provides that the boundaries of school districts shall remain as then constituted until changed by the county court.

Each district is vested with corporate powers and holds in its corporate name all lands and property required for school purposes.

The annual school meeting of the district is to be held on the third Saturday of August, at 2 o'clock P. M. All residents of the district qualified to vote for State and county officers are voters in the district meetings. At such meeting they elect the directors (who must be able to read and write), designate sites for school-houses, determine the time that school shall be taught in excess of three months and the amount of tax to be levied by district tax not to exceed one-half of 1 per cent., and, if sufficient money cannot be raised to support a school for three months, may by ballot determine that no school shall be kept.

Three months' school is required by the law. A school month is four weeks of five days each.

Teachers are required to attend the public examinations held by county examiners and to attend teachers' institutes, and no deduction of pay can be made for loss of time when so attending. Teachers' wages have preference over other claims.

CALIFORNIA.

The constitution of 1849 provided for a State superintendent, the creation of a school fund for the endowment of a State university, and for the establishment of a system of common schools by which a school should be taught in each district at least three months in every year.

The new constitution requires the schools to be maintained at least six months in every year and authorizes two counties to unite for school purposes under one superintendent. It declares that the public school system shall include all public schools, but the entire State fund is to be applied for the support of primary and grammar schools, and remits the selection of text books and examination of teachers to the local authorities.

The code in force in 1878 provided for a State board of education, to consist of the governor, State superintendent, principal of the State Normal School, and the superintendents of San Francisco, Sacramento, Santa Clara, Alameda, Sonoma, and San Joaquin Counties, with power to adopt rules for their own government and the government of the public schools and district libraries, and to prescribe the course of study in the public schools.

The State superintendent is elected by the people at the general election, with the usual powers and duties. He is a visitor of orphan asylums and all incorporated literary institutions. His duty is to visit schools in different counties, to report to the controller each year the number of children in each county between 5 and 17 years of age, and to the governor biennially preceding each session of the legislature.

A county superintendent is elected in each county biennially, unless under the new constitution two counties choose to unite for such election. He is to apportion school money to the districts, draw his warrants therefor, and keep record of the same. He is to visit each school in his county at least once in each year, and for every school not visited forfeits $10 from his salary. He is to preside over teachers' institutes, enforce prescribed course of study in schools, approve or reject plans for school-houses, and in all counties of 20,000 inhabitants to devote his whole time to the duties of his office. In connection with three professional teachers appointed by him he is to examine persons who wish to teach in the county schools. He may require the district trustees to repair school buildings, and if they neglect to provide a school in any district he may appoint the teachers, open the schools, and draw his warrant for the expenses.

There are three trustees in each district, one to be elected each year for three years. They have power to prescribe and enforce rules for the government of the schools, to control and manage the school property of the district, purchase furniture and apparatus, to build school-houses, and purchase lots when authorized by district, employ teachers and fix their compensation, exclude from schools children under 6 years of age, enforce prescribed course of study, keep a register of all children entitled to admission to the schools, and maintain all schools established by them an equal length of time during the year, as far as practicable with equal rights and privileges, and each trustee must visit every school at least once each term. They must use all school moneys exclusively for schools under their direction for the year until at least eight months' school has been maintained. County school money may be used for any purpose authorized by law, but all State moneys, less 10 per cent. for library, are to be applied exclusively to the payment of teachers.

Writing and drawing paper, pens, ink, and lead and slate pencils for the use of the schools are furnished under direction of the trustees and paid for out of district fund. Books for the children of indigent parents may be also furnished.

Each county, city, or incorporated town, unless subdivided, forms one school district. Each district is designated by name and possesses corporate powers.

Every elector of the county who has resided in the district thirty days is a district voter.

The school census of each district is to be taken annually in June by a census marshal appointed by the trustees. The school year begins July 1, and the school month is four weeks of five days each.

Every school, unless otherwise specially provided, must be open for the admission of all white children residing in the district between 5 and 21 years of age. Children of African descent or Indians are to be taught in separate schools, but if separate schools are not provided they shall be admitted to the other schools.

Unless otherwise specially provided, the schools are to be of three grades, no school to continue in session over six hours a day, and pupils under 8 years are not to be kept over four hours; pupils are admitted in the order of registry.

In cities having graded schools beginners must be taught by teachers of at least four years' experience.

Ten per cent. of the State school fund apportioned to the district, not, however, to exceed $50, together with any sum added thereto by donation, is to be expended annually by the district board for library and apparatus. Libraries are to be kept in the school-houses when practicable and free to all pupils of suitable age. Any member of the district may become entitled to the privileges on payment of life membership or such monthly fee as may be prescribed.

The county school tax is to be estimated at $500 for each teacher in the county, deducting therefrom 90 per cent. of the State fund apportioned. The board of supervisors must levy the county school tax, not to exceed 50 cents on each $100, and not less than $3 for each census child. If the supervisors fail to levy, the auditor must add the amount to the assessment roll.

The district may by vote raise an additional tax not to exceed 70 cents on each $100 for building purposes in any one year, and not to exceed 30 cents for other purposes.

The State school moneys are apportioned to the counties in proportion to the number of children 5 to 17 years old. The county superintendent apportions to the districts according to the number of teachers, estimating one teacher to each 100 census children or fraction not less than 15,

$500 to each teacher. Districts having over 10 and less than 15 census children receive $300. Any balance remaining goes pro rata to districts having over 50 census children.

To entitle a district to the apportionment there must have been at least six months' school the preceding year, the prescribed text books and course of studies must have been used and teachers holding legal certificates employed.

Female teachers are to receive the same compensation allowed males for like services, and women are eligible to school offices.

Parents or guardians having control of children between 8 and 14 years of age are required to send them to school at least two-thirds of the time the schools are taught. Parents of children deaf and dumb or blind are to send same to State institution for such classes for not less than five years.

Teachers' institutes are held in each county of 20 or more districts annually, and in other counties at discretion of county superintendent. The sessions are to be not less than 3 nor more than 5 days, and teachers are required to attend, and $100 may be used for expenses.

COLORADO.

Article IX of the constitution requires the maintenance of a uniform system of free public schools throughout the State, wherein all residents between 6 and 21 years of age shall be educated gratuitously, one or more schools to be maintained in each district at least three months in each year.

It also provides for a State board of education, to consist of the State superintendent, secretary of state, and attorney general, a county superintendent in each county to be elected for two years. The legislature is to provide for the organization of school districts of convenient size, in each of which shall be a board of three or more directors, to be elected by the qualified voters of the district, who shall have control of instruction in the public schools of their districts.

The school laws are compiled to 1877.

The State and county superintendents are elected biennially at the general election, with the usual powers and duties.

The districts are divided into three classes: Those containing a school population of over 1,000 are of the first class; those containing a population of less than 1,000 and not less than 350, of the second class; and those of less than 350, of the third class.

Districts of the first class are to elect a board of six directors, and those of the second and third class, three directors, with terms so arranged that one-third shall be elected each year.

Voters at State elections who have resided in district 30 days may vote in district meetings. No resident is denied the right to vote on account of sex.

Each organized district is a body corporate. New districts may be formed on petition of parents or guardians of not less than ten children of school age.

The district board may employ and dismiss teachers, fix and pay their salaries; prescribe rate of tuition for non-residents, the course of study exercises, and text books to be used; enforce rules and regulations of State superintendent, the length of schools in excess of three months, the number of teachers to be employed, the time for opening and closing the schools; require all pupils to be furnished with the prescribed books; provide books for indigent children and exclude all sectarian books. Text books once prescribed are not to be changed for four years

The school boards of districts of the first and second class may establish high schools and determine the qualifications for admission thereto.

Teachers must hold license from State or county authority.

A public school is one that derives its support wholly or in part from money raised by State, county, or district tax.

Every public school must be taught in the English language, and, except the high schools, be open at least three months in each year for the admission of all children of school age resident in district.

The school year begins September 1. The school month is 4 weeks of 5 days of not more than 6 hours each. The school age is over 6 and under 21 years.

The scholastic census is to be taken by the secretary of the district board annually.

Teachers' institutes are to be held in each judicial district when the county superintendents of two or more counties in the district give assurance to the State superintendent that at least 25 teachers desire to attend one, and $100 may be applied annually for expenses.

CONNECTICUT.

The constitution provides for a school fund, the interest of which is to be applied to the support of the public schools for the equal benefit of all the people of the State, and prohibits it from being diverted to any other purpose.

The laws as in force in 1879 provide for a State board of education, consisting of the governor, lieutenant governor, and four persons chosen by the legislature—one from each congressional district—for four years, one to be elected each year.

The board has the general supervision of the educational interests of the State and appoints a secretary who acts substantially as State superintendent.

There is no county school organization. Each town, at its annual meeting, elects a board of school visitors, consisting of 3, 6, or 9, one-third to be chosen each year for the term of 3 years, and the town may vest the employment of teachers in this board.

The board are to choose a chairman and secretary and have power to prescribe rules for the classification, management, discipline, and studies of the public schools, and, subject to the State board, determine the text books to be used. They are to examine and issue certificates to teachers, and may appoint acting school visitors, to consist of the secretary and one or more of the members of the board.

Each town has power to form, alter, unite, or dissolve school districts, but no new district can be formed unless it contains 40 children of school age. Any town may, by vote at annual meeting, abolish all school districts and assume the control of all the schools therein, and for this purpose shall constitute a single school district.

School districts are bodies corporate and hold annual meetings. Qualified voters in the town resident in district are voters, and shall choose a district committee of not more than three, who are the executive officers of the district, and are annually to take census of all children in the district between the ages of 4 and 16.

Public schools are required to be established in every district for at least 30 weeks in each year where the number of persons of school age is 24 or more and at least 24 weeks in other districts. No school is required to be maintained where the average attendance is less than 8.

The schools are to be open to all children over 4 years of age, but the board of visitors may exclude all under 5 years. No person is to be excluded on account of race or color.

If the districts neglect to employ teachers and keep open a school, the board of visitors are to do so, and the expense is to be paid by the town.

Each district or town maintaining a high school, which shall raise by tax or otherwise $10 or more for a library in any year, shall be entitled to receive in addition $10 from the State, and the board of visitors are to select the books therefor.

Districts have power to vote taxes for school purposes, but no district is entitled to any share of the State fund unless a school has been kept up as required by law during the preceding year.

DELAWARE.

The constitution requires the legislature to provide by law for establishing schools and promoting arts and sciences.

The school laws as amended to 1875 provide for a State board to consist of the State superintendent, the president of Delaware College, and the State auditor. The State superintendent is appointed annually by the governor.

The State board are to hear appeals and determine finally all matters of controversy between the superintendent and the commissioners or teachers or between commissioners and teachers, prescribe text books, issue uniform series of blanks for use of teachers, and require records to be kept and returns made in accordance therewith.

The State superintendent is charged with the usual duties and is to engage in no other business. He may also examine teachers, grant certificates, and suspend or withdraw the same for cause, subject to appeal to the State board. The certificates are not to be available until a fee of $2 is paid to the county treasurer and the certificate countersigned by him. The State superintendent may redistrict or consolidate districts in Sussex County, but not interfere with consolidated districts or incorporated boards.

At the annual stated meeting of each district, after the first, one of a board of 3 school commissioners[1] is to be elected for a term of three years. This provision does not apply to Wilmington or to districts 45 and 46 in New Castle.

The school commissioners shall annually, without regard to any vote therein, levy and collect $100 in each district in New Castle and Kent Counties and $60 in each district in Sussex for the support of schools.

The commissioners are to make assessment lists for their districts of all white male inhabitants, receive and collect all moneys of the district, select sites, lease or purchase necessary grounds or buildings, and provide schools for the district when and as long as the funds will enable them to employ teachers.

Teachers are to hold certificates of State superintendent; but this does not apply to schools or districts controlled by an incorporated board, unless by special request of such board.

The act provides that the districts shall remain as constituted at the time of its passage, but they might be altered or divided by the levy court; but no district should be divided unless each part should contain 35 scholars over 5 years of age. Two or more districts may unite for the support of schools for their common benefit.

The stated meeting of the district is to be held in April each year. The district has power to determine by a majority vote what sum shall be raised for school purposes. If the majority so vote, it may be raised by tax; otherwise, by subscription. The tax is not to exceed $400, exclusive of the fixed sum required to be levied without reference to vote. Districts No. 9 in New Castle County and No. 3 in Kent may raise $500 and No. 5 in Kent $400 by taxation. Any district raising $300 by tax may levy such further sum as may be required for a good school therein, on the rate bill system, by quarterly apportionment on the persons sending scholars to school. Any district which shall raise $25 in any year by tax or subscription may draw its proportion of State school money.

The State school fund consists of the surplus revenue, 5,000 shares Farmers' Bank, loan of $80,793.83 to the P., W. & B. Railroad, and loan of $5,000 to Sussex County, the clear income to be divided equally among the counties. The income of other stocks and securities belonging to the fund, fees for marriage and auction licenses, and other income

[1] These commissioners are termed also a school committee.

of said fund to be distributed to the counties in proportion to the population by the census of 1830, after deducting $30 from share of each county for printing for school convention; the city of Wilmington is to receive one-seventh of the share of New Castle County.

The schools are to be free to all white children over five years of age.

By special act the city of Wilmington is made an independent district, controlled by a board of education of two from each ward. The board are given corporate powers; may rent, purchase, or build houses, and do all acts necessary for instituting and sustaining schools, and may increase the number until they are sufficient to accommodate all white children.

There was no law providing for the education of colored children until the act of March 24, 1875.

By that act the levy court was required to levy annually a tax of 30 cents on each $100 of the assessments of real and personal property and polls of colored persons as they stand on the lists, the proceeds of the tax to be set apart as a separate and distinct fund for the support of colored schools in the State. This fund was to be paid over to the Delaware Association for the Education of Colored Children and applied by them to the support of colored schools, each county to have the benefit of the amount collected in it.

A subsequent act prohibits the use of any part of this fund by the association for the payment of salaries or expenses of its officers.

FLORIDA.

The constitution declares it to be the paramount duty of the State to make ample provision for the education of all children residing within its borders without distinction or preference, and requires the legislature to provide a uniform system of common schools; for a university and the liberal maintenance of the same; instruction in both to be free.

In addition to the income of the State fund, it requires the levy of an annual State tax of not less than one mill on the dollar and an annual county tax of not less than one-half of the amount apportioned from the State fund. No district is to be entitled to any apportionment unless a school has been sustained therein at least three months.

The school code, as in force in 1877, provides for a State board consisting of the State superintendent, secretary of state, and attorney general.

The State superintendent is appointed by the governor for four years, and is ex officio president of the State board.

The State board has charge of all school lands and funds, and is to use appropriations to the university or seminary fund in establishing one or more departments of the university, commencing with a department of teaching and a preparatory department, to which each county may send pupils in ratio of number of representatives, free of charge for tuition.[1] It is also to decide upon questions and appeals referred to it by the State superintendent.

The State superintendent is charged with the usual duties of supervision of school interests and apportionment of funds, and is to entertain and decide upon appeals, or refer the same to the State board, as well as to prescribe text books and rules for the management of the department of education.

The county board consists of not more than five, to be appointed by the State board, on nomination of the State superintendent, upon recommendation of the representatives of the county.

The county superintendent is appointed by the governor, with other county officers, for a term of 2 years, and is to serve as secretary and agent of the county board, is to inspect county, ascertain localities in which schools should be established, the number who will attend each, and amount of aid citizens will contribute, present plans for school buildings, and visit and examine schools.

The county board hold and manage all property acquired by county for educational purposes, select sites for school-houses of not less than one acre in rural districts and as near that as possible in cities and villages, purchase, rent, construct, and repair school-houses, locate and maintain schools to accommodate as far as possible all youth between 6 and 21 years of age, employ such teachers as may be satisfactory to the local trustees, grade and classify pupils, establish schools of higher grades when the advancement and number of pupils require, establish and maintain school libraries, apportion school moneys to the districts in proportion to the average attendance, examine teachers, and do all acts necessary for the promotion of the educational interests of the county.

The district trustees are to consist of one and not more than three persons. They are to be recommended by the patrons of the school, selected by the county superintendent, and appointed by the county board, and have special charge of the schools for which they are appointed.

Each county constitutes one school district. Any county or school district neglecting to support a school for three months in the year forfeits its proportion of the State fund.

The county school tax is not to exceed one-half of 1 per cent. in any one year.

Teachers' certificates are granted by the State board, State superintendent, and county board, or by county superintendent when authorized by county board. Certificates may be suspended by the county superintendent and annulled by the authority issuing the same.

The school day is not to exceed six hours; school month, 22 days; school term, 3 months; school year, 3 terms.

---

[1] Neither of these departments had been established up to the close of 1878, nor apparently in 1879.

The tax assessor is every four years to take census of children between 4 and 21 and between 6 and 21, reporting all deaf-mutes.

GEORGIA.

The constitution of 1877 provides for "a thorough system of common schools," "as nearly uniform as practicable," to be sustained "by taxation or otherwise," and to be free to all the children of the State, but limits the instruction to be given in them to "the elementary branches of an English education only," and requires separate schools for the white and colored races. This last is the only constitutional provision of its kind thus far except in Alabama and Texas.

The school law is the act of 1872 as subsequently amended.

The governor, secretary of state, and State school commissioner constitute a State board, who are an advisory body with whom the State commissioner may consult; also a body in the nature of a court to hear appeals from the State commissioner on any question of construction or administration of the school laws, their decisions to be final and conclusive.

The State commissioner is appointed by the governor, with consent of the senate, and charged with the general duties pertaining to the office. He is to apportion the State school revenue to the counties, upon the basis of the number of youth between 6 and 18 and of confederate soldiers under 30 years of age. His report is to include the statistics of private schools and colleges, as well as those of public schools.

The county board consists of five freeholders—3 to hold for 2 years and 2 for 4 years—who are selected by the grand jury. The county board appoints a secretary, who is to act as county commissioner, with a term of four years.

The county boards are to lay off the counties into subdistricts, and may alter these when necessary. They have the same control of the schools as the county boards in Florida. But where the counties are subdistricted they must appoint 3 intelligent and upright citizens of each subdistrict to act as school trustees for their subdistrict, to serve at first for one, two, and three years, one being subsequently appointed each year.

The county commissioner is to examine teachers, and when approved recommend to county board for license; he is the medium of communication between subofficers and the State commissioner and has general supervision of the schools.

The county board may establish evening schools for the instruction of youth over 12, and may organize one or more manual labor schools in each county on such plan as will be self-supporting. Ambulatory schools are also provided for in counties with sparse population, to continue for 2 months each in contiguous neighborhoods, and to have their terms successive, so that one teacher may serve several schools.

Each county is one school district. Any city of over 2,000 inhabitants or any county, under authority of the legislature, may organize a public school system independent of this system, but the same reports are required of them as of other districts.

The school census is to be taken every four years, to embrace all children between 6 and 18.

The academic and calendar years are the same. The minimum school term is three months each year.

Admission to all public schools of the State is gratuitous to all children residing in the subdistrict in which the school-houses are located. Schools for white and colored children are to be separate, but, so far as practicable, equal facilities are to be secured to both in respect of the abilities of teachers and length of time taught.

ILLINOIS.

Article VIII of the constitution requires the general assembly to provide a thorough and efficient system of free schools whereby all children of the State may receive a good common school education.

Laws to 1879.

A State superintendent of public instruction is elected by the people every four years and is charged with the usual powers and duties. A county superintendent is also elected for four years, with general supervision of county schools and to have charge of school lands therein.

Every congressional township is made a township for school purposes under control of a board of three trustees, to be elected by legal voters; term of office, 3 years. Must be 21 years of age and residents of township. No two, when elected, to be residents of the same school district. Women over 21 are eligible. Board vested with perpetual corporate powers. Meetings to be at least semiannual.

They are to lay off township into one or more districts, and upon petition of 50 voters establish high school. School fund to be apportioned to district in proportion to number of children under 21; in new districts set off from older ones, in proportion to the amount of taxes collected in them the year before the division. Trustees to report to county superintendent usual school statistics.

Annual meeting of school districts to be holden in April each year. A board of three directors to be elected for 3 years' terms, one each year, subject to change or reëlection.

The directors may levy a tax annually, not to exceed 2 per cent. for educational and 3 per cent. for building purposes, for establishing and maintaining schools for not less than 5 nor more than 9 months each year, and defraying expenses of same. After necessary school expenses are paid they may appropriate surplus to libraries and apparatus. The directors and not the district are the body corporate.

They are to establish and keep in operation for at least 110 days a sufficient number of schools for the accommodation of all children over 6 and under 21, and shall secure to such children the right and opportunity for an equal education in such schools;[1] may adopt and enforce necessary rules and regulations; appoint all teachers and fix their compensation; assign pupils to the several schools; direct studies and text books to be used; shall strictly enforce uniformity of text books, but not permit changes in same oftener than once in four years; no child excluded on account of color.

No teacher to be employed unless he holds proper certificate. Teachers' wages are payable monthly on return of report; not required to teach on Saturdays or legal holidays, nor to make up time of special holidays ordered by directors. School month, calendar month.

The State common school fund consists of 2 mills tax, 3 per cent. of net proceeds of sales of public lands, and interest on surplus revenue fund, to be apportioned to counties on the first Monday of January each year by the State auditor.

In school districts of over 2,000 inhabitants, instead of directors a board of education of 6 may be elected, with 3 to be added for every additional 20,000 inhabitants.

In cities of over 100,000 inhabitants the schools are under the control of a board of education, with a city superintendent. The purchase of lots and erection of houses to be with the concurrence of the city councils.

The presidents or principals of all colleges, academies, and educational institutions to report to State superintendent. The State superintendent may visit all educational and charitable institutions, and superintendents of same are to report to him.

State and county normal schools are established and provided for.

INDIANA.

Article VIII of the constitution declares that "knowledge and learning, generally diffused throughout a community, being essential to the preservation of a free government, it shall be the duty of the general assembly * * * to provide by law for a general and universal system of common schools wherein tuition shall be without charge and equally open to all."

Laws to 1879.

The State superintendent is elected for two years and has general supervision of State system.

The governor, State superintendent, the presidents of the State University and Purdue University, principal of State normal school, and superintendents of the three largest cities to constitute State board of education, of which the State superintendent is ex officio president.

The county superintendent is elected biennially by vote of township trustees in convention, and, with township trustees, constitutes county board of education.

---

[1] Exclusion of children on account of color is expressly forbidden.

Each civil township and each incorporated town or city are school districts with corporate powers.

The common council of each city and board of trustees of each incorporated town, at their first meeting in June each year, are to choose school trustees to serve three years, one to be chosen each year.

The school trustees are to organize by the election of a president, treasurer, and secretary of their own number.

Trustees are to receive revenue and keep account of same; to take charge of school affairs of township; employ teachers; procure or build houses and furniture; establish and grade schools; and have care and management of all school property. In incorporated cities or towns may employ superintendent, and trustees of two or more municipal corporations may establish joint graded schools. May levy tax for any school purpose, except tuition, not to exceed 50 cents on $100, and $1 poll tax, and are to make annual enumeration of children between 6 and 21, distinguishing between white and colored. All taxpayers of the district and persons transferred for school purposes are voters at school district meetings, except minors and married women. The voters are to meet annually in October and elect a director who is a voter, and may determine time school is to be taught and what additional branches.

The school year begins on the first Monday in July, and the tuition revenue is to be expended in the school year. No teacher to be employed or to commence school unless licensed by State or county authority.

Text books are prescribed by county board; formerly were not to be changed for three years after adoption. By a law of 1879 may not be changed till the end of the time for which they were adopted, and then new adoptions must be for 10 years.

Township institutes to be held one Saturday in each month, county institutes in each county annually.

The school term is 60 days; month, 20 days; week, 5 days.

Schools to be taught in the English language. German may be taught on request of parents of 25 children.

Township trustees may organize separate schools for colored children, having same rights, privileges, and advantages as the other schools. If no separate schools are provided, they are to be admitted to other schools. Any colored child sufficiently advanced is entitled to enter the higher grade provided for white children. There is to be no distinction in same on account of race or color.

In cities of 30,000 or more, each district is to elect one commissioner to be a member of the board of city school commissioners. The common council is to divide city into districts. City board to organize and elect president, secretary, and treasurer. One-third of board to be elected each year for term of three years. The board to have full charge and control of schools in city. Cities of less than 30,000 may adopt this system.

IOWA.

The constitution requires that a system of common schools shall be provided for, under which a school shall be kept up and supported in each district for at least three months in every year.

The State superintendent is elected for two years by the people, and is charged with general supervision of schools and county superintendents.

County superintendents are elected by people for two years.

In addition to usual duties, they are to report to the superintendent of college for blind names, age, and residence of all persons blind to such an extent as to be unable to acquire an education in the common schools, and also of deaf and dumb in same condition to the superintendent of the institution for deaf and dumb.

Each civil township and each independent district organized prior to the act is declared to be a school district with corporate powers.

Each district township to hold annual meeting on the second Monday in March. In townships comprising one district three directors are to be elected. When divided into subdistricts, one director is elected for each and one at large, who are to constitute the township board of school directors. The township board may divide town into subdistricts. Subdistrict meetings for choice of directors are held the first Monday in March annually. No subdistrict for less than 15 pupils is to be created. Women are eligible to school offices.

Township boards are invested with charge and control of schools and school-houses, but cannot change text books oftener than once in three years except by vote of electors.

In each subdistrict shall be taught one or more schools for the instruction of all youth between 5 and 21 for at least 24 weeks, of 5 days each, every year. Any person who was in the military service of the United States during his minority may be admitted.

Contracts with teachers to be in writing. No person to be employed unless holding certificate of county superintendent.

School month of 4 weeks of 5 days each. Schools to be closed during sessions of institute and teachers required to attend. By vote at any legal meeting, electors may direct German language to be taught.

The county supervisors are to levy a county tax for support of schools of not less than one nor more than three mills on the dollar; also the district tax which may be voted; the district tax for school-house fund not to exceed ten mills; contingent fund not to exceed $5 per pupil; teachers' fund, including semiannual apportionment, not to exceed $15 for each pupil residing in the district. May levy $75 for contingent fund and $270, including semiannual apportionment, for teachers' fund each year for each subdistrict.

The county auditor is to apportion semiannually to the several districts the county school tax and interest on permanent school fund in proportion to number of persons between 5 and 21, and county treasurer to pay to district treasurer quarterly.

Cities or towns of not less than 300 inhabitants may be constituted independent districts. Independent districts of less than 500 to elect 3 directors—of 500 and over, 6 directors—one-third each year, with powers of township boards.

Counties with a population of 2,000 may establish high schools, to be controlled and managed by 6 directors chosen at a general election, the county superintendent to be president of board. Tax therefor not to exceed five mills.

County superintendent to visit schools once and subdirector to visit them twice each term; enumeration to be made by subdirector.

The State university is governed by a board of regents, consisting of the governor, State superintendent, president of university, and one person from each congressional district, elected by general assembly. The course of study to commence at points where completed in high schools.

KANSAS.

Article VI of the constitution provides that the legislature shall encourage the promotion of intellectual, moral, scientific, and agricultural improvement, by establishing a uniform system of common schools, and schools of a higher grade, embracing normal, preparatory, collegiate, and university department.

Laws to 1879.

The State board of education consists of the State superintendent, chancellor of State University, president State Agricultural College, and principals of normal schools at Emporia and Leavenworth, who may issue State diplomas and certificates to professional teachers.

A State superintendent is elected biennially, charged with usual duties and to recommend list of approved text books.

County superintendents elected biennially by people to have charge of school interests of the county, to divide county into convenient school districts, and may change and alter the same, but no new district to be formed unless it contains 15 scholars of school age.

Every district is a body corporate, and deemed to be duly organized when district board is elected and qualified. Annual meetings of district to be held in August. All persons who are qualified electors and females over 21 are voters in district. The district board consists of a director, clerk, and treasurer, one to be elected each year.

The district by vote determines sites of school-houses; may raise tax not exceeding 1 per cent. for building purposes and 1 per cent. for teachers' fund; determines time school is to be taught, not to be less than 3 months, and whether by male or female teachers; appropriates money for summer or winter school or both; and may direct sale of lot when not needed for school purposes. Two or more districts may unite to establish graded schools by major vote, and have powers of district. May vote tax not exceeding 2 mills for a district library, to consist of works of history, biography, science, and travels. The district clerk to make annual report to the annual meeting, which he is to submit and read to the legal voters of the district. The district board are to employ and may dismiss teachers; to visit schools at least once each term; shall require uniform text books to be used in each branch of schools; when adopted, no change to be made for five years, unless upon petition of four-fifths of legal voters of district.

Common English branches to be taught in every school district, with such others as district board may direct.

School month, 4 weeks of 5 days of 6 hours each.

Schools to be at all times equally free and accessible to all children over 5 and under 21 resident in district, subject to such regulations as district board may prescribe. Whenever the public money is not sufficient to support schools for the length of time determined by the district, the district board may assess a tuition fee upon each scholar attending, to meet such deficiency, but not until the entire 1 per cent. for teachers' fund has been assessed.

A normal institute for the instruction of teachers is to be held annually in each county.

The county superintendent and two persons appointed by county commissioners are to constitute a county examining board for examination of teachers.

Cities of over 15,000 inhabitants are denominated cities of the first class, and the schools are controlled by a board of education of three from each ward, elected by voters of ward, one each year. Board may elect a city superintendent and appoint their own examining committee. The whole city is to constitute one district for purposes of taxation, but may be divided into subdistricts by the board. Cities of over 2,000 and not exceeding 15,000, of second class, with board of two from each ward, one elected each year, with similar powers.

KENTUCKY.

The constitution provides for the preservation of the school fund and the distribution of the revenue from it, with any sum raised by tax or otherwise in aid of common schools, and for the election of a superintendent of public instruction to hold office for four years.

The school code, as amended up to 1878, provides for a State board of education, to consist of the State superintendent, secretary of state, attorney general, and two professional teachers elected by them, who are made a body corporate; the State superintendent and two professional teachers to be a standing committee to propose rules and determine text books to be adopted at discretion by trustees. The State board may organize and keep in existence a State teachers' association, but no money is to be paid out of the treasury or common school fund therefor. The State superintendent is charged with the usual duties.

A county commissioner of common schools for each county, with one for the city of Louisville, is to be appointed for a term of two years by the court of claims.

The county commissioner may lay off and abolish districts, examine and pay teachers, suspend or remove same for cause, and have general charge of schools of county; may select uniform series of text books from the list furnished by State board, not to be changed for two years and the district trustees are bound by the selection when made;[1] and shall hold a teachers' institute in his county annually. Teachers, and all persons holding certificates as such, are required to attend.

Persons applying for examination are to pay $1 to county board, or $3 if to State board. Every person attending institute to pay fee of $2.

The county commissioner, with the consent of the white voters of any district, may condemn school-house, and a per capita tax of not exceeding $2 on each white male over 21 may be levied to rebuild the same. Where such amount is inadequate, the trustee may warn in the hands liable to work on the highways for the purpose of rebuilding. The house may be built of logs, stone, brick, or plank, but must be of sufficient size to accommodate the children. If a fireplace is used, the chimney must be of stone or brick; if a stove is to be used, the pipe must be so protected as to be secure against liability from fire.

School districts are to remain as constituted until changed as provided by the act. No district to include more than 100 white children between 5 and 20 years of age, unless it contains a town or village or there be established a high school, academy, or college entitled to a share of the State fund, and none with less than 40 such children.

Cities and towns establishing and maintaining schools adequate for all white children in it shall be deemed one district.

Each district is a body corporate, and its affairs are managed by three trustees, one to be elected annually. Aside from the usual duties, they are charged to invite and encourage all white scholars to attend the schools, to instruct parents that it is their right for which the State pays, even though they may contribute nothing; and their annual report must show that they have performed this duty. They must not make any arrangement for the benefit of some individuals to the exclusion of others. They are to take a census of *white* children between 6 and 20 in April of each year.

Colleges and educational institutions exclusively devoted to the education of white children may be made school districts and receive State school funds for teaching youth of school age.

Where, by contribution or otherwise, 40 volumes can be procured, the trustee may organize a district library; but no part of school revenues derived from general taxation can be used for the purchase of

[1] In the examination of teachers and choice of text books, the commissioner has the aid of two assistants, selected by himself.

books, maps, or charts for the same. The library to be free to all white pupils of suitable age belonging to the district.

A poll or per capita tax of not more than 50 cents per annum may be levied on each patron of the school for fuel and contingent expenses.

The income of the State fund is distributed pro rata for each white child between 6 and 20.

A majority vote of qualified white voters is required to levy a district tax. Any resident widow or alien taxpayer or person having children of school age may vote. District tax not to exceed 25 cents on $100 in any year, and in graded school districts not to exceed 30 cents. Under a law of April 9, 1878, a tax, after due notice to the district, may be voted for five successive years.

No school to be deemed a common school or entitled to contribution out of the school fund unless the same has actually been kept by qualified teachers for five months, or in districts having minimum number (40) of school children, three months during the school year, and at which every white child between 6 and 20 has had the privilege of attending. The school year begins July 1; school month, 22 days.

Prior to 1874 there was no law providing for the education of colored children. At that time an act was passed providing for a uniform system of common schools for colored children, to be supported exclusively by taxes to be levied upon colored people.

The revenue arising from this source is distributed annually by the State superintendent to the counties, and the county commissioner is responsible for its proper distribution.

The county commissioner is to lay off his county into suitable districts, not to exceed 100 nor less than 20 children of school age, and appoint three colored trustees for each district. The teachers are required to hold certificates the same as for white schools. No colored child is allowed to attend a white school, nor any white child a colored school. No house for colored school can be erected within one mile of a white school, except in cities and towns, and there not within 600 feet. The officers and teachers of colored schools may organize State and county associations. The census of colored children is to be taken in the same manner and at the same time as that of the white children.

The State board is to prescribe the course of study and rules for the government of such schools. The State superintendent is to furnish blanks, and is authorized to employ an additional clerk at $700 per annum, paid out of fund collected. Five per cent. of the tax is deducted for collection. The county commissioner is allowed 1 per cent for disbursing, and $3 for each colored school visited are also to be paid out of colored fund. The fund is thus subject to large reduction.

LOUISIANA.

The constitution of 1868 required the establishment of at least one free public school in every parish, free to all children of the State between 6 and 21, without distinction of race, color, or previous condition. It forbade the establishment of any separate schools or institutions of learning by the State exclusively for any race, and provided that institutions for the education of the deaf and dumb should be fostered by the State.

The new constitution of 1879 requires schools to be established for the education of all children between 6 and 18, to be under the control and direction of parish boards of directors. Each parish board is authorized to appoint a superintendent of its schools, who shall be secretary of the board; the entire system to be under the supervision of a State superintendent chosen for four years.

It requires the general assembly to provide for the support of schools by taxation or otherwise, but at the same time provides that the State tax for all purposes shall not exceed 6 mills. A poll tax is to be levied of from $1 to $1.50 on every male over 21. Four per cent. interest on the full school fund of $1,130,867.50 is to be paid annually to the several parishes for the support of schools, but this interest is to be paid out of the tax to be levied and collected for the general purposes of education. Schools are to be taught in the English language, but in parishes where the French predominates they may also be taught in that language. Women over 21 are made eligible to office under the school laws.

The school law of 1877 provides for a State board of education, to consist of the governor, lieutenant governor, secretary of state, attorney general, State superintendent, and two citizens. They are to prescribe text books and apparatus, not to be changed oftener than once in four years, contract for same with lowest bidder, to be furnished pupils at lowest prices; also, to appoint a board of directors of not less than 5 nor more than 9 for each parish except New Orleans for terms of four years, and fix the branches to be taught in public schools.

The State superintendent is charged with the usual duties.

The parish board appoint from their own number an examining committee, and no teacher can be employed without their certificate. They are required to limit the annual expense of the schools to the revenue derived from the State, parish, or from contributions. They are to divide the parish into subdistricts, provide school-houses, employ teachers, and have control and supervision of schools. Annual and monthly visiting committees are to be appointed by the board, and each school is to be visited monthly.

The public schools of New Orleans are under the control of a board of 20 directors, 8 appointed by the State board and 12 by the city board of administrators. The city board appoint a superintendent for a term of four years, who is ex officio a member of the board, but without vote. They may establish night schools and two or more normal schools.

City and parish boards are to establish schools; no school to be of less than 10 pupils, and not over 60 pupils to be in charge of one teacher. The State board prescribe branches to be taught.

The directors may levy a parish tax of not exceeding 2 mills, but parish tax not to exceed 1 per cent. for all purposes. May levy tax in New Orleans of 2 mills, but not to exceed $275,000.

Enumeration of children of school age to be taken biennially in each district.

The new constitution apparently omits some important requirements of the old, and leaves them in the discretion of the parish board. Until they shall take action in the premises, it cannot be known what changes will be made, nor what effect they may have upon the present system.

MAINE.

The constitution makes it the duty of the legislature to require the several towns to make suitable provision for the support of schools, and from time to time, as circumstances may authorize, to encourage and suitably endow academies, colleges, and seminaries of learning.

School laws as in force, 1878.

The officers of the school system are a State superintendent, appointed by the governor and council, town superintending committees, or town supervisor with same powers, and district agents.

The term of office of State superintendent is three years, and he has general supervision over all public schools of the State. The towns at their annual meeting are to choose a superintending committee of 3, one to be elected each year to serve 3 years.

The town may determine number and limit of school districts, or abolish the same, and assume control of all schools within its limits; may choose agents for districts, or authorize districts to choose them, and may authorize agents to employ teachers instead of superintending committee.

When the town has abolished the district system, the superintending committee have control and management of schools; where divided into districts, the general supervision of same.

Towns are required to raise not less than 80 cents for each inhabitant, exclusive of income of corporate school fund, State moneys, &c., under penalty of forfeiture of not less than twice nor more than four times the amount; and may make provision for free industrial or mechanical drawing in day or evening schools.

They may also raise money to purchase text books for pupils or sell them to pupils at cost.

School districts that have exercised privileges and franchises for one year to be deemed legally organized; all districts, corporations; qualified voters of town resident in district, voters therein.

Annual meetings to be held to choose moderator, clerk, and agent, unless agent is chosen by town.

The district by vote at its legal meetings controls all its affairs; but if it refuse to keep up the school for the required time or to provide proper houses, the town is authorized to interfere and do it, assessing cost on the district.

Where the minority are of opinion that the amount raised by the district is insufficient, they may appeal to the town, who may raise the money required.

The superintending committee of the town have the general supervision of the schools, examine teachers, select and prescribe text books, not to be changed for five years, visit and examine schools twice each term, classify and determine description of scholars who are to attend each school.

The agent is to take school census of children between 4 and 21 annually. If he neglects to make return the school committee must make the enumeration.

The towns alone are responsible for the support of schools and payment of instructors. The school district agent is the agent of town for the transaction of business in the district. (26 Me. Rep. 56.)

Any town establishing and maintaining a high school for not less than ten weeks in any year is entitled to receive from State one-half the expense thereof, not to exceed $500 to any one town.

Normal schools for education of teachers are provided for.

MARYLAND.

The constitution requires a free school system uniform throughout the State, with schools to be kept open in each district for at least six months each year.

The school law of 1872, *as subsequently amended.*

The State board of education consists of the governor, principal of State normal school, and four others, to be appointed by the governor from the presidents and examiners of county boards.

The State board has the care and supervision of public school interests; is to see that the law is executed, issues uniform series of blanks for returns, makes by-laws for administration of school system; may grant certificates to professional teachers, and the members of the board are ex officio trustees of State normal school, and all schools and colleges receiving State aid are to report to the board.

The county board of commissioners consists of three, or, in counties of over 100 schools, five persons appointed by the circuit court of the county for a term of two years.

The county board, a body corporate to take and hold all property now vested in the public school authorities of any county, is to have control and management of all schools in county; fix salaries of teachers, purchase and distribute text books; when the county is not properly divided into districts, to appoint a committee to divide the same. The commissioners are to select sites and prescribe plans of school-houses; may authorize German language to be taught, and employ assistant teachers in schools numbering over 50 scholars—one teacher for every additional 40 scholars. May establish graded schools in districts of over 100, and may close schools when average attendance is less than 10. Shall adopt and may prescribe text books; may authorize delivery of books to pupils under such rules as they may adopt, no pupil to pay more than $1 per quarter for use of same.

The county examiner is appointed by the board, and, if required, must receive the certificate of State board. He is to examine teachers, but no male under 19 or female under 17 can receive a certificate. He must visit schools three times each year if the number is 50 or less, and twice if the number is over 50, and report quarterly to the board. A public examination of each school is required twice each year.

Three trustees are appointed for each district by the county board, who are to have care of school-houses and attend to repairs of same, the amount of repairs to be determined by the county board before being made; appoint qualified teachers, subject to confirmation of county board, and report quarterly to county board.

One or more schools to be kept up in every district, if possible, for ten months each year, free to all white children between 6 and 21. To the ordinary elementary branches the trustees may add algebra, book-keeping, natural philosophy, vocal music, physiology, and laws of health and domestic economy.

The schools are to be kept open each week day except Saturday, six hours each day. The school year consists of four terms—fall, winter, spring, and summer—time of commencement and close to be fixed by the county board.

High schools may be established by the county board, to be under care of 3 high school commissioners appointed by the board, with powers of district trustees.

The mayor and council of the city of Baltimore are authorized to establish in said city a system of free public schools, and do any and every act necessary therefor; may delegate supervision and control thereof to a board of school commissioners, and may levy and collect tax to defray expenses thereof.

A State normal school is established, supported by annual State appropriations. The principal of normal school to hold teachers' institute in each county annually. District, county, and State teachers' associations are recommended, and district libraries, for which latter the county board is to pay $10 annually, provided the district shall raise an equal amount or more.

The county board are also to establish schools for colored children between 6 and 20 years of age, to be kept open the same length of time as other schools, each to be under control of a special board of trustees, to be appointed by the county board. The State moneys are to be apportioned to colored schools at same time and in same manner as to other schools. The total amount of taxes paid for school purposes by the colored people of any county or in Baltimore also to be devoted to the support of colored schools.

The State tax for school purposes is 10 cents on each $100, no money to be apportioned to any county unless the schools are kept open at least seven and one-half months in the year.

MASSACHUSETTS.

The constitution declares that "wisdom and knowledge, as well as virtue, diffused generally among the body of the people, being necessary for the preservation of their rights and liberties; and as these depend on spreading the opportunities and advantages of education in the various parts of the country, and among the different orders of the people, it shall be the duty of legislatures and magistrates, in all future periods of this Commonwealth, to cherish the interests of literature and the sciences, and all seminaries of them; especially the university at Cambridge, public schools, and grammar schools in the towns."

It further ordains that all moneys appropriated by the State or raised by taxation in the towns and cities for the support of public schools shall be applied to and expended in no other schools than those conducted according to law, and under the order and superintendence of the authorities of the town or city in which the money is to be expended, and never appropriated to any religious sect for the maintenance exclusively of its own school.

Another amendment precludes from voting and from eligibility to office all who cannot read the constitution in the English language and write their names, unless from physical disability, but not taking away their existing right to vote.

School laws as amended to 1878.

The board of education consists of the governor, lieutenant governor, and eight persons appointed by the governor and council for the term of 8 years, one retiring each year in the order of appointment. It appoints a secretary, who is the executive officer of the board, substantially performing the duties of a State superintendent. It may also appoint agents to visit the towns, inquire into condition of schools, and confer with committees or teachers, and generally perform same duties as the secretary might do if present. It prescribes the form of school registers to be kept in the schools, the forms of blanks and inquiries for returns of school committees, has general supervision of school matters, and reports each year to the legislature. The State board also has charge of State normal schools. The other officers are the town school committee, to consist of any number divisible by 3—one third to be elected by ballot each year for the term of 3 years, at the annual town meeting—who are to have general charge and superintendence of all public schools in the town. No person is ineligible on account of sex.

The school district system has been generally abolished in the State, but is retained in a few of the towns, and the schools are substantially carried on under the town system.

Every town is required to maintain at the expense of said town, for at least six months each year, a sufficient number of schools for the instruction of all children who may legally attend public school therein, under a teacher or teachers of competent ability and good morals.

The branches to be taught are orthography, reading, writing, English grammar, geography, arithmetic, drawing, history of the United States, and good behavior, to which the school committee may add, in such schools as they deem expedient, algebra, vocal music, agriculture, physiology, and hygiene.

Any city or town may, and every city or town having over 10,000 inhabitants must, annually make provision for giving free instruction in industrial or mechanical drawing to persons over 15 in day or evening schools, under the direction of the school committee.

Every town may, and every town of 500 families or householders must, besides the schools heretofore prescribed, maintain a school to be kept by a master of competent ability and good morals, who, in addition to the branches before mentioned, shall give instruction in bookkeeping, general history, surveying, geometry, natural philosophy, chemistry, botany, civil polity, and the Latin language; such school to be kept for the benefit of the whole town 36 weeks at least in each year, exclusive of vacations, and in every town of 4,000 inhabitants the teachers of such school shall be competent to instruct in astronomy, geology, rhetoric, logic, intellectual and moral science, political economy, and in the Greek and French languages.

Cities and towns may establish industrial schools to be under the control of the school committee, but attendance on such schools is not to take the place of attendance upon the public schools required by law.

One or more female assistants are to be employed in every school having an average of 50 or more scholars, unless the town by vote dispense with such assistants.

Towns neglecting to raise money for the support of the schools required by law shall forfeit a sum equal to twice the highest sum ever before voted for schools therein. Towns neglecting to choose school committee forfeit not less than $500 nor more than $1,000, forfeitures to be paid into county treasury, and three-fourths of same to be turned over to school committee, if any, or to selectmen, and used for support of schools in same manner as if raised by tax.

The school committee are to supervise schools, direct what books are to be used, prescribe as far as practicable the course of study and exercises to be pursued, procure at expense of town sufficient supply of text books to be furnished to pupils at cost; may procure at expense of town such apparatus, books of reference, and other means of illustration as they may deem necessary in accordance with appropriations made therefor. Cities or towns may authorize committee to purchase text books for use in schools, to be the property of the city or town, and to be loaned to pupils under such regulations as they may prescribe.

Any city or town may require committee to appoint a superintendent who, under their direction, shall have care and superintendence of the schools.

Towns not divided into districts to provide and maintain a sufficient number of school-houses for the accommodation of all children therein entitled to attend.

School census to be taken in May each year of all children between 5 and 15. No person excluded from schools on account of race, color, or religious opinions of applicant or scholar.

There are compulsory requirements as to sending to school children from 8 to 14 years of age, and through the aid of truant officers in towns these laws have been made remarkably effective, the enrolment in the schools for several years past having considerably exceeded the number of children of school age.

MICHIGAN.

The constitution requires the legislature to provide for and establish a system of primary schools to be kept without charge for tuition at least three months each year in every district.

It also provides for a superintendent of public instruction and a State board of education, of three members, one to be elected at each biennial election for the term of six years. The State superintendent is ex officio a member and secretary of board, which has especial supervision of the State normal school. The constitution further directs the legislature to provide for township libraries, and applies for the support thereof all fines for breach of the penal laws of the State.

The State superintendent is elected biennially, and charged with general supervision of public instruction: to visit and report upon the State university, all incorporated literary institutions, primary and normal schools, and State reform school; to prepare list of books best adapted to use of schools and for township libraries.

There is no county organization under the present law, the office of county superintendent having been abolished in 1875.

At the annual meeting of each township in April are to be elected a school inspector and school superintendent, who, with the township clerk, are to constitute the township board. The superintendent is chairman of board, is to examine teachers, visit schools at least twice each year, is subject to rules and regulations of State superintendent and to report to him. Each organized township to maintain a library, which may be divided into district libraries.

The township board is to divide township into convenient districts, and may alter and regulate boundaries. No district to be divided and no two districts consolidated without vote of a majority of taxpayers.

Every person over 21 who has been a resident for three months and holds property liable to tax, is a voter. All persons entitled to vote at township meetings who have resided in district three months are eligible to office and may vote on all questions, except when raising of tax is in question. School districts are deemed to be organized when any two of the three officers have filed acceptance of office.

The district by vote provides school-houses, imposes taxes, determines length of schools, whether to be taught by male or female teachers, and provides for repairs, purchase of apparatus, libraries, and for payment of debts and liabilities.

The tax for building purposes in any one year is limited to $250 in districts containing less than ten children of school age, to $500 in districts of over ten and less than thirty, and to $1,000 unless over fifty. Schools must be maintained not less than nine months in districts of 800 children of school age, five months in districts of from 30 to 800, and three months in districts of less than 30. In districts of less than 30 children of school age amount raised for entire support of schools, including share of school fund and two mill tax, not to exceed $50 per month. If district refuses or neglects duties, town board are to perform same. The director, or such person as the board may appoint, is to take census of children between 5 and 21. District board to employ qualified teachers.

The school year commences on the 1st Monday of September in each year; school month, 4 weeks of 5 days each.

Town boards to adopt text books not to be changed for 5 years; no money to be paid to towns until books so adopted are used, and proportion of 2 mill tax forfeited if schools not maintained as provided by law.

All residents of a district five years of age have equal right to attend any school therein, and no separate school or department to be kept for any race or color. This provision not to prevent grading of schools.

Graded schools may be established in districts of more than 100 children by two-thirds vote, to be controlled by board of trustees, one-third to be elected each year, with powers of district board. By act of April 17, 1871, a State public school for dependent and neglected children was established and placed under supervision of a board of control of eight persons appointed by the governor, one to be appointed every two years.

Its object is to receive children over 4 and under 16 years of age who are in a suitable condition of mind and body to receive instruction and who are neglected and dependent, especially those maintained in county poorhouses or who are abandoned by parents, orphans, or whose parents have been convicted of crime.

Such children are to be maintained and educated in the branches taught in the common schools, and to have proper physical and moral training. The declared object is to provide temporary homes until homes can be found in families. It is the duty of the board of control to provide suitable places for them when sufficiently educated, and it is made the legal guardian of such children and may bind them out.

Whenever there is a vacancy in such school the superintendents of the poor are to bring the children in the poorhouses, or other children in want or suffering, or abandoned or improperly exposed, or in any orphan asylum whose officers desire to surrender them, for examination before the judge of probate, who is to determine the facts as to dependency. The superintendents of poor are to forward children to such school.

MINNESOTA.

Article VIII of the constitution recites that, "the stability of a republican form of government depending mainly on the intelligence of the people, it shall be the duty of the legislature to establish a general and uniform system of public schools;" and it requires that "the legislature shall make such provisions by taxation or otherwise as, with the income arising from the school fund, will secure a thorough and uniform system of public schools in each township of the State."

Laws to 1877.

The State superintendent is appointed by the governor, with consent of senate, for 2 years, charged with usual duties.

A county superintendent is elected for each county for 2 years, who is to examine teachers and have general supervision of schools of his county. In counties containing over 100 districts he may appoint an assistant.

The district system has been adopted in this State. Every district is presumed to be legally organized after it shall have exercised the privileges and franchises for one year. Districts are classified as follows: First, common school districts; second, independent districts; and, third, special districts. The county commissioners may form new districts.

Legal voters of district are to choose moderator, director, clerk, and treasurer; the director, treasurer, and clerk to constitute the district board. Women may vote in district meetings.

The district to provide houses and grounds, establish schools, and raise money by tax. Tax for building purposes not to exceed 8 mills in any one year, but may raise $600 if it does not exceed 25 mills. Districts of less than ten voters may raise $200 only.

District board may levy tax if district neglects, hire teachers, and have charge of schools.

Independent districts to be under the control of six directors, two elected each year; to keep schools in operation not less than 12 nor more than 44 weeks each year; to appoint board of examiners, who are to examine teachers and visit and examine schools in such districts.

All schools supported wholly or in part by the State school fund to be deemed public schools, and admission to the same shall be free to all persons between 5 and 21 residing in the district; none to be excluded on account of color, nationality, or social position.

School month, 4 weeks of 5 days each.

A county tax of 1 mill, all fines for breach of penal laws, and amount of liquor licenses to be county school fund.

The State contracts for text books; the counties to pay for amount ordered by them at the prices fixed. Books so procured are to be used in schools and not changed for five years; $50,000 set apart as a text book fund for this purpose.

The State normal schools are under control of board of 6 directors, 3 appointed every 2 years by governor and senate; supported by State appropriations; tuition free to State pupils who engage to teach for two years.

MISSISSIPPI.

The earlier constitutions contained the declaration that, "religion, morality, and knowledge being essential to good government, the preservation of liberty, and the happiness of mankind, schools and the means of education shall forever be encouraged."

Article VIII of the constitution of 1868 required the legislature to establish a uniform system of free public schools for all children between the ages of 5 and 21, and as soon as practicable schools of a higher grade, one or more schools to be maintained in each school district at least four months in every year. It also provided for a State board, State superintendent, county superintendent, and for the establishment of a common school fund; and in addition thereto the legislature was authorized to levy a poll tax not exceeding $2 and provide for the levy of such other taxes as should be required to properly support the school system, all school funds to be divided pro rata among children of school age.

School laws to 1878.

The State board have the management and investment of the school fund, and are to report its state and condition each year. The State superintendent is elected every four years, has general charge and superintendence of school system, and is to determine true intent and meaning of school laws, rules, and regulations, his decision to be final unless reversed by State board.

The county superintendent is appointed by the State board for two years, has supervision of schools in county; he is to arrange the schools of his county so that suitable school facilities shall be afforded to every child of school age, to examine teachers, and open and close schools so that equal number of days shall be given to all schools in the county.

The patrons of the school are to elect 3 trustees to manage district affairs. In incorporated towns the mayor and aldermen are to appoint trustees.

Every county constitutes a school district. Towns of 1,000 may constitute an independent district.

County superintendents are to procure certificates of qualification from the county board of examiners, consisting of 3; one appointed by county supervisors, one by chancellor of district, and one by the judge of the circuit court.

Ample free school facilities are to be furnished to all of school age, but white and colored are to have separate houses. Schools to be taught five months in each year, but the time may be reduced to four months when the aggregate tax would exceed $7.50 on the $1,000.

Private high schools may educate State students and receive $2 monthly from the school fund for each one's tuition.

School year commences January 1. The school month is 20 days of not less than 6 nor more than 8 hours each.

The county assessor takes census of school children.

The pay of teachers is regulated by statute and based upon the average attendance. In schools of first grade, where the average attendance is 25, the pay is 8 cents per scholar; in the second grade, 6 cents, and in the third grade, 5 cents. If the average attendance is over 12 and less than 25, the pay is the same for number actually attending, and one-third of above rates for the difference between number actually attending and 25. But the total amount paid out of school fund shall not exceed 7½ cents for principal and assistants.

The above rates may be increased one-tenth or diminished one-tenth in cities and towns constituting separate school districts.

The State school fund not to be less than $200,000 each year. The county tax not to exceed 3 mills.

In the city of Columbus the mayor and aldermen are made school trustees, and, with the county superintendent, constitute the city board and control city schools.

Text books, not to be changed for 5 years, are to be selected by the teachers of county, in convention.

MISSOURI.

Constitution, Article XI: "A general diffusion of knowledge and intelligence being essential to the preservation of the rights and liberties of the people, the general assembly shall establish and maintain free public schools for the gratuitous instruction of all persons in this State between the ages of 6 and 20 years."

If the public school fund provided and set apart for the support of free public schools should be insufficient to sustain schools at least four months in each district, the general assembly are to provide for the deficiency. In no case shall there be set apart less than 25 per cent. of the State revenue, exclusive of the interest and sinking fund, to be applied annually to the support of schools.

It further provides for a State superintendent and a State board, consisting of the governor, secretary of state, attorney general, and State superintendent, the latter to be president of board.

Code of 1874.

The State superintendent is elected for four years and charged with usual duties.

The county commissioner is elected for two years.

The county courts have management and care of township and county school funds, and annually apportion moneys to districts according to enumeration of children of school age.

Subdistricts, as now organized and bounded, are continued as school districts.

The control is vested in 3 directors chosen by the qualified voters for terms of 3 years, one elected each year, who are to meet and organize within five days after election. They have the general powers of district boards, and are to take annual enumeration of children between 5 and 21.

Teachers are to hold certificates from State superintendent or county commissioner, and are required to attend institutes.

Cities, towns, and villages may be organized into school districts, under control of six directors. After first election, one-third to be elected each year, to constitute the board of education.

Central schools may be established, to be under control of a board consisting of the presidents of district boards. Two or more districts by majority vote may unite for this purpose and form a central school district.

The presidents of boards of cities, towns, and villages, and directors of districts, to meet in convention every five years and adopt text books.

The annual rate of tax in districts for school purposes not to exceed 40 cents on $100, but may be increased by a majority vote to 65 cents, and in districts formed of cities and towns to $1. The school year commences on the first Tuesday of April. School month, 4 weeks of 5 days; school day, 6 hours. The income of State, county, and town funds to be used for teachers' wages.

Where the number of colored children in any district exceeds 15, schools are to be established for them. The tax for the maintenance of any colored school shall be levied and collected from the taxable property of the township in which such school is located. Two or more districts may be united to maintain a colored school where each has less than minimum number. The State superintendent is to provide for the same if the local board neglect.

NEBRASKA.

Article VIII of the constitution requires the legislature to provide for the free instruction in the common schools of all persons between the ages of 5 and 21, the school fund to be equally distributed among the districts. The government of the State university is vested in six regents, to be elected by people for 6 years; a State superintendent of public schools, to be elected for 2 years, is provided for.

It also authorizes the legislature to provide for a school or schools for the safe keeping, education, employment, and reformation of all children under 16 who, from want of parental care or other cause, are growing up in mendicancy or crime.

School laws, 1879.

The State superintendent is charged with usual duties.

The county superintendent is elected for 2 years, and has general supervision of schools in his county and examination of teachers.

The counties are divided into school districts. Districts that shall have exercised privileges and franchises for one year are to be deemed legally organized.

Districts are to hold annual meetings in April of each year, and elect at the first meeting a moderator, for 3 years; director, for 2 years; and treasurer, for 1 year; and thereafter one each year, to serve 3 years, who are to constitute district board.

Every male citizen and unmarried woman of 21 years of age residing and owning property in district subject to tax for school purposes may vote in district meetings.

Districts of more than 150 children of school age (5 to 21) may elect a district board of 6 trustees, if so determined by a majority vote, at annual meeting, one-third to retire each year.

The district provides houses and grounds, regulates length of schools, and raises taxes therefor; but to entitle district to any part of State fund the schools must be kept up 3 months in districts of less than 75 scholars, 6 months in those of from 75 to 200, and 9 months when over 200.

The State tax is 2 mills, and is apportioned to counties by State superintendent according to enumeration.

The county superintendent apportions to districts, one-fourth divided equally and three-fourths pro rata, according to enumeration.

Text books are selected by State superintendent.

NEVADA.

The constitution, Article XI, § 2, requires the legislature to provide "for a uniform system of public schools, by which a school shall be established and maintained in each school district at least six months in every year," and also for a State tax to aid in sustaining them.

Laws of 1877.

The governor, State superintendent, and surveyor general constitute the State board. The State superintendent is elected for four years and a county superintendent in each county for two years, all with the usual powers and duties.

The State superintendent is to apportion interest on school fund to counties in proportion to children between 6 and 18; the county superintendent apportions to districts, 25 per cent. according to the number of teachers and the balance pro rata according to number of census children listed and reported each year. The county board of examiners consists of county superintendent and two persons appointed by him.

Qualified teachers are such as have certificates from State or county board. Text books are determined by State board.

County school tax not less than 15 nor more than 50 cents on each $100. One-half mill State tax and 5 per cent. of all State taxes to be set apart semiannually.

Each village, town, or incorporated city constitutes but one district. At the general county election the voters of each district are to elect trustees, to consist of 3 when the votes cast at the last election did not exceed 1,500, one for 4 years and two for 2 years, and of 5 where voters exceeded 1,500, two for 4 and three for 2 years, and thereafter their successors, with usual powers of district boards.

If the State money is not sufficient to keep up six months' school, they must levy tax for deficiency.

Rate bills on parents of scholars are authorized for schools in excess of six months.

The school year commences September 1. The school month is 4 weeks of 5 days each.

Districts failing to keep up school for 3 months under qualified teachers to forfeit proportion of semiannual apportionment.

The trustees are to furnish teachers with a list of all children in the district, and the teacher to report monthly those attending. If at end of four months non-attendance is shown, the trustees are to demand the penalty of parents, &c., which is not less than $50 nor more than $100 for the first offence, and not less than $100 nor more than $200 for second and subsequent offences. Sixteen weeks' school required for all children between 8 and 14.

Both State and county teachers' institutes are provided for, the former annual, the latter one or more each year.

NEW HAMPSHIRE.

The constitution contains the usual provisions of those of the New England States.

The law provides for a State superintendent appointed by the governor and council for two years, who has general supervision and control of educational interests of the State.

The towns at annual meetings are to choose a superintending school committee to supervise schools of town, raise money for schools—not less than $350 for each $1 of the State apportionment—to be assigned to districts according to valuation or in such other mode as town may determine.

Towns may divide into districts or they may abolish districts. Districts composed of the whole town must elect and any other district in any town in which there are 50 children may elect a board of education of 3, 6, or 9, one-third to retire each year. High school districts may be established by a two-thirds vote of the town or of any district of 100 scholars, and two or more districts may, by concurrent votes, unite to support a high school or other schools.

When town is divided into districts each district is to elect a prudential committee, who is the executive officer of the district and employs teachers holding certificates of town committee.

The districts have the usual powers under the district systems. Women are voters and eligible to school offices.

Town committee determine text books, are to visit schools at least twice each term, and are to report to the town at its annual meeting, and also to the State superintendent.

NEW JERSEY.

The constitution requires the legislature to provide for the maintenance of a thorough and efficient system of free public schools for the instruction of all children in the State between the ages of 5 and 18.

School laws, 1879.

The general supervision and control of public instruction is vested in a State board of education, consisting of the trustees of the State school fund and of the State normal school. The trustees of the school fund are the governor, president of the senate, speaker of the house, attorney general, secretary of state, and controller. The trustees of the normal school are two from each congressional district, appointed by the governor, with consent of the senate, one in each district appointed each year for the term of two years.

The State superintendent is appointed by the State board for a term of two years. He is to carry out the instructions of the board; is ex officio a member of the normal school board, and with principal of normal school constitutes State board of examiners.

County superintendents are appointed by State board, subject to approval of chosen freeholders, and hold during pleasure of board.

Each school district elects 3 trustees, to serve 3 years, one to be elected each year, with usual powers of district boards. Females are eligible.

The district trustees constitute the township association; the county and city superintendents form a State association, of which the State superintendent is president.

The county superintendent and 3 teachers appointed by him are a county board of examiners. In cities governed by special law, the city board appoint examiners and a city superintendent.

The county superintendent is to fix boundaries of districts, and may divide or unite the same, but no new district is to be formed unless it contains 75 children of school age. Each incorporated city or town forms one district.

Any two or more districts may unite to establish graded schools, to be governed by joint board and entitled to share of school fund.

Every district to provide its own school-houses, and forfeits right to any share of school appropriation unless nine months' school is maintained.

The State school tax is two mills; $100,000 from income of school fund to be paid to the counties in two or more instalments; $100 for each county, for teachers' institutes. If the State fund is insufficient for a nine months' school, a township tax may be levied.

The legal voters of district may levy a tax. All moneys received by district, other than district tax, over $20, to be used for teachers' salaries.

Tuition free to all residents of district between 5 and 18, and all from 8 to 14 years of age are required to attend school at least 12 weeks each year. Corporal punishment in schools is prohibited.

Districts raising $20 for a library are entitled to same amount from the State.

An act of March 14, 1879, provides that districts theretofore receiving $350 shall thereafter receive but $300 from State apportionment.

Every county is entitled to send to State normal school, free of charge for tuition, 3 pupils for each representative elected.

Applicants for admission to State agricultural college are to be selected by the county superintendent on examination.

NEW YORK.

By the constitution, the capital of the common school fund, of the literature fund, and of United States deposit fund is to be preserved inviolate; $25,000 of the revenues of the deposit fund are to be annually added to capital of common school fund; the revenues of the literature fund are to be applied to support of academies; the revenues of common school fund, to support of common schools.

School laws, 1878.

A State superintendent is elected by joint ballot of senate and house for three years. He is ex officio trustee of Cornell University, a regent of the State university, general supervisor of State normal schools, and trustee of State Asylum for Idiots; provides for education of Indian children, and visits institutions for deaf and dumb and blind, with usual powers and duties in reference to common schools, and may appoint a deputy.

The State is divided into districts, having no special reference to county or township lines, in each of which is to be elected triennially a school commissioner, with the ordinary powers and duties of a county commissioner in his district, and is to define the boundaries of school districts in his jurisdiction, divide territories into districts when necessary, and, with consent of trustees, may alter the same.

School districts are at annual meetings to elect one or three trustees, clerk, tax collector, and librarian. Where there are three trustees, one is to be elected each year. District officers must be qualified voters.

Every resident male of 21 years of age who owns or hires real property liable to school tax; every resident authorized to vote at town meetings, having a child of school age who has attended eight weeks the preceding year; owner of personal property exceeding $50 in value, exclusive of such as is exempt from execution, liable to school tax, and no others, are qualified voters in district meetings.

The district, by vote, may designate sites, levy tax to build, purchase, or repair houses, and to raise money for district purposes, not to exceed $25, for purchase of maps, apparatus, &c., and not to exceed same amount for anticipated deficiency in contingencies, and the taxable inhabitants may vote annual tax of $50 for library.

The trustees have usual powers of district board, and are to report number of children in district between 5 and 21.

The common schools are to be free to all over 5 and under 21 resident in district; and children between 8 and 14 years old are required to be sent to some school at least 14 weeks in each year, but no Indian children may be admitted to the public schools in districts where a separate school is provided for them.

Teachers must hold diploma from State normal school, or certificate of State superintendent, school commissioner, or the proper school officer of city or village.

Union free schools may be formed, to be controlled by not less than 3 nor more than 9 trustees, one-third elected each year, who are to constitute board of education. Such union district to be recognized as a school district in distribution of school moneys. The board has power of trustees; may grade schools.

District school authorities may, if they deem it expedient, establish separate schools for colored children, to be supported in same manner and to same extent as other schools.

Boards of education or school districts, by two-thirds vote, to designate text books, not to be changed for five years.

An act of May 13, 1878, requires the trustees to be elected by ballot in all districts of over 300 children of school age.

NORTH CAROLINA.

The constitution requires the legislature to "provide by taxation or otherwise for a general and uniform system of public schools, wherein tuition shall be free of charge to all children between 6 and 21 years of age." White and colored are to be in separate schools, but no discrimination to be made in favor or to the prejudice of either race.

It also provides for a State superintendent and a State board of education, to consist of the governor, lieutenant governor, secretary of state, treasurer, auditor, attorney general, and State superintendent.

It provides that each county shall be divided into school districts, and that a school shall be maintained in each district at least four months each year, and makes any county commissioner failing to comply with this requirement liable to indictment. It provides for an irreducible educational fund, makes the University of North Carolina a State institution, and directs that its benefits shall, as far as practicable, be extended to the youth of the State free of charge for tuition. It gives the State board full power to legislate and make all needful rules in relation to the free public schools and the educational fund of the State, subject to amendment or repeal by the legislature, and empowers the legislature to enact that every child of sufficient mental and physical ability shall attend the public schools during the period between 6 and 18 not less than 16 months, unless educated by other means.

Laws in force, 1877.

The county commissioners of each county constitute the county board of education. They are to appoint one resident examiner to examine teachers; lay off county into districts; employ teachers; if money insufficient for 4 months' school, may levy tax for deficiency; and appoint school committee of three for each district.

Every school to which aid shall be given from State shall be deemed a public school, to which children between 6 and 21 only shall be admitted. Moneys are to be apportioned to the districts according to the number of children between 6 and 21. Teachers are to hold certificates, which are three grades. Teachers of the first grade are not to be paid over $2 a day; teachers of the second grade, not to exceed $1.50; and of the third grade, not to exceed $1. No teacher to be paid for less than one month of twenty days.

Course of study and text books are prescribed by the State board. School committees take an annual school census of their districts.

Laws of 1876–'77 provide for normal instruction of both white and colored teachers, and authorize townships having within their limits cities of 5,000 or more inhabitants to levy taxes for the support of graded public schools.

OHIO.

The constitution contains the usual requirement that a thorough and efficient system of common schools shall be provided for by taxation or otherwise.

The law is taken from the last compilation of the State commissioner, 1879. The State commissioner is elected triennially, and is to appoint a State board of examiners.

A county board of examiners of three is appointed in each county by the probate judge, who hold for two years; city boards of examiners, by the city boards of education.

School districts are classified as city districts of first class, city districts of second class, village districts, and township districts.

Cities of 10,000 or more inhabitants are of first class, and under control of a board of education of one or two from each ward, elected by voters. Cities of less than 10,000 are of second class, and with incorporated villages are controlled by a board of three or six, elected by voters.

Each township constitutes one district and is under control of a board consisting of the township clerk and the clerks of the subdistrict boards. The township clerk is clerk of board, but without vote.

Townships are divided into subdistricts. The qualified voters of each subdistrict elect a board of three directors; one elected each year, to serve three years. The directors elect one of their number clerk, and manage the district affairs under direction of township board, employ qualified teachers, and take census of children between 5 and 21.

The township board control central or high schools when established; may grade subdistrict schools, assign scholars to primary schools, and regulate admission to graded schools. They may appoint an acting manager and establish one or more separate schools in each district for colored children when the number exceeds 20, but if the number is too small for a separate school they may be admitted to other schools. They may exclude children under six in cities or towns of 1,000 or more inhabitants.

Township and city boards prescribe the studies to be pursued and the text books to be used.

The State school fund is to be used for payment of teachers, but no teacher is entitled to pay until reports are made; no township is entitled to apportionment unless at least 24 weeks' school has been kept up, and no district, unless an enumeration of its youth has been taken and returned.

Cities of less than 40,000 may levy a school tax of 4 mills; of 40,000 and less than 100,000, 3 mills; of 100,000 or more, 2 mills; and are to maintain schools not less than 24 nor more than 44 weeks each year.

The school month is 4 weeks of 5 days each. Upon demand of 75 voters, German is to be taught. The schools are to be free to all children resident in district between 6 and 21 years of age, and persons having children between 8 and 14 years of age are required to send them to a common school at least 12 weeks in each year, unless otherwise instructed or excused by the school board. Without such schooling no child under 14 may be employed for labor during school hours.

City and county teachers' institutes are provided for, and during the session of the former all teachers of common schools within the county may dismiss their schools to attend the institute. City boards may also allow their teachers to attend.

OREGON.

The constitution requires the establishment of "a regular and uniform system of common schools," and that the income of the school fund shall be distributed to the districts according to the number of children therein between the ages of 4 and 20 years, to be applied to the support of the common schools and the purchase of suitable libraries and apparatus.

School laws, 1878.

The State superintendent is elected by the people for four years, with usual powers and duties.

The governor, secretary of state, and State superintendent constitute the State board, who are to prescribe rules for the general government of schools, to secure regularity of attendance, prevent truancy, and promote the interests of the schools, to sit as State board of examiners and grant State diplomas and certificates.

A county superintendent is elected by people for two years, who has supervision of schools in county; is to lay off county into districts and change or alter same and examine teachers.

Organized districts are to hold their annual meeting in March and choose a clerk and three directors, one director to be elected each year for 3 years.

The directors are to provide school-houses, take care of and furnish the same, when instructed by major vote of district; employ teachers, and maintain high school six months in districts where the number of school children is 1,000 or more.

Any citizen who has resided in the district 30 days next preceding the meeting may vote. Widows having children of school age and taxable property may also vote.

The schools are to be free to all persons resident in district between 6 and 21. A school quarter is 12 weeks or 60 days, and no district may receive its portion of the school fund unless it reports, by the first Monday of March, that it has had a school of that duration.

Text books determined by State board on vote of majority of county superintendents.

Institutions for deaf and dumb and blind are provided for under control of State board.

Enumeration of children between 4 and 21 taken by district clerk.

PENNSYLVANIA.

The constitution requires "the support and maintenance of a thorough and efficient system of common schools, wherein all the children of this Commonwealth above the age of six years may be educated," and an appropriation of at least one million dollars each year for that purpose. Women 21 years of age and upwards are eligible to office under the school laws. Appropriations to sectarian schools are forbidden.

Laws as compiled by State superintendent.

The State superintendent is appointed by the governor for term of four years, with usual powers and duties.

County superintendents are elected triennially by viva voce vote in convention of district directors.

Cities and boroughs of over 7,000 inhabitants may have their own superintendent, to be elected for 3 years by school directors of same.

Every township, borough, or city constitutes a school district. In every city or borough which consists of more than one ward, each ward is a school district. Independent districts may be formed and abolished by the court of quarter sessions.

School districts are bodies corporate, and may purchase and hold real and personal estate necessary for the support and establishment of schools, and sell and dispose of the same when not needed for such purpose.

Each district is to elect six directors, one-third to be elected each year for three years. The directors are to organize and choose a clerk[1] and treasurer.

The board exercise general supervision over the schools; appoint all teachers and fix their compensation. They shall establish a sufficient number of schools for the education of all persons between 6 and 21 in their districts who may apply for admission. The number, location, size, and arrangement of school-houses are in their discretion. They shall direct what branches are to be taught and the books to be used—books not to be changed oftener than once in five years.

They may grade schools and prescribe qualifications of admission thereto; establish separate schools for colored children whenever they can be located so as to accommodate 20 or more scholars.[2]

The school month is 22 days. Less than 110 days of school will not entitle a district to share of State moneys.

The directors determine the amount of school tax to be levied, which, with amount received from State appropriation and from other sources, must be sufficient to maintain schools for not less than 5 nor more than 10 months each year.

State moneys are apportioned according to the number of taxables in each district.

In cities or boroughs divided into wards the ward directors exercise the powers and duties of school directors as regards the erection and repair of houses and providing lots, and the levy of taxes therefor. All other duties are to be performed by a board of controllers, consisting of the directors of each ward. Whenever the directors of each district shall convey to such board of controllers all district property, the city

[1] In practice, the clerk is the acting superintendent of the schools of the district.

[2] The law seems to require the establishment of separate schools where 20 or more scholars can be accommodated. Where this number cannot be collected into one school there is no law which excludes them from the other public schools.

or borough shall thereafter constitute but one district, the number of directors from each ward not to exceed 3.

RHODE ISLAND.

The constitution declares that, "the diffusion of knowledge, as well as of virtue, among the people being essential to the preservation of their rights and liberties, it shall be the duty of the general assembly to promote public schools, and to adopt all means which they may deem necessary and proper to secure to the people the advantages and opportunities of education."

School laws, 1874.

The State board of education consists of the governor, lieutenant governor, and one member from each county except Providence, which has two, to be elected by the general assembly, two each year.

The board elect annually a State commissioner, who is charged with the usual duties and under direction of State board is to secure uniformity in text books.

Any town may establish and maintain schools with or without forming school districts, and may provide suitable houses in all the districts, but districts which have provided suitable houses are not to be again taxed for such purpose.

Each town is to elect a school committee of not less than 3, one-third to be elected each year for term of three years,[1] and may elect a superintendent of schools; failing to do so, its school committee must appoint one. Districts elect a moderator, clerk, treasurer, collector, and one or three trustees. Joint school districts with 2 trustees are provided for. Voters in town may vote in district of residence; none but taxpayers may vote on question of tax or expenditure of money raised thereby. The powers of districts when formed, or of the towns when not divided, are the usual powers under the New England system. The voters of the district, whether it be a part only or the whole town, control the school affairs. The district trustees are the executive officers of the district, while the town committee have general supervision of schools and, where town is not divided, powers of trustees.

No person can be excluded from any public school in the district of residence on account of race or color, or on account of being over 15 years of age, or otherwise, except by some general regulation applicable to all. Every school aided by the State is to be visited by the town committee, State board, or State commissioner.

If any districts neglect to organize, or for seven months neglect to employ teachers and establish schools, the town committees are to act for them.

Schools in the city of Providence are governed by ordinances of city authorities.

[1] Women are eligible to school committees.

Of the income of the State school fund $90,000 are to be apportioned annually, $63,000 according to the number of children under 15 and $27,000 according to number of districts. This State money goes to teachers only. No town is entitled to any share unless it shall raise an equal amount by tax. When the schools are maintained by organized districts, the town's proportion of the $63,000 is to be divided among the districts, one-half equally and one-half in proportion to average attendance, and its share of the $27,000 equally among the districts.

State assistance towards the formation of town libraries as means of education is authorized by a law of 1875.

SOUTH CAROLINA.

The constitution provides for a State superintendent to be elected as other State officers, also for the election of a commissioner for each county biennially, said commissioners to constitute the State board of education, with the State superintendent as chairman. It also requires the legislature to provide for a liberal and uniform system of free public schools, to provide for the compulsory attendance at some public or private school of all children between 6 and 16, not physically or mentally disabled, for a term equivalent, at least, to 24 months, to levy a tax for support of schools on all taxable property and a per capita tax of $1 on every male over 21. It also provides for the establishment of a State normal school, the education of the deaf and dumb and blind, a State reform school for juvenile offenders, for the organization of an agricultural college in connection with the State university, and, further, that all universities, colleges, or public schools supported, in whole or in part, by the State shall be free and open to all the children and youth of the State without regard to race or color.

School laws, 1878.

The State board is an advisory body to State superintendent, and hears appeals from county boards. The State superintendent and four persons appointed by governor constitute State board of examiners.

The board of examiners prescribe and enforce course of study in public schools and uniform series of text books, not to be changed for five years without permission of the general assembly.

The county commissioner and two persons appointed by State board constitute county board of examiners.

The county board lay off county into convenient school districts and appoint for each school district a board of 3 trustees to serve 2 years, who are to provide houses, employ qualified teachers, and have care of district affairs.

The school year begins November 1. The county board are to limit school terms according to fund. All contracts in excess of funds apportioned are void.

The schoo commissioner of the county of Charleston is to organize and have charge of schools outside of the city.

For the city of Charleston there is a city board, consisting of one from each ward, who are to elect a chairman, clerk, and superintendent, and have charge and control of the city schools.

The State school tax is one mill and the poll tax of $1.

TENNESSEE.

The constitution of 1870 declares it to be "the duty of the general assembly in all future periods of this government to cherish literature and science." It provides for a perpetual school fund, the interest of which is to be applied "to the support and encouragement of common schools throughout the State, and for the equal benefit of all the people thereof;" no part of said fund to be diverted to any other purpose. It further provides that "no school established or aided under this section shall allow white and negro children to be received as scholars together in the same school."

School laws of 1873, *as amended to* 1879.

The State superintendent is appointed by the governor and senate for a term of two years, and charged with the usual duties.[1]

A county superintendent is appointed by the county court biennially, with general supervision of county schools. One of his duties is "to suggest to district directors such changes as may be necessary to secure uniformity in the course of study, when it can be done without expense to parents."

Districts to be constituted as now or as they may hereafter be established.

On the first Thursday in August the qualified voters of each district are to elect a board of three directors for the term of three years, one to be elected each year. If the district fails to elect, the county superintendent to appoint. Directors are to be residents of the district; teachers not eligible. The directors have charge and control of schools in district under supervision of county superintendent.

The schools are to be free to all persons between 6 and 21 resident in the district; white and colored to be separate.

The branches to be taught are orthography, reading, writing, arithmetic, grammar, geography, elementary geology of Tennessee, history of the United States, vocal music, and elementary principles of agriculture. No other branches to be introduced except by local taxation or payment of tuition.

Where the number of scholars is sufficient, preference is to be given to graded schools. The consolidation of public schools with private

[1] A State board of education for the establishment and care of normal schools was created in 1875, and succeeded in establishing a good normal college at Nashville, but the legislature has failed to render it any pecuniary aid.

schools is authorized, provided the required public school branches be taught in the latter and the authority of the State school officers over those studying these branches shall be as full as in the ordinary public schools.

The State school fund amounts to $2,512,500, on which the State is to pay interest at 6 per cent. semiannually; also, a poll tax of $1 to be paid to county in which it is collected, and a State tax of 1 mill—each county to have the amount collected in it.

When the money derived from State fund and taxes is not sufficient to keep up a public school for five months, the county trustees are to levy additional county tax.

The moneys apportioned according to scholastic population; school census to be taken by district clerk.

Under the present law the districts have no power to levy taxes for the purchase of real estate and school furniture, for building houses, prolonging the schools, or for any school purpose. The directors have no revenues except the State moneys and county taxes.

The county superintendent is the auditor of all school accounts, and all warrants must be approved by him; and the county trustee must pay directly to the party entitled, and not to clerk of district.

TEXAS.

The constitution of 1875 makes it "the duty of the legislature to establish and make suitable provision for the support and maintenance of an efficient system of public free schools." It provides for a permanent school fund; requires that there shall be set apart annually not more than one-fourth of the general revenue of the State and a poll tax of $1 on each male 21 years of age and under 60 for the benefit of free schools, these taxes and the interest on the permanent fund to be the available school fund to be distributed to the counties according to the scholastic population.[1] Separate schools are to be provided for white and colored children, but impartial provision is to be made for both.

School laws, 1879.

The governor, secretary of state, and comptroller constitute a State board, who have charge of and invest State school fund.

The board appoint a secretary, whose duty it is to keep a record of the proceedings, file and index reports, advise and counsel with school officers of counties, cities, and towns, issue regulations and instructions binding on officers and teachers. He seems to take the place of the State superintendent, who under the former law was elected by the people for four years.

The former law provided for a county board of five directors, elected

[1] The census of this population is required to be taken annually by the tax assessor of each county.

by the people for four years. For these the present law substitutes a board of examiners, appointed by the county judge, who also distributes blanks, receives and passes upon petitions for the organization of school communities, appoints trustees therefor, distributes available school fund, receives and passes upon all applications for the erection of school-houses, approves warrants and contracts with teachers, and licenses as teachers persons who have been passed by the board of examiners appointed by him. Under the former law the trustees were elected by qualified voters of district.

Parents and guardians may now unite and organize as a school community upon petition to county judge, approved by county board. In towns not exceeding 1,500 inhabitants but two school communities can be organized for whites and two for colored. The trustees are to contract with teachers if a school-house has been provided. When there is no school-house, the available fund may be used for erecting house, provided the members of the community contribute an equal amount in labor and means and land is donated.

All children of the scholastic age are entitled to tuition free in orthography, reading, writing, English grammar, composition, geography, and arithmetic. The school age under the old law was 6 to 16 years; under the present law it is 8 to 14.

Children not of scholastic age may attend the community school upon payment of tuition, as agreed upon between parents and teachers; but the trustees are not to permit any contract which interferes with the interests of State pupils.

Trustees are to contract with teachers on the basis of the number of children of scholastic age registered. No teacher is entitled to full pay unless the average daily attendance amounts to 75 per cent. of the whole number registered on the community list. If the average attendance is 50 and less than 75 per cent., the teacher may receive 75 per cent. of contract compensation. If the attendance is less than 50 per cent., the teacher may be paid for the actual daily attendance, or trustees may discontinue the school. Teachers of the first grade are not to receive over $2 a month per capita; of the second grade, not to exceed $1.50, and of third grade not to exceed $1—in no case to exceed $60 a month for first grade, $40 for second grade, and $25 for third grade.

The former law required the trustees to provide houses and schools for the scholastic population of their districts, employ competent teachers, and to see that the schools were taught and properly conducted for at least four months in the year; and if the income derived from the public fund apportioned to any district was insufficient for this purpose, the board of directors were required to levy an ad valorem tax upon all taxable property in the district sufficient to supply the deficiency.

The former law also provided that all the scholastic population of the State should be required to attend the public free schools at least four months in each year, unless prevented by ill health, feeble physical constitution, or by reason of danger from hostile Indians or prevalence of contagious or infectious disease. No indication of such requirement appears in the new law.

VERMONT.

The constitution declares that "laws for the encouragement of virtue and the prevention of vice ought to be constantly kept in force and duly executed. And a competent number of schools ought to be maintained in each town for the convenient instruction of youth, and one or more grammar schools be incorporated and properly supported in each county in the State."

School laws of 1874, *as subsequently amended.*

A superintendent of education is elected biennially by the legislature for the State. Each town also elects a superintendent of common schools, and these superintendents in each county are to meet annually at the county seat, prepare a series of questions for the examination of teachers, fix a standard of qualifications, and choose by ballot one of their number and two practical teachers of the county to constitute an examining board to determine upon a series of text books.

Each organized town is to maintain and support one or more schools under competent teachers, and may establish central or high schools for advanced pupils and elect prudential committee therefor; each pupil from other towns to be charged tuition fee, to be fixed by such committee.

The towns are the primary authority, but may form school districts.

When districts are formed they are to elect officers, among which is a prudential committee of one or three; all officers must be legal voters. Voters in town meetings may vote in district of residence.

The powers of the town superintendent and district and prudential committee are the same as in the other New England States.

If the district neglects to comply with the requirements of the laws, the selectmen of the town are to appoint new officers, who are to open and keep up schools at expense of district, and assess tax therefor. A town tax of nine cents on each $1 of the list is to be levied, including one-half the interest on the United States deposit fund. Towns may raise such additional sum as they please. No district entitled to share unless schools are taught two terms of 10 weeks each. School week, 5 days; school month, 4 weeks. Towns may abolish districts and assume control of schools.

VIRGINIA.

The constitution provides for the election by the general assembly of a State superintendent for a term of four years; for a board of education, to consist of the governor, attorney general, and State superintendent; for county superintendents, to be appointed by the State board, subject to confirmation by the senate, and for division of townships into school districts of not less than 100 inhabitants, and in each district a board of three trustees, with terms so arranged that one shall be elected each year.

It also requires the general assembly to establish a uniform system of free public schools, to be introduced into all the counties of the State; authorizes laws to prevent parents and guardians from allowing their children to grow up in idleness and vagrancy; the establishment of normal and agricultural schools and such grades of schools as may be for the public good. It requires the State board to provide for uniformity of text books and the furnishing of school-houses with the necessary apparatus and a library; makes provision for a State literary fund, the interest of which, with the capitation tax and an annual tax of from 1 to 5 mills, is to be for the equal benefit of all the people of the State, to be divided according to the number of children between 5 and 21.

It requires provision to be made for the supply of text books to pupils whose parents are unable to supply them and authorizes each district to raise additional sums by tax for support of public schools, not to exceed 5 mills in any one year, the general assembly to fix salaries of school officers and make all needful laws to carry these provisions into effect.

School laws, 1878.

The State board is authorized to make by-laws and regulations for carrying into effect the school laws, decide upon appeals from decisions of State superintendent, regulate all matters arising under school system not otherwise provided for, invest school fund, and audit all claims paid out of State fund.

The State superintendent is to determine true intent and meaning of the school laws, see that laws and regulations are faithfully executed, and has general charge and supervision of system.

County superintendents are charged with the usual duties. There is also provision for a county school board composed of the county superintendent and district trustees, to care for county school property. District trustees are to be appointed by joint action of the county superintendent, county judge, and attorney. They are to be residents of the district, elect a president and clerk of their own number, and have charge of district affairs. They are to provide suitable school-houses and appurtenances according to exigencies of the district and means at their disposal, no house to be erected unless with approval of county superintendent. Incorporated towns of 500 to 5,000 inhabitants may constitute school districts, and through their councils appoint boards of school trustees.

No district is entitled to share of school fund until houses are provided, nor unless five months' school has been maintained the current year.

The public schools are to be free to all residents of the district between 5 and 21. White and colored are to be separate, but under the same general regulations as to management, usefulness, and efficiency.

Schools must have an average attendance of not less than 20, to be wholly supported by the State, but the trustees, with consent of county superintendent, may legalize a school where the average attendance is not less than 15. An average of attendance of not less than 10 may be allowed where two-thirds of support is from other than State funds.

The branches taught are limited to orthography, reading, writing, arithmetic, grammar, and geography, unless by special regulation of State board. Preference to be given to graded schools where number is sufficient.

Any district board may admit into any one of the public schools instruction to qualify pupils to become teachers or to enter colleges or the higher institutions of learning, and require therefor a tuition fee not exceeding $2.50 a month.

County and district taxes are not to exceed 10 cents on $100, except in Alexandria County, where 50 cents may be levied by a three-fourths vote.

The number of schools is to be according to the available funds to be distributed by the State board in proportion to number of children between 5 and 21.

Cities of 10,000 or more inhabitants are of the first class; cities of less than 10,000 are of the second class.

Every city is a district, or, if divided into wards, each ward is a district. All the trustees constitute the city board.

The State board to appoint a superintendent for cities of the first class. The city boards are to prescribe the number and size of districts until divided.

The city school tax is not to exceed 3 mills.

WEST VIRGINIA.

Article VII of the constitution provides for a State superintendent, to be elected for four years, for a poll tax of $1, and State tax not to exceed 95 cents on $100. Article XII, for a thorough and efficient system of free schools, to be under supervision of State superintendent; authorizes leg, islature to provide for county superintendents and other officers; provides for State school fund, and makes governor, State superintendent- auditor, and treasurer the board of school fund; directs present school districts to remain until changed by law; requires legislature to appropriate for support of free schools the interest of school fund, net proceeds of all fines and forfeitures and of taxes provided for by constitution, and to provide that the people in each county and district shall raise such proportion as shall be prescribed by law; white and colored schools to be separate; and that no independent school district shall be formed without the consent of the district or districts out of which it shall be formed.

School laws, 1877.

The term district is defined to mean that division of territory which under the old constitution was known as a township, and is to be presided over by a board of education; independent district, a division of territory designated by special act of legislature; a subdistrict is a subdivision of a district, presided over by a trustee.

The county superintendent is to be elected biennially at the general election. At the same time the voters of each district are to elect a president and two commissioners, who are to constitute the district board, and also by vote determine question of tax or no tax.

The district board are to appoint 3 trustees for each subdistrict, one to be appointed each year for 3 years.

The district board are to determine number and salary of teachers, to appoint a secretary not a member of board, and shall cause to be kept up a sufficient number of schools for all persons entitled to attend; i. e., all youth between 6 and 21.

The trustees are under supervision and control of board. Trustees appoint teachers to be approved by board, and may remove same, subject to appeal to board. One or more schools to be established in every subdistrict for colored children when the number exceeds 25. The trustees of two or more districts may unite to establish colored schools. Whenever the benefit of free schools is not secured as aforesaid to colored children, the fund is to be divided in proportion to white and colored and their proportion expended by district board for the benefit of the colored children.

The school year commences September 1; school month is 22 days—20 days school and 2 days institute. The district board may establish graded and high schools, but must first submit question to voters of district.

The county superintendent and 2 teachers constitute a board of examiners to examine teachers; an examination fee of $1 is charged and applied to payment of two examiners. Teachers required to have certificate of county examiners, diploma of State normal school, or certificate from State board. Each teacher required to attend institute 2 days each month.

The president of board to examine school-houses once each year and report condition to board. Plans for new houses to be approved by county superintendent. District board may levy tax not exceeding 40 cents on $100 in any one year for building fund; also, to levy such tax as with State funds will keep up schools for 4 months each year, but not to exceed 50 cents on $100. Voters may authorize school for more than 4 months, and board levy tax therefor. Text books for the State schools are prescribed by statute, and county superintendents are to see that these are used and no others introduced. The State school tax is 10 cents on each $100, to be added to the interest on the State school fund and other sources of revenue and applied to the support of free schools, and to no other purpose whatever.

WISCONSIN.

Article X of the constitution provides for a State school fund; requires the legislature to provide for a system of district schools, as nearly uniform as practicable, to be free to all children between 4 and 21; that each town and city shall raise for public school purposes an amount equal to one-half of amount received from State, and vests supervision of public instruction in a State superintendent and such other officers as the legislature may direct.

Law of 1878.

The State superintendent is elected by the people biennially, and county superintendents in same manner.

The district system is in force in this State. A town, if it so votes, may be one district, and the districts in it subdistricts, or it may be divided into districts. In the one case the town, and in the other the district, controls the schools.

Each district elects a director, treasurer, and clerk for three years, one to be elected each year.

The district may levy tax for teachers' wages of $350 for 15 scholars or less, $450 when over 15 and less than 30, and $500 when from 30 to 40; for maps, &c., $75; and for library, $100.

The director, treasurer, and clerk constitute district board, and must act as a board. May levy tax, if district neglect; determine text books, not to be changed for three years; employ teachers; and exercise general powers of district boards.

Any town may by vote establish high schools, the officers to be the same as in a district and to constitute a high school board.

When town system is adopted the subdistricts are to choose a clerk, and the clerks constitute the town board. The town board are to choose a president, vice president, and secretary, who are to be the executive committee, the secretary to supervise the schools. Ample powers for the establishment, maintenance, and control of schools are given to such town boards.

ARIZONA.

School laws, 1875-1879.

The governor, superintendent of public instruction, and treasurer constitute the territorial board of education, the governor being president and the superintendent secretary. The probate judge of each county is ex officio county superintendent.

A board of examiners is appointed by the territorial superintendent for each county, the county superintendent to be chairman of the board.

Counties are divided into districts. The county superintendent may form new districts upon petition.

The territorial superintendent is to apportion school money to the counties under the supervision of the territorial board, according to the average attendance for the three months prior to January 1 of each year, and the county superintendent to the districts in same manner.

At each general election the voters of the district are to elect three trustees, who elect a clerk and treasurer of their own number and control district affairs.

Schools are to be kept open three months each year. The school month is four weeks of five days each.

Text books are prescribed by board of education. The territorial tax is 15 cents on $100 and the county tax not less than 50 nor more than 80 cents.

A census of children between 6 and 21 is taken annually by census marshal appointed by trustees.

DAKOTA.

Laws of 1877.

A territorial superintendent is appointed for two years by the governor and council.

A county superintendent is elected by people biennially.

He is to divide county into districts and apportion money to same according to number of children between 5 and 21, examine teachers, and have general supervision of schools of county.

Each district at its annual meeting elects a director, clerk, and treasurer, who are to be qualified voters and constitute the district board, one to be elected each year for three years.

The districts locate houses and have control of schools. May vote tax not to exceed 2 per cent. for building fund, 2 per cent. for teachers' fund, 1 per cent. for furnishing houses, and $25 for library. A scholastic census is made annually by the clerk of each district. A county tax of $1 on each elector and 3 mills on the dollar of taxable property to be levied annually for school purposes, and to be distributed to districts in the proportion of their school population.

County teachers' institutes are to be held, and an annual territorial one.

Text books may be prescribed by the territorial and county superintendents and district school officers in conjunction, not to be changed for three years.

DISTRICT OF COLUMBIA.

The school laws of the District of Columbia are found in acts of Congress and the ordinances of the cities of Washington and Georgetown prior to June 1, 1871, the acts of the legislative assembly from that date to June 20, 1874, when it was abolished, and orders of the District commissioners since that date. At that time the white schools were under the control of three boards of trustees, one for Washington, one for Georgetown, and another for the county. The colored schools were placed by act of Congress under a special board of trustees, with almost unlimited powers.

Subsequent to July 1, 1874, the District commissioners assumed the authority to consolidate these four boards into one consisting of 19 trustees, 11 to be residents of Washington, 3 of Georgetown, and 5 of the county. This continued until the act of Congress of June 11, 1878, section 6 of which, so far as it relates to the public schools, provides—

That from and after July 1, 1878, * * * the board of school trustees shall be abolished, and all the powers and duties now exercised by them shall be transferred to the said commissioners of the District of Columbia, who shall have authority to employ such officers and agents and to adopt such provisions as may be necessary to carry into execution the powers and duties devolved upon them by this act.

This is plain and explicit, and no doubt could arise as to its meaning if it had stopped there, but this clause follows:

And the commissioners of the District of Columbia shall from time to time appoint 19 persons, actual residents of the District of Columbia, to constitute the trustees of public schools of said District, who shall serve without compensation and for such terms as the commissioners shall fix. Said trustees shall have the powers and perform the duties in relation to the care and management of the public schools which are now authorized by law.

In one breath the existing board of trustees is abolished and their powers and duties transferred to and vested in the commissioners of the District, who may employ the necessary officers and agents to carry the same into effect; and in the next it restores the board and provides that they shall have the powers and perform the duties which are now authorized by law. Does the last repeal the first, or are the trustees merely the "agents and officers" through whom the commissioners may act? Taking either clause by itself there is no difficulty of construction, while taking both together there is a manifest conflict.

As a matter of fact, the schools have continued under the system which has grown up under the action of the old boards of trustees. The order of September 9, 1874, consolidating the then existing boards, was a virtual repeal by the commissioners not only of then existing District laws but of acts of Congress; and if they are vested with this authority it may not be easy to define what laws are in force.

IDAHO.

The school laws in force in 1879 make the controller of the Territory ex officio superintendent of education and the county auditor county superintendent.[1]

The county commissioners are to appoint an examiner, who, with the county superintendent, is to examine teachers.

Each county may be divided into convenient districts, and each district is authorized to elect three trustees for term of one year.

[1] In two counties the probate judge is superintendent.

All actual resident taxpayers are voters in district, except married women and minors.

The county school tax is not to be less than two nor more than eight mills. All fines for breach of penal laws are applied to support of schools.

The interest on proceeds of sales of public lands is apportioned to the counties by the treasurer of the Territory in the ratio of number of children between 5 and 21.

The county superintendent apportions money to the subdistricts, one-half equally and one-half per capita. No subdistrict having less than 10 children of school age entitled to share.

Teachers must hold certificate from county examiners, and are charged a fee of $3 therefor.

MONTANA.

School laws to 1877.

A superintendent of public instruction is to be appointed by the governor and council for two years, with power to adopt a course of study, as well as rules and regulations, for the schools.

A superintendent is elected by the people for each county biennially.

Counties are divided into school districts, and new districts may be formed by county superintendents on petition.

Each district elects a board of three trustees and a clerk. The trustees are elected, one each year, to serve three years. Vacancies are filled by county superintendent. Taxable electors are voters in the district.

The clerk is to take census of children between 4 and 21, Indians not included.

The schools are to be open for the admission of all children between 5 and 21, residents of the district. Separate schools may be provided for colored children.

The school month is 20 days, or 4 weeks of 5 days each. The school day is 6 hours, but teachers may dismiss all under 8 years after 4 hours.

County institutes are to be held annually in counties of 10 or more districts, sessions from 2 to 5 days, and teachers are required to attend. Teachers must hold certificates from the county superintendent.

The trustees may establish high schools by vote of district.

The school revenue is the interest on proceeds of sales of public lands, and of fines, a county tax of from 3 to 5 mills, and an optional district tax.

No district is entitled to share unless 3 months' school has been kept up and a duly licensed teacher has been employed.

NEW MEXICO.

No district school system appears to have been adopted in this Territory, and whatever laws are found are fragmentary and crude.

There is a provision for the election of four supervisors for each county, who are to have sole and entire control of the schools and school funds.

A poll tax of $1 is imposed upon every male over 21, to be applied exclusively for schools, and there is a further provision that in the settlement of the accounts of each county at stated periods any surplus remaining to credit of county in excess of $500 is to be transferred to the school fund.

A few years since a bill for the establishment of a free public school system passed one branch of the legislature, but was defeated in the other. Apparently there is a sharp contest between sectarianism and the friends of the free school system.

UTAH.

School laws to 1878.

The territorial superintendent is elected biennially and a superintendent for each county at the same time.

The county court is to divide each county into school districts.

Each district elects a board of three trustees, with the usual powers and duties, to serve for 2 years.

The county court also appoints a board of examination to examine and license teachers.

Text books are prescribed by the territorial and county superintendents and the president of the University of Deseret, meeting in convention for that purpose. School terms are arranged by the consentient action of the county superintendents and the trustees of their several counties.

The territorial school tax is 3 mills. The district trustees assess a tax of $\frac{1}{4}$ of 1 per cent., which may, by a two-thirds vote of district, be increased to not exceeding 3 per cent.[1]

The territorial tax is apportioned by superintendent according to the number of children between 6 and 16, which number is ascertained by an annual school census taken by the district trustees.

WASHINGTON.

School laws to 1877.

A superintendent of public instruction is appointed by the governor and council for a term of two years, also one person from each judicial district, who with the superintendent constitute the board of education

The board are to prescribe text books and rules for the government of the schools, sit as a board of examination, and grant teachers' certificates.

[1] Apparently to supplement the sums derived from these two sources there is an annual territorial appropriation of $20,000, with the proceeds from a tax on railroads and from the sale of estrays.

The county superintendent is elected biennially, who with two persons selected by him constitutes a county board of examination.

Districts are established by the county superintendents on petition of residents.

Each district elects a board of three directors, one to be elected each year for three years. Every person who has resided in the district for three months next preceding the meeting may vote, whether male or female.

Two or more districts may unite to establish graded schools, or any single district may have them. A city or town of 500 or more school children is required to establish such schools, and one with 400 inhabitants may compel the attendance of children between 8 and 16 years old at least 6 months each year.

Every district of 15 or more children of school age must maintain at least three months' school each year to entitle it to apportionment. The school month is 4 weeks of 5 days each. The school day, 6 hours; for primary schools, 4 hours.

Teachers' institutes are to be held in each county with 10 or more districts annually and one for the whole Territory must also be held annually by the territorial superintendent. Text books, when adopted, are not to be changed for five years.

Districts may vote tax, not to exceed 10 mills, to maintain their schools or furnish additional school facilities; meetings for this purpose not to exceed two in any year. All other school moneys are apportioned to the districts in proportion to their number of youth of school age (4–21), as reported by the district clerks.

WYOMING.

School laws to 1878.

The territorial librarian is superintendent of schools. The county superintendent is elected by people, and is to divide his county into districts.

Each district is to elect a board of three trustees, one to be elected each year for three years. The trustees are to choose of their own number a director, treasurer, and clerk.

All citizens and taxpayers over 21 who have resided in district for 30 days are voters, women included. Women may also hold office.

The district determines number and length of schools, provides houses and may vote money therefor, and may raise not exceeding $100 for library.

The district board are to make all contracts, and, with county superintendent, may establish graded schools.

The schools are to be free to all children between 7 and 21.[1] Where

[1] Three months' attendance annually in some school is made a duty (unless in the case of invalids and others excused by the school board) for all children of school age; and parents or guardians who neglect or refuse to send to school children between 7 and 16 years of age are liable to a fine of $25 for every offense against this rule.

there are 15 or more colored children in any district separate schools may be provided.

No discrimination in pay of teachers is to be made on account of sex.

A county tax of 2 mills is to be levied annually.

CONCLUSION.

Like all other statutes, the school laws of the States are subject to change or amendment at the will of the legislatures.

In no State is the system claimed to be perfect; but, on the contrary, the reports of the State and other supervisory officers freely criticise the workings of the systems and frequently suggest amendments.

In the Report of the Commissioner of Education for 1875 will be found a brief statement of the system in each of the States. A comparison of these with the present will show that few changes have been made in many of the States, and that where they have occurred they are mainly in details. In a few States changes have been made which are not in the direction of progress.

The history of the common school system, however, shows that wherever the free school system has once obtained a foothold no retrograde movement can be permanently successful. Local or sectional prejudices may retard its progress, but the good sense of the people will in the end triumph over all obstacles.

ON SOME CHANGES IN THE LEGAL STATUS OF THE CHILD SINCE BLACKSTONE

Florence Kelley

THE

INTERNATIONAL REVIEW.

AUGUST, 1882.

ON SOME CHANGES IN THE LEGAL STATUS OF THE CHILD SINCE BLACKSTONE.

THE child's position under the law at this time is unique in the extent to which care for his welfare is carried.

Whereas the State, through its judicial function, gives to the adult protection in the enjoyment of life, liberty, property, and the pursuit of happiness, to the child it gives the same protection of life, with additional favorable provisions—the same protection in the enjoyment of liberty to an extent restricted only for his good,[1] and the same protection in the enjoyment of his property under legislation rich in provisions for his interests.[2]

Primarily, the law assumes that parental affection secures this threefold protection, and therefore upholds parental rights and enforces parental duties; yet it recognizes the fact that parents may be dead or delinquent, and provides for this contingency by instituting the quasi-parental relations of guardianship and adoption, and by providing for the transfer of custody and the settlement of pauper and illegitimate children, while, wholly apart from the paternal relation, the State now, as never before, takes cognizance of and bestows favor upon the child in systems of public education provided by the State, in the development of factory acts, in legal disabilities imposed and special provisions enacted for the child's protection.

In the case of dependent and delinquent children, too, recent statute law provides modified treatment quite in the spirit of the old common law provision, which pronounced a child under seven years conclusively incapable of crime, and a child under fourteen prima facie so.[3]

1 See Schouler, Dom. Rel. Custody.

2 Bl. ch., 17, 3: "Infants have various privileges and various disabilities; but their very disabilities are privileges, in order to secure them from hurting themselves by their own improvident acts."

3 Bl., ch. 17.

This extremely favored position of the child under the law has not always existed. It is chiefly the product of the present century, and is, therefore, of statute origin,[1] and it has been attained by legislation involving consequences not perhaps wholly foreseen. The existing mass of laws affecting children has been created in ever-increasing recognition of the child's welfare as a direct object of legislation, apart from the family relation; and herein lies the cardinal distinction between the status of the child to-day and its status under Blackstone.

In the Commentaries, although the principle of especially caring for childhood was recognized, it was expressed chiefly in laws which benefited the legitimate child within the family, and which acted in and through the family or its substitute, the guardian; and at best the development of the principle was merely germinal. One evidence of this is that Blackstone has no chapter upon Infancy. The domestic relations of the child are discussed under the head Parent and Child; the relation of the young criminal is dismissed with a brief discussion of the age at which criminal responsibility is attained; the disposition of pauper children falls naturally under the Poor law, and the maintenance of the illegitimate child is summarily devolved upon the father or the parish, as circumstances decide, without reference to the good of the child. Nowhere in the Commentaries is there a hint that the common law regarded the child as an individual, with a distinctive legal status. The nearest approach, perhaps, to this is in the discussion of legal disabilities, where it is stated: "Infants have certain privileges and certain disabilities, but their very disabilities are privileges preserving them from the consequences of their own rash acts;"[2] but even here the child is viewed in connection with the ownership of property—somewhat as an appendage to it—and the discussion has reference more to the property than to the child.

So throughout the Commentaries the child is merely an incidental phenomenon, and his moral welfare is ignored. This is well illustrated by the relation of custody. Perhaps no relation of childhood is so universal as this; but Blackstone discusses it under the head Parent and Child, regarding it purely as a paternal right, ignoring the welfare of the child, and emphasizing only the absolute ownership of the father.

The child's welfare being in no sense an object to be secured, there is in the Commentaries no provision for granting to the legitimate child the benefit of transfer from the custody of a delinquent father to

[1] See Schouler, Dom. Rel., Introduction.

[2] Bl., ch. 17, § 3.

that of its mother,[1] or to that of any other person. The father owned his legitimate child. It was his chattel, to be kept or given according to his whim. So absolute was the paternal possession that, though a minor, the father could give or bequeath away his child's custody despite its mother, though it were an infant in arms, or even before its birth;[2] and, though the father died a minor, he could deprive his child of its mother's care by appointing testamentary guardians, with absolute power.

The growth of this branch of the law is marked. The first change was made in England by the Wills act,[3] which debarred a minor from appointing testamentary guardians. Next, in 1839, the Custody of Infants act[4] provided for giving to the mother access to her children under the age of seven, or possession of them to that age, under certain specified circumstances Finally, in 1873, the Infants' Relief act[5] provided for the access or possession of the mother until the child should reach the age of sixteen, under the same circumstances as before.[6] And it is now laid down that "the Court of Chancery (English) will interfere with the rights of a father to the custody of his children, the object of the interference being, of course, the benefit of his children, not the punishment of the father, on grounds of unfitness of character and of conduct,"[7] while the American authority, Schouler, writing in 1870, affirms that.[8] "In this country the doctrine is universal that the courts of justice may in their sound discretion, and when the morals or safety or interests of the children strongly require it, withdraw their custody from the father and bestow it upon the mother, or take the children from the parents and place the care and custody of them elsewhere."[9] The rule as to legal preference is essentially that of the common law, with, however, an increasing liberality in favor of the mother, strengthened in no slight degree by positive legislation.

[10]The father has then the paramount right to the custody of the children, independent of all statute to the contrary. But this right he may forfeit by his misconduct. "It is an entire mistake," says Judge Story, "to suppose that the court is bound to deliver over the infant to its father, or that the latter has an absolute vested right in the custody." The cardinal principle in such matters is to make the

1 Bl. Com., ch. 16, § 2: "A mother, as such, is entitled to no power, but only to reverence and respect."

2 Simpson's Law of Infants (1875), p. 144.

3 1 Vict., ch. 26 (Wills act).

4 2 and 3 Vict., ch. 54.

5 36 and 37 Vict., ch. 12.

6 Simpson, Law of Infants (1875), p. 137.

7 Simpson, Law of Infants (1875), p. 139.

8 Schouler, Dom. Rel., pp. 338–9.

9 Kent Com., § 205, and cases cited.

10 Dom. Rel., p. 342.

welfare of the children paramount to the claims of either party. And judicial precedents, judicial dicta and legislative enactments all lead to one and the same irresistible conclusion." So far has the care for the child's individuality grown that the same authority adds:[1] "The practice is to give the child the right to elect where he will go if he be of proper age."

And, in New York, to prevent the father's depriving his legitimate child of its mother's care and custody after his death, the consent of the mother is required to an appointment of testamentary guardians.[2] To this point has the recognition of the child's welfare grown in the time since Blackstone; and incidentally has grown with it this recognition of the child's need of legal power in the mother, making a change very marked since the dictum of Blackstone that the "mother, as such, is entitled to no power, but only to reverence and respect."[3]

Great, however, as is the change in provision for the custody of the legitimate child within the family, its effects, in changing the actual circumstances of children, are probably far less than the effects of the growth of provision for custody of children outside of the legal family.

Care for the welfare of the child in legislation governing the custody of illegitimate children has grown perhaps in equal proportion. In the Commentaries no provision whatsoever is made for this matter of vital importance to the child except the negative one that "he hath no father."[4] In this respect the English law has changed comparatively little; for the English authority, Simpson, writing in 1875, says:[5] "In the eye of the law the illegitimate child is *filius nullius*, and, consequently, has no legal guardians—not even the mother or putative father." But the American authority, Schouler, writing in 1870, says: "American policy is in general more favorable than that of England as to the mother's rights. In New York it is broadly ruled that the mother, as its natural guardian, is bound to maintain an illegitimate child, and that she is entitled to control it,"[6] a provision of infinite value to the child where mother and child are victims of bigamy; and of value to it in any case as securing to it fixed, definite, legal guardianship.

The growing care for the child has changed in a most marked way its position when, unhappily thrown out of the domestic relations by

[1] Schouler, Dom. Rel., p. 342.

[2] N. Y. Stat., 1862, ch. 187, § 2.

[3] Bl., ch. 16, § 2.

[4] Bl., ch. XVI., § 3.

[5] Simpson, Law of Infants, p. 126.

[6] Schouler, Dom. Rel., p. 384.

reason of pauperism or the absence of legal guardians, it is left to the care of the public. Of this class of children Blackstone merely says that overseers of the poor were appointed in each parish "to raise competent sums for the maintenance of the poor, impotent, old, blind, and such other, being poor and not able to work"[1]—terms including pauper children, without specifying anything whatsoever concerning their custody. Later, he tells us, "a board of three commissioners was appointed, empowered to issue all such rules and regulations as they think proper for the maintenance, education and apprenticing of the children of poor persons."[2] The custody which resulted from this law is known to readers of "Oliver Twist." Here also, as in the case of the custody of the illegitimate child, there is less change in England than is seen in our American law; for at present "pauper children, whether legitimate or not, are, under the English law, made inseparable from the mother within the years of nurture"[3]—*i. e.*, from birth to the age of seven.

In Massachusetts, on the contrary, whose legislation affecting pauper children is believed to be the most enlightened yet attained, it is now, by statute, illegal to permit any child to remain in any almshouse after reaching two years of age, at which time a State Primary School receives the child, or an individual home is found for it.

In the primary school the child becomes a ward of the State, and is in the legal custody of the State Board of Health, Charity and Lunacy, thus legally, as well as personally, removed from the adult pauper population.

So far as is possible the child under two years of age, also, is removed from the almshouse, being placed in the personal care of one woman, and the legal custody of the women in charge of the Massachusetts Infant Asylum.[4]

In all legal provisions for pauper children in Massachusetts, which is cited as embodying in its legislation the best expression of the modern view of the child, the effort of the State is toward making custody the means of securing the child's welfare. The law assumes that a parent unable to keep his child out of the almshouse forfeits the trust of guardianship, and the State finds a home and other

[1] 43 Eliz., ch. 2.

[2] 4 and 5 Wm. IV., ch. 76, § 15; continued by 3 and 4 Vict., ch. 42; 5 Vict., ch. 10, and 5 and 6 Vict., ch. 57, to July 31, 1847.

[3] Schouler, Dom. Rel., p. 382.

[4] See Mass. Gen. Acts, 1867; Incorp. Mass. Inf. Assy., and Sup. Acts, 1870 and 1880.

guardians for such children,[1] making all possible effort to supply the lost parental relation by the pseudo-parental relation of adoption. That is, the law assumes that every parent normally retains custody of his child; but the pauper parent, proving that he cannot maintain it, forfeits the trust of custody; and the impersonal custody of the almshouse being morally and physically injurious, the personal relations of home life are substituted so far as possible.[2] But, where the State makes this transfer of the child on these grounds, it asserts its recognition of the moral welfare of the child over the legal right of the family, and furnishes evidence of the altered position of the child destitute of property since Blackstone's day, as now the mere fact of childhood brings the young pauper under elaborate specific provisions of law made for the express purpose of securing his moral welfare.

Again, in the case of children removed from parental custody by reason of juvenile crimes and misdemeanors; according to Blackstone, under the common law the child susceptible of sentence[3] of incarceration seems to have undergone the same custody as the adult, Blackstone making no mention of provision for supplying any different custody. Indeed, as late as 1823, under Sir Robert Peel's "Consolidated Jails act," legal offense was made the basis of classification without regard to age, character or conduct in prison.[4] And Mary Carpenter wrote bitterly,[5] "the only school provided in Great Britain by the State for her children is the jail."

In Massachusetts, on the contrary, at the present day, if a child appear before a magistrate and is liable to commitment in default of bail, agents of the State Board of Health, Charity and Lunacy have instructions to be present and offer themselves as bail,[6] in order that this individual care may prevent the child's falling into public custody. Should the child, however, be committed, he or she goes to an industrial school under legislation which pays respect not only to the grade of offense of the minor, but to its age and sex.[7] The

1 3d An. Rep. Mass. St. Bd. Health, Ch. and Lunacy.

2 3d An. Rep. Mass. Bd. Health, Ch. and Lunacy.

3 In stating limitations under which children are susceptible of capital punishment, Bl. 469, gives a good illustration of the principle that the child's life is additionally protected, since certain capital crimes cannot be punished if committed by children.

4 Wines, Prisons and Child-Saving Institutions.

5 Carpenter, Reform Schools, p. 261.

6 3d An. Rep. St. Bd. of Health, Charity and Lunacy.

7 See Mass. General Statutes for acts of incorporation of Westborough and Lancaster schools, and the State Primary School at Monson, 1848, 1855. See, further, act of July, 1879, by which these schools are all under care of a board of five trustees, of whom two are women.

delinquent child, becoming by this commitment a ward of the State, is withdrawn from the school at the earliest possible moment and placed in an individual home[1] (under the care of a member of an auxiliary board, composed of women, if the offender be a boy under fourteen years or a girl under twenty-one); and his ever finding his way into a jail depends upon such repeated evil-doing as proves the offender adult in crime, if a child in years.[2]

In this provision for the custody of delinquent children, all growth has tended toward supplying to the child who has proved his natural guardian unfit to restrain him, and by being committed has forfeited his normal legal custody, such home life and personal care as shall replace, as far as possible, the lost normal relation. Leaving such children to the actual guardianship and custody of the State, as embodied in the jail, proved destructive; and present legislation in Massachusetts gives, instead, quasi-parental home life under the guardianship of a board of public officials of whom by law some must be women. Here, too, is growing care for the child's welfare, and growing recognition of his individuality with its need of individual care. Here is also the assertion by the State of its power and will to decide the home of the child, and of the superiority of the moral over the legal qualification of the home in securing the child's welfare. Such legislation is an acknowledgment that the personal relation of home life must be provided by the State for its wards as better than the impersonal custody of the jail,[3] but it is indirectly a blow to the legal family; for in practice it relieves the parent or guardian from further responsibility, not attempting to reach the child through the legal domestic relations. This last mentioned, possibly undomestic, feature is, however, the sole point in which the present legislation of Massachusetts affecting children resembles the view of the delinquent child derivable from Blackstone; and the custody of delinquent children indicates perhaps better than anything else the total emergence of the child from his former legal oblivion. In view of the growth, in complex provision, of law governing the child's custody, Blackstone's discussion of custody as a parental right has become inadequate. Present legislation proceeds upon the principle that custody rests not on any parental vested right, but on the right of the child to be in the care most fit to secure his welfare, whether that of father, mother,

1 Mass. Gen. Statutes. See act of 1880.

2 See 3d An. Rep. State Bd. Health, Charity and Lunacy.

3 Proceeding of Convention of Associated Charities, Boston, 1881.

guardian or board of charity, or board of women visitors, or some adoptive parent; and nothing is more significant than the growing recognition of the child's need of and right to be in the care and custody of women.[1]

Under the Commentaries the legitimate child was a chattel dependent for custody upon its owner's whim; the illegitimate child was without legal custody; the pauper child was not different from the pauper adult—childhood was swallowed up in pauperhood; the delinquent child's childhood was merged in his delinquency, and his custody upon that basis was the adult delinquent's custody.

Now, the child is a child in the eye of the law, be he legitimate or illegitimate, or pauper or delinquent, and his custody is arranged in recognition of the fact. But that is also a blow struck at the legal family, since it tends toward bridging in some measure the gulf which separates the child within normal domestic relations and the child without, not diminishing the happiness of the former but letting the latter approach it, and so diminishing in some measure the legal prestige of the child within the family.

Another right of the child which was slightly treated by Blackstone, and has grown gradually into recognition, is the right of protection. A survey of the legal provision for this relation gives further evidence that the child, as such, was slightly guarded under the common law; for, vitally essential to every child as this protection is, Blackstone discusses protection, like custody, as a purely paternal function, observing merely that a parent "may justify an assault and battery in defense of the persons of his children." Indeed, he regards protection as a "natural right, rather permitted than enjoined by any municipal laws, nature working so strongly in this respect as to need rather a check than a spur."[2] Since Blackstone, however, the child's welfare has demanded that this parental duty and right should be supplemented by positive legislation punishing the suppression of the fact of the child's birth,[3] making child-stealing a felony, giving the father the right of action for injury to the child's person,[4] making vaccination obligatory, insuring to the pauper child more healthful care than is given to the pauper adult, prohibiting the sale of liquor and of obscene literature to children, restricting the hours of the child worker, and incorporating societies for protecting children from cruelty, sometimes that of the parent himself. More distinctly here than in most cases

[1] Mass. Gen. Stat. 1868–82.

[2] Bl., § 450.

[3] Geo. IV., ch. 21.

[4] Schouler, Dom. Rel., p. 358.

the law makes two fold provision for the care of the child by arranging for upholding the father in his right of caring for his child, and for enabling other agencies to enforce his own performance of his duties as parent. Here, too, the process of generalization goes on and the legal paternal right of protecting one's chattel becomes the universal right of the child to be protected. Inherent in every child is the need of protection, and when the paternal function fails the law charters a society, giving to the orphan and the illegitimate child what substitute it can for the lost safety of the legal family.

But that also is a blow struck at the legal family, since that also helps the child outside the family.

A third right, which illustrates the growth of legal provision for the child, as such, and independent of the family, is the right to such education as shall make him an intelligent citizen.

In this country education had been acknowledged as a function of the State throughout the New England colonies a century before the Commentaries were written,[1] and the growth of legal provision for the performance of the function has been chiefly geographical, one State after another imitating New England more or less exactly according to circumstances, during two centuries and a half, the growing provision for education holding a rough proportion to the extent of suffrage.

In England, however, education was still a purely paternal function in Blackstone's time,[2] and the development of legal provision for education during the present century has been thoroughly organic, illustrating more strikingly than either of the functions hitherto discussed the extremely gradual recognition of the child as a being possessed of distinct and individual status independent of domestic relations.

Of education Blackstone observes:[3] "The last duty of parents to their children is that of giving them an education suitable to their station in life, a duty pointed out by nature as of far the greatest importance of any. Yet the municipal laws of most countries seem to be defective on this point by not constraining the parent to bestow a proper education upon his children."

He further mentions that, in respect to one sort of education, the children of poor persons are better off than the children of the rich, since the overseers of the poor are legally bound to have them apprenticed to a trade.

Thus education was in general the prerogative of the child pos-

[1] See Lodge, Short Hist. U. S., ch. 22.

[2] See Bl. Parent and Child.

[3] Bl. § 451.

sessed of normal domestic relations and sufficient property to permit his receiving the training of one of the so-called public schools, while the pauper child received such manual training, by means of apprenticeship, as removed him at the earliest possible moment from the care and cost of the parish, and the laborer's child received nothing.

[1] Here the matter rested until 1802, when the elder Sir Robert Peel carried a bill[2] through Parliament "compelling masters and mistresses of cotton and woolen mills employing more than a fixed small number of spindles, to furnish apprentices instruction in reading, writing and arithmetic, or either of them, according to the abilities of the apprentice, a part of each day, within working hours, for the first four years."

This bill is most significant. In commenting upon it the Duke of Argyle says:

"It is characteristic of the slow progress of new ideas in the English mind, and of its strong instinct to adopt no measure which does not stand in some relation to preëxisting laws, that Sir Robert Peel's bill was limited strictly to the regulation of the labor of apprentices. * * * The notion was that, as apprentices were already under statutory provisions, and were subjects of a legal contract, it was permissible that their hours of labor should be regulated by positive enactment. * * * Through this narrow door the first of the Factory acts was passed. * * * If the evils of the factory system had not begun to be observable in the labor of apprentices, there is no saying how much longer those evils might have been allowed to fester without even an assertion of the right to check them."[3]

Of course, the assumption was that all children not apprenticed were sufficiently educated through paternal care and affection, but the reverse of this is shown by the áuthor referred to, as follows:

"The earnings of children became an irresistible temptation to the parents. They were sent to the factory at the earliest age, and they worked during the whole hours that the machinery was kept at work."

[4]"To meet this the act of 1819 was passed, which, being the first measure restricting the labor of unapprenticed children, was, properly

[1] 2 Geo. IV., ch. 73.

[2] For the futility of this act (except as a wedge,) see Jules Simon, "Ouvrier de huit ans," Rev. d. d. Mon., Dec. 1864.

[3] Argyle, Reign of Law, ch. VII.

[4] Arthur Young, Labor in Europe and America, p. 182.

speaking, the first of the Factory acts. This act and the one of 1825 remained practically dead letter for want of adequate enforcing clauses; and it was not until Lord Ashley's bill, in 1833, establishing a stringent system of government inspection, that any progress was made in mitigating the evils which the factory system developed."

Three years after Lord Ashley's bill, in 1836, another bill—not a factory act—was passed, which was almost as significant of the growing legal care for the education of the child as Sir Robert Peel's bill of 1802. Almost as slight a wedge, and quite as trivial in its immediate effects, this bill permitted gifts to be made of parts of waste lands and commons for sites for poor schools, limiting the gift to one statute half acre.[1]

Such was the legal provision for education at the accession of Queen Victoria. Two wedges had been inserted, and one of them, the first Factory act, had already resulted in the extension of care for their education to factory children employed in worsted, hemp, flax, tow, linen or silk manufacture, in addition to the cotton and wool workers, first provided for.[2] Every legal provision for the education of the English child beyond these limited and inefficient beginnings is included in the Victoria Statutes, and hardly a year has passed without adding to their scope and efficiency. Year after year, one industry after another has been brought under the Factory acts, until all the textile and metal industries, and, after a long and bitter struggle, the brick and tile makers, are forced to supply half-time schools or furnish at the demand of the government inspector the certificate of attendance at a certified school of every child employed. So, too, the mining industries, and, last of all, the young canal drivers, are included under special provisions of these acts.

Hand in hand with this extension of the child's legal claim to education has gone the extension of legal provision for furnishing him the means of training.

Five years after Victoria's accession the Permissive act[3] of 1836 was extended to permit any number of half-acre grants for separate schools, and this, in turn, is extended in 1844[4] by provision for encouragement to the making of such schools by grants of public money provided a government inspector be admitted and in 1849[5] the half-acre restriction is removed.

[1] 1, 6 and 7 William IV., ch. 70.

[2] Young, Labor in Europe and America.

[3] 6 and 7 William IV., ch. 70.

[4] 4 and 5 Vict., ch. 38.

[5] 12 and 13 Vict., ch. 49.

In 1855,[1] guardians are permitted to grant relief, to enable poor persons to educate their children in any school approved by the guardians.

In 1856,[2] education becomes for the first time a recognized function of the State, and the Queen is empowered to appoint a vice-president of the Council of Education from the Privy Council, who shall sit and vote as a Member of Parliament in Commons.

That is to say, in 1855 the recognition of the child's right of being educated had so far grown that the pauper child could not be deprived of it, while the administration of the means of education had been transferred bodily to the State.

Subsequent legislation governing education has proceeded in the same direction, and the adoption of the principle of compulsory education was the culmination of the development of the principle of caring for the welfare of the child, as a child, which was first embodied in Lord Ashley's bill of 1832.

In a comparison of the legal provision for the education of the child in England and in America, one striking fact presents itself.[3] New England in the seventeenth century was the purest democracy then on the face of the globe, and New England made the most thorough legal provision for the education of every child. In old England suffrage was restricted; and, in the absence of legal provision for education, the children educated corresponded pretty nearly to the number of families whose property secured them suffrage. After the introducing of steam, philanthropy accomplished in thirty years (1802-32) almost nothing in securing education to the one class of children with whose education philanthropy concerned itself.

On the introduction of more general suffrage followed steadily increasing legal provision for the child, until to-day the English suffrage roughly corresponds to the suffrage of New England in the seventeenth century, and the present legal provision for education in England secures a degree of universally compulsory education also roughly corresponding to the education of New England at that time.[4]

It is doubtless true that the same liberal spirit which maintains a general suffrage would naturally maintain a system of general educa-

[1] 18 and 19 Vict., ch. 34.
[2] 19 and 20 Vict., ch. 116.
[3] See Lodge, Short Hist. U. S., ch. 22.
[4] MacMillen, August, 1876. Eng. Factory Act and Compulsory Education.

tion as well; but it is also true that where suffrage is general the State must make education so in self-defense.[1]

It would seem, therefore, that the growth of care for the moral welfare of the child, and the removal of the duty of education from the family to the State, must receive a decided impulse from every extension of suffrage, and the foregoing comparison would seem to offer confirmation of the theory.

From a survey of the changes of status of the child as affected by custody, protection and education, it would seem that the position of the legitimate child within the family is substantially as it was in the time of Blackstone. Domestic affection sufficed then, as now, for securing these three necessaries for the child within the family, and legal provision need be made only as the family itself altered, and then only in giving to the father's love and care the reënforcement of legal power in the mother as she emerged from legal nonentity. Hence the chief change in the status of the legitimate child is negative, his legal position being partially and gradually approached by the status of the illegitimate[2] and of the pauper child, and somewhat of the prestige and prerogative of the legitimate child is lost.

Only when the family itself sustains an injury through divorce, or pauperism, or cruelty, or the emergence of the child too early into the field of the laborer, can the strong arm of the law prove itself tender and merciful also by directly sustaining and defending the hapless children.

Inevitably, therefore, care for the welfare of the child has asserted itself chiefly in legislation touching children directly and outside the domestic relations. But in so doing it has extended many safeguards formerly wholly domestic. The relations of childhood discussed by Blackstone as domestic were the paternal rights of custody, possession of the child's earnings, and maintenance in indigent old age; with the paternal duties of maintenance, education, and protection. We have seen that the discussion of custody as a merely paternal right is wholly inadequate; the legal[3] provision for the child's maintenance is revolutionized by the extended duties of the mother, and, though parental, is no longer wholly paternal. Present legislation proceeds upon the principle that every child, whether in a family or not, must be protected, and whosoever will may protect him, while

1 See Horace Mann, Lect. on Ed., Vol. I.

2 Schouler, Dom. Rel. on the Illegitimate Child.

3 See A. J. Spencer in Pop. Sci. Mo., Apr. 1881, on Leg. Stat. Married Women.

the once paternal duty of education has been transferred bodily to the State.

The illegitimate child's position is somewhat modified by direct legislation; but, apart from the recognition by statute of his need of and right to be in his mother's custody, and to have her responsible for his maintenance, his status improves with every growth of legislation touching children as individuals removed from the domestic relations and directly responsible to the State. As a pauper, the illegitimate is treated as the legitimate pauper child is treated; as future citizen, he is trained in the public schools, profiting by the growth of law, which removes education from the family to the State; through societies chartered by law he is restrained from overworking in the factory, and from buying intoxicating liquor and obscene literature; and he, too, profits by the municipal ordinances which recognize in the newsboy and the bootblack industrial beings whose rights demand the protection of municipal license. So far is his condition assimilated to that of the legitimate child that the statement is now true that "the chief legal disadvantage of the illegitimate child is his inability to inherit."[1]

Indeed, every new law which guards all children, acting on them directly as human beings responsible to itself without the intervention of parent or guardian, by including the orphan and the illegitimate child, and improving their condition, diminishes the proportion in which the legitimate child living in normal legal relations is especially cherished, and strikes a blow at the legal family. This, statute law since Blackstone has increasingly done, guarding all children without reference to the family, diminishing paternal power, and making the child more and more nearly the ward of the State.

This[2] tendency it is which is characteristic of the nineteenth century legislation governing minors, and the same movement which has generalized custody, protection and education until they have ceased to be paternal duties and rights, and have become tacitly acknowledged as rights of the child without reference to the family, is evident elsewhere. Two mighty forces impelling legislation in this direction are steam, which has given to the child the novel rôle of industrial being, and enfranchisement, which has forced the State in self-preservation to compel his education as future citizen. But not these two forces

[1] See Schouler, Dom. Rel. Illegitimate Child.

[2] See British Statutes 1802–82, as illustrating this tendency better than our scattered legislation affecting children.

alone have forced the child's partial emergence from its former position in which it existed (according to the legal hypothesis) almost solely within the family, governed wholly in and through the family, to its present position in which it is in great measure subject to the direct action of legislation.

Underlying all child-governing legislation of the present century is the same impulse toward guarding unrepresented classes which has altered the status of women, made legal provision for the dependent and defective classes, ameliorated the condition of the Indian, and lifted the Negro bodily out of the unrepresented condition. This tendency has acted both directly and indirectly; directly, in altering legislation, and indirectly, in bringing the influence of women[1] to bear upon legislation affecting children. The extent of the change wrought in this way cannot, of course, be calculated; but the influence of Mary Carpenter upon penal and reformatory legislation affecting children in Great Britain is a conspicuous example of what is taking place unobserved elsewhere.

A third force which has contributed to secure the recognition of the child as an individual possessed of legal status independent of his family ties, is the growing value attached to human life and to human personality, and the attendant respect for individuality in every form. At present this does in practice so shape the law as to make individuality superior to the unity of the family. This is clearly seen in the relation of custody. When the law breaks by divorce the legal family, giving the child its choice of abode with either parent, it emphatically asserts this supremacy of the individual. When the law removes a delinquent child from the family relation into which it was born, and places it, through the working of reformatory legislation, in a home selected by the agents of the law, emphatically does it assert the precedence of the child's moral welfare over the legal unity of the family, and the precedence of the moral over the legal aspect of the home, in the eye of the law itself. This is perhaps the one dangerous force of all which have been molding infancy legislation; for the child's prime safeguard is the family, and whatsoever strikes the family wounds the child.

In the wish to state fairly this one possible harm to the child among the many improvements in his status, the assimilation of the status of the "other" child to that of the child normally placed has perhaps been exaggerated in the foregoing discussion in the effort to give due

[1] See Life of Mary Carpenter, by Philip Estlin Carpenter.

weight to the dangerous, as well as to the helpful, features of development of the principle in legislation of caring for every child's moral welfare. So marked, however, is the emphasis now laid by the law on the individuality of the child that one writer has said that the child's present position as "favorite of the law" is attained largely at the expense of the family, the proportion of truth diminishing constantly in the statement, "the law secures the welfare of the child by upholding parental rights and enforcing parental duties."

Nevertheless, allowing due gravity in this danger, and assuming the whole body of legislation for education and the child's welfare to have been accomplished by mere statecraft, inspired only by the wish to train quiet citizens for the State, with large, too, allowance for every dangerous tendency, the result, as it stands written in the statutes of the nineteenth century, is yet, in its far-reaching care for the fatherless and the oppressed, a noble embodiment of the tender spirit of Him who said of the helpless little child: "Of such is the kingdom of Heaven."

FLORENCE KELLEY.

THE LAW
AND
THE AMERICAN CHILD

Thomas Charles Carrigan

THE

PEDAGOGICAL SEMINARY

Founded and Edited by G. STANLEY HALL

VOL. XVIII JUNE, 1911 No. 2

THE LAW AND THE AMERICAN CHILD[1]

By THOMAS CHARLES CARRIGAN, A. M., Clark University

CONTENTS

(1) INTRODUCTION

Beneath the Children's Institute at Clark University, there is a statue of the late George Frisbie Hoar—a former Trustee

[1]The writer is indebted for assistance to President G. Stanley Hall, Dr. William H. Burnham, Dr. Theodate L. Smith and Librarian Louis N. Wilson, of Clark University, also to Thomas J. Homer, Esq., of Boston, Rev. John J. McCoy, LL. D., of Worcester, Dr. George E. Wire, of the Worcester County Law Library, and Librarian Robert K. Shaw, of the Worcester Free Public Library.

of the University, a United States Senator and a Jurist. To some interested in Child Welfare this statue symbolizes that courage, hope and humanity which characterized the Senator's life and which were manifested in his prevention of the deportation of the Syrian children in 1901, and in 1903 led the second session of the Fifty-seventh Congress to enact Sec. 37 of Chap. 1012 of the United States Statutes, which provides "Whenever an alien shall have taken up permanent residence in this country and shall have filed his preliminary declaration to be a citizen and thereafter shall send for his wife or minor children to join him, if said wife or either of said children shall be found to be affected with any contagious disorder, and it seems that said disorder was contracted on board the ship in which they came, such wife or children shall be held under such regulations as the Secretary of the Treasury shall prescribe until it shall be determined whether they can be permitted to land without danger to other persons; and they shall not be deported until such facts have been ascertained." (19, 2, 298.)

Near the northern terminus of the same street on which the University is located, stands the Worcester County Court House. Within a few steps beyond the entrance, the visitor comes to an arch on which is emblazoned: "Here Speaketh the Conscience of the State Restraining the Individual Will."

On Thursday, January 26, 1911, in an address to the young men and women of the Worcester Evening High School another who measures up to the best traditions of the Massachusetts Supreme Court Bench, Mr. Justice Rugg, said: "I believe those words of Senator Hoar at our Court House make the best definition of law extant." Law, then, in the United States at the beginning of this second decade of the twentieth century, may be assumed to be that legislative and judicial expression of the public conscience by which the individual is governed. And as our people are the State, it would seem to follow that our laws are never better nor worse than the American people demand.

The term "child" in this study is synonymous with the legal term "infant" and is intended to include all the years of minority.

The following pages contain a brief survey of some laws that concern the American child. It is not the purpose of this paper to follow out any of these laws in detail, to do so would require a separate volume for each of several of the laws outlined. The recency of the laws mentioned in this study is noted under the topics through references to the bibliography. Statutes, later than those cited by some of the authorities enumerated in the bibliography, have been inserted. Obviously no claim can be made that the latest revisions have been presented—the legislatures of most of the states are now in session and new laws are being enacted daily.

(2) Marriage

Just as infancy is the legal status of persons under age, marriage is the legal status of husbands and wives. After a valid marriage man and woman are husband and wife, and their offspring are legitimate children.

Professor Stimson in his "Popular Law Making" says "It is always to be remembered that the law of marriage, and divorce as well, was originally administered by the Church. Marriage was a *sacrament;* it brought about a status; it was not a mere secular contract, as is growing to be more and more the modern view. Indeed, the whole matter of sexual relations was left to the Church, and was consequently matter of sin and virtue, not of crime and innocence. Modern legislation has, perhaps, too far departed from this distinction. Unquestionably, many matters of which the State now takes jurisdiction were better left to conscience and to the Church, so long as they offend no third party nor the public." (39, 324-5.)

Capacity of Parties in General.. A person may be generally incapable of contracting marriage because of (a) want of age; (b) want of mental capacity; (c) want of physical and sexual capacity; (d) relationship by blood or marriage with the other party; (e) being of a different race from the other party; and (f) having been married before and that marriage not being at an end.

(a) Want of age. At common law the marriage of a male over fourteen and a female over twelve was valid. At least "thirty states, including the District of Columbia have by statute prescribed a higher age limit for marriageable consent, and in those states the marriage of a minor below the common law age of consent and the statutory age of consent is voidable by the minor on arriving at the statutory age of consent.

"In Minnesota and Wisconsin the statutory age of consent is fixed at 18 for the male and 15 for the female, but the statute does not declare that marriages under such ages, shall be void, therefore the courts have held them to be voidable, only. In the remaining 17 states the ages of consent remain the same as at common law. Three of these states, Kentucky, Louisiana and Virginia, having adopted said ages by statute" (1,1136).

The lowest statutory age for a male is fourteen. The states in which marriage can be contracted by a male at fourteen years are Kentucky, Louisiana, and Virginia. The states in which the statutory limit is fifteen years are Kansas and Missouri. Those in which it is sixteen years are the District of Columbia, Iowa, North Carolina, Texas and Utah. Those in which it is seventeen years are Alabama, Arkansas, and Georgia; those in which it is eighteen years are Arizona, California, Delaware, Idaho, Illinois, Indiana, Michigan, Minnesota, Montana, Nebraska, Nevada, New Hampshire, New Mexico, New York, North Dakota, Ohio, Oklahoma, Oregon, South Dakota, West Virginia, Wisconsin and Wyoming; and twenty-one in most of the remaining states.

Age limit for females. The lowest age at which a valid marriage can be contracted by a female is twelve years. The states in which the statutory limit of twelve obtains are Kansas, Kentucky, Louisiana, Missouri and Virginia. In the following states it is fourteen years: Alabama, Arkansas, District of Columbia, Georgia, Iowa, North Carolina, Texas and Utah. The states in which the statutory limit is fifteen are Minnesota, New Mexico, North Dakota, Oklahoma, South Dakota and Wisconsin.

The states in which the statutory limit is sixteen years are Arizona, Delaware, Illinois, Indiana, Michigan, Montana, Nebraska, Nevada, New Hampshire, Ohio, West Virginia and Wyoming. The statutory limit is eighteen years in Idaho, Massachusetts, and New York. In other states for which no minimum marriageable age is given the provisions of the common law seem to apply.

The age below which parental consent is required for the marriage of a male is twenty-one years in forty states and territories in three states it is 18, and in one state 16. In Tennessee it is sixteen years, and in Idaho and North Carolina eighteen years.

In Georgia, Michigan and South Carolina no age is fixed for parental consent for the male. The age below which parental consent is required for the marriage of a female is fixed at 21 in 9 states, at 18 in 34 states (including D. C.), and at 16 in 3 states. (1.1137.) It is sixteen in Maryland and Tennessee. It is twenty-one years in Connecticut, Florida, Kentucky, Louisiana, Pennsylvania, Rhode Island, Virginia, West Virginia, and Wyoming. No statutory limit is established in New Hampshire, New York, and South Carolina. In all the other states and territories it is eighteen years. In Massachusetts, permission from the Probate Court is required for the marriage of a male under eighteen or of a female under sixteen.

(b) *Mental Capacity*. The marriage of the insane, persons absolutely *non compos*, was always void both at Common law and the Church law as well. By recent laws Connecticut and Minnesota prohibit the marriage of an epileptic, imbecile, or feeble-minded woman under 45 years of age or cohabitation by any male of this description with a woman under 45 years of age, and marriage of lunatics is void in the District of Columbia, Kentucky, Maine, Massachusetts, Nebraska.

(c) *Physical and Sexual Capacity*. Marriage of impotent persons has always been void; Michigan prohibits the marriage of persons having sexual diseases; by recent laws Indiana and California refuse marriage licenses to persons under the influence of intoxicants or drugs or infected with certain transmissible diseases; and "finally most startling of all the proposal looms in the future to make every man contemplating a marriage submit himself to an examination, both moral and physical, by the state or city officials as to his health and habits, and even that of his ancestry, as bearing upon posterity." (39.327-8.)

(d) *Consanguinity and Affinity*. Marriage between first cousins is forbidden in Alaska, Arizona, Illinois, Indiana, Kansas, Missouri, Nevada, New Hampshire, North Dakota, Ohio, Oklahoma, Oregon, Pennsylvania, South Dakota, Washington and Wyoming, and in some of them is declared incestuous and void, and marriage with step-relatives is forbidden in all states except Florida, Hawaiian Islands, Iowa, Kentucky, Minnesota, New York, Tennessee and Wisconsin. In Hawaii, Porto Rico and the Philippines marriages are prohibited within the fourth degree of consanguinity.

(e) *Miscegenation*. Marriages between whites and persons of negro descent are prohibited and punishable in Alabama, Arizona, Arkansas, California, Colorado, Delaware, Florida, Idaho, Indiana, Kentucky, Louisiana, Maryland, Mississippi, Missouri, Nebraska, North Carolina, Oregon, South Carolina, Tennessee, Texas, Utah, Virginia and West Virginia. Marriages between whites and Indians are void in Arizona, North Carolina, Oregon, and South Carolina; between whites and mongolians in Arizona, California, Mississippi, Oregon and Utah.

(f) If one has been married before and that marriage is not at an end, he of course cannot contract another marriage. If he goes through the form of a second marriage under such circumstances, he is guilty of bigamy, which is an offense punishable in all states. In nearly all states and territories the statutes provide that a person may contract marriage after the disappearance of a former husband or wife (the former marriage not having been dissolved by divorce or annulled) if the latter has been continuously absent for a specified number of years and has not been known to be living during this period. The length of time which the absence without news has continued is three years in Florida, Iowa, and New Hampshire. It is two years in Pennsylvania. It is seven years in Maine, Maryland, Massachusetts, Mississippi, Missouri, North Carolina, Oregon, Rhode Island, South Carolina, Vermont, Virginia, West Virginia and Wisconsin. It is five years in Alabama, Arizona, Arkansas, California, Colorado, Delaware, District of Columbia, Georgia, Idaho, Illinois, Indiana, Kansas, Kentucky, Louisiana, Michigan, Minnesota, Montana, Nebraska, Nevada, New Jersey, New Mexico, New York, North Dakota, Ohio, Oklahoma, South Dakota, Tennessee, Texas, Utah, Washington, Wyoming.

Marriage Licenses. "Wisconsin seems to be the only state requiring the license to be taken out several days before the marriage. Only two states, Louisiana and Maine, appear to have any provision for the filing of objections, by parents, guardians or others, to a contemplated marriage. In Louisiana the license issues immediately upon the making of the application. In Maine notice of the intention to apply for a license must be made at least five days before the issuing of the license." (1.1138.) New Hampshire has just adopted this Maine plan. All the states and territories, except South Carolina, require marriage licenses, and also, except South Carolina require every marriage solemnized to be reported to some official specified by law. However, in Maine, Maryland, Iowa and Kansas a license is not required for the marriage of members of the Society of Friends, or Quakers. In Pennsylvania, Delaware, Maryland, Georgia and Ohio the parties, instead of securing a license, may have recourse to the publication of banns. There are also other minor exceptions in certain states.

3. Divorce

The American people are divided on matters pertaining to divorce. Those opposed to any divorce, that carries the legal right of remarriage during the life time of the divorced husband or wife, sometimes combine with those urging the fewest legal causes of divorce, and the coalition presents a united front against the exponents of "the open door" in divorce legislation. Some of the divorce reformers maintain that there are insidious influences planning to amend the marriage vows, so as to read "Till *divorce* doth us part;" that such a modification can be expected of an age that has legally evoluted or devoluted or devilized unto progressive fragmentary polygamy and polyandry on the installment plan. They tell us that divorce is a modern institution; that is divorce by the secular courts; that such "divorce as the Roman Church, recognized (without the right of remarriage) or was granted by the act of Parliament, was the only divorce existing down to the year 1642, when one Hannah Huish was divorced in Connecticut by the General Court, 'with liberty to marry again as God may grant her opportunity,' and about that time the Colony of Massachusetts Bay enacted the first law (with the possible exception of one in Geneva permitting divorces by ordinary courts of law" (39, 326). The divorce reformers allege that the advance in present methods beyond those of the seventeenth century is shown by many a modern Hannah Huish, who believing that God helps her who helps herself, makes her own "opportunity" by keeping on her waiting list at least one "minute man," who, too often, is himself waiting anxiously for some divorce mill to grind out the welcome refrain—"Off with the old, on with the new." They call our attention to the pathetic figure in some of these cases, *the child* learning the shifting designations for his father's former wife—his mother, his father's present wife—his stepmother, his mother's former husband—his father, his mother's present husband—his stepfather, with perchance a few other stepmothers and stepfathers intervening to complicate the task. They assure us that whatever the pedagogical value in the mastery of such a lesson, the child's ideals of "family life," "home," "mother," and "father" can hardly contribute much to his moral uplift before or his country's after his arrival at manhood. The adherents of latitude in divorces, on the other hand, have their array of arguments for their position. One or two typical replies are: "Many clergymen argue that to have only one cause, adultery, is the worst law of all, as it drives the parties to commit this sin when otherwise they might attain the desired divorce by simple desertion" (39,323). Again they ask, "How can the child be possibly benefited in a home of parents, that are agreed that their particular "marriage is a failure," but are willing to try other marriages? Moreover, the difference in condition, education, religion, race and climate is so great throughout the Union that it is unwise, as well as impossible to get all of our forty-eight States to take the same view on this subject, the Spanish Catholic as the Maine free-thinker, the settler in wild and lonely regions as the inhabitant of the old New England town over-populated by spinsters" (39, 323). "Nevertheless, it is not questionable that modern American legislation, particularly in the code States, in California, New York, and the west generally, is based upon the view that marriage is a simple contract, whence results the obvious corollary that it may be dissolved at any time by mutual consent. No state has thus far followed the decision to this logical end, on the pretended assumption that the rights of children are concerned but the rights of children might as well be conserved upon a voluntary divorce as after a scandalous court proceedings.

One possible view is that the Church should set its own standard, and the State its own standard, even to the extreme of not regulating the matter at all except by ordinary laws of contract and laws for the record of marriage and divorce and for the custody, guardianship, support, and education of children, which would include the presumption of paternity pending an undissolved marriage, but all divorce to be by mutual consent. It is evident to any careful student of our legislation that we would be rapidly approaching this view but for the conservative influence of Massachusetts, Connecticut, Pennsylvania, New Jersey, and the South, and but for the efforts of most of the churches and the divorce reform societies. Which influence will prove more powerful in the end it is not possible to predict." (39.325.)

Weak must be the grievance, and arrested must be the ingenuity of that husband or wife, in some parts of our country, who cannot discover relief in one or more of the thirty-five causes for divorce now on the statute books of the states of the Union.

Causes of Divorce

South Carolina has no divorce for any cause.

The following table of causes for absolute divorce and some of the States recognizing each cause is of interest:

(1) Abandonment or desertion—In all except New York, District of Columbia, North Carolina and South Carolina.

(2) Adultery—Sexual Immorality—In all states but South Carolina.

(3) Attempt to take Life—Illinois, Tennessee and Louisiana.

(4) Causes deemed sufficient by courts—Washington.

(5) Civil Death—Rhode Island.

(6) Consanguinity—Pennsylvania, Georgia, Florida and Mississippi.

(7) Crime—Conviction or Imprisonment—All except Maine, Rhode Island, New York, New Jersey, Maryland, District of Columbia, North Carolina, South Carolina and Florida.

(8) Crime against nature—Alabama.

(9) Cruelty—Extreme Cruelty—Maine, New Hampshire, Vermont, Massachusetts, Rhode Island, Connecticut, Delaware, Georgia, Florida, Ohio, Indiana, Illinois, Michigan, Wisconsin, Minnesota, North Dakota, South Dakota, Nebraska, Kansas, Kentucky, Tennessee, Mississippi, Louisiana, Oklahoma, Texas, Montana, Idaho, Wyoming, Colorado, New Mexico, Arizona, Utah, Nevada, Washington, Oregon, and California.

(10) Defects of Disposition—Violent temper—Florida and Kentucky.

(11) Fraud or Fraudulent Contract—Connecticut, Pennsylvania, Georgia, Ohio, Kansas, Kentucky, Oklahoma and Washington.

(12) Fugitive from Justice—Virginia and Louisiana.

(13) Habitual Use of Drugs—Maine, Massachusetts, Rhode Island and Mississippi.

(14) Illegality of Marriage—Bigamy—Pennsylvania, Florida, Ohio, Illinois, Missouri, Kansas, Tennessee, Mississippi, Arkansas, Oklahoma and Colorado.

(15) Illicit carnal intercourse—Maryland, Virginia and West Virginia.

(16) Incapacity to contract Marriage—Mental Incapacity—Georgia, Mississippi, Idaho, Utah and Washington.

(17) Indignities and Defamation—Pennsylvania, Missouri, Tennessee, Louisiana, Arkansas, Wyoming, Washington and Oregon.

(18) Intolerant Religious Belief—New Hampshire and Kentucky.

(19) Intemperance—Habitual Drunkenness—Maine, New Hampshire, Massachusetts, Rhode Island, Connecticut, Delaware, Georgia, Florida, Ohio, Indiana, Illinois, Michigan, Wisconsin, Minnesota, Iowa, Missouri, North Dakota, South Dakota, Nebraska, Kansas, Kentucky, Tennessee, Alabama, Mississippi, Louisiana, Arkansas, Oklahoma, Montana, Idaho, Wyoming, Colorado, New Mexico, Arizona, Utah, Nevada, Washington, Oregon and California.

(20) Lack of real consent to marriage—Duress or force—Pennsylvania, Georgia, Kentucky and Washington.

(21) Loathsome Disease—Kentucky.

(22) Lewd Conduct—Kentucky.

(23) Misconduct—Rhode Island and Wisconsin.

(24) Neglect of duty—Ohio, North Dakota, South Dakota, Kansas, Oklahoma, Montana, Idaho and California.

(25) Neglect to provide—Maine, Vermont, Massachusetts, Rhode Island, Delaware, Indiana, Michigan, Wisconsin, Nebraska, Tennessee, Wyoming, Colorado, New Mexico, Arizona, Utah, Nevada, and Washington.

(26) Other causes—Void and voidable Marriages (not otherwise specified)—Rhode Island and Maryland.

(27) Personal unfitness to contract marriage—Impotency—All except Vermont, Connecticut, New York, District of Columbia, South Carolina, Iowa, South Dakota, South Dakota, Texas, Montana, Idaho, and California.

(28) Pregnancy before Marriage—Virginia, West Virginia, North Carolina, Georgia, Iowa, Missouri, Kansas, Kentucky, Tennessee, Alabama, Mississippi, Wyoming, New Mexico and Arizona.

(29) Previous Divorce in Another State—Florida, Ohio and Michigan.

(30) Presumption of Death—Rhode Island and Connecticut.

(31) Refusal to move to State—Tennessee.

(32) Vagrancy—Missouri and Wyoming.

(33) Voluntary Separation—Rhode Island, after ten years; Kentucky, after five years.

(34) Violence endangering life—Pennsylvania, Iowa, Missouri, Kentucky, Alabama and Arkansas.

(35) Want of age—Delaware.

Limited Divorces

Limited divorces or separations from bed and board are granted in Alabama, Arkansas, Delaware, District of Columbia, Georgia, Indiana, Kentucky, Louisiana, Maryland, Michigan, Minnesota (in favor of wife only), Rhode Island, New Jersey, New York, North Carolina, Pennsylvania (in favor of wife only), Rhode Island, Tennessee (in favor of wife only), Vermont, Virginia, West Virginia and Wisconsin.

Children of the Divorced

The United States Census Bureau issued in 1910 a report of the results of a compilation of statistics of divorces granted in the courts in the United States for a period of twenty years: being from 1887 to 1906, both years inclusive. In the cases included in the report, in 376,694 or 39.8 per cent. of the whole number, there were children of the parties to the divorce, and in 380,608 or 40.2 per cent, no children were reported. In 188,323 cases or 19.9 per cent, no mention was made of children and the presumption is that no children were involved.

Alimony

At least eighteen states have statutory provisions on alimony which make the wife "equally with husband, liable for the maintenance of the minor children, while in others such liability of the wife will attach only where she has been adjudged the guilty party. A few statutes provide that the separate estate of the wife shall be taken into consideration, and that alimony may be refused if she has sufficient property for her needs. A tendency has appeared in the newer legislations to limit the amount which either party may receive to an alimentary pension payable only so long as it may be needed." (29, 151-2.)

A synopsis of the marriage and divorce Statutes of the various states is contained in "The law of Marriage and Divorce" by Frank Keezer, Boston, 1906, pages 193-343.

(4) Employment of Mothers

Diligent search has failed to find a single law in any American state regulating when a pregnant mother shall cease working or how soon she may return to her employment after her child is born. On this subject Professor Stimson writes as follows:

"Now all these laws arbitrarily regulate the hours of labor of women at any season without regard to their conditions of health, and are therefore far behind the more intelligent legislation of Belgium, France, and Germany, which considers at all times their sanitary condition, and requires a period of rest for some weeks before and after childbirth. The best that can be said of them, therefore, is that they are a beginning. No law has attempted to prescribe the social condition of female industrial laborers, the bill introduced in Connecticut that no married woman should ever be allowed to work in factories having failed in its passage." (39.219.)

The following (from the Quarterly Bulletin of the International Labor office) is a fairly complete list of the foreign countries having regulations:

(1) The period in Spain after confinement is from 4 to 6 weeks, and another phrase in the law adds, "A woman in the

eighth month of pregnancy may ask leave to cease work, which shall be granted if medical opinion supports her application." (24.2.20.)

(2) In Austria also a law provides that in stone quarries, lime, sand and gravel pits women who are approaching their confinement shall not be employed. (24.3.139.)

(3) In the German Empire the law provides that women shall not be employed for eight weeks, including the time before and after confinement, and at least six weeks must intervene between childbirth and return to work. (24.3.335.)

(4) In Italy the prohibited period is one month after confinement, and in the rice fields one month before and after confinement. A medical certificate as to the length of pregnancy is required, and the law adds, "It shall be sufficient if such certificates show that the women in question have not yet reached the last month of their pregnancy." (24.1.486, 24.2.580 and 24.3.183-195.)

(5) Following is a list of the countries which prohibit the employment of women after confinement, and the length of the prohibited period.

Denmark—4 weeks, unless by permission of medical officer. (24.1.181.)
Appenzell, Canton of Switzerland, 6 weeks. (24.3.124.)
Argentina—30 days. (24.3.28.)
Berne, Switzerland—from 4 to 8 weeks. (24.3.119.)
Bosnia and Herzgovina—4 weeks. (24.4.7-193.)
Norway—6 weeks. (24.4.346.)
New Zealand—4 weeks. (24.4.30.)
Roumania—3 to 4 weeks. (24.4.46.)

(6) In most of these countries the woman's position must be kept open for her until her return. In most of these cases where the state provides sick insurance, the women are permitted to apply for this assistance during the period of prohibited employment.

(5) En ventre Sa Mere

"A child is the living offspring of human parents either before or after birth. A child *en ventre sa mere* is a child while yet unborn. Although the point was formerly in doubt, it is now settled in this country, that from the time of conception the infant is *in esse*, for the purpose of taking any estate which is for his interest, whether by descent, devise or under the statute of distributions; provided, however, that the infant is born alive, and after such a period of fœtal existence that its continuance in life might reasonably be expected." (2.10.625.) Beck, Medical Jurisprudence, Vol. I, P. 407 (12 ed.), says, "As a general rule, it seems now to be generally conceded that no infant can be born viable, or capable of living, until one hundred and fifty days, five months after conception. There are however cases mentioned to the contrary. In such cases we should recollect that females are liable to mistakes in their calculations and that conceptions may take place at various times during the menstrual intervals, and thus vary the length of gestation. Such early births are at the present day very generally and very properly doubted. . . We may . . . . . conclude that between five and seven months, there have been instances of infants living, though most rare; and even at seven, the chance of surviving six hours after birth is much against the child," and see Chitty, Med. Jur. 406. On the other hand, by statute, a child born ten months after the death of the father comes within the rule. Massie v. Hiatt, 82 Ky., 314. (11.10.626.) See also "(7) Birth." The divorce libel of Schwartz v. Schwartz now pending in Boston, Suffolk County, Massachusetts, is remarkable. The libellant, the wife, in petitioning for the dissolution of the marital tie also requests the Court to grant her the custody of her unborn child.

(6) Abortion

"Abortion is defined to be the delivery or expulsion of the human fœtus prematurely, or before it is yet capable of sustaining life. . . . The defendant's intent to cause or produce an abortion controls and constitutes an essential element of the offense." (11.1.170.) At common law it is a criminal offense to cause or procure an abortion upon a woman who has become quick with child, but as to whether a common law offense is committed by causing or procuring, with the consent of the woman, an abortion before such a quickening, there is a conflict of authority. To the effect that such an abortion constitutes no criminal offense are the following authorities:

Iowa—Hatfield v. Gano, 15 Iowa, 177; Maine—Smith v. State, 33 Me., 48; Maryland—Lamb v. State, 67 Md., 524; Massachusetts—Com. v. Bangs, 9 Mass., 387; Michigan—People v. McDowell, 63 Mich., 229; New Jersey—State v. Cooper, N. J. L., 52; New York—Evans v. People, 49 N. Y., 86.

But contra, see the following cases:

Arkansas—State v. Reed, 45 Ark., 333; North Carolina—State v. Slagle, 83 N. C., 630; Pennsylvania—Mills v. Com., 13 Pa. St., 631.

"Quick with child" and "with quickchild" are synonymous terms. The words "big" and "great" are tantamount to the word "quick." In Evans v. People, 49 N. Y. 86, 90, Allen, J., says: "Quick is synonymous with 'living', and both are the opposite of 'dead. The woman is not pregnant with a living child until the child has become quick. If the child is a living child from the instant of conception, then all the authorities, medical and legal, are sadly at fault in their attempts to distinguish between mere 'pregnancy' and 'pregnancy with a quick child,' and legislators have been laboring under the same hallucination in legislating upon the subject for all the acts passed in reference to abortion in this country and in England recognize the fact that the child does 'quicken,' that is, becomes endowed with life, at a certain period, longer or shorter, after conception, and that there is a period during gestation when although there may be embryo life in the fœtus there is no living child. And to the same effect see Smith v. state, 33 Me., 48; Com. v. Parker, 9 Met. (Mass.), 263. (11.1.172.) Dwight in his Medical Jurisprudence writes "By the term quickening are described certain peculiar sensations usually noted by the mother at about four and one-half months following conception." (12.147.) To many, the better rule would be that of the Catholic Church, namely, that there is life "*ipso momento conceptionis*" and that an abortion even then is murder. The woman on whom the abortion is produced is not a principal. In some states, however, by statute, the woman is made punishable; but her offense is separable from that of the person administering the drug or performing the operation. But in Smith v. Gaffard, 31 Ala., 45, it was held that a statute prohibiting the administration by any person, to a pregnant woman, of any drug or substance with intent to procure her miscarriage, does not make it an offense for a woman to take a drug with intent to produce a miscarriage. (11.174.) Section 15 Chap. 212, Revised Laws of Massachusetts provides that whoever administers, advises, prescribes, aids or assists in an abortion shall, if the woman dies, be punished by imprisonment in the state prison for not less than five nor more than twenty years; and if the woman does not die, by imprisonment in the state prison for not more than seven years and by a fine of not more than two thousand dollars. Massachusetts and other states have provided penalties of "three years imprisonment and a fine of not more than a thousand dollars for advertising, giving or conveying any notice, hint or reference to any person, or to the name of any person, from whom, or to any place where anything or means whatever, or any advice or knowledge, may be obtained for the purpose of causing or procuring the miscarriage of a woman pregnant with child." (Mass. Revised Laws—Chap. 212—Sec. 16.)

(7) Birth

Continuing the subject treated under topic (5) *En ventre sá mere*, as to the degree of life necessary for inheritance Dwight says: "Modified by certain conditions, that will be spoken of later, a child whether of full term or not, whether or not affected by disease or conditions which make it impossible that life shall be prolonged, providing there is evidence of life, is capable of inheriting. It is not necessary that respiration should be established. It is not necessary that the child should cry. Neither is it necessary to prove that a complete, independent circulation was established. Pulsation of the umbilical cord after delivery, a slight active motion in one of the extremities, or pulsation in an artery, is in itself proof of life to a sufficient extent for the purposes of inheritance. It is usually necessary to demonstrate that complete birth has taken place. Some, however, have held that the partial birth of a living child is all that is necessary. Such rulings, however, have been contradicted, as they bring up rather difficult questions as to the extent of birth necessary to inherit. Crying and respiration may occur before birth is complete, but this evidence is of doubtful value." (12.198.)

"Not a single state, not even a single city, in the entire United States possesses complete registration of births. Boston claims to have about the best, only 96 per cent. . . The era of modern sanitary civilization may be marked by the dates upon which various countries began to record infant mortality. Some countries—China, Turkey and the United States—even yet possess no records of infant mortality. Unless the American people wake up, China and Turkey will have satisfactory data for infant mortality long before the United States. . . The omission of the United States from the international data for births is on account of our almost entire lack of effective birth registration.

"Talk about the registration of births in the United States. Why for not more than one-half (55.3 per cent) of the total population of the United States is there even fairly accurate registration of deaths alone. Many states—practically the entire South—make no more records of the deaths of their citizens than if they were cattle; not even so much, for blooded cattle have their vital events recorded, while human beings are thrown into their graves without a trace of legal registration. And even the states that have fairly good registration of deaths, and that have had such registration for many years, grossly neglect the equally important, or even more important, registration of births. . . Our native born children of native parents are as worthy of protection as the children of any other country, and the children born to foreign parents in this country should have the same safeguard as about their cradles as if they had been born in a foreign land. America should not mean barbarity in its relation to infant life. The ægis of protective civilization should rest upon the infant of American birth, and a proper record be made of the vital events of his life for his personal protection, legal use and for the most important sanitary information which can alone be obtained from such records." (Dr. Cressy L. Wilbur, in Report of the Committee on Birth Registration. Proceedings of The American Association for Study and Prevention of Infant Mortality, Johns Hopkins University, Baltimore, November 9-11, 1910.)

(8) Midwives

In the following states midwives are examined and licensed by law:—Connecticut, District of Columbia, Illinois (violators prosecuted) Indiana, Minnesota, Missouri, New Jersey, Ohio, Wisconsin and Wyoming (practice exempted in cases of emergency). The practice of midwives is exempted in Arizona, Arkansas, Idaho, Kentucky, Maryland, Mississippi, North Carolina, Oklahoma, South Carolina, Virginia and West Virginia. The states having "no law" regulating the practice of midwives are Alabama, California, Colorado, Delaware, Florida, Georgia, Iowa, Kansas, Louisiana (law does not apply to midwives in rural districts and plantation practice), Maine, Massachusetts, Michigan, Montana, Nebraska, Nevada, New Hampshire, New Mexico, New York, North Dakota, Oregon, Pennsylvania, Rhode Island, South Dakota, Tennessee, Texas (no specific law, examination provided for those who wish to practice obstetrics alone). The act "does not apply to those who do not follow obstetrics as a profession, and who do not advertise themselves as obstetricians or midwives, or hold themselves out to the public as so practicing," Utah (no specific law. Those desiring to practice obstetrics are examined and licensed, but the law permits practice "in case of emergency," and it exempts "persons practicing obstetrics in communities where there are no licensed practitioners"), Vermont and Washington. (23.103-431.)

(9) Infanticide

By infanticide is understood "the destruction of life in newborn children." The law assumes, as a rule, that an infant whose dead body was found was born dead unless proof is brought that the opposite is the case. This crime is one of the most common among all nations, especially among the poorer classes, and these problems are very frequently presented for medico-legal investigation. There are three questions which are perhaps of the greatest importance in connection with them. Under the English as under that of most nations, the crime of murder does not vary, and is subject to the same punishment whether the victim is an infant or of more mature age. It is treated under a different heading in works on legal medicine, as it presents different problems for solution. The law requires that it should be proved:

1. That sufficient uterine age and development has been reached to allow of a separate existence on the part of the child.
2. That the child was born alive.
3. Proof of the manner of death. (12.173.)

(10) Prevention of Blindness

Connecticut, Illinois, Indiana, Maine, Maryland, Massachusetts, Michigan, Missouri, New Jersey, New York, Ohio, Oregon, Pennsylvania, Rhode Island, Tennessee, and West Virginia have laws requiring cases of ophthalmia neonatorum to be reported. In Connecticut midwives and nurses are liable to a fine of $200 or imprisonment not to exceed six months, or both, "Should one or both eyes of the baby become inflamed, swollen or reddened at any time within two weeks after birth and the midwife or nurse fails to report in writing within six hours to health officers or legally qualified practitioner of city, town or district where parents reside that such inflammation, etc., exists." Minnesota requires the parent as well as the nurse and midwife to report within twelve hours to local health officers if one or both eyes of an infant, under two months, become inflamed, reddened and diseased. Ohio has a law making the treatment of ohpthalmia neonatorum by midwife or general practitioner without notifying an occulist or sending the child to a hospital, a misdemeanor with a heavy fine and an imprisonment clause. Unfortunately the law is reported as "not operative." (43.52.2047-2056.)

(11) Vital Statistics

The American Medical Association Bulletin, Vol. 6, No. I, September 15, 1910, contains a model bill on vital statistics patterned, in the main, after the Pennsylvania law. (42.) Section 6 requires that stillborn children or those dead at birth shall be registered as births and also as deaths. Midwives, under this model bill, are not allowed to sign certificates of death for stillborn children. Section 13 provides that the physician or midwife, "and if there be no attending physician or midwife, then it shall be the duty of the father or mother of the child, householder or owner of the premises, manager or superintendent of public or private institutions in which the birth occurred, to notify the local registrar, within ten days after the birth, of the fact that a birth has occurred." Section 21 makes failure to register cause of death, false certification of cause of death and failure to file a proper certificate of birth misdemeanors punishable by fines of from five to two hundred dollars. This model bill has become the law of some twenty states, and has been endorsed by the following: The Census Department, Department of the United States Government, the American Medical Association, the American Bar Association, the American Association for the Study and Prevention of Infant Mortality and in 1910 by the general officers of the American Federation of Labor." Registration of births, is urged, as "a necessary part of any plan for the study of infant mortality, because without such registration we have no means of ascertaining definitely the relation between the annual death rate and birth rate. In other words it enables us to find out where we are. It is an essential part of any plan for the reduction of infant mortality because the prompt registration of births increases the possibility of preventing certain infantile diseases and blindness. The registration of births is also of the utmost importance for legal reasons, as a means of establishing the identity of the individual." (Leaflet issued by the American Association for Study and Prevention of Infant Mortality, September 1, 1910.) When it is remembered that Bulletin 104 of the year 1909 of the United States Bureau of Census shows that the death of babies less than a year old constitutes one-fifth of our total mortality, it would seem that even the most indifferent and the laziest will not begrudge the effort necessary to record the child's entrance into and his departure from this world. Yet so much notice is denied to the child in too many states.

(12) Legitimacy and Illegitimacy

Under the common law only the child born in wedlock was legitimate. The Canon law, which is the law of the Church, decreed that the child born before the marriage became legitimate on the marriage of the parents, and as "Canon law lies at the base of much American law" (27.356), the rule has come to be universal in the United States that a child whose parents marry after its birth, no matter how long (39.140), becomes legitimate. So also, a child is legitimate when born within a competent time after the termination of marriage by death or divorce (11.5.525). And finally most of our states consider that a child, born during a void marriage entered into in good faith, is legitimate. Of course even the child born during marriage may be shown to be illegitimate and it must be remembered that any legal presumption of legitimacy stands only until the contrary is shown. However, our courts have placed the burden of proof on the one alleging illegitimacy and on the grounds of public policy and decency ordinarily will not allow any father or mother to testify that a child, presumed to be legitimate, is, as a matter of fact, illegitimate. Thus far it will be noted that marriage controlled legitimacy. But our legislators have conceived or known of situations where the father of an illegitimate child might not want or be able to marry the mother but was anxious to remove the stain of illegitimacy from the child. Such a legal process is called legitimation, and differs from adoption which usually refers to strangers in blood. Professor Stimson's American Statute Law reads: "In several states, the father of an illegitimate child, by publicly acknowledging it as his own, receiving it as such (with the consent of the wife, if married) into his family, and otherwise treating it as legitimate, thereby rendered it legitimate for all purposes"—at least in California, Nevada, Dakota and Idaho. (37.756.) "In several states, the putative father (if he was unmarried at the birth of the illegitimate child) has a process in court by which he might legitimate the child"—in North Carolina, Tennessee, Georgia, New Mexico, Alabama and Mississippi. (37.757.) In 1887 Maine enacted the law that an illegitimate child is heir if the father adopts him into his family, or in writing makes acknowledgment that he is the father before a justice or notary; and he inherits from the kindred of such father, whether lineal or collateral, and they from the child, as if legitimate: Maine 1887, 14. (38.98.) Massachusetts permits the father to adopt his illegitimate child with the consent of its mother, and thereby make it his heir. This is considerable progress since "all the earls and barons answered with one voice that they would not change the laws of England." (39.40.) Florence Kelley in 1882 in commenting on the changes in the legal status of the illegitimate child since Blackstone, wrote: "So far is his condition assimilated to that of the legitimate child that the statement is now true that the chief legal disadvantage of the illegitimate child is his inability to inherit." (26.96.) The mother has a superior right to the custody of her illegitimate child but she may lose her right by abusing or neglecting the child. The putative father seems to be entitled to the custody against all but the mother. However, the best interests of the child will be the controlling factor in deciding the question of custody in any court. (11.5.637.) The statutory liability of the putative father for the support of the legitimate child is to-day universal. Alabama, Georgia, Illinois, Indiana, Maine, Massachusetts, Michigan, New Hampshire, New York, North Carolina, Ohio, Oklahoma, Pennsylvania, Rhode Island, South Carolina and Wisconsin authorize their courts to imprison the putative father as one means of enforcing an order for the maintenance of the illegitimate child. (11.5.670.)

(13) Milk Laws

Dr. Henry L. Coit, of Newark, New Jersey, seems to have been the first to urge legislation "on the subject of milk production designed for clinical purposes." Abandoning the effort to get a state law on this subject Dr. Coit organized a Medical Milk Commission which worked independently of state authorities as a professional body and from year to year his plan was duplicated in various parts of the country until now there are seventy-two such Milk Commissions. In many instances these commissions have started a crusade through municipal activities for the improvement of the general supply of milk. These commissions are professional bodies without pecuniary interests or commercial relations with the production of milk and have as their general object, the obtaining of milk suitable for sick-room purposes and infant feeding. The Medical Milk Commissions has been recognized by the Government through the Departments of Agriculture and the Marine Hospital Service, both departments having issued bulletins on the history of the "Pure Milk Movement." Four years ago, the Medical Milk Commissions then at work (of which there were only twenty-two) were federated for the purpose of extending the propaganda and influencing the organization of this movement in other centres of population. This work has been carried on from the office of the Secretary of this federation, by Dr. Otto P. Geier, of Cincinnati. Both Dr. Coit and Dr. Geier insist that "certified milk has a definite meaning as outlined in the plans for the original Commission and it has not only received federal recognition but in three states has been protected by law." These three states are Kentucky, New York and New Jersey, and the Michigan legislature has a similar bill before it for passage. The New Jersey Law as the law of the state in which certified milk had its origin, is considered the most comprehensive and is entitled "An Act providing for the incorporation of medical milk commissions and the certification of milk produced under their supervision. "This act will be found in State of New Jersey Laws of 1909. Four sections of this law follow:

"8 Every such association shall have power to enter into agreement in writing with any dairyman or dairymen for the production of milk under the supervision of such association for the purposes enumerated in section one hereof and to prescribe in such agreement the conditions under which milk shall be produced, which conditions, however, shall not be below the standards of purity and quality for 'Certified Milk' as fixed by 'The American Association of Medical Milk Commissions,' and the standards for milk now fixed or that may hereafter be fixed by the Board of Health of the State of New Jersey. In any contract entered into by any such commission with any dairyman or dairymen, it may be provided that such medical milk commission may designate any analsyts, chemists, bacteriologists, veterinarians, medical inspectors or other persons who in its judgment may be necessary for the proper carrying out of the purposes of such commission for employment by such dairyman or dairymen and to prescribe and define their powers and duties, and that such persons so employed by such dairyman or dairymen may be discharged from employment whenever such medical milk commission may request such discharge or removal in writing.

"9. All containers of any kind or character used in the carrying or distribution of milk produced by any dairyman or dairymen under contract with any medical milk commission shall have attached thereto or placed thereon a certificate or seal bearing the name of the Medical Milk Commission with which such dairyman or dairymen producing such milk shall be under contract, which certificate shall have printed, stamped or written thereon the day or date of the production of the milk contained in any such container and the words 'Certified Milk' in plain and legible form.

"10. The work and methods of any Medical Milk Commission organized under this act and of the dairies on which milk is produced under contract with any such commission shall at all times be subject to investigation and scrutiny by the Board of Health of the State of New Jersey. The Secretary of said State Board of Health shall be an ex-officio member of every milk commission organized under this act.

"11. No person, firm or corporation shall sell or exchange or offer or expose for sale or exchange as and for certified milk, any milk which is not produced in conformity with the methods and regulations prescribed by and which does not bear the certification of a medical milk commission incorporated pursuant to the provisions of this act or organized or incorporated in some other state for the purposes specified in section one hereof, and which is not produced in conformity with the methods and regulations for the production of certified milk from time to time adopted by the American Association of Medical Milk Commissions, and which is below the standards of purity and quality for certified milk as fixed by the American Association of Medical Milk Commissions; and any such person, firm or corporation violating any of the provisions of this section shall be guilty of a misdemeanor."

The Milk Commission appointed by the Mayor of Philadelphia enumerates the essential points (see The Worcester Gazette, Saturday, March 18, 1911).

"Of course, pure milk—comparatively speaking—is to be had. But as a rule there is a menace all along the line.

"Take, for instance, the farm where milk is produced. Unless modern and improved sanitary principles are enforced, the beginning of the danger is right there.

"Then comes the railroad journey to the city.

"Next the handlers come in and eventually the milk is served at the home.

"Now there is not a step from farm to customer that is not of the highest importance to guard.

"The cow must be milked by cleanly hands in a cleanly place.

"The milk must never for a moment be exposed to unsanitary conditions, for milk is a tremendous absorbent of everything that is impure.

"It must be sent to railway station in a cooled condition, and it must be transported to the city platform in cooled cars.

"The dealer must transfer the cans in wagons that will maintain the low temperature.

"Finally the milk must be delivered in a cooled state, Then it is up to the housekeeper to see to it that the bottles shall be placed in iced receptacles.

"To put it briefly, milk must be under constant supervision and direction and control from the time the cow yields her milk to the time of delivery to the purchaser.

"That is the problem that confronts not only the commission but City Councils and the Legislature. For there must be hearty co-operation from start to finish.

"When we can have milk under such constant inspection we shall be sure of having a pure supply. And that is precisely what we must have. No matter what the cost is, we must have it."

"True, Pure Milk at any cost. Every baby in every home throughout the country demands it, and when the King commands his subjects must obey. But more than that the public health and posterity demand it."

The Report of the United States Commissioner of Education for the year ending June 30, 1910, Vol. I, at page 141, says that "in order to provide a supply of pure milk, cream, and butter for pupils who procure luncheons at the schools, the St. Louis School board prepared for the year 1909-10 a special contract embodying such sanitary precautions as they thought necessary to insure purity in the dairy products supplied." (44.1.141.) If the St. Louis plan is copied generally throughout the country the movement for pure milk is destined to be successful at an earlier date than has been expected.

(14) Compulsory School Attendance Laws

The statutory provisions relating to compulsory education and child labor throughout the United States are compiled in the Report of the United States Commissioner of Education for the year ending June 30, 1910, Vol. I, pages 148-153 inclusive, and in Monroe's Cyclopædia of Education, Vol. I, pages 289-93 inclusive. The Cyclopædia contains an excellent article of about ten pages on "Compulsory Attendance" by Dr. David Snedden, Massachusetts Commissioner of Education. Recourse should be had to Dr. Snedden's article for much information that cannot be condensed into the space assigned to the subject in this paper. The compilations mentioned show that Alabama, Florida, Georgia, Louisiana, Mississippi, South Carolina and Texas have no compulsory education law. In North Carolina and Tennessee legislation applies only to certain sections, and in Virginia "compulsory attendance law is optional with the voters of any county, city or town (36.1.293), with these exceptions: "A. Throughout almost the entire United States some school attendance is compulsory from 7 or 8 years of age to 14. B. Massachusetts, New York, Idaho, New Hampshire and others require certain educational qualifications, otherwise attendance is compulsory to 16. The 1908 law of New Jersey sets an upper limit of 17 for all who have not completed the eight grades; those finishing the elementary school course may not leave until 15. C. A number of states require, especially in cities, that children under 16 must attend school regularly unless definitely employed. Illinois, Maryland, Pennsylvania, and Missouri (St. Louis and Kansas City only) are examples. D. Laws on compulsory education have frequently been nullified because the amount of attendance each year was not specified, and consequently evasions were easy. Even yet some states prescribe a minimum amount, *e. g.*, Iowa, 16 consecutive weeks; Missouri (outside of St. Louis), not less than half the term; Nebraska, two thirds of term. The majority of states having well-developed legislation now making attendance obligatory for the entire term during which school is in session. E. Recently special legislation in some states provides for compulsory attendance from 8 to 20, at State School for Deaf. Nebraska, Minnesota, and North Carolina (for whites), have somewhat similar legislation. In early stages poverty of parents paved the way for exemptions, but the modern tendency is away from this. Many states provide for supplying free books to needy children. In Ohio and Colorado boards of education must give aid in clothing where it is necessary. In some large cities philanthropy has secured the provision of scholarships for those whose parents need aid in keeping children at school." (36.1.293.)

The maximum penalty on parents for neglect to comply with the compulsory education law is as follows:

Delaware, first offense: $2 or 2 days imprisonment, subsequent offenses: $5 or 5 days imprisonment; Connecticut, $5 for each week's absence; Maryland $5; Pennsylvania, first $2, subsequent $5; West Virginia, first $2, subsequent $5; Virginia, first $10, subsequent $20; District of Columbia, Illinois ("and stand committed until paid"), Iowa, Massachusetts, Montana, New Hampshire, North Dakota, Ohio, Rhode Island, South Dakota ("costs and stand committed till paid") fall within the group authorizing the imposition of a fine of $20. In Kentucky the delinquent parent can be fined for the first offense $20 and $50 for subsequent offenses. The $25 group includes Arizona, Arkansas, Colorado, Kansas,

Nebraska, North Carolina, Vermont, Washington and Wyoming. Nevada has a penalty of $100 for the first and $200 with costs for subsequent offenses. The states where parents can be sentenced to imprisonment are New York, which has a provision for five days or $5 for the first offense and 30 days and $50 for subsequent offenses; Missouri, 10 days and $25; New Mexico, 10 days or $25; Oregon, 10 days and $25; California, 25 days and $50; Maine, 30 days or $25; Minnesota, 30 days or $50; Indiana, 90 days and $25; Michigan, 90 days and $50; Wisconsin, 3 months and $50; and Idaho judges can make stubborn parents take notice by imposing a sentence of 6 months and a fine of $300.

"The American states are obviously moving toward certain standards in compulsory attendance which will partly depend upon development of additional school facilities. For example, child labor legislation is increasingly closing up industries to youths under 16. The raising of educational standards will compel many children to attend school until they are 16. The state will provide for those who are demonstrably needy, rather than allow dependent parents to withhold from children their educational heritage. The increasing appreciation of the need of vocational education will result in the provision of special school facilities for imparting either the whole or part of this education. It is not improbable that the advanced position of Germany in this respect (*i. e.* compelling children from fourteen to eighteen to give part time to continue education of a vocational or other character), will be imitated. Special schools will be provided for defectives and delinquents, and attendance at these made obligatory. Ultimately a complete system of registration of all children must be provided, to be carried on by attendance officers, and centralized in each limited school area, not only for the enforcement of attendance but for obtaining compliance with child labor legislation, and the provision of medical or other aid." (36.1.295.)

(15) Truancy

In the last section we saw that a parent, whose child does not attend school as required, may be fined and imprisoned in most states. And the law usually states the minimum amount of the child's absence that will make the parent liable. In Massachusetts every person, who fails to cause a child under his control to attend school for five day sessions or ten half day sessions within any period of six months, is liable to a fine of not more than twenty dollars. An "Attorney General of New York has ruled that more than two unexcused absences in four consecutive weeks constitute a violation of the law" (4.190), for which the parent can be fined and imprisoned.

Concerning the prosecution of parents, Bardeen's School Law says: "A child should not be arrested unless an *habitual* truant or disorderly and insubordinate while in attendance at school. Frequently parents are only too glad to have their children committed as truants and cared for at town or county expense until they are permitted by law to go to work. The most direct and effective method of reaching parents and forcing upon them the duty of keeping their children in school is by penalizing the parent as provided in the statute. Where parents are prosecuted the most, truancy exists the least." (4.191.) Massachusetts and other states provide that "whoever induces or attempts to induce a child to absent himself unlawfully from school, or employs or harbors a child who, while school is in session, is absent unlawfully from school, shall be punished by a fine of not more than fifty dollars."

The law makers of our states passed through childhood before they were called to serve as legislators. Some of them will acknowledge that the truant schoolboy has become the able legislator. Realizing that the majority of truants do not take their parents into their confidence when "playing hookey," the members of our legislatures have also enacted laws relative to habitual truancy. And provision has been made for boarding truant schools, sometimes called "Training Schools," to which *only* habitual truants, habitual absentees and habitual school offenders are committed by our courts. The inmates of our boarding truant schools are usually children that have got beyond the control of their parents or those that come from "broken homes." The child must be discharged from the boarding truant school upon becoming sixteen years of age. Dr. Snedden believes that "much good legislation relating to children breaks down because of poor machinery of enforcement. In Connecticut there is a state agent with assistants who attends to the execution of laws on compulsory education and child labor. In all other states the enforcement of the law is local. In nonurban areas school boards and local constables are authorized to proceed against parents failing to keep children in school; in cities it is now common to constitute special attendance officers with limited police powers. Most of this machinery is yet very defective." (36.1.293.) He maintains that four different types of special class or school are necessary in any city to procure the adequate carrying out of the law. (a) Those pupils who have become quite incorrigible, and whose parents have lost control of them, must be sent to an institutional school, committed for a term of years. Only thoroughgoing reform is adequate. (b) A day truant school, where hours are long and manual work abundant. This school, while allowing pupils to sleep at home, should aim primarily to keep them off the street and away from contagion of bad company. Such schools do not exist in American, but are found in English cities. (c) Special classes should be provided for pupils who cannot easily be brought under the ordinary school discipline. These classes may have the same programmes as the ordinary classes, but should be under charge of teachers of sufficient maturity, experience, and personal character to cope with this type of child. (d) Possibly a fourth type of class should be for those who by irregular attendance have hopelessly fallen away from the regular class attainments." (36.1.294). Some states by legislation make the parents in part responsible for the support of their children in truant schools.

(16) Medical Inspection of Schools

The legal aspects of medical inspection of schools is treated in Chapter II, "Medical Inspection of Schools" by Gulick and Ayres. (16.159.183.) The statutes cited by Gulick and Ayres were those in operation about the year 1908. At the time "Medical Inspection of Schools" was written, Massachusetts had the distinction of being the only state in the Union having a "mandatory medical inspection law." (16.159.) By a mandatory medical inspection law is meant a law enacted by the state legislature whereby cities and towns are compelled to provide for medical inspection in their schools. Under date of March 7, 1911, Dr. Ayres writes: "Legal provision is made for Medical Inspection in thirteen states and in the District of Columbia. Four are compulsory laws. They are the laws of Colorado, Massachusetts, New Jersey and Indiana. In the last state the law refers to Indianapolis only. Permissive laws exist in California, Connecticut, Maine, New York and the District of Columbia. Permissive laws applying to cities exist in Ohio and Washington. Laws applying to sight and hearing are in force in Louisiana, Vermont and Virgina."

The abstracts of the Medical inspection laws that follow are, in the main, taken from a forthcoming paper on Medical Inspection of Schools," by Mr. George H. Shafer, of Clark University:

Colorado. The responsibility here rests with the teachers, they note defects and inform the principal, who notifies parents. Parents are compelled to have the child examined; if they neglect, they are turned over to the Bureau of Child and Animal Protection for prosecution. If parents are indigent, the child is referred to the county physician.

Massachusetts. The school Committee of every city and town in the commonwealth shall appoint one or more school physicians, shall assign one to each public school within its city or town, and shall provide them with proper facilities for the performance of either duties as prescribed in this act, and shall assign one or more to perform the duty of examining children who apply for health certificates in accordance with this act; provided, however, that in cities wherein the board of health is already maintaining or shall hereafter maintain substantially such medical inspection as this act requires, the board of health shall appoint and assign the school physician. Every school physician shall make a prompt examination and diagnosis of all children referred to him, and such further examination of teachers, janitors and school buildings as in his opinion the protection of the health of the pupils may require." Teachers make examinations of eyes and ears. The statutes provide First, for a general examination of all the children in the public schools at least once a year for any defect or disability tending to interfere with their school work. Second, for a special examination of children (a) who show signs of being in ill health or of suffering from infectious or contagious diseases (b) who are returning to school after absence on account of illness or from unknown causes, also the examination of pupils who apply for health certificates. The school committee shall notify parents of all defects found.

New Jersey. "Every board of education shall employ a competent physician to be known as the medical inspector and fix his salary and term of office." Every board of education shall adopt rules for the government of the medical inspector which shall be submitted to the State Board of Education for approval."

The medical inspector shall examine every pupil, to learn whether any physical defects exist, and keep a record from year to year of the growth and development of such pupil, which record shall be the property of the Board of Education, and shall be delivered by said medical inspector to his successor in office. Said inspector shall lecture before the teachers at such times as may be designated by the Board of Education, instructing then concerning the methods employed to detect the first signs of communicable disease, and the recognized measures for the promotion of health and the prevention of diseases. The law also compels parents to remedy defects. It went into effect April 13, 1909.

California. The Training School for September, 1910, published at Vineland, New Jersey, has an article on "Health and Development Supervision in California." On pages

248-9 one reads, "Mr. George L. Leslie, director of the medical inspection of the Los Angeles schools, who is chiefly responsible for the passage of the law, summarizes its provisions as follows:

"1. The establishment (under the direction of boards of educaton or boards of school trustees) of annual physical examinations of school pupils and a follow-up service to secure the correction of defective development, thus maintaining continuous health and growth supervision of children and youth. "2. The requirement of physical examination of all candidates for teachers' positions in the public schools to determine vitality and efficiency and make possible further examination of teachers as may be advisable to determine continued fitness for work, and to determine the amount of work to be required of the teaching force of the schools consistent with efficiency and continued service. "3. The adjustment of school activities to health and growth needs and development processes of pupils. "4. The special study of mental retardation and deviation of pupils in the schools. "5. Expert sanitary supervision. "6. It provides for a class of educators—experts in physiology, hygiene, and practical psychology—who can skillfully diagnose defective growth and development, and take more intelligent steps to grow children and youths. It provides for the co-operation of this class of educators and all educators with skilled physicians."

New York provides for the medical inspection of all children in attendance upon schools under their supervision, whenever in their judgment such inspection shall be necessary, and to pay any expense incurred therefor out of funds authorized by the voters of the district or city or which may properly be set aside for such purpose by the common council or the board of estimate and apportionment of a city. (Subd. Added by L. 1910, chap. 602.)

Ohio has a law as follows: Section 7692. Any board of education in a city school district may provide for the medical inspection of pupils attending the public schools. For that purpose it can employ competent physicians, nurses, and provide for and pay all expenses incident thereto from the public school funds, or by agreement with the board of health or other board or officer performing the functions of a board of health for such city. It may provide for medical and sanitary supervision and inspection of the schools which are under the control of such board of education and of the pupils attending such schools, by a competent physician selected by the parent or guardian of the child, but on failure of the parent or guardian, then by the district physicians and other employee to be appointed by such board of health. (R. S. Sec. 4018a.)

The District of Columbia has a permissive law. State of Washington has a permissive law for districts of first class.

In 1907 *Connecticut* passed a law authorizing the board of education or town committee of any town, or the board of education or committee of any school district to appoint one or more school physicians.

The school physician is to examine all pupils referred to him by principals, and teachers, janitors and school buildings as in his opinion the protection of the health of the pupils may require." The law further says: "The school authorities of any town or school district which has appointed a school physician in accordance with the provision of this act shall cause every child attending the public schools therein to be separately and carefully tested and examined at least once in every school year to ascertain whether such child is suffering from defective sight or hearing, or from any other physical disability tending to prevent such child from receiving the full benefit of school work, or requiring a modification of such school work in order to prevent injury to the child or to secure the best educational results. Notice of defects of diseases are to be sent to parents with such advice or order relating thereto as the physician may deem advisable." Provision is also made for the employment of *school nurses*.

The law of Maine is largely copied from that of Massachusetts. It differs in that it is permissive in case of the town. And further the following articles make it altogether permissive.

Expenses which a city or town may incur by virtue of the authority herein vested in the school committee shall not exceed the amount appropriated for that purpose in cities by the city council and in towns by a town meeting. (March 16, 1909.)

Further the law of Maine makes no mention of examination for employment certificate.

Utah has a law as follows: Board of Health has jurisdiction in matters pertaining to health in schools. The local boards of health shall have jurisdiction in all matters pertaining to the preservation of the health of those in attendance upon the public and private schools in the state, to which end is hereby made the duty of each of the local boards of health.

1. To exclude from said schools any person, including teachers, suffering with any contagious or infectious disease, whether acute or chronic, or liable to convey such disease to those in attendance.

2. To make regular inspection of all school buildings and premises, etc.

Vermont has a law requiring inspection of eyes and ears by teachers.

It will be noted that a penal provision applying to neglectful parents of defective children is mentioned as occurring in the laws of Colorado and New Jersey. This penal provision is endorsed by many, if not all, of those in sympathy with medical inspection of schools—Also Connecticut authorizes the employment of school nurses. Relative to the school nurse, Gulick and Ayres say:

"Dr. S. W. Newmayer, of Philadelphia, terms the school nurse 'the most important adjunct to medical inspection'" Dr. John J. Cronin, of New York, in writing of the work of the school nurse says: "It is most highly endorsed by teachers, principals, educators, parents, and children. Since this innovation many cities throughout the world have copied our nursing system as far as possible, up to the standard set by this city." Dr. Ernest J. Lederie, formerly Commissioner of Health of New York City, says, "The school nurse has been voted a success from the day she began work." Dr. Walter S. Cornell says of the school nurses in Philadelphia, "As a rule, in the foreign, poverty stricken sections they are invaluable." Dr. Thomas F. Harrington, Director of the Department of School Hygiene of Boston, writes, "It does not seem possible to conceive a more satisfactory arrangement or a more effective piece of school machinery than the school nurse under school supervision."

"Citations from the best authorities on the subject, similar in tone to those quoted, might be indefinitely multiplied. It may be said, indeed, that there is no division of opinion on the subject. The leading authorities without exception advise and recommend school nurses in connection with the work of medical inspection" (16. 66). Dr. John J. Cronin, Assistant Medical Inspector of the New York City Board of Health, is of the opinion that there should be one medical inspector and one nurse for each two thousand pupils" (16.143). As to Dr. Cronin's right to speak on this question, Gulick and Ayres write, "Dr. John J. Cronin, of New York City, has made most wise, extensive, able and best known medical inspection from the standpoint of education" (16.6). New York pays its nurses $75 per month and employs them for twelve months in the year. Boston pays the supervising nurse $924 for the first year, which is increased by an annual increment of $48 to a maximum of $1,116. The assistant nurses receive $648 per year and an annual increase of $48 until the maximum of $840 is reached. New Haven pays its nurses $600 per year" (16.143-4). A very interesting and instructive "table collected by the bureau of municipal research of New York City, April 1, 1910, and intended to show what school authorities are doing to promote the physical welfare of school children in cities having a population of 8,000 or more," appears in the Report of the U. S. Commissioner of Education for 1910, Vol. 1, pages 141-7. In the same volume at pages 140-1 "Dental Inspection in the Cleveland Public Schools" is mentioned. The final paragraph reads "As a result of the investigation the board of education accepted a proposition of the Cleveland Dental Society to conduct gratis for the year 1910 the following work: To make one dental examination of all pupils in the public schools within the year; to establish for the year four centrally located clinics for the treatment of the indigent poor; and to conduct a series of practical and illustrated talks on oral hygiene." The Statute Laws on the Practice of Medicine in all states are complied in "Legal Medicine and Toxicology" by R. L. Emerson, M. D., New York, 1909.

(17) Laws for Child Protection

(1) *Societies.* Under this topic, after glancing at the organized movement for the prevention of cruelty to children, some of the laws for child protection will be considered. To any one at all acquainted with the vast amount of legislation on even "the neglected child," no excuse will be required for the omission of much important legislation in a paper of this kind. And as the scope of the topic—Laws for Child protection—is broader than commonly understood from the words: "neglected child," it follows that only the broken and disjointed outlines of the topic can be here sketched.

"The Humane Movement" by Roswell C. McRea, of Columbia University, contains a "Summary of State Laws for the Protection of Children" (31.389-431). Chapter V in the same work (31.135-146) gives much valuable information relative to the organized movement for the prevention of cruelty to children. Societies for the Prevention of Cruelty to Animals were organized in 1866, eight years before similar societies for children were formed.

"In 1874, the officers of the American Society for the Prevention of Cruelty to Animals were confronted with a case of cruelty to a child. This little girl, Mary Ellen, had been daily beaten by a stepmother and tormented in other cruel ways. The attention of charitable people was called to Mary Ellen's plight and they took up her case. It was discovered that the child could have no protection under the law until the guilt of her persecutor was established under existing legal forms. Under these circumstances they turned to the American Society for the Prevention of Cruelty to Animals, which handled the case. The investigation of other children's cases suggested the desirability of an organization that could do for children what was already being done for animals by a number of organizations. Mr. Bergh, Mr. Elbridge T. Gerry and Mr. John D. Wright who were already interested in the work for animals, launched the new venture, and Mr. E. Fellows Jenkins was drawn away from the American Society to become Superintendent of the new organization, a post just resigned by him. The Society was formed to rescue children from vicious and immoral surroundings and to prosecute offenders, to prevent cruel neglect, beating or other abuse of children, to prevent the employment of children for mendicant purposes or in theatrical or acrobatic performances and for the enforcement of all laws for the protection of minors from abuse.

The Society, during all its thirty-five years of work, has consistently avoided all alliances that would bring its activities into co-operation with other organized work for the improvement of the conditions surrounding child life. Meanwhile, the movement thus inaugurated has become world-wide. In the United States, other societies followed the New York society in the following order: 1875—Rochester, 1876—Portsmouth, N. H., 1876—San Francisco, 1877—Philadelphia, 1878—Boston, 1878—Baltimore, 1879—Buffalo, 1879—Washington, Del., 1880—Brooklyn, 1880—Richmond County, N. Y. These all adopted the New York model, as other local societies have since done, principally in the states of New York and New Jersey. The large majority of protective societies, however, combine work for children with that for animals. Indeed, aside from two California societies, two in Virginia, one in Rhode Island, one in Tennessee, one in Michigan and one in Louisiana, those above mentioned in addition to New York and New Jersey societies are the only ones in which the work for children is not combined with that for animals. This of course excludes those instances in which child protection is made a phase of the activities of societies doing general charity work." (31.135-6.)

No less authority than Professor Stimson says, "Perhaps the most dangerous tendency, at least to conservative ideas, is the increasing one to take the children away from the custody of the parents, or even of the mother, and place them in state institutions. Indeed, in some western states it would appear that the general disapproval of the neighbors of the method employed by parents in bringing up, nurturing, educating, or controlling their children, is sufficient cause for the state authorities to step in and disrupt the family by removing the children, even when themselves unwilling, from the home to some state or county institution. Any one who has worked much in public charities and had experience with that woeful creature, the institutionalized child, will realize the menace contained in such legislation" (39.337-8). And Professor Stimson's opinion seems to be indorsed in the attitude of the Pennsylvania Society for the Prevention of Cruelty to Children, according to the following: The Pennsylvania Society is another that has come to share "the modern economic thought that the normal condition of the child is in the home, even though the home be a poor one; the children often help their parents to reform, and the father and mother can in many instances be made to realize and feel that upon them is the burden of responsibility to see that their children do not become in any sense a charge upon the community. Its belief in this theory is evidenced by the fact that in the year just closed 1,522 cases have been passed over to what is technically known as 'Supervision,' cases in which perhaps on the first the breaking up of the family seemed justifiable. Endeavors have, therefore, been made in every case to preserve the family as a whole. The results obtained by visitors and agents in this work of reconstruction have been beyond belief." (31.143.)

A piece of legislation worthy of note is found in the Maryland Code P. G. L. art. 6, sec. 24, as printed on page 9 of the 6th Edition of the Manual of the Maryland Society for the Protection of Children, compiled by Lewis Hochheimer, Esquire. It reads as follows: "2. Sheltering Children—Persons who receive into their homes or employ children who have left their parents, guardians or other custodianson account of actual or supposed illtreatment are protected against vexatious suits by express provision of law. No person who in good faith receives, harbors, persuades away or removes from a parent, guardian or master any minor for the purpose of sheltering or protecting such minor from illtreatment or suffering can be held to incur any liability therefor." (21.9.)

(II) *Offense Against Children forbidden under Penalty.* (a) *General.* According to Mr. McRea's "Summary of State Laws for Child Protection" there are general statutes in some states. It does not follow that, even in the states where no such general statutes exist, the strong arm of the law cannot be invoked for child protection. Mr. McRea found four offenses mentioned in some general statutes namely: "To willfully cause or permit (a) life or health of any child to be endangered, (b) or unnecessarily expose to weather, (c) or cruelly torture or punish, (d) or neglect or deprive of necessary food, clothing and shelter." Kansas (boy under 14 or girl under 16. Search warrant may be issued and child removed.), Michigan (officers may search on issuance of warrant), Utah (boys under 14, girls under 16), and Wyoming seem to be the only states that can be credited with general statutes enumerating the four offenses. Twenty states have no general statutes and the remaining states include all those having from one to three of the four general statutes mentioned.

(b) *Abandonment, Desertion, Non-Support.* Here is included (a) abandonment, (b) or willful failure to provide food, care, shelter, etc., to minor, (c) sentence may be suspended under bond to observe conditions imposed by court, (d) failure to comply with such conditions leads to execution of sentence, Illinois (under 12) Iowa, Maryland, Minnesota (under 15). Nebraska, North Dakota, Ohio, Pennsylvaia (under 16), Texas (under 12) and Wyoming have so legislated. Alabama, Arkansas, Mississippi and Nevada are reported as without laws. Michigan has a law that if the parent is imprisoned, the earnings, if any shall be paid to family (1907 No. 44). In Arizona it is deemed abandonment to send a child to a saloon or house of ill-fame.

(c) *Exhibitions and Employments* (*not child labor*). To apprentice, exhibit or use any child under——years (a) in any place where intoxicants are sold, (b) as gymnast, acrobat, dancer, etc., (c) for obscene or immoral purposes, (d) for begging, (e) in any business or exhibition dangerous to life or limb, (f) for peddling, (g) at rag-packing, junk gathering, etc., (h) exception made of church, school, musical or other entertainments for educational or scientific purposes. Wyoming, for children under 14, seems to be the only state that has specific laws on the entire eight subdivisions. Sixteen states are reported as having no legislation. The remaining states include Illinois that has legislation covering seven of the eight divisions of our topic, New York and Ohio with six provisions each.

(d) *Obscene Literature, etc.* (a) To show, publish, give or sell literature, prints, etc., (b) or permit a child to distribute such: Illinois, Minnesota (to show in public to minor), Montana (or criminal news to minor under 16), Nebraska (or criminal news to minor), New Hampshire, New York, and North Dakota (under 18) have enacted laws. Arizona makes it an offense to use indecent language before a minor; Florida penalizes the marking of school places in obscene way by others than pupils; Iowa prohibits the introduction of obscene literature into home, or give to minor, or use phonograph for indecent songs; and Kansas by statute excludes minors from trials where vulgar evidence is produced.

(e) *Admittance to Resorts.* District of Columbia, Kansas, Louisiana, Maryland, Oklahoma, South Carolina, Utah and Virginia are reported as having no laws on the admittance of children to resorts. Twelve states are reported as forbidding their admittance to resorts, unaccompanied by parent or guardian. The following forbid the admittance of children to places where intoxicants are sold: Arizona (under 16), California (under 18), Colorado, Connecticut (unlawful for a minor to loiter about a saloon), Delaware (under 18), Idaho (under 16), Illinois, Indiana (male under 16, female under 17), Iowa, Maine, Michigan, (under 17), Nevada (loiter in), New Hampshire, New Jersey (to play games), New York, North Carolina (under 18 or billiard room, or bowling alley, when adverse notice has been served by parent or guardian), Ohio, Oregon, Pennsylvania (under 18; or any place dangerous to health or morals—1885, Act. of May 28, see 1907, Act of May 29—under 16 in house of prostitution or opium den), South Dakota, Vermont, West Virginia (under 18, or any place dangerous to health or morals) and Wisconsin (or girl under 17 to dance or ball), California makes it an offense to send or direct a minor under 18 to saloon, gambling or immoral place. Colorado forbids admittance to places where obscene plays are performed or where game of chance or for playing for wager is in progress. Massachusetts forbids a child under

14, to be admitted to any resort, after sunset, unaccompanied by adult and under 17, to any dance hall or skating rink unaccompanied by adult, school or church dances excepted. Michigan prohibits the admission of a child under 17 to theatre, dance hall or show place or billiard or ten-pin room; or for a minor to remain in; school pupils included, 1907, No. 55. Minnesota makes it criminal to admit or invite a minor under 18 to a house of ill-fame. In New Jersey the child under 16 cannot be admitted to theatres, dance-halls or show-places and the fines for violations go to the poor fund. It is a crime in the State of Washington to allow a minor to play cards in one's home without consent of parent or guardian, Ball. Code, Sec. 7314.

(f) *Sales of intoxicants to Minors.* Relative to selling liquor to minors, Lewis Sutherland's Statutory Construction reads: "Statutes forbidding the sale of liquor to minors are common, for a treatment of the subject see Black on Intoxicating Liquors, No. 415-422. Some courts hold that an honest and well founded belief that the minor was of lawful age is a good defense to a prosecution under the statute. Other courts hold that such a belief is no defense and that the vendor must ascertain at his peril whether the person to whom he sells is a minor. Where the statute made it unlawful to sell, furnish or give liquor to a minor, a saloon-keeper who allows an adult to treat a minor in his saloon is guilty of furnishing liquor to the minor within the statute. In such a case the saloon-keeper has also been held to deal or traffic in liquor with the minor. But such a transaction is held not to be a sale or gift to the minor. Where a minor expressly buys liquor for an adult, pays for it with the adult's money and delivers it to him, it is not a sale to the minor. Where sales on the written order of the parent, guardian or family physician were expected, it was held that a general order from a parent to sell or give his son from day to day and at all times as much liquor as he wanted was not such an order as the statute contemplated. An act forbidding the sale of liquor to minors provided that a sale by an agent should be deemed and taken to be the act of his master. It was held that a sale by an agent was not conclusive, but only *prima facie* evidence of a sale by the master, and that it would be a good defense that the master had in good faith forbidden such sales. (28.1276-7.) In the following states the sale of intoxicants to minors is forbidden: Alabama (parent has right of action), Arizona (under 16; or to give without consent of parent or guardian), California (under 18), Colorado, Connecticut (and minor is punishable for misrepresentation of age). Delaware (or to procure for), Florida, Georgia (father has right of action against person who furnishes without his permission. Sale forbidden without permission of parent or guardian), Idaho (or to give), Illinois (to give, without order of parent or physician, or to buy or procure for, without such order), Indiana (and misrepresentation of age punishable, loitering in saloon not to be permitted), Iowa (or to give to, or to procure for, except on order of parent or physician), Kansas (treating or giving by any parent, guardian or physician), Kentucky (without order of parent), Louisiana (or to furnish or to obtain for, or to allow to loiter in saloon), Maine, Massachusetts (whoever sells or gives to a minor either for his own use, the use of parents or of other person, or allows a minor to loiter on premises shall forfeit one hundred dollars for each offense to be recovered by parent or guardian in an action of tort), Minnesota (or pupil except by licensed pharmacist), Mississippi (and minor punishable for false representation of age), Missouri (without permission of parent or guardian), Montana (or gives), Nebraska (or gives), Nevada (and false representation of age punishable), New Hampshire, New Jersey (or give, under 18), New Mexico, New York, North Carolina (to unmarried minor, or to make purchase for), North Dakota (or give, or treat except by order of parent or physician), Ohio (or furnish), Oregon (deliver to, or allow to loiter. Penalty, loss of license. Misrepresentation of age punishable), Pennsylvania (and misrepresentation of age punishable), Rhode Island, South Carolina (or furnish), South Dakota, Tennessee (or to furnish or entice to place where sold), Texas (or to give, without consent of parent or guardian), Utah (or to furnish or procure for), Vermont, Virginia (to sell or procure for pupil in school or college of State), Washington (or give, without consent of parent or guardian, minor between 18 and 21 punishable for misrepresentation of age), West Virginia (unless by prescription, or loitering about saloon), Wisconsin (misrepresentation of age by minor over 18 punishable), and Wyoming. The sale of candy containing liquor or flavor of same is forbidden. Massachusetts (more than 1% of alcohol under 16), Vermont (1906, No. 50) and Wisconsin (1907 Ch. 168).

(g) *Tobacco Laws*. Ten states now have on their statute books laws prohibiting the manufacture and sale of cigarettes and cigarette papers. They are as follows: Tennessee (1897), Wisconsin, Minnesota, South Dakota, Iowa (with $300 mulct provision), Nebraska, Kansas, Arkansas, Oklahoma and Washington. The sale of cigarettes to children is forbidden in the following states: Alabama (or furnish; or materials for such), Arkansas (or tobacco in any form, manufacture and sale of cigarettes forbidden), Arizona (under

16, tobacco in any form; or furnished), Colorado (or gift of tobacco in any form to minors under 16), Connecticut (use of tobacco in public place by minor under 16 forbidden), Delaware (or furnish, or materials for such to minor under 17), Florida (or furnish or procure, or materials for such, for minor under 18), Georgia (or furnish or materials for such), Idaho (or give or materials for such), Illinois (under 16, or tobacco in any form without written order of parent or guardian), Indiana (or furnish, or materials for such, or tobacco in any form to minor under 16, or to advise to use), Iowa (under 16, tobacco in any form. Manufacture and sale of cigarettes forbidden), Kansas (under 21, tobacco, opium or narcotic in any form). Under date of March 18, 1911, Superintendent Lucy Page Gaston of the Anti-cigarette League wrote, "The Kansas law forbids the use of tobacco in any form by minors under 21." Manufacture and sale of cigarettes are forbidden in Kentucky (under 18; or furnish such or materials for such or council to smoke), Louisiana (or material for such), Maine (or give), Maryland (under 15; tobacco in any form without permission of parent or guardian, unless acting as agent of employer). Other persons may not purchase cigarettes for a minor in Massachusetts (under 18; or not being parent or guardian gives to minor under 18; tobacco in any form under 16; or not being parent or guardian gives to minor under 16 shall be punished by a fine of not more than fifty dollars). Michigan (or furnish tobacco in any form to minor under 17, except on order of parent or guardian), Minnesota (furnishing to tobacco or allowing about premises to smoke, manufacture and sale of cigarettes forbidden), Mississippi (or furnish tobacco in any form to minor under 18 without consent of parent), Missouri (or furnish, or materials for such, to minor under 18), Montana (or give tobacco in any form), Nebraska (give or furnish tobacco in any form to minor under 18, manufacture and sale of cigarettes forbidden), Nevada (or give; or cigarette paper. Tobacco in any form to minor under 18, except on order of parent or guardian), New Hampshire (giving tobacco to minor under 18), New Jersey (cigarettes under 18; or furnish, or paper for such, under 14 tobacco in any form), New Mexico (or give; or tobacco in any form, minor under 18, or pupil, without consent of parent or guardian), New York (under 16, minors under 16 not to smoke in public places), North Carolina (minor under 17, or aid in getting, or materials for such), North Dakota (or furnish tobacco in any form), Ohio (or furnish under 16), Oklahoma (manufacture and sale of cigarettes forbidden or gift of cigarettes to any one), Oregon (under 18; or give tobacco in any form without consent of parent or guardian, and such minor may not smoke in public), Pennsylvania (under 16, tobacco in any form; or furnish cigarettes or paper to any minor), Rhode Island (unlawful for minor under 16 to use tobacco in public), South Carolina (or furnish; or materials for such. Half fine goes to informer), South Dakota (sale or manufacture of cigarettes forbidden. Unlawful for minor to smoke in public, or for any one to abet same), Tennessee (tobacco in any form without consent of parents to minor of 17, manufacture and sale of cigarettes forbidden), Utah (under 18; or furnish tobacco, opium or narcotic in any form), Vermont (under 16, or furnish tobacco without consent of parent or guardian, or furnish cigarettes or wrappers), Virginia (under 16), Washington (and of materials for such forbidden; or furnish tobacco in any form to minor; unlawful for minor to smoke cigarettes or to counsel him to smoke, manufacture and sale of cigarettes forbidden), West Virginia (or opium or furnish), Wisconsin (tobacco in any form, manufacture and sale of cigarettes forbidden), and Wyoming (under 16).

(h) *Carnal Abuse.* The carnal abuse of a female child is a felony punishable under extreme provisions for rape. "In some jurisdictions it is held that a statute punishing for rape any person who shall have carnal knowledge of any woman forcibly and against her will, or any person who shall carnally know or abuse any female under a certain age with her consent, defines but one crime and not two distinct crimes; but in others the statute is construed as defining two distinct crimes" (11.33. 1418). Statutory provisions applying to the carnal abuse of a female child are as follows: Alabama (girl under 12 by male over 16; girl between 12 and 14), Arkansas (girl under 16), Arizona (male over 14 with girl under 17), California (under 16), Colorado (male over 18 with girl under 18. If male is under 20, sentence may be commuted to commitment to State Reform or Industrial School), Connecticut (under 16; any parent or guardian who consents to the detention of a female under 21 for prostitution or carnal intercourse may be fined $1,000 and imprisoned for one year), Delaware (under 18; lascivious playing with girl under 16), District of Columbia (under 16), Florida (under 10; capability of boy under 14 shall be determined by the jury), Georgia (under 12; punishment may be death or on jury's recommendation of mercy twenty years imprisonment), Idaho (under 18, by male over 14), Illinois (under 15, by male over 17), Indiana (under 16), Iowa (under 18; also lewd act of person over 18 with child under 13), Kansas (under 18), Kentucky (under 12; under 16 over 12 lighter penalty), Louisiana (between 12 and 18 by male over 17), Maine (under 14, also between 14 and 16, lighter penalty), Maryland (under 14; also male over 18 with female between 14 and 16), Massachusetts (under 16), Michigan (under 16; male over 14 with girl 14; also to debauch a male under 15, or take a girl under 17 to house of prostitution), Minnesota (under 16; under age of 10 punished by imprisonment for life; of girl between 10 and 14 imprisonment from 7 to 30 years; of girl between 14 and 16 three months to a year in county jail or one to seven years in state prison), Mississippi (under 12), Missouri (under 14; between 14 and 18), Montana (minor 16 by male over 16), Nebraska (with chaste girl under 18, by male over 18), Nevada (under 14 by male over 15), New Hampshire (to willfully and deceitfully entice or carry away a female child under 18 for purpose of prostitution of illicit intercourse), New Jersey (under 16), New Mexico (under 10; under 14 by male over 14), New York (under 18), North Carolina ("virtuous" female between 10 and 14), North Dakota (under 18, by male over 14), Ohio (under 16 by a male over 18), Okalahoma (under 14 , male over 14, also female between 14 and 16 of previously chaste character), Oregon (under 16 by male over 16), Pennsylvania (under 16, of good repute), Rhode Island (under 16), South Carolina (under 14 and under 16, by male over 14, after abduction), South Dakota (under 18 by male over 14), Tennessee (under 12), Texas (female under 15 by male over 14), Utah (between 13 and 18), Vermont (of girl under sixteen by a male over 16; a male under 16 with a consenting female under 16 are guilty of a misdemeanor and may be committed to the Vermont Industrial School), Virginia (under 14), Washington (under 18), West Virginia (under 14. Does not apply to male under 14 with female over 12 with free consent), Wisconsin (under 18, previously chaste), and Wyoming (under 18).

(i) *Corporal punishment in Schools.* Bardeen's School Law has twenty pages on corporal punishment. After discussing the common law right of the teacher to inflict corporal punishment, Mr. Bardeen says. "A change of sentiment is manifest in recent decisions. The teacher will not find it safe to rely upon modern confirmation by courts of many decisions once rendered and long considered good authority (4.234). Every year this tendency is becoming more and more marked, and the teacher who cannot govern *without* severe corporal punishment will do well to retire from teaching before he is forced out" (4.235). The Laws of 1909 in New York read: "To use or attempt, or offer to use force or violence upon or toward the person of another is not unlawful when committed by any guardian, master or teacher in the exercise of a lawful authority to restrain or correct his child or scholar, and the force or violence used is reasonable in manner and moderate in degree" (88.1909, N. Y.). "But even here," says Mr. Bardeen, "the teacher is subject to the rules established by the trustees. When the trustees have made a rule forbidding corporal punishment, the teacher may not inflict it" (4.223). New Jersey, and some cities like New York and Syracuse forbid corporal punishment (4.221). "In 1889, Arizona dropped the enactment expressly authorizing corporal punishment" (4.236). Prior to 1899 in Arizona any teacher before inflicting corporal punishment upon a pupil must first notify the parent or guardian and one member of the board of trustees of his or her intention at least one day before such punishment is to be inflicted stating the day and hour at which the punishment will be inflicted and extending an invitation to such parent and one trustee to be present" (4.229). The law just mentioned is not reported to have required engraved invitations with "R. S. V. P." nor the presence of the coroner or a representative of the Associated Press. Cyc., (v. 35, p. 1137) reads, "As a general rule, a school teacher, in so far as it may be reasonably necessary to the maintenance of the discipline and efficiency of the school, and to compel a compliance with reasonable rules and regulations, may inflict reasonable corporal punishment upon a pupil for insubordination, disobedience, or other misconduct, but a teacher cannot inflict corporal punishment to enforce an unreasonable rule, to compel a pupil to pursue a study forbidden by his parent, or to compel him to do something which his parent may have requested that he be excused from doing, although the teacher may be justified in refusing to permit the attendance of the pupil whose parent will not consent that he shall obey the rules of the school. The infliction of corporal punishment by a teacher is largely within his discretion; but he must exercise sound discretion and judgment in determining the necessity for corporal punishment and the reasonableness thereof, under the varying circumstances of each particular case, and must adapt the punishment to the nature of the offense, and to the age and mental condition and personal attributes of the offending pupil, and, considering the circumstances and conditions of the particular offense and pupil, the punishment must not be inflicted with such force or in such a manner as to cause it to be cruel or excessive, or wanton or malicious" (11.35.1137-9). After reading this quotation one is forced to remark that the ever increasing responsibilities of the office have not yet led the public to pay the average teacher as high a wage as the average brick-layer, carpenter and plumber receive. May be it is because the brick-layer, carpenter and plumber first organized unions, and then persistently followed the injunction: "Ask and you shall receive." What has been said on corporal punishment thus far, applies to cases where the teacher has not been attacked by the pupil. The legal right of self-defense is possessed by every teacher and no legislature will attempt to take it away. Finally as to corporal punishment, Dr. Snedden says, "As in the public schools, there is a general belief that the complete prohibition of whipping would have a bad moral effect, but that by the proper development of other means of control, its use may or ought to be almost entirely dispensed with" (35.147). President G. Stanley Hall and many others subscribe to this belief.

(j) *The Neglected Child.* Judge Baker, of the Boston (Mass.) Juvenile Court in a paper read at Massachusetts Conference of Charities, Fitchburg, October, 1910, said, "Probably the case ordinarily thought of when neglected children are mentioned is that of children who have no regular meals, get only scraps of food and are constantly hungry; who are clad only in dirty, ragged outer garments, without stockings, shoes or under clothes; whose flesh is encrusted with dirt; whose hair is infested with vermin; whose parents are seldom sober, usually idle and frequently in jail. Our statutes, however, authorize interference in a much larger class of cases" (3.3). Judge Baker went on to describe the larger class by giving examples of sober, industrious parents failing to have the child's eyes treated for ophthalmia neonatorum, not providing glasses, surgical attendance or living in unhygienic quarters when able to afford better, as illustrating cases of children who "by reason of the neglect of parents are growing up without proper physical care" mentioned in the Massachusetts statutes. Other cases included the child "excellently fed and clothed and the pink of neatness" but if its parents are selling liquor illegally or letting rooms in their house for immoral purposes, the child can be taken away because in the words of the statute 'by reason of the crime of its parents' it is growing up 'under circumstances exposing it to lead an idle and dissolute life' (3.5). Again, Judge Baker said, "Children may be properly fed, clothed and fairly well cleaned but be suffered by their parents to be frequently tardy and absent from school, and spend all their time when out of school running the streets all over the city because the mother not satisfied with the husband's steady earnings of $18.00 a week, insists on going out to work herself. Such children can be brought to court because 'by reason of neglect of their parents' they are 'growing up without salutary control' " (3.5). These examples from the paper of Judge Baker, with what has been already said on "Laws for Child Protection" in this study, will give a general idea of the legal problem known as the "neglected child." In the introduction to "Juvenile Court Laws in the United States," Expert Special Agent John Koren, of the United States Bureau of the Census, wrote: "In addition to hearing cases of delinquency these courts (Juvenile Courts) are charged with the disposition of dependent and neglected children. In many instances the laws prescribing the authority and duty are so bound up together that they cannot very well be separated. Moreover, the functions of the juvenile courts and their peculiar place in the community cannot be correctly estimated if viewed solely in relation to delinquency cases. It therefore seemed wisest to incorporate in the summary the legislation relating to dependent and neglected children, so far as the juvenile courts are concerned with them." (18.3.) The various efforts in several states, and especially in large cities, to care for neglected children are summarized by Mr. Homer Folks in his monograph on the Care of Destitute, Neglected and Delinquent Children. (New York, 1902.)

(18) Juvenile Court Laws

Juvenile Court Laws "have in recent years come in for the larger share of attention in all of our state legislation. Radical changes, with a view to recognizing the independence of the child and the desirability of treating it both apart from the usual rules of procedure and punishment applicable to adult criminals and also with a view to holding the parent or guardian responsible for the wrong doing of the child as well as to secure better environmental conditions by removing it entirely from the custody of the parent, have found a place in the law of most states." (32.1.624.) "Juvenile Court Laws in the United States—A Summary by States, by Thomas J. Homer; A topical abstract by Grace Abbott; Edited by Dr. Hart, of the Russell Sage Foundation, appeared in 1910, and should be consulted by every one interested in the subject. It is a book of 150 pages, and its comprehensiveness and compressibleness become evident the more it is tested and examined. This section in touching on only some of the salient points can at the most only serve as an indicator pointing to "Juvenile Court Laws in the United States Summarized" (18). Twenty-three states have enacted juvenile court laws, and they are Alabama, California, Colorado, Georgia, Idaho, Illinois (1899), Indiana, Iowa, Kansas, Kentucky, Louisiana, Massachusetts, Michigan, Minnesota, Nebraska, Ohio, Oregon, Pennsylvania, Tennessee, Texas, Utah, Washington, Wisconsin—and in the

District of Columbia. "Under the common law a child of seven was regarded as responsible for his acts and was treated as a criminal in the charge, the trial, and the disposition made of him after the trial. Under the new theory the child offender is regarded not as a *criminal* but as a delinquent, 'as misdirected and misguided and needing aid, encouragement, help and assistance;' he is kept entirely separate from the adult offender, and the probation system is used whenever practicable. These are the most important features of the new legislation which has been adopted in the states enumerated" (18.122). District of Columbia, Colorado, Indiana, Louisiana, Massachusetts, Michigan, Maryland, Missouri and Utah have created special courts which are given jurisdiction over juvenile offenders alone. "Most states have found, however, that it presented fewer legal difficulties to use some court already established in this jurisdiction." (18.123). "In the great majority of states the jurisdiction of the Juvenile Court extends to children 16 or 17 years of age. But in Illinois and Kentucky the limitation is for boys 17 and girls 18, in Louisiana, Nebraska and Oregon 18 for both, and in Utah 19 for both boys and girls" (18.125). The more inclusive laws of Alabama, Colorado, Illinois, Indiana, Kentucky, Louisiana, Michigan, Minnesota, Missouri, Nebraska, Ohio, Tennessee, Texas, Utah and Washington regard "as a delinquent any child who (a) knowingly associates with thieves, vicious or immoral persons, (b) absents itself from home without the consent of its parent or guardian or without just cause, (c) is growing up in idleness or crime, (d) knowingly visits or enters a house of ill repute, (e) visits or patronizes gambling houses, saloons, or bucketshops, (f) wanders about the street at night or about railroad yards or tracks, (g) jumps on and off trains, (h) enters a car or engine without lawful authority, (i) uses vile, obscene or indecent language or is (j) immoral or indecent" (18.126-7).

The subdivisions of delinquency conceive the child as actively at fault, while the laws covering the neglected child and the dependent child look upon them as more passive or the victims of the faults of others. And it is to be remembered that juvenile courts are concerned not only with the delinquent but also with the neglected and dependent child. The procedure in juvenile courts may be "initiated" on a petition in California, Illinois, Iowa, Kansas, Kentucky, Louisiana, Michigan, Minnesota, Nebraska, New Hampshire, Ohio, Oregon, Tennessee and Wisconsin. In Alabama, Colorado, Massachusetts, Missouri, Texas, Utah and Washington, the old word "complaint" is used. (18.127.) A "summons" issues on the filing of the "petition" or "complaint" in many states. This "summons" is addressed to the parent or guardian and directs him to appear with the child in court on a certain date. The laws in force in Indiana, Iowa, Kansas, Kentucky, Minnesota, Missouri, New Hampshire, New Jersey, Ohio, Oregon, Washington and Utah make "the trial quite informal so that an intimate friendly relationship may be established at once between the judge and the child." New Jersey and New York follow the regular criminal procedure as does also Michigan when the child is charged with a felony" (18.129). The District of Columbia and eight states reserve the right of appeal from the decision of juvenile judges. Twenty-one states require a separate Juvenile Record. A dozen states require the juvenile court to be held in a separate room and Chicago and Milwaukee have separate Juvenile Court Buildings. (18.131.) Six states "provide that the trial shall not be public and all persons not necessary to it shall be excluded." (18.132.) Pending trial no child under twelve shall be committed to jail in Illinois, Michigan and California, under fourteen in Colorado, Idaho, Kentucky, Massachusetts (except when arrested in the act of violating a law of the commonwealth or on a warrant; if over 14 may be comitted to jail if court thinks he will not otherwise appear for trial, Montana, Nebraska, Ohio, Tennessee, Washington and Wisconsin, under sixteen or seventeen in Kansas, New Hampshire, Texas and Utah (18.133.) Fifteen states have a detention "home" or "school" instead of a jail for juveniles awaiting trial. The juvenile Judge in "most states can continue the hearing from time to time, leaving the child, under the supervision of the probation officer, in its home or in some suitable family or commit it to some detention school or House of Reform or to any institution willing to receive it and having for its object the care of delinquent children" (18.134.) Connecticut, District of Columbia, Indiana and Massachusetts provide that the court may fine or imprison the child for the original offense (seldom done in Massachusetts) or for violating the conditions of probation—Illinois, Massachusetts (if child is over 14), Ohio, Oregon and Texas leave a loophole for a return to the old system by providing that the judge may order the child to be proceeded against and sentenced under the existing criminal laws of the state (18.135.) Illinois, Missouri and Wisconsin select the probation officers for their juvenile courts from eligible lists determined by competition civil service examination. In most of the states the juvenile Judge has the appointment of the Juvenile Probation officer (18.136). "The duties of the probation officers, the law provides in almost all the states having Juvenile Court Laws, shall be (a) to investigate any child to be brought before the Court, (b) to be present in court to represent the interests of the child, (c) to furnish such information as the judge may require and (d) to take charge of any child before and after trial." (18.137.) The following states have statutes punishing by fine or imprisonment parents or others who contribute to the child's delinquency: Colorado ($1,000 fine or 12 months imprisonment or both), Connecticut ($500 fine or 6 months imprisonment or both), District of Columbia ($200 fine or 3 months or both), Idaho ($500 or 6 months or both), Illinois $200 or 12 months or both), Indiana ($500 or 6 months or both), Kansas ($1,000 or one year or both), Kentucky, Massachusetts ($50 or 6 months or both), Minnesota ($500 or 6 months or both), Missouri, Nebraska ($500 or six months or both), New Jersey ($1,000 or 12 months or both), Louisiana, New York, Ohio ($1,000 or 12 months or both), Texas ($1,000 or 12 months or both), Utah, Washington ($1,000 or 12 months or both) and Wisconsin ($500 or one year or both) (21.138-9). In the following states, with the exceptions noted, a child "in no case may be sent to a common jail but to a special place of detention:" Alabama (may be so placed if captured for a felony, in nighttime, or in exceptional cases for safe-keeping until home can be found), Arizona (but no child under 12 may be committed to the Industrial School unless this seems best after probation), California (under 12. Others must be kept separate from adults), Colorado (under 14), Georgia (under 16), Idaho (under 14), Illinois (under 12,) Indiana (boys under 16, girls under 17), Iowa (under 17), Kansas (except in case of felony), Kentucky (children at jails must be looked after by matron. Dependent and neglected must be kept apart from delinquent, boys under 17, girls under 18), Louisiana (neglected and delinquent under 17), Maryland (under 16), Massachusetts (lock-up or house of detention to be avoided, whenever possible—under 14, except for offense ordinarily punished by death or life imprisonment), Michigan (under 12 or with adults if under 17), Minnesota (under 14; between 14 and 16, to be separate from adults), Montana (under 14), Nebraska (under 14; between 14 and 16 not with adults), New Hampshire (under 17), New York (under 16 no longer than necessary for the purpose of transfer. Not with adults except in presence of proper officials), Ohio (under 12); Oregon (under 14 and others must be kept apart from adults), Pennsylvania (under 12, not to be sent to any correctional institution pending hearing, not to be confined in institution for adults), Rhode Island (under 16, older ones at discretion of court. State probation officer may have custody of girl under 16, not longer than six months), South Dakota (under 16), Tennessee (under 14, and not to be incarcerated except to guarantee appearance in court), Utah (boys under 14, girls under 16), Vermont (under 16, not to be sent to the house of correction for first offense, but to state industrial school), Washington (under 14, and none shall be placed with adults) and Wisconsin (under 14; and between 14 and 16, not with adults) (18.395-431). Finally it should be stated that a child in most states becomes an adult, before the criminal law, earlier than he does before the civil law, that the juvenile age fixed by the legislation of the states does not correspond to the age of majority; that when the juvenile age is passed the child is subject to treatment as an adult, although many states are not unmindful of the possibility of reformation taking place even in manhood.

(19) Child Labor Laws

A summary of the child labor laws in force in 1910 has been prepared by Laura Scott, and will be found in "Legislative Review, No. 5, American Association of Labor" (34).

All states and territories except Nevada have enacted laws on child labor. The following have laws prohibiting any child labor whatever: Arizona (under 14 during school hours without proof that child is excused from school attendance), Arkansas (under 14 without age and dependency certificate or schooling certificates), Colorado (under 14 during school term without school certificate; 14 to 16 who cannot read and write, without schooling certificate), Connecticut (under 14 when school is in session; 14 to 16 who cannot read must attend night school), Delaware (under 14 in any gainful occupation), Florida (under 12 when school is in session), Idaho (in any gainful occupation under 12; 12 to 14 during school session; 14 to 16 without required school instructions), Illinois (under 14; 14 to 16 who cannot read and write, without age certificate; 14 to 16 who cannot read and write, without age certificate and night school certificate if there is a night school held in such place), Kansas (under 14 when school is in session), Kentucky (under 14 during school hours; 14 to 16 without employment certificate), Maryland (under 12; 12 to 16 without permit), Massachusetts (under 14 while school is in session), Minnesota (under 14 when school is in session; 14 to 16 without employment permit and medical certificate if demanded), Missouri (under 14, 14 to 16 without age certificate), Montana (during school term under 16 without schooling certificate), Nebraska (during school hours under 14), New York (during school term under 14; 14 to 16 in cities of first and second class without employment certificate or school certificate), North Dakota (under 14 during the term of public school), Oregon (under 14 during school hours), Washington (under 15 without schooling certificate) and Wisconsin (under 14; 14 to 16 without permit). Night labor for children under twelve is prohibited from 8 P. M. to 6 A. M. in South Carolina in factories: mines and textile establishments—under *fourteen* in Arkansas (7 P. M. to 6 A. M. in factory manufacturing), Georgia (7 P. M. to 6 A. M. in factory, manufacturing), North Carolina (7 P. M. to 6 A. M. in any), Texas (6 A. M. to 6 A. M. in any), Virginia (6 P. M. to 7 A. M., manufacturing, mechanical mining), under *sixteen* in Alabama (from 7 P. M. to 6 A. M. in factories and mills), California (10 P. M. to 6 A. M. in hotels, laundries, manufacturing, mercantile, messenger, office, place of amusement, restaurants and workshops),

Connecticut (after 10 P. M. in mercantile), Delaware (6 P.M. to 7 A. M. in any gainful occupation), District of Columbia (10 P. M. to 6 A. M.), Idaho (9 P. M. to 6 A. M. in any occupation), Illinois (7 P. M. to 7 A. M. in any gainful), Iowa (9 P. M. to 6 A. M. in elevator, factory, laundry, manufacturing, mercantile, mill, mine, packing house, shop, slaughter house, store), Kansas (6 P. M. to 7 A. M. —distribution of messages or merchandise, elevator, factory, messengers, mine, packinghouse, theatre, workshop), Kentucky (7 P. M. to 7 A. M. in any gainful occupation), Louisiana (male under 16, female under 18—7 P. M. to 7 A. M. in any work), Michigan (male under 16, female under 18—6 P.M. to 6 A.M. in manufacturing, messengers [except for telephone, telegraph or post office], mine, workshop), Minnesota (7 P. M. to 7 A. M. in any gainful occupation), Mississippi (7 P. M. to 6 A. M. in manufacturing), New York (5 P. M. to 8 A. M. in factory; under 16—10 P. M. to 7 P. M.—under 16 after 7 P. M.; cities of first class—in apartment house, business office, distribution of messages or merchandise, hotel, mercantile establishment, messenger, restaurant, telegraph office, transmission of messages or merchandise), North Dakota (7 P.M. to 7 A.M. any), Ohio (male under 16, female under 18—6 P. M. to 7 A. M.), Oklahoma (male under 16, female under 18—6 P. M. to 7 A. M.), Oregon (6 P. M. to 7 A. M. in any), Pennsylvania (9 P. M. to 6 A. M.), Rhode Island (8 P.M. to 6 A. M. in business establishment, factory, manufacturing, except mercantile establishments on Saturday and four days preceding Christmas), Vermont (after 8 P. M. in factory, messenger, mill, quarry, railroad, workshop), Washington (8 P. M. to 5 A. M.) and Wisconsin (9 P. M. to 6 A. M. in any); under *eighteen* in New Jersey (7 P.M. to 7 A.M. in factory, manufacture of goods of any kind, mill, workshop), New York (male 16 to 18 from 12 midnight to 4 A. M., and female 16 to 21 from 9 P. M. in factories); under *twenty-one* in Massachusetts (between 10 P. M. and 6 A. M. in mercantile, and manufacturing.

Florida, Missouri, Montana, Nebraska, Nevada, New Mexico, South Carolina, Texas, Utah, Vermont, Washington, West Virginia and Wyoming have no legislation on the number of hours that a child shall work per day or per week. Legislation in the other states as to the maximum hours of child labor is as follows: Alabama (under 14, 60 hours per week), Arkansas (under 14, 60 hours per week 10 per day), California (under 18, 54 per week 9 per day) Colorado (under 16, 8 per day), Connecticut (under 16, 58 per week), Delaware (under 16, 54 per week 9 per day), District of Columbia (under 16, 48 per week), Idaho (under 16, 54 per week 9 per day), Illinois (under 16, 48 per week 8 per day), Indiana (male under 16 female under 18, 60 per week 10 per day, under 14, 8 per day), Iowa (under 16 10 per day), Kansas (under 16, 48 per week 8 per day), Kentucky (under 16, 60 per week 10 per day), Louisiana (under 18, 60 per week 10 per day), Maine (male under 16, female under 18, 58 per week 10 per day), Maryland (under 16, 10 per day), Massachusetts (under 18 in mercantile 58 per week; under 18 in manufacturing 56 per week 10 per day, under 18 in any other employment for wages or other compensation 58 per week with average for year 56 per week), Michigan (under 18, 54 per week 10 per day) Minnesota (under 16, 60 per week 10 per day), Mississippi (under 16, 58 per week 10 per day), New Hampshire (under 18, 58 per week 9 hours 40 min. per day), New Jersey (under 16, 55 per week 10 per day), New York (under 16 in factory 6 days per week 8 hours per day; under 16 in other occupations 54 per week, 9 per day; male 16 to 18, female under 21, 60 per week 10 per day), North Carolina (under 18, 66 per week), North Dakota (under 16, 60 per week, 8 per day), Ohio (male under 16, female under 18, 48 per week 8 per day), Oklahoma (under 16, 48 per week 8 per day), Oregon (under 16, 6 days per week 10 hours per day), Pennsylvania (males under 16, females under 18, 58 per week 10 per day), Rhode Island (under 16, 56 per week 10 per day), South Dakota (under 18 10 per day), Tennessee (under 16, 60 per week) and Wisconsin (under 18, in cigar factory 48 per week 8 per day; under 18 in any other, 6 days per week 10 hours per day).

To enumerate the many occupations prohibited to children in the various states would take too much space. The prohibited occupations to children of certain ages generally include the dangerous, injurious, unhealthy, acrobatic, mendicant, immoral, hazardous, standing, manufacturing, mercantile, mechanical, workshop, and many states have a general prohibition for any gainful employment (34.132). "The laws as to labor in mines are naturally more severe; although in some they are covered by ordinary factory laws (Colorado, Florida, Iowa, Kansas, Kentucky, Louisiana, Michigan, Minnesota, North Dakota, Oregon, South Carolina, South Dakota, Tennessee, Vermont, Virginia, and Wisconsin). Female labor is absolutely forbidden in mines or works under ground in Alabama, Arkansas, Illinois, Indiana, Missouri, New York, North Carolina, Oklahoma, Pennsylvania, Utah, Washington, Wyoming and West Virginia—in short, in most of the states except Idaho, Kansas, Iowa, Kentucky, Virginia, Wyoming, where mines exist; and the limit of male labor is usually put at fourteen (Alabama, Arkansas, Idaho, Indiana, Missouri, Ohio (fifteen during school year), South Dakota, Tennessee, Utah and Wyoming), to sixteen (Illinois, Missouri (of those who can read and write), Montana, New York, Oklahoma, Pennsylvania and Washington); or twelve (North Carolina, South Carolina and West Virginia), even in states which have no such legislation as to factories. The laws as to elevators (Indiana, Massachusetts, New York, Rhode Island, Kansas and Oregon), dangerous machinery (Connecticut, Iowa, Missouri, Oregon, Louisiana and New York), or dangerous employment generally (Illinois, Kansas, Kentucky, Massachusetts, Michigan, Minnesota, Missouri, Montana, New Jersey, New York), Ohio, Oklahoma, Pennsylvania, and Wisconsin), are even stricter, and as a rule apply to children of both sexes; the Massachusetts standard being, in the management of rapid elevators, the age of eighteen, in cleaning machinery in motion, fourteen, etc.; sixteen to eighteen in Indiana, Iowa, Louisiana, New Jersey, New York and South Carolina. The labor of all women in some states, and of girls or women under sixteen or eighteen in other states, is forbidden in occupations which require continual standing Illinois (under sixteen), Michigan (all), Minnesota (sixteen), Missouri (all), New York (sixteen), Ohio (all), Oklahoma (sixteen), Wisconsin, sixteen), Colorado (all over sixteen). Females in Iowa, Louisiana, Michigan, Missouri, New Hampshire, New York, Vermont, Washington (except wife of the proprietor or a member of the family), or minors in Arizona, Connecticut, Georgia, Pennsylvania, Idaho, Maryland, Michigan, Missouri, New Hampshire, South Dakota and Vermont, or young children in Florida, Illinois, Massachusetts, Missouri and Nebraska, are very generally forbidden from working or waiting in bar-rooms or restaurants where liquor is sold, and in a few states girls are prohibited from selling newspapers or acting as messengers (New York, Oklahoma and Wisconsin). The Northern States have a usual age limit for the employment of children in ordinary theatrical performances, and an absolute prohibition of such employment or of acrobatic, immoral, or mendicant employment. But in some states it appears that there is only an age limit as to these (California, Kentucky, Maine, Maryland, Michigan, Missouri, Montana, New York, Oregon, Rhode Island, (sixteen years); Colorado, District of Columbia, Florida, Illinois, Kansas, New Hampshire, Virginia, Wisconsin, Wyoming (fourteen); Connecticut, Georgia (twelve); Delaware, Indiana, Louisiana, Massachusetts, West Virginia (fifteen); Minnesota, New Jersey, Pennsylvania, Washington (eighteen). The hours for railroad and telegraph operators are limited in several states, but rather for the purpose of protecting the public safety than the employees themselves (Colorado and New York). The following other trades are prohibited to women or girls: Bootblacking or street trades generally (District of Columbia and

Wisconsin); work upon emery wheels, or wheels of any description in factories (Michigan); and in New York no female is allowed to operate or use abrasives, buffing wheels, or many other processes of polishing the baser metals, or iridium. Selling magazines or newspapers in any public place, as to girls under sixteen (New York, Oklahoma, Wisconsin), public messenger service for telegraph and telephone companies as to girls under nineteen (Washington)" (39.225,-6).

(20) RIGHTS OF THE CHILD

"Legislation always means an attempt to define and express rights which society is ready to recognize, guarantee, and make universal in their application. Among the more important rights of childhood that are now generally given legislative protection are: (1) The right to be well born. (2) The right to parental name, support and protection. (3) The right to leisure, play, and recreation. (4) The right to education. (5) The right to exemption from work, until physically and mentally equipped for the specific tasks with which the work life may properly begin, and, for a longer period the right to protection from any temptation to enter upon extra-hazardous or dangerous trades or to work under conditions inimical to health and morals. (6) The right to protection from inhumane treatment. (7) The right to protection of health and morals. (8) The right to a chance in a decent environment, both physical and social, when guilty of any infraction of the law" (36.621). Most of these rights have been discussed in the preceding pages There are many other privileges and disabilities that the law confers. In Oliver vs. Houdlet, 13 Mass., 237, Justice Wilde said, "In all cases the benefit of the infant is the great point to be regarded; the object of the law being to protect his imbecility and indiscretion from injury, through his own imprudence or by the craft of others." "Hence, although the infant may avoid his contract, yet it is binding on a person of full age who contracts with him. Every person deals with an infant at arm's length, at his own risk, and with a party for whom the law has a jealous watchfulness" (46.10). Some contracts bind the infant, or minor as we shall call him henceforth. A minor's contract to marry, his contract for necessaries for himself or his wife and children, and his contract to enlist seem to be binding. The prices he will have to pay for necessaries, will not be what the merchant charges but what the necessaries are reasonably worth. "Of course food, clothing and house rent, especially if the minor is a young man who is married, are necessaries. Dentist's bills for filling teeth, and even a watch and chain, have been judicially held to be necessaries for certain well-to-do lads, who, after running up these bills, refused to pay them. More unhandsome still was the conduct of the youthful Kentucky bridegroom who tried to elude payment for his wedding suit of clothes, on the ground that it was a luxury and not a necessity. But he, and the young Englishman who bought a wedding present for his bride and then tried to escape paying for it, found that the jury considered these things necessaries and not luxuries. On the other hand, cigars and tobacco, wine suppers, and diamond and ruby cuff-buttons worth $60 apiece, are held in law to be luxuries, and in no possible way necessaries for any minor; not even for fashionable young men in college who wish to lead their 'set'" (15.84-5). The safest rule in business transactions seems to be for the adult to deal with the minor's parent or guardian. Of course a minor can take and hold property of all kinds during minority but the vendor or grantor is usually liable to have the minor refuse to confirm the sale or conveyance on attaining full age. There are so many conflicting decisions on this whole subject that "the layman, who is his own lawyer usually has a fool for a client." What has been said on this topic applies to the minor, who has property in his own name and who is not living at home. Ordinarily, if the minor has property of his own and his father is not so fortunately circumstanced, the minor's support can be made a charge on the minor's property. But this whole subject has been so diversely regulated by statute that it seems impossible to frame a short rule that will be found universal. The husband or father who fails to provide reasonable support and maintenance for his wife and minor children can be punished by a fine (in Massachusetts and other states payable to the wife) or imprisonment.

The child adopted is usually not related by nature to those assuming the legal relations of maternity or paternity, and "the consent of the child or other person to be adopted must in most states be obtained if such person be over fourteen years of age or over twelve years in the states of New York, California, Nevada, the Dakotas, Idaho and Arizona. Generally any woman being an inhabitant of the state and twenty-one years of age may adopt. The adopter must be forty years of age in Louisiana; competent to make a will in Iowa. If the adopter has a wife or husband, he or she must consent or join in the petition or other instrument, if competent, in the states of New Hampshire, Massachusetts, Maine, Vermont, Rhode Island, Connecticut, New York, New Jersey, Ohio, Illinois Michigan, Wisconsin, Minnesota, Delaware, Kentucky, Missouri, California, Oregon, Nevada, Colorado, Washington, the Dakotas, Idaho, Utah and Louisiana. In Massachusetts and Louisiana the person adopted must be younger than the person adopting; and it must be a child in the States of New Hampshire, Maine, Rhode Island, Pennsylvania, Illinois, Wisconsin, Minnesota, Nebraska, Delaware, Missouri, Oregon, Nevada, Colorado, Utah, Alabama, Florida, Louisiana, and the Territory of New Mexico. No woman can adopt her own husband in Massachusetts; or her own child in Illinois, Wisconsin, Iowa, Minnesota and Washington; a brother or sister, whether of the whole or half blood, or an uncle or aunt in Massachusetts; nor in Louisiana can a man adopt his illegitimate children, whom the law prohibits him from acknowledging. By the law of the state of Nevada no mongolian can either adopt or be adopted. It would seem by the law of Illinois that only an orphan can be adopted, or a child both of whose parents have deserted it for at least one year. In New Jersey, Idaho, and Louisiana the person adopting must be at least fifteen years older than the person adopted, and at least ten years older in California, Nevada, and the Dakotas. In North Carolina an adoption may be made either for life or during the minority of the child (5.50-2).

A digest of the apprentice laws of the states will be found in "The apprenticeship System in its relation to Industrial Education" by the late Carroll D. Wright, President of Clark College, Worcester, Massachusetts, United States Bureau of Education, Bulletin, 1908, No. 6. (47.) "Besides the general power of a parent to bind his infant child as an apprentice, an orphan whose estate is insufficient for his support, or an infant pauper, whether an orphan or not, may be apprenticed by the overseers of the poor or other similar officers" (11.3.542). In some jurisdictions, as in New York, an infant may bind himself, while in others this power is denied. The usual rule is to require the child's consent to his apprenticeship.

In the United States the child's capacity to make a will is looked upon with disfavor according to the following: "Modern legislation repudiates largely the wills of all infants, male or female, with obvious disfavor. And the latest enactments of the majority of American states are to the same purport, establishing the age of twenty-one as that at which a person of either sex ceases to be disqualified from making a will of either real or personal estate. States still vary in provisions, however, concerning the testamentary capacity of infants. Eighteen years is sometimes taken as the testamentary age for both males and females; while various codes adopt a still earlier standard of discretion, distinguishing in some instances between males and females, or even between females married and unmarried. Sometimes, too, the line is drawn between the kinds of property, so that an infant's personality but not his real estate may be disposed by testament before he reaches the age of twenty-one" (33.21).

The code of Georgia, Seventh Title, Chap. 2, Art. 1, 3265 reads "Infants under fourteen years of age are considered wanting in that discretion necessary to make a will." In New York, a female at 16 and a male at 18 can dispose of their personal property by will.

(21) Rights of Parents

The parents have the natural right to the control and custody of the child. The common-law rule was that the father's right to custody of a legitimate child was superior to that of the mother. But the common-law rule has been modified in most, if not all, states. "General rules cannot be laid down for the determination of cases affecting the custody of infants, there can be no legal standard by which the courts must be governed. The general result of American cases may be characterized as an utter repudiation of the notion that there can be such a thing as a proprietary right or interest in or to the custody of an infant. The terms "right" and "claim," when used in this connection, according to their proper meaning, virtually import the right or claim of the *child* to be in that custody or charge which will subserve *its* real interest" (20.22). Colorado, Connecticut, Idaho, Kentucky, Maryland, Massachusetts, Minnesota, Mississippi, Montana, New Hampshire, New Mexico, New York, Ohio, Oklahoma, Rhode Island, South Dakota, Texas, Vermont, Washington and Wisconsin allow a married woman to be appointed guardian of her own or other people's children, to have charge of their persons and property, even though she lives with her husband. In Arkansas, Missouri and Utah, she can be appointed guardian of a child's person only and in California of its estate. In New Jersey she and her husband may be jointly appointed (15.91). Statutes in every state provide for the support of the child by the parent, and when the child is an orphan, statutory provision exists in some states for his support by the grandparents, if they have sufficient means. The marriage of a minor daughter excuses her father from supporting her as that is one of the duties assumed by her husband. In all cases where a child has property, the parent before using the property, even for the child's benefit, should apply for permission to the proper court. If the parents have custody of the child, the child's earnings belong to the parents. "Under some statutes the parent, if he intends to claim the child's earnings, must notify the child's employer, and in absence of such notice payment to the child is valid and he has good title to the money" (11.29.1624). The parent may emancipate the child by "giving him his time," and "the effect of this is to throw the child upon his own exertions for support and legally absolve the father from further obligation" (15.76).

Religious Convictions. The peculiar religious convictions of a father form no ground for removing the child from his custody, nor does a father forfeit his right to custody of his child by being or becoming an atheist. But where a father belongs to a sect which entertains opinions, obnoxious to society, adverse to civilization, opposed to the usage of christendom, and in some respects contrary to the express commands of the Bible, the court will not award him the custody of the child. In determining the custody of a child as between persons other than parents the court regards its temporal welfare as paramount to questions of religious doctrine; but the child will be delivered to the custody of persons of its father's faith if its temporal interest will be as well conserved by the custody of such persons as by that of others of a different faith or indifferent in religious matters" (11.29.1600).

(22) Majority

At common law all persons under twenty-one are infants or minors but this rule has been modified in some states by statute. The age of majority in some states is eighteen years for married females while in other states eighteen is the age of majority for all females, and in Utah all minors attain majority on marriage. Provisions in some states are made whereby a minor can be relieved of legal non-age by the court. The statutory provisions as to majority follow: Alabama (21, except married females; over 18 may be relieved of non-age by the court), Alaska (21 except "all female persons when married according to law"), Arkansas (males 21, females 18), Arizona (males 21, females 18), California (males 21, females 18), Colorado (males 21, females 18), Connecticut (21 for all persons), Delaware (21 for both sexes), District of Columbia (males 21, females 18), Florida (21 non-age may be removed by court over 18), Georgia (males and females 21), Idaho (male 21, female 18), Illinois (male, 21 female 18), Indiana (21), Iowa (male 21, female 18, and also attains majority by marriage), Kansas (21 male, and female 18), Kentucky (21,) Louisiana (21), Maine (21), Maryland (males 21, females for most purposes 18), Massachusetts (21), Michigan (21), Minnesota (males 21, females 18), Mississippi (21), Missouri (male 21, female 18), Montana (males 21, females 18), Nebraska (males 21, females 18), marriage ends minority of female), Nevada (male 21, female 18), New Hampshire (both sexes come of age at 21), New Jersey (21), New Mexico (21, guardianship over both ceases on marriage), New York (21),

North Carolina (21), North Dakota (males 21, females 18), Ohio (male 21, females 18), Oklahoma (males 21, females 18), Oregon (males 21, females 18), Pennsylvania (21), Rhode Island (21), South Carolina (21), South Dakota (males 21, females 18), Tennessee (21), Texas (21, females 18 also becomes of age on marriage), Utah (males 21, females 18, all minors attain their majority on marriage), Vermont (male 21, female 18), Virginia (21 for both or when female marries), Washington (males 21, females 18), West Virginia all persons (21), Wisconsin (males 21, married women over 18), Wyoming (males 21, females 18 or until they marry).

(23) Summary

1. Federal legislation seems to be chiefly concerned with the alien child. Professor Stimson intimates that the Constitution may have to be amended to make Federal legislation possible (39.215).

2. Each state legislates for the children within its jurisdiction, and there is a wide diversity in the child-laws of the states.

3. It seems to be legally settled "that the legislature must be the sole judge of the expediency of such legislation" (39.215); and "the state is the ultimate parent of the child."

4. Parents and children have been deprived of their natural rights through the legislation of some states. "Indeed, in some Western states it would appear that the general disapproval of the neighbors of the method employed by parents in bringing up, nurturing, educating or controlling their children, is sufficient cause, for the state authorities to step in and disrupt the family by removing the children, even when themselves unwilling, from the home to some state or county institution. Any one who has worked much in public charities and had experience with that woeful creature, the institutionalized child, will realize the menace in such legislation" (39.337-8).

5. The laws on marriage and divorce are not uniform throughout the states.

6. No state has laws regulating the employment of pregnant mothers.

7. Nine states have no laws on the practice of midwifery.

8. Sixteen states have laws requiring cases of ophthalmia neonatorum to be reported. In Connecticut midwives and nurses are liable to a fine of $200 or imprisonment not to exceed six months or both for failure to report in writing within six hours to health officers the fact that one or both eyes of a child has become inflamed, swollen or reddened at anytime within two weeks after birth.

9. The Pennsylvania law relative to vital statistics has been adopted by twenty states and should become universal in this country.

10. The legal status of the illegitimate child closely approximates that of the legitimate child in some states.

11. The New Jersey law on "certified milk" is most comprehensive. (State of New Jersey, Laws of 1909.)

12. Seven states have no compulsory education law. "Throughout almost the entire United States some school attendance is compulsory from 7 or 8 years of age to 14" (36.1.293). Thirty-five states impose penalties on parents for neglect to comply with the compulsory education law.

13. Some states have certain laws, as for example school laws, that minimize the functions of the home, but also emphasize parental responsibility through penalizing provisions.

14. There is a tendency to coddle the child in some states and the absolute prohibition of corporal punishment in schools seems to be illustrative of the tendency.

15. Thirteen states have legal provisions on medical inspection of schools. Four are compulsory laws. They are the laws of Colorado, Massachusetts, New Jersey and Indiana (refers to Indianapolis only). The New Jersey law compels parents to remedy defects. Connecticut provides for the employment of school nurses.

16. The District of Columbia and seven states seem to have no laws on abandoment, desertion and non-support. Michigan has a law that provides if the parent is imprisoned, his earnings if any shall be paid to the family.

17. Sixteen states seem to have no laws regulating exhibitions and employments (not child-labor) of children.

18. Three states seem to have no laws on the publication or sale of obscene literature to children.

19. The District of Columbia and seven states are reported as having no laws governing the admittance of children to resorts.

20. The sale of intoxicants to children is prohibited generally throughout the country.

21. Ten states prohibit the manufacture and sale of cigarettes and cigarette papers. Massachusetts and other states prohibit the sale or gift of cigarettes to minors under eighteen years of age; at least fourteen states prohibit sale of tobacco, in any form, to minor under 16, and Kansas prohibits the sale of tobacco, opium or narcotic in any form to a minor under twenty-one years of age.

22. The legal age of consent to carnal intercourse for a female child varies from ten years in one state to eighteen years in thirteen states.

23. Twenty-three states have enacted Juvenile Court Laws. In the great majority of the states the jurisdiction of the Juvenile Court extends to children of 16 or 17 years of age; in two states to boys 17 and girls 18; in three states it is 18 for both; and in one state 19 for both. In 19 states and the District of Columbia parents or others contributing to the child's delinquency may be punished by a fine or imprisonment.

24. Nevada is the only state without child labor laws. Nineteen states forbid employment of children under 14 in factories, stores, offices, laundries, hotels, theatres and bowling alleys. In six states the labor of a child under 16, in 18 states of a child under 14 and in 8 states of a child under 12 in mines is forbidden. Twenty-three states forbid employment of children during school hours. Night work is prohibited in 23 states under 16, in 7 states under 14 and 2 states under 12. Legislation is tending to prohibit the industrial employment of a child under sixteen.

25. Tendencies that are common in the legislation of a group or groups of states have been noted already in these pages. Broader inferences at this time seen unwarranted.

26. Some states have laws that are inoperative because the legal machinery for their enforcement is lacking; other states, though legally well equipped, are not enforcing laws on their statute books. In every community much depends on the men behind the law. An automatic law has not been discovered in this study.

27. A common result of a disaster or a grave scandal is a new law, which is sometimes so necessary that the wonder is that its need was not met by earlier remedial legislation. Preventive laws should be enacted before great expenditure of life, health or morals make legislation imperative. When a National Children's Bureau is established in this country, preventive legislation will receive deserved attention. Apart from the laws relating to birth registration, midwives, ophthalmia neonatorum, milk, and medical inspection, strangely few preventive laws were found in the legislation of the states.

(24) SUGGESTIONS

To be an American citizen in this year of our Lord, one thousand nine hundred eleven, is the greatest privilege on earth—except one, that of the American child, the American citizen of to-morrow. The words of Dr. McCoy, who has given over thirty years to both study and practical work in child-welfare, follow: "Have you ever given a moment to this great thought? The young people of America are the heirs to all the values of the ages, and what a marvellous heritage that is. They are of a certainty, too, the men and women of destiny. In their hands in a short time will be all the interests of life and those that concern eternity. Religions, system of government, the armies and navies of the world that even now are shaking earth and sea and sky in thunderous throwing of the 'grim dice of the iron game,' the ceaseless breathings of the mighty engines of our industries, the passing ships of commerce, swift almost as the lightning from shore to shore, the courts, the schools, the philosophies, the arts, literature, the knowledge of natural forces and the power of their application—all will be theirs.

"The old or the middle-aged either have finished or are putting the last touches to their life-work. They are up or over the mountain and are going down into the soft glory of the sunset; but the young with glad shout are breasting the eastern hills with all the radiance of a new morning in their eyes and with the fires of a new purpose glowing in their hearts.

"And they must be fitted for their mission. For this reason the citizens come and deliberate together; for this reason they pile the public gold whereby to raise the school walls; for this reason they call scholarly men and women to guide and rule; for this reason have the book presses been groaning in labor this many a year; and for this reason are eager searches of enlightenment going down to the sea, and into the earth, and up in the sky, seeking new truths to bring back for their betterment" (30.11-12).

1. The first suggestion, the need of systematic legislation for children, will not meet with much opposition. Almost every one acknowledges the need of systematization which will preclude "crank laws" and make for sanity in child legislation.

2. The question how legislation for the children of the United States may be systematized is unsolved. The Federal right to legislate for the children of the several states is questioned under the present constitution. Until the Federal right is established by judicial decision or legislative amendment to the constitution, expediency must devise other methods.

A National Children's Bureau, which will do for the entire field of child-laws what the United States Bureau of Education is doing for school-laws, seems essential.

3. And a National Association for Child Legislation would be of inestimable assistance in the solution of the problem. Such an organization might serve to correlate the many independent organizations now urging child legislation. The union of the existing organizations would make a National

Association for Child Legislation a sturdy infant from birth, and the propaganda of the present organizations should become more effective throughout the entire country. A National Association for Child Legislation must be democratic. In this country no organization can succeed permanently and be controlled by any aristocracy—not even an aristocracy of learning. The success of the American Association for Labor Legislation, in one of its chosen fields, that of child-labor, might be studied to advantage by a National Association for Child Legislation.

4. To maintain even the semblance of the primacy of the home, legislation, that minimizes the functions of the home, should also emphasize the responsibility of parents. In some jurisdictions this tendency appears in the school laws and juvenile delinquency laws penalizing parents. It is a principle that should be kept in mind in child-legislation. Dr. Burnham writes: "A few pretty definite practical principles follow from this idea of the primacy of the home in education. They are enforced, too, apparently by the teachings of experience. We may formulate them as follows:

"First, the aim of school education is to supplement the education of the home.

"Second, the best of institutions is a poor substitute for a good home. Other things being equal, put the delinquent or neglected child in a home rather than a school.

"Third, charitable institutions are likely to be successful in the degree in which they approximate in their management the conditions of home life.

"Fourth, schools and other institutions should not as a rule usurp functions that belong to the home. In case this is desirable, it should be done in such a way that it will not be permanently necessary to do so.

"Fifth, teachers should always recognize the authority, the responsibility, and the general expert character of parents in the education of their own children. The numerous exceptions to this can be treated all the better by one who recognizes this general truth. On the whole, perhaps we may say that parents are not much more inefficient than we teachers, and certainly we can learn much from a child's parents in regard to the best methods for his education.

"Sixth, for the child's misdemeanors the parents as well as the child should be held responsible. This is coming to be recognized in child legislation, as, for example, in the Colorado law." (8.487.)

5. The welfare of the child and the parents demand that the home shall not be eliminated except as the last resort. The Pennsylvania Society is another that has come to share

"the modern economic thought that the normal condition of the child is in the home, even though the home be a poor one; the children often help their parents to reform, and the father and mother can in many cases be made to realize and feel . . . that upon them is the burden of responsibility to see that their children do not become in any sense a charge upon the community. Its belief in this theory is evidenced by the fact that in the year just closed 1,522 cases have been 'passed' over to what is technically known as 'supervision' cases, in which, perhaps, on the first visit the breaking up of the family seemed justifiable. Endeavors have, therefore, been made in every case to preserve the family as a whole. The results obtained by the visitors and agents in this work of reconstruction have been beyond belief" (31.143). And Dr. Chamberlain adds the following: "Indeed whatever can create a home environment, or something closely approximating to it, must be beneficial, as it is the most human method of 'reform' or 'regeneration'" (9.1.629).

6. As well intentioned but over-indulgent parents sometimes rear "the spoiled child," legislation that tends to coddle the child should be discussed for at least a year before its enactment.

7. The report of the Committee of the Commissioners on Uniform State Laws Entitled "An act relating to and regulating marriage and marriage licenses; and to promote uniformity between the state in reference thereto" (1.1130-1153), should be read by every legislator.

8. The recommendations of the Commissioners on Uniformity relative to migratory divorce and to divorce procedure and divorce from the bonds of marriage are deserving of serious consideration (39.323-324).

9. The "Act relating to desertion and non-support of wife by husband, or of children by either father or mother, and providing punishment therefor; and to promote uniformity between the states in reference thereto" (1.1179-1181), provides in Sec. VII for the payment "for the support of such wife, child or children, a sum equal to . . . for each day's hard labor performed by said person (the husband or father) so confined," and is an act that seems worthy of adoption throughout the Union.

10. Some statutory provision should be made in all states relative to the employment of mothers before and after childbirth.

11. Legislation should be enacted making it criminal to advertise any illegitimate child for adoption without first receiving permission from the State Board of Charity.

12. The school age should be raised so that any child under seventeen, who is neither attending school regularly or working, could be required to attend some school. Industrial schools or special schools would be required for this class. While statistics from a single city are far from establishing a norm, the writer's study of Juvenile Delinquency in Worcester, Massachusetts, may be of interest in this connection.[1] From June 1, 1907, to April 1, 1910, sixty-five per cent. of the boys and sixty-eight per cent. of the girls arrested for delinquency were between fourteen and seventeen years of age. There were 493 boys and 32 girls. Of the boys, 67 were attending school, 191 were working, and 236 or 49.7% were neither attending school or working, "just loafing around." Among the girls 22 girls or 68.7% were also "loafing," 9 girls were working and only one girl in the group was attending school. Both the boys and girls who were "loafing" were before the court for the more serious offenses.

Relative to the need of day truant schools in this country, in the same study 85% of the Worcester boys and girls in the Lyman School at Westboro and the State Industrial School at Lancaster stated that a connection existed between their own truancy and their own delinquency; and the majority of delinquents of school age studied were also truants.

13. Each child attending school should receive a physical examination at least once a year under the direction of an occulist, aurist, physician and dentist, and legislation should be enacted compelling parents to take reasonable remedial measures.

14. Laws should be amended to enable authorities to have supervision over all female school offenders until their majority is reached. In some jurisdiction this class of girls must be released at the age of fourteen and they return to environments that are sometimes especially dangerous at that age. These girls are really "neglected children." Relative to this age, President Hall writes: "In fine, puberty for a girl is like floating down a broadening river into an open sea. Landmarks recede, the water deepens and changes in its nature, there are new and strange forms of life, the currents are more complex, and the phenomena of tides make new conditions and new dangers. The bark is frail, liable to be tossed by storms of feeling, at the mercy of wind and wave, and if without chart and compass and simple rules of navigation, aimless drifting in the darkness of ignorance, amidst both rocks and shoals, may make of the weak or unadvised, wrecks or castaways" (17.507-8). Again President Hall says, "Caldo

[1]Juvenile Delinquency in Worcester, Massachusetts, by Thomas C. Carrigan, No. 54, 562, Library Clark University, Univ. Case C. 316.

finds that most prostitutes fall between the ages of fifteen and eighteen, which he terms the period of sexual vulnerability toward which chief effort should be directed." (17.431.)

15. Parents, when of sufficient means, should pay a reasonable amount for the support of their delinquent children confined in corrective State Institutions.

16. Superintendent of Institution, Chief of Police, Superintendent of Schools and Juvenile Probation Officer of the child's city or town, or a majority of them should have power at any time to release from any corrective institution any child not committed for a felony.

17. In order to give an opportunity to the working public, which is unable without loss of pay to meet the school authorities during the day, legislation should require the following offices in all cities to be open at least one evening in each week:

(1) Office of the superintendent of schools
(2) Office of the truant officer
(3) Office of the principal of all large grammar schools.

18. To better acquaint the teacher with the child's disadvantages out of school, legislation should provide that each teacher should be allowed to visit, *during the hours school is in session,* the home of each pupil at least once a month during the school-year. Teachers, generally, are overworked and underpaid, and the writer would be the last to suggest the imposition of another "fad." The suggestion on this page was born from investigating the unheralded and noble work of a woman principal. That her visits to the homes of her pupils have unmeasureably benefited both pupils and parents, many can testify; and that her teaching has steadily gained in common-sense tempered by sympathetic insight is the report of an expert, the writer has not the honor of her acquaintance. The divorce of the school and home is almost absolute in many places. Rarely any mother visits the school except to discuss discipline in some extraordinary case. Fathers are seldom visitors, and that is not surprising when it is remembered that most fathers would have to lose a part of a day's wages to visit school. The home and school are strangers too often as far as parents and teachers are concerned. This suggestion aims at making parents and teachers acquaintances, and then friends, in hope that both will mutually profit.

19. Records of all absences without excuse should be kept by every principal.

20. Every principal should be supplied with the name, age and address, and the school attending of every child of school age in his district.

21. Co-operation of school and police departments on truancy seem advisable in some places..

22. A juvenile census should be taken annually in cities and towns.

23. Every city should establish a free employment bureau for the purpose of securing positions for children above the school age, who need employment. To-day much is being said and written about vocational training. In most cities, when the working boy and girl, no matter how deserving, leave school, they must find their own positions and they generally take what they can get. This tends to make "misfits." The suggested bureau could have on file the names of employers in shops, stores, etc., who want worthy young people in their establishments. Think of the moral lever that the recommendation of such a bureau might be to the minds of the older school children, who are looking forward to "a good job." If diplomas, medals, etc., have been effective in moral education, it seems that the prospect of "a good job" at the end of school-life might be made at least as potent with the American child.

Bibliography

The first citation, on page 1, is followed by these figures (19.2.298), which are to be interpreted:—19. Hoar, George F. Autobiography of Seventy Years. 2. Volume II. 298. Page 298. This will serve as a key to the other references.

1. American Bar Association. Report of the 33rd Annual Meeting, Baltimore, 1910. 1197 p.
2. American and English Encyclopedia of Law. Northport, Long Island, N. Y., 1896. 31 volumes.
3. Baker, Harvey H. What constitutes a neglected child under the Massachusetts Statutes. Boston, 1911. Address. 8 p.
4. Bardeen, C. W. A Manual of Common School Law, Syracuse, N. Y., 1910. 496 p.
5. Bayles, George J. Woman and The Law. New York, 1901. 274 p.
6. Black, Henry C. Handbook on the Construction and Interpretation of the Laws. St. Paul, Minn., 1896. 499 p.
7. Blackstone, Sir William. Commentaries on the Laws of England (Sharswood's Edition). Philadelphia, 1875. 2 volumes, 531 p., 739 p.
8. Burnham, William H. The Home in relation to the other Factors in Education. *The Pedagogical Seminary,* December, 1909. Volume XVI, No. 4, pp. 485-91.
9. Chamberlain, Alexander F. Criminality in Children. Monroe's Cyclopædia of Education, Volume I, pp. 625-30. New York, 1911.
10. Clark, Hannah B. Sanitary Legislation affecting Schools in the United States. U. S. Commissioner's Report, 1893-4, Volume 2, Chapter X, pp. 1300-1349.
11. Cyclopedia of Law and Procedure. (Cyc.) Volume I (published 1901). Volume XXXVI (published 1910). 4 volumes forth coming. The American Law Book Company, New York.

12. DWIGHT, EDWIN W. Medical Jurisprudence, Philadelphia, 1903, 249 p.

12a. DUTTON and SNEDDEN. The Administration of Public Education in United States, New York, 1908, 598 p.

13. EWELL, MARSHALL D. A Manual of Medical Jurisprudence (Second Edition), Boston, 1909, 407 p.

14. GRAY, JOHN C. The Nature and Sources of the Law. New York, 1909. 332. p.

15. GREENE, MARY A. The Woman's Manual of Law. Boston, 1902. 284 p.

16. GULICK and AYERS. Medical Inspection of Schools. New York, 1908. 276 p.

17. HALL, G. STANLEY. Adolescence, Its Psychology and its Relations to Physiology, Anthropology, Sociology, Sex, Crime, Religion and Education. New York, 1904. 2 volumes, 589 p. 784 p.

18. HART, HASTINGS H. HOMER, THOMAS J. ABBOTT, GRACE. Juvenile Court Laws in the United States. Summarized, New York, 1910. 150 p.

19. HOAR, GEORGE F. Autobiography of Seventy Years. New York, 1903. 2 volumes, 434 p. 493 p.

20. HOCHHEIMER, LEWIS. The Law Regulating the Custody of Infants. Baltimore, 1899. 148 p.

21. —— ——. Manual of the Maryland Society for the Protection of Children. Baltimore, 1909. 28 p.

22. HOLMES, O. W., JR. The Common Law. Boston, 1881. 422 p.

23. Illinois State Board of Health. Summary of the Laws and Regulations Governing the Practice of Medicine in the States and Territories of the United States, Monthly Bulletin, October, 1910. 402-31 p.

24. International Labor Office. Quarterly Bulletin, American Association for Labor Legislation, John B. Andrews, Secretary, Metropolitan Tower, New York City.

25. KEEZER, FRANK. The Law of Marriage and Divorce (with a synopsis of the Statutes of the various States). Boston, 1906. 609 p.

26. KELLEY, FLORENCE. On some Changes in the Legal Status of the Child since Blackstone. The International Review. August, 1882, pp. 83-95.

27. LEE, GUY CARLETON. Historical Jurisprudence. New York, 1900. 517 p.

28. LEWIS, JOHN. Sutherland's Statutes and Statutory Construction (second edition). Chicago, 1904. 2 volumes, 603 pages, 1416 p.

29. LOEB, ISIDOR. The Legal Property Relations of Married Parties. New York, 1900. 200 p.

30. MCCOY, JOHN J. The Playground Movement. The Catholic Educational Review, Brookland, D. C. Volume I, No. I. January, 1911. pp. 10-23.

31. MCREA, ROSWELL C. The Humane Movement. New York, 1910. 444 p.

32. MONROE, PAUL. Cyclopædia of Education. Volume I, New York, 1911. Compulsory Attendance, etc.

32a. MORRIS, M. F. An Introduction to the History of Development of Law. Washington, 1909. 315 p.

33. SCHOULER, JAMES. Laws of Wills and Administration. Boston, 1910. 648 p.

34. SCOTT, LAURA. Child Labor—Summary of Laws in force in 1910. Legislative Review, No. 5. American Association for Labor Legislation. New York, 1910. 139 p.

34a. SHIELDS, THOMAS E. The Making and Unmaking of a Dullard. Washington, 1910. 296 p.

35. SNEDDEN, DAVID S. Administration and Educational Work of American Juvenile Reform Schools. New York, 1907. 206 p.
36. —— ——. Compulsory Attendance, Monroe's Cyclopædia of Education, Volume 1, New York, 1911. 285-95 p.
37. STIMSON, FREDERIC J. American Statute Law. Boston, 1886. 2 volumes, 779 p. 622 pages.
38. —— ——. American Statute Law. First Supplement, Boston, 1888. 122 pages
39. —— ——. Popular Law-making. New York, 1910. 390 p.
40. SWETT, MAUD. Summary of Labor Laws in Force, 1909, Woman's Work, Legislative Review, No. 4. American Association for Labor Legislation, New York, 1910. 16 p.
41. TAYLOR, HANNIS. The Science of Jurisprudence. New York, 1908. 676 p.
42. The American Medical Association. The Present Situation in Vital Statistics Legislation (with model bill on vital Statistics). Bi-monthly Bulletin, Volume 6, No. I, September 15, 1910. Chicago. 31 p.
43. The American Medical Association. Report of the Committee on Ophthalmia Neonatorum. Journal of the American Medical Association, Volume 52, p. 2047-2056, Chicago, June 19, 1909.
44. UNITED STATES COMMISSIONER OF EDUCATION. Report for year ended June 30, 1910. Washington, 1910. Volume I, 622 p.
45. WILBUR, CRESSY L. Report of Committee on Birth Registration, Proceedings of the American Association for Study and Prevention of Infant Mortality. Baltimore, 1910.
46. WILCOX, S. M. Legal Rights of Children, United States Bureau of Education, No. 3. Washington, 1880. 96 p.
47. WRIGHT, CARROLL D. The Apprenticeship System in its Relation to Industrial Education. United States Bureau of Education Bulletin No. 6. Washington, 1908. 116 p.

THE CHILDREN'S CHARTER, 1930

U.S. Children's Bureau

THE CHILDREN'S CHARTER

PRESIDENT HOOVER'S WHITE HOUSE CONFERENCE ON CHILD HEALTH AND PROTECTION, RECOGNIZING THE RIGHTS OF THE CHILD AS THE FIRST RIGHTS OF CITIZENSHIP, PLEDGES ITSELF TO THESE AIMS FOR THE CHILDREN OF AMERICA

I For every child spiritual and moral training to help him to stand firm under the pressure of life

II For every child understanding and the guarding of his personality as his most precious right

III For every child a home and that love and security which a home provides; and for that child who must receive foster care, the nearest substitute for his own home

IV For every child full preparation for his birth, his mother receiving prenatal, natal, and postnatal care; and the establishment of such protective measures as will make child-bearing safer

V For every child health protection from birth through adolescence, including: periodical health examinations and, where needed, care of specialists and hospital treatment; regular dental examinations and care of the teeth; protective and preventive measures against communicable diseases; the insuring of pure food, pure milk, and pure water

VI For every child from birth through adolescence, promotion of health, including health instruction and a health program, wholesome physical and mental recreation, with teachers and leaders adequately trained

VII For every child a dwelling-place safe, sanitary, and wholesome, with reasonable provisions for privacy; free from conditions which tend to thwart his development; and a home environment harmonious and enriching

VIII For every child a school which is safe from hazards, sanitary, properly equipped, lighted, and ventilated. For younger children nursery schools and kindergartens to supplement home care

IX For every child a community which recognizes and plans for his needs, protects him against physical dangers, moral hazards, and disease; provides him with safe and wholesome places for play and recreation; and makes provision for his cultural and social needs

X For every child an education which, through the discovery and development of his individual abilities, prepares him for life; and through training and vocational guidance prepares him for a living which will yield him the maximum of satisfaction

XI For every child such teaching and training as will prepare him for successful parenthood, home-making, and the rights of citizenship; and, for parents, supplementary training to fit them to deal wisely with the problems of parenthood

XII For every child education for safety and protection against accidents to which modern conditions subject him — those to which he is directly exposed and those which, through loss or maiming of his parents, affect him indirectly

XIII For every child who is blind, deaf, crippled, or otherwise physically handicapped, and for the child who is mentally handicapped, such measures as will early discover and diagnose his handicap, provide care and treatment, and so train him that he may become an asset to society rather than a liability. Expenses of these services should be borne publicly where they cannot be privately met

XIV For every child who is in conflict with society the right to be dealt with intelligently as society's charge, not society's outcast; with the home, the school, the church, the court and the institution when needed, shaped to return him whenever possible to the normal stream of life

XV For every child the right to grow up in a family with an adequate standard of living and the security of a stable income as the surest safeguard against social handicaps

XVI For every child protection against labor that stunts growth, either physical or mental, that limits education, that deprives children of the right of comradeship, of play, and of joy

XVII For every rural child as satisfactory schooling and health services as for the city child, and an extension to rural families of social, recreational, and cultural facilities

XVIII To supplement the home and the school in the training of youth, and to return to them those interests of which modern life tends to cheat children, every stimulation and encouragement should be given to the extension and development of the voluntary youth organizations

XIX To make everywhere available these minimum protections of the health and welfare of children, there should be a district, county, or community organization for health, education, and welfare, with full-time officials, coördinating with a state-wide program which will be responsive to a nationwide service of general information, statistics, and scientific research. This should include:

(*a*) Trained, full-time public health officials, with public health nurses, sanitary inspection, and laboratory workers
(*b*) Available hospital beds
(*c*) Full-time public welfare service for the relief, aid, and guidance of children in special need due to poverty, misfortune, or behavior difficulties, and for the protection of children from abuse, neglect, exploitation, or moral hazard

FOR EVERY CHILD THESE RIGHTS, REGARDLESS OF RACE, OR COLOR, OR SITUATION, WHEREVER HE MAY LIVE UNDER THE PROTECTION OF THE AMERICAN FLAG

CHILDREN AND THE LAW

Henry H. Foster, Jr.
and
Doris Jonas Freed

Children And The Law

HENRY H. FOSTER, JR. AND DORIS JONAS FREED*

(The following article is reprinted with permission from the latest volume of the ANNUAL SURVEY OF AMERICAN LAW. It is the first article ever to appear in the ANNUAL SURVEY on the law as it affects children.)

The past year has produced an unusual amount of ferment and public concern regarding children and the law. Child custody became a subject of widespread discussion by the mass media due to the Iowa decision, *Painter* v. *Bannister*.[1] Adoption law and placement policies were subjected to extensive editorial comment due to the *Liuni* case in New York.[2] So-called "battered child" statutes were enacted in several states, leaving only Hawaii and the District of Columbia without such legislation.[3] New York by statute adopted the Wisconsin device of providing for guardians in matrimonial actions to protect the interests of children.[4] The most important case in the history of the juvenile court movement was argued before the United States Supreme Court.[5]

---

*Henry H. Foster, Jr. is a Professor of Law at New York University School of Law. Doris Jonas Freed is a Member of the Maryland and New York bars.

1. 140 N.W.2d 152 (Iowa), *cert denied*, 385 U.S. 949 (1966).

2. In re St. John, 51 Misc. 2d 96, 272 N.Y.S.2d 817 (Family Ct. 1966), rev'd, sub. nom Fitzsimmons v. Liuni, 26 App. Div. 2d 980, 274 N.Y.S.2d 798 (3d Dep't 1966). See also N.Y. Times, Nov. 11, 1966, p. 46, col. 5.

3. For a discussion of the problem, see Foster & Freed, *The Battered Child*, 3 TRIAL 33 (1966-67); Hansen, *Child Abuse Legislation and the Interdisciplinary Approach*, 52 A.B.A.J. 734 (1966); McCoid, *The Battered Child and Other Assaults Upon the Family*, 50 MINN. L. REV. 1 (1965) Paulsen, Parker & Adelman, *Child Abuse Reporting Laws*, 34 GEO. WASH. L. REV. 482 (1966).

4. See N.Y. Divorce Reform Law § 215-c, which in effect provides that special guardians may be appointed in matrimonial actions to protect the interests of minors, handicapped or incompetent children.

5. Application of Gault, 99 Ariz. 181, 407 P.2d 760 (1965), rev'd and remanded with direction, 87 Sup. Ct. 1428 (1967). Since this article was set in type the case has been decided in favor of requiring constitutional due process in juvenile proceedings.

Recent concern about poverty and family law has led to a re-evaluation of the policies and administration of welfare law, especially as it relates to children.[6]

I

Child Custody

Since the time of Solomon, judges have quite properly regarded the resolution of disputed custody cases as a most difficult task. Fortunately, conscientiousness and humility ordinarily mark such decisions.[7] Occasionally, however, prejudice or ignorance become evident where there is an abuse of judicial discretion. Such may occur when standards or guidelines are injudiciously applied as absolute rules or there is insufficient data for intelligent judgment. In the past, judicial error most frequently has been due to a blind acceptance of the shibboleth that "blood is thicker than water" or an automatic and sentimental preference for the mother over the father whatever the circumstances of the case.[8]

It is perfectly obvious that natural parents ordinarily should be preferred over strangers and that usually the mother is the best custodian for young children. But neither proposition is inevitably and unvariably true. If, for example, parent substitutes have had custody for a substantial period of time, the best interests of the child may be substantially impaired by a transfer of custody. Nonetheless, the usual rule in the United States is that the natural patient not only is to be preferred over a "stranger" but that such preference is automatic barring parental unfitness.[9] Moreover, it is usually held that, at least in the case of children of "tender years," the mother prevails over the father, even though the "best interests" test theoretically affords each parent an equal claim to custody.[10]

6. See ten Broeck, *California's Duel System of Family Law,* 16 STAN. L. REV. 257, 900 (1964); Symposium, *Law of the Poor,* 54 CAL. L. REV. 319 (1966); 17 STAN. L. REV. 614 (1965).

7. "A judge agonizes more about reaching the right result in a contested custody issue than about any other type of decision he renders." Botein, *Trial Judge* 273 (1952).

8. See Foster & Freed, *Child Custody,* 39 N.Y.U.L. REV. 423, 615 (1964).

9. *Id.* at 425.

10. Although in New York, for example, DOM. REL. LAW § 70 provides that in habeas corpus suits for child custody there shall be no prima facie right to the

Since, in the past, questionable custody decisions usually have been those where insufficient regard was shown for the best interests of the child, it is indeed ironic that the custody *cause celebre* of recent years involves an overcompensation for the more common error. The Iowa court in *Painter* v. *Bannister*[11] purported to make the best interests of four year old Mark the controlling consideration in a custody contest between the father and the maternal grandparents. However, in avoiding a mechanical application of the usual preference for the natural parent over a stranger, the Iowa court made a rigid application of the "best interests" test without regard for the fact that Mark had been placed with the grandparents temporarily until the father re-established a suitable home. In effect, one absolute or inflexible rule replaced another due to a failure to give sufficient weight to both the father's interest in his son and the circumstances of the placement with the grandparents.

Moreover, in addition to erroneously treating a guideline as an inflexible rule, the Iowa court may be faulted for its excessive reliance upon the testimony and conjectures of a child psychologist who was subjected to inept direct and cross-examination. Again, the more common judicial omission is a failure to receive or sufficiently consider the evaluation and recommendations of experts rather than an uncritical acceptance of such testimony.[12] The Iowa court (in contrast to the trial judge who characterized the expert testimony as "exaggerated") abandoned that healthy skepticism.

Of course, the most regrettable aspect of *Painter* was the odious

---

custody of the children but the court shall determine what is for the best interests of the child and § 240 provides that as between parents "there shall be no prima facie right to the custody of the child in either parent," in practice the mother usually prevails where daughters or children of tender years are involved. See FOSTER & FREED, LAW AND THE FAMILY—NEW YORK, § 29:5 (1966); Oster, *Custody Proceeding,* 5 J. FAM. L. 21 (1965).

11. 140 N.W.2d 152 (Iowa 1966). Compare Foster & Freed, *Child Custody,* 39 N.Y.U.L. REV. 615, 628-629 (1964), where it is concluded that the welfare of the child should be the primary factor in awarding custody and that "any person who has had de facto custody of the child in a stable and wholesome home and is a fit and proper person shall prima facie be entitled to an award of custody." The above guideline was not advocated as a rigid inflexible rule and was prefaced by the statement that "custody may be awarded to persons other than the father or mother whenever such serves the best interests of the child."

12. See Foster & Freed, *Child Custody,* 39 N.Y.U.L. REV. 615, at 615-22 (1964).

comparison of rural Iowa with the "bohemian" atmosphere of the San Francisco Bay area. The court forgot the adage "the Godly trust not their own righteousness." The language and reasoning of the opinion were so extreme that it is easy to lose sight of the fact that perhaps Mark's best interests *were* served by keeping him with his grandparents. But even though such may be true, it must be reiterated that both the interests of the father and the circumstances surrounding the placement with the grandparents should be taken into account.

The conclusion that the Iowa court was correct in giving substantial weight to the best interests of the child, albeit incorrect in giving insufficient weight to other relevant factors, is reinforced by an examination of Iowa custody decisions subsequent to the *Painter* case. In *Alingh* v. *Alingh*,[13] the Iowa court was obviously correct in its decision that the best interests of two children controlled and that custody should be awarded to the paternal grandparents rather than the father. After a mentally ill mother had physically abused them, the children in question had been turned over to the grandparents who had cared for them nine or ten years. Similarly, a twelve year old boy's "best interests" were held paramount to the mother's claim in *Halstead* v. *Halstead*,[14] where the child had lived with his paternal grandparents for ten years, was happy and well adjusted and preferred to remain with them in the home they provided rather than moving in with their estranged mother and her new husband.

The factors which distinguish the later Iowa cases from *Painter* v. *Bannister* are (1) the length of time the child had been with parent substitutes, (2) the circumstances and conditions of the initial placement and the conditions agreed upon for its termination, and (3) the reasonableness of the inference that another change in custody would be harmful to the child. Although the above variables should not be assigned a precise weight, the *Painter* case is disturbing because of the cumulative effect achieved when one weighs such factors. The placement was temporary until the father found a suitable home. He requested Mark's return within a relatively short period, and although a child psychologist speculated about the grandfather having become a "father figure" and the harmful effects a return to the father might occasion, the undeniable fact was that Mark, after an initial period of

13. 144 N.W.2d 134 (Iowa 1966).
14. 144 N.W.2d 861 (Iowa 1966).

poor adjustment, had shown himself capable of adaptation to a different milieu.

To disagree with the result in *Painter* v. *Bannister* is not to reject the great weight that should be given to the best interests of the child. In many cases, the child's best interests will coincide with his removal from unfit parents. *In re Morrison,*[15] another Iowa decision, terminated the parental rights in three small children because their best interests required their removal from an extremely bad home. Both parents had been diagnosed as "emotional unstable personalities," and had long records of amorous and criminal escapades. Although the children in question were clean, well fed and attended church regularly, the father was an ex-convict and the mother had gone through a series of love affairs. The household was in a turmoil and the marriage was marked by constant friction, physical violence and infidelities. It makes little difference whether the termination of the parental rights of such parents is rationalized in terms of "best interests" or "unfitness."

The fact that *Painter* v. *Bannister* is unique among custody disputes between parents and strangers, is shown by recent decisions from Alabama,[16] Connecticut,[17] Massachusetts[18] and Nebraska[19] all of which, despite the placement of children for a substantial length of time with "strangers" such as grandparents, ruled in favor of the parent. These cases, applying the "unfit parent" test, gave insufficient attention to the best interests of the children in question. The Nebraska decision in *Raymond* v. *Cotner,*[20] although it did not receive the publicity accorded to *Painter* v. *Bannister,* is an egregious example of disregard of the wishes and best interests of the child. A father who had not had any meaningful contact with his eleven year old daughter since her birth, was awarded custody in preference to maternal grandparents, the only real "parents" the child had ever known. The parents had been divorced shortly after the daughter's birth, and the mother had moved in with her parents. Because she worked, they raised the

15. 144 N.W.2d 97 (Iowa 1966). For other extreme cases where a mother lost custody, see Commonwealth v. Powers, 421 Pa. 2, 219 A.2d 460 (1966); Barrie v. Costello, 401 S.W.2d 707 (Tex. Civ. App. 1966).

16. Kewish v. Brothers, 181 So.2d 900 (Ala. 1966).

17. Stiwinter v. Roberts, 153 Conn. 240, 215 A.2d 413 (1965).

18. Ridgeway v. Cels, 214 N.E.2d 31 (Mass. 1966).

19. Ball v. Ball, 180 Neb. 145, 141 N.W.2d 449 (1966).

20. 175 Neb. 158, 120 N.W.2d 892 (1963).

child. The mother was killed when the child was eleven and the father, then remarried, sought and obtained custody. The daughter testified that she had never seen her father and wanted to remain with her grandparents. Under such circumstances, a little dose of *Painter* v. *Bannister* would have been beneficial for the majority of the Nebraska court.[21]

While on the one hand, courts should not regard a child as chattel, adopting neither a property right nor a "natural right" approach to custody determinations,[22] on the other hand, natural parents have paramount rights and responsibilities as to their children. Major difficulties arise, where, because of association and affection for a substantial period of time, custodians have become real "parents." In such situations, if the contest is between "strangers," courts ordinarily give decisive weight to the best interests factor and are extremely reluctant to change the child's environment.[23] However, where a natural parent seeks to take custody from some other relative or stranger, ordinarily the parent will prevail unless "unfit."[24] In the case of the father, abandonment, nonsupport, prior disinterest in the child's welfare, immorality and criminality may be sufficient to deprive him of custody.[25] In the case of the mother, relinquishment of her claim to custody and in some instances immorality or criminality may work a similar deprivation.[26] Other courts, however, insist that immorality, alcoholism or similar unfitness must be directly detrimental to the child and that

21. See the vigorous dissent by White, C.J., *id.* at 166, 120 N.W.2d at 896.

22. See FOSTER & FREED, LAW AND THE FAMILY—NEW YORK, § 29:14 (1966); Simpson, *The Unfit Parent,* 39 U. DEL. L.J. 347 (1962); Note, *Alternatives to "Parental Right" in Child Custody Disputes Involving Third Parties,* 73 YALE L.J. 151 (1963).

23. For example, see Whetsell v. Wallizer, 241 Md. 711, 216 A.2d 571 (1966), and In re Wheeler, 26 App. Div. 2d 616, 271 N.Y.S.2d 840 (4th Dep't 1966).

24. Compare Cox v. Young, 405 S.W.2d 430 (Tex. Civ. App. 1966) (transfers custody after mother's death from stepfather to natural father), with Clark v. Jelinek, 414 P.2d 892 (Idaho 1966) (stepfather prevailed over father who had abandoned and refused to support his children).

25. Clark v. Jelinek, 144 P.2d 892 (Idaho 1966).

26. See Commonwealth v. Powers, 421 Pa. 2, 219 A.2d 460 (1966); 401 S.W.2d 707 (Tex. Civ. App. 1966). See also Peck v. Shierling, 222 Ga. 60, 148 S.E.2d 491 (1966), reversing an award of custody of a nine year old to his aunt and uncle and remanding for purpose and ascertaining whether mother had lost her parental rights by abandonment and because she was unfit.

"unfitness" must relate to the parent-child relationship and the child's upbringing.[27]

Perhaps the most sensible rule is indicated by the Illinois court in *Nichols* v. *Nichols*,[28] where it was held that in a custody dispute between the father and a married daughter over four minor children, the father should prevail unless his parental rights had been forfeited or the best interests of the children required their removal from him. In any event, the decision in *Painter* v. *Bannister* makes it abundantly clear that a weighing and balancing process is required and that no single factor should be isolated so as to automatically determine custody. Moreover, at least where children are old enough to express a sound preference, their wishes as to custody should be respected and given great weight unless their choice would clearly be detrimental to their best interests.[29]

There are a number of recent cases where the mother lost custody, usually to the father, either because she was found to be an unfit parent or due to extraordinary circumstances.[30] Also there are several cases

27. See Oster, *supra* note 10. See also Simpson, *supra* note 22.

28. 70 Ill. App. 2d 376, 216 N.E.2d 690 (1966).

29. See Herron v. Herron, 141 N.W.2d 562 (Iowa 1966), holding that wishes of seven, eight and ten year old children should be given little if any weight; State ex rel. Waslie v. Waslie, 143 N.W.2d 634 (Minn. 1966), holding that testimony as to preference of sixteen year old should be secured in custody dispute between parents and grandparents.

30. Bailey v. Bailey, 3 Ariz. App. 138, 412 P.2d 480 (1966) (remarried father prevailed over mother); Cochran v. Cochran, 49 Cal. Rptr. 670 (Dist. Ct. App. 1966) (father had *de facto* custody for three years); Crow v. Crow, 49 Hawaii 257, 414 P.2d 82 (1966) (custody transferred from mother to father because mother had denied visitation rights and poisoned child's mind against father); Froman v. Froman, 218 N.E.2d 808 (Ill. App. 1966) (alcoholic mother neglected children); Hahn v. Hahn, 69 Ill. App. 2d 302, 216 N.E.2d 229 (1966) (adulterous mother); Herron v. Herron, 141 N.W.2d 562 (Iowa 1966) (remarried father prevailed over mother who had men visiting home); Whisman v. Whisman, 401 S.W.2d 583 (Ky. 1966) (ten year old boy transferred to remarried father from mother's crowded home where she had two illegitimate children); Poole v. Arculeer, 190 So. 2d 75 (La. Ct. App. 1966) (two young daughters awarded to father where mother had "a total disregard for her own reputation as well as that of her family"); Duplantis v. Bueto, 186 So. 2d 424 (La. Ct. App. 1966) (mother had relinquished custody to father for over four years); Camarata v. Schroeder, 184 So. 2d 75 (La. Ct. App. 1966) (adulterous mother); Craft v. Craft, 184 So. 2d 758 (La. Ct. App. 1966) (mentally unstable mother); Portman v. Portman, 181 So. 2d 429 (La. Ct. App. 1965) (adulterous mother); Andrews v. Andrews, 242 Md. 143, 218 A.2d 194 (1966) (mother relinquished custody); Hodge v. Hodge, 186 So. 2d 748 (Miss. 1966) (adulterous mother);

which held that the mother prevailed, again usually over the father, even though an award of custody to her may not have been in the child's best interests.[31] These cases exemplify that rather than both parents having equal claims to custody, the mother's claim is superior unless she is an unfit person or has relinquished *de facto* custody of her children. Concentration on her claim or right to custody tends to downgrade the child's-best-interest-test which, according to the avowed rules, is applicable.[32]

In the case of illegitimate children, ordinarily the mother is viewed as the natural guardian. It is unusual for the natural father to seek custody. However, in a recent New York Family Court decision,[33] the natural father was awarded custody of an illegitimate child, when the court announced the abolition of the presumption in favor of the natural mother's right to custody and ruled that the father's claim was superior under the facts of the case. The mother, from age thirteen, had given birth to several illegitimate children, showed no signs of mother love, and in general was an unfit parent. California followed

---

Copenhaver v. Copenhaver, 402 S.W.2d 612 (Mo. Ct. App. 1966) (mother in poor health); Wood v. Wood, 400 S.W.2d 431 (Mo. Ct. App. 1966) (mother worked and had to leave children alone with maid); Goodman v. Goodman, 180 Neb. 83, 141 N.W.2d 445 (1966) (unfit mother); Sweet v. Sweet, 25 App. Div. 2d 805, 269 N.Y.S.2d 530 (3d Dep't 1966) (permanent custody of four children continued in father); In re Godinez v. Russo, 49 Misc. 2d 66, 266 N.Y.S.2d 636 (Family Ct. 1966) (custody of illegitimate child awarded to natural father); State v. Winters, 413 P.2d 425 (Ore. 1966) (parental rights of mother in three illegitimate children transferred where mother unfit); Dannelly v. Dannelly, 405 S.W.2d 141 (Tex. Civ. App. 1966) (mentally ill mother); Shannon v. Newman, 400 S.W.2d 861 (Tex. Civ. App. 1966) (alcoholic stepfather); Bukovich v. Bukovich, 399 S.W.2d 528 (Tex. 1966) (modification action); Todd v. Superior Ct. 414 P.2d 605 (Wash. 1966) (mentally ill mother); Larson v. Larson, 30 Wis. 2d 291, 140 N.W.2d 230 (1966) (adulterous mother).

31. Recent cases where mother prevailed over father: Murley v. Murley, 24 Ark. 70, 398 S.W.2d 68 (1966); Moffit v. Moffit, 51 Cal. Rptr. 683 (Dist. Ct. App. 1966); Julian v. Julian, 188 So. 2d 896 (Fla. Dist. Ct. App. 1966); Wills v. Glunts, 222 Ga. 122, 149 S.E.2d 106 (1966); Jones v. Sutton, 388 S.W.2d 596 (Ky. 1966), 54 Ky. L.J. 811 (1966); Garbee v. Garbee, 400 S.W.2d 193 (Mo. Ct. App. 1966); Kimble v. Kimble, 399 S.W.2d 630 (Mo. Ct. App. 1966) (wishes of twelve year old daughter to live with father disregarded); Moyer v. Moyer, 206 Va. 899, 147 S.E.2d 148 (1966); King v. King, 29 Wis. 2d 586, 139 N.W.2d 635 (1966).

32. For a questionable decision, see Wise v. Gillette, 408 P.2d 806 (Idaho 1965).

33. In re Godinez v. Russo, 49 Misc. 2d 66, 266 N.Y.S.2d 636 (Family Ct. 1966).

the usual rule and awarded custody of an illegitimate child to her mother rather than to her aunt and uncle,[34] but Pennsylvania granted permanent custody of an illegitimate child to foster parents where the mother had surrendered the child several times and had been guilty of neglect when she did have custody.[35] The mother or foster parents of illegitimate children usually prevail in custody disputes with state or voluntary agencies.[36]

From the standpoint of convincing evidence to overcome judicial preference for the mother or for parents over strangers, abandonment or relinquishment of the child is the strongest countervailing factor,[37] though serious physical abuse[38] may have equal force. Immorality,[39] mental illness[40] or physical disability including alcoholism,[41] are less certain factors, depending in some measure upon whether it is an urban or rural court that is determining custody. An adulterous mother, for example, may or may not be awarded custody, depending upon the particular court and also upon whether she was promiscuous or brought "uncles" into the home.[42] Relatedly, courts are inclined to accord vis-

---

34. Miller v. Hudmon, 53 Cal. Reptr. 211 (Dist. Ct. App. 1966).

35. Commonwealth ex rel. Gunther v. Powers, 421 Pa. 2, 219 A.2d 460 (1966.)

36. See Olney v. Gorden, 240 Ark. 807, 402 S.W.2d 651 (1966), holding that natural parents have a right to custody of their children as against strangers and the state cannot interfere with that right simply to better the moral and temporal welfare of the child as against an unoffending parent. Hence, the natural father's consent to adoption was essential and the mother's consent alone was insufficient. See also Home of the Holy Infancy v. Kaska, 397 S.W.2d 208 (Tex. 1965), 19 Sw. L.J. 855 (1965), 44 Texas L. Rev. 1028 (1966), where father of legitimated child prevailed over adoption agency; in re Werling, 181 So. 2d 872 (La. Ct. App. 1966).

37. See Cochran v. Cochran, 49 Cal. Rptr. 670 (Dist. Ct. App. 1966); Duplantes v. Bueto, 186 So. 2d 424 (La. Ct. App. 1966); Andrews v. Andrews, 242 Md. 143, 219 A.2d 194 (1966).

38. Shannon v. Newman, 400 S.W.2d 861 (Tex. Civ. App. 1966) (father allowed to retain full custody of four year old daughter where mother was married to an unstable man who drank and had been violent to his three former wives).

39. See cases cited note 30 *supra.*

40. *Ibid.*

41. *Ibid.*

42. Schroeder v. Schroeder, 184 So. 2d 75 (La. Ct. App. 1966) (custody to father where mother had been proved guilty of adultery on two occasions and was visited in her home in presence of children by paramour); Portman v. Portman, 181 So. 2d 429 (La. Ct. App. 1965) (adulterous wife lost custody of two

itation rights to a father, even in doubtful cases,[43] but are reluctant to award this same privilege to grandparents or other "strangers."[44] In both these areas many states continue a strict adherence to the rules of adversary procedure and the hearsay rule which impede the use of background investigations and reports that are needed for intelligent decision.[45]

In addition to the criteria and rules pertaining to an award of custody and their sensible application, there also is the problem of "child snatching" in violation of court order under pretense of seeking a modification of a prior award. Although a few courts apply the clean hands doctrine and refuse to modify a prior award at the petition of one who has violated a prior order,[46] perhaps most courts blandly continue to assert jurisdiction on the basis of real or feigned changes in circumstances, to show partiality for the local petitioner, and to overlook the effect on the child, made a pawn in a power struggle between contentious adults.[47] Since the applicability of the full faith and credit obligation to prior custody orders is in considerable doubt,[48] judicial restraint rather than a *parens patriae* assertion of custody jurisdiction is urgently needed. At the present time, the Commissioners on Uniform State Laws are working on a custody jurisdiction model act. It is to be hoped that their statute and recommendation will be forthcoming within the near future so that this most serious inadequacy of law may be corrected.

---

sons to their father); and Herron v. Herron, 141 N.W.2d 563 (Iowa 1966) (remarried father prevailed over mother who had man visiting her every week-end and also during visits of the three children).

43. See Hill v. Hill, 404 S.W.2d 641 (Tex. Civ. App. 1966); Raible v. Raible, 242 Md. 586, 219 A.2d 777 (1966).

44. Shriver v. Shriver, 7 Ohio App. 2d 169, 219 N.E.2d 300 (1966), holding it was an abuse of discretion to award visitation rights to paternal grandparents over objections of mother.

45. See Edwards v. Kibler, 24 App. Div. 2d 1076, 265 N.Y.S.2d 831 (4th Dep't 1965). Compare Johnson v. Johnson, 25 App. Div. 2d 672, 268 N.Y.S.2d 403 (2d Dep't 1966). See also Note, 19 Okla. L. Rev. 193 (1966).

46. See Ratner, *Legislative Resolution of the Interstate Child Custody Problem,* 38 So. Cal. L. Rev. 183, 184 (1965).

47. For recent examples, see In re Guardianship of Rodgers, 100 Ariz. 269, 413 P.2d 744 (1966), and Crow v. Crow, 414 P.2d 82 (Hawaii 1966). The classic example is New York ex rel. Halvey v. Halvey, 330 U.S. 610 (1947).

48. See Ratner, *Child Custody in a Federal System,* 62 Mich. L. Rev. 795 (1964).

II

Child Support

The parental duty of child support is perhaps the most extensively enforced obligation arising out of the family relationship. To make up for the uncertain antecedents of the common law in this regard,[49] most states have adopted an assortment of statutes, procedures and remedies to shore up the obligation, particularly that of the father. Although the primary duty of child support rests upon him, the mother by statute frequently is made secondarily liable for family necessities.[50] Moreover, in addition to the liability of the father of legitimate children for child support, a natural father may be held accountable, and a step-father, a foster father or one standing in loco parentis, may also be held accountable.[51]

Although there is general agreement as to the duty of child support, there is disagreement as to the measure of the duty and as to what (if any) circumstances other than emancipation of the child may relieve the father. The problem as to measure involves the question of whether the father must support his children according to his financial means—a test roughly comparable to his obligation to pay alimony—or according to their needs. The precise question which has brought this conflict to the fore is whether a father, if able, must provide a college education for a child who has the ability to benefit from it. The issue of suspension or termination of the father's duty of child support, in the absence of emancipation, is illustrated by the conflict in the cases as to whether or not the mother's violation of the father's visitation rights will relieve him from the duty of child support.[52]

49. See Foster, *Dependent Children and the Law,* 18 U. PITT. L. REV. 579 (1957). See also Strange v. Strange, 222 Ga. 44, 148 So. 2d 494 (1966), for a recent discussion of the father's common law duty to support his children.

50. See County of Alameda v. Kaiser, 238 Cal. App. 2d 815, 48 Cal. Rptr. 343 (Dist. Ct. App. 1966), holding mother must reimburse county for care of mentally ill twenty year old son.

51. See Katz, *Foster Parents Versus Agencies,* 65 MICH. L. REV. 145, 160 (1966). See also Chestnut v. Chestnut, 147 S.E.2d 269 (S.C. 1966), holding that foster parent may terminate relationship at will and with it the obligation of child support.

52. Compare Kane v. Kane, 154 Colo. 440, 391 P.2d 361 (1964), 42 Denver L.C.J. 182 (1965); Fleischer v. Fleischer, 25 App. Div. 2d 901, 269 N.Y.S.2d 270 (3d Dep't 1966).

Recent decisions in Missouri[53] and New York[54] have held that children were entitled to be supported according to their father's financial standing rather than limiting child support to the needs of the children.

The trend noted last year, obligating a father, upon divorce, to pay for a child's college education,[55] has been continued, and this year decisions in Michigan[56] and Pennsylvania[57] reiterate the duty, although the latter decision excused the father because of heavy expenses in supporting his eighty-five year old mother. Judges noted that college education is a necessity not a luxury for young people of ability. An order, therefore, may be made against a father of sufficient means to help a child receive an education beyond high school when the child is able and willing.

Regarding the problem of termination of support, an Arizona case recently held that support payments are for the benefit of the child, but suspension of this obligation because of deprivation of visitation rights, rests in the discretion of the trial court.[58]

The usual rule is that the father's child support obligation cannot be contracted away, as for example by the terms of a separation agreement.[59] Interesting on its facts is a criminal support case from Alabama where the father appealed a sentence of one year at hard labor.[60] The defendant in 1948 had married a fifteen year old girl who bore a son the following year. Although the paternity of the son was in doubt, he was assumed to be the child of the defendant. In 1950 the defendant secured a divorce for the wife's abandonment. They entered into an agreement, incorporated into the divorce decree, that she would be wholly responsible for the support and maintenance of the child. About

---

53. 402 S.W.2d 263 (Mo.Ct. App. 1966).

54. Schwartz v. Schwartz, 48 Misc. 2d 859, 265 N.Y.S.2d 820 (Family Ct. 1966), construing N.Y. Family Ct. Act § 413.

55. See 1965 Ann. Survey Am. L. 403-04. See also Inker & McGrath, *College Education of Minors,* 6 J. Fam. L. 230 (1966).

56. Mowrer v. Mowrer, 3 Mich. App. 516, 143 N.W.2d 144 (1966). See also Chapin v. Superior Ct., 239 Cal. App. 2d 851, 49 Cal. Rptr. 199 (Dist. Ct. App. 1966).

57. Commonwealth ex rel. Brown v. Weidner, 208 Pa. Super. 114, 220 A.2d 382 (1966).

58. Reardon v. Reardon, 3 Ariz. App. 475, 415 P.2d 571 (1966).

59. See Smith v. Smith, 7 Ohio App. 2d 4, 218 N.E.2d 473 (1964).

60. Rouse v. State, 184 So. 2d 839 (Ala. Ct. App. 1966).

five months after the divorce the former wife moved to another state and lived with another man for eleven years. Two to three years before the criminal prosecution she returned to Alabama and remarried. At the time she swore out the warrant for the arrest of the defendant she had a weekly income of sixty dollars and the defendant had a net income of $158 every two weeks plus military retirement pay. The conviction was reversed on the ground that the provision of the divorce decree wherein the mother agreed to support the child was prima facie a refutation of willful neglect on the defendant's part, and that there should have been resort to civil processes before invoking the criminal remedy. Since there was no showing of destitution but merely that the child needed braces for his teeth, and since the child was living with his mother and stepfather, one may wonder why any civil or criminal sanction was applicable where a court decree purported to relieve him of the duty of child support.

California courts engaged in some hair splitting over the liability for institutional care given to relatives and the duty to reimburse the state. In the *Kirchner* case[61] it was held that equal protection principles precluded imposition of such indemnification where the institutionalization was for the protection or benefit of the public. Recent decisions indicate that if the institutionalization is for the benefit of the family, or for the benefit of both the family and the public, reimbursement may be exacted from the relative.[62] Thus, a father was charged with the cost of maintaining his son at a "juvenile hall" and a county "boy's camp" where he had been sent by order of the juvenile court, the sum amounting to $1,208.00.[63] It is difficult to comprehend the glib distinction between public and private benefit that the California courts are making, and it would seem that concern for saving welfare expenditures is diminishing the constitutional principle adopted in the *Kirchner* case.

The New York Court of Appeals recently held that parties to a separation agreement may agree to arbitrate their differences as to

61. Department of Mental Hygiene v. Kirchner, 60 Cal. 2d 716, 388 P.2d 720, 36 Cal. Rptr. 488 (1964).

62. County of Alameda v. Espinoza, 52 Cal. Rptr. 480 (Dist. Ct. App. 1966); County of Alameda v. Kaiser, 232 Cal. App. 2d 815, 48 Cal. Rptr. 343 (Dist. Ct. App. 1965).

63. County of Alameda v. Espinoza, 52 Cal. Rptr. 480 (Dist. Ct. App. 1966).

amount of support money and that there is no legal requirement that child support be fixed by a court rather than by an arbitrator.[64] The reasoning is that although the arbitration award may not be given res judicata consequences against a child who was not a party to the arbitration, it does effectively bind the parents insofar as the award did not adversely affect any substantial interest of the child.

III

Adoption

The most important recent developments in the adoption field are the public concern over placement criteria engendered by the *Liuni* case,[65] and the Supreme Court's decision in *Armstrong* v. *Manzo*[66] regarding the due process requirement of notice to a natural father before his child may be adopted by a stepfather.

In the *Liuni* case a county welfare commissioner sought to block adoption and to regain custody of a four and one-half year old girl who had been in the care of foster parents since she was five days old. The New York official, who had legal custody due to the surrender of the child to him by the natural parents, gave several reasons for opposing adoption by the foster parents including the welfare policy against adoption by foster parents and the prior mental illness of the foster mother. However, the reasons publicized in the press were the physiological mismatching of the foster parents and child and the age of the foster parents. The child was blonde and blue eyed, the foster parents dark, of Italian extraction, and forty-eight years old. Despite conclusive evidence as to the love and affection that existed between the child and the foster parents, the commissioner prevailed upon the trial court to order the return of the child to him so that she might be placed for adoption with some other couple who more nearly met the placement criteria.

The decision received a great deal of publicity, rivaling *Painter* v. *Bannister*. An appeal was taken to the appellate division which ordered

---

64. Schneider v. Schneider, 17 N.Y.2d 123, 216 N.E.2d 318, 269 N.Y.S.2d 107 (1966).

65. In re St. John, 51 Misc. 2d 96, 272 N.Y.S.2d 817 (Family Ct. 1966), rev'd. sub. nom. Fitzsimmons v. Liuni, 26 App. Div. 2d 980, 274 N.Y.S.2d 798 (3d Dep't 1966). See also N.Y. Times, Nov. 11, 1966, p. 45, col. 5.

66. 380 U.S. 545 (1965).

a new trial. The Governor of New York requested that the Department of Public Welfare make a complete investigation of the case. The investigation resulted in the recommendation that the foster parents be permitted to adopt the child. At the retrial that recommendation was accepted and the adoption by the foster parents finally was approved.[67]

Although critical comment as to the arbitrary criteria applied by the commissioner and his indifference to the bonds and attachment between the child and the foster parents was wholly justified, by and large there was a failure to note that the *Liuni* case was not merely an isolated example of bureaucratic bungling. In the background there were substantial issues relating to the social value of generally accepted placement criteria, the unthinking and unreasonable application of such criteria and the traditional agency opposition to adoption by foster parents. Also, there were important issues regarding judicial review of agency discretion and the goal or goals of placement. In other words, the *Liuni* case was significant because it dramatically exposed how the relatively trivial may override the basically important unless courts check administrative discretion, and because it raised fundamental questions as to the purpose of legal adoption.

It is unfortunate but true that in bureaucratic hands mere factors to be weighed and balanced may assume the character of absolutes and that for petty officials, general standards may become inflexible rules rather than guidelines to decision. The misuse of criteria and the abuse of discretion can be avoided only if the decision process is goal directed. The most important goal in adoption is not the matching of complexions, but placement of the child in a loving and wholesome home. In New York, however, there is unfortunate precedent for giving priority to the legal status of those contending for custody and agency authority.

In the Matter of Jewish Child Care Association[68] was a four-to-three decision by the Court of Appeals which refused to permit foster parents to keep a child over agency objections. The agency's main argument was that despite the agreement of the foster parents that they would not seek to adopt the child, (which agreement had been coerced from them by threats to remove the child) they nonetheless continued their efforts to secure an adoption. The agency contended

67. N.Y. Times, Jan. 17, 1967, p. 37, col. 4.

68. 5 N.Y.2d 222, 156 N.E.2d 700, 183 N.Y.S.2d 65 (1959).

that the foster parents had become too emotionally attached to the child, and that by indulging her with too much love, they created a strain on her relationship with her natural mother (who had seen her only twice in three years) and that the child needed a "neutral environment" where foster parents would be called "aunt" and "uncle" rather than "mother" and "father." The majority opinion gave priority to the interests of the natural mother and to the authority of the agency, attaching only secondary significance to the child's welfare and the extra-legal claim of the foster parents based upon love and affection.

Professor Sanford N. Katz, a most perceptive commentator on adoption and custody matters, recently published a valuable critique on the *Child Care Association* case and has suggested some practical guidelines for the resolution of conflicts between agencies and foster parents.[69] Professor Katz recommends that courts keep in mind the specific community goals of the parent-child relationship and the best interests of the child rather than the legal status of the claimants and the authority of welfare agencies. The guidelines and emphasis suggested by Professor Katz would result in the placement of the child with the foster parents in each of the cases under discussion. From the welfare agency point of view, however, it is important to have foster homes which will serve on a temporary basis and foster parents who comply with regulations.

As previously pointed out in the discussion of *Painter* v. *Bannister*, to subscribe to the doctrine that ordinarily the best interests of the child should control placement or a custody award, does not require a total preclusion of other considerations which in a given case may be crucial. *Armstrong* v. *Manzo*[70] involved another consideration that cannot be ignored. The Supreme Court held that procedural due process applied to adoption proceedings, and that an adoption decree secured by a stepfather without notice to the natural father was invalid. Although the natural father subsequently obtained a hearing on his motion to vacate the adoption decree, and was allowed to present evidence; the

69. See Katz, *Foster Parents Versus Agencies: A Case Study in the Judicial Application of "The Best Interests of the Child" Doctrine*, 65 MICH. L. REV. 145 (1966). It should be noted that the last part of the title is not apropos since the New York court did not apply the best interests of the child doctrine but instead sacrificed such to the legal status of the parent and the authority of the agency.

70. 380 U.S. 545 (1965).

decree, nonetheless, was held invalid because he was entitled to a procedural preference. The court felt that the burden of proving unfitness should have been placed on the stepfather who sought to adopt the child over the natural father's objections. His absence in the adoption proceedings gave the stepfather an undue advantage, since the latter did not have to carry the burden of proving his own qualifications as well as the natural father's unfitness. Of course, the case did not affect the *de facto* status of the child who remained in the custody of his mother and her second husband.

The Supreme Court's holding as to due process in adoption proceedings received prompt application in an interesting case which arose in Arkansas. That state refused to recognize an Oklahoma adoption decree which was entered with the consent of the mother but without notice to the natural father. The natural parents had been divorced a few months earlier in Kansas. The child's birth had been concealed, and within nine days after birth, the Oklahoma adoption proceeding had been completed. Since Oklahoma statutes dispenses with consent for adoption where the parent in question has been divorced for cruelty, no attempt was made to notify the father.[71] The father, after learning of his son's birth and that an attorney had arranged for the adoption, was forced to carry his case to the Kansas Supreme Court before the names of the adoptive parents were revealed to him.[72] Upon learning that they had moved to Arkansas, he immediately brought a writ of habas corpus to obtain custody of the child.

The lower court held that the Oklahoma adoption was entitled to full faith and credit, but the Arkansas Supreme Court reversed upon the authority of *Armstrong* v. *Manzo* awarding custody to the natural father.[73] A dissenting opinion took the position that the Oklahoma adoption, although void as to the father, was valid as to the mother, and that because the adoptive parents stood in the natural mother's shoes, the best interests of the child should determine the custody issue.

---

71. 70 OKLA. STAT. ANN. §§ 60.6.-7 (1966). Compare § III of the N.Y. DOM. REL. LAW, discussed in In the Matter of the Adoption of Ekstrom, 24 App. Div. 276, 265 N.Y.S.2d 727 (3d Dep't 1965), which provides that consent to adoption shall not be required of a parent who has been divorced for his or her adultery except that notice of the proposed adoption shall be given to such a parent.

72. Olney v. Hobble, 193 Kan. 692, 396 P.2d 367 (1964).

73. Olney v. Gordon, 402 S.W.2d 651 (Ark. 1966).

The intriguing problem of adult adoptions arose in a recent California case which decided that an heir had standing to collaterally attack an adult adoption on the basis of fraud.[74] A further study of this phase of adoption, and whether or not there should be a minimum age difference as a requisite, has appeared in a valuable article by Professor Wadlington.[75] Recently there has been a proliferation of statutes concerning adoption. California has eliminated the need for parental consent to adoption where a father has been guilty of nonsupport for one year, or a mother has placed a child with an agency and has not been heard from for one year.[76] Alaska has removed the requirement of consent or notice to the natural father of an illegitimate child.[77] Three states—California, Oklahoma and South Carolina—recently enacted statutes permitting the termination of parental rights prior to adoption proceedings.[78] Fees for adoption services[79] and the confidentiality of adoption records have also been regulated.[80] Oklahoma and Nevada have joined other states in inhibiting "black market" adoptions,[81] and Nebraska, New York and West Virginia have new provisions regarding consent to adoption and what constitutes relinquishment of parental rights to a child.[82]

IV

Rights of Children

The period of gestation for new torts is an uncertain one. A successful delivery may never be achieved. Since 1963, when the *Zepeda*

74. In re Adoption of Sewall, 51 Cal. Rptr. 367 (1966).

75. Wadlington, *Minimum Age Difference as a Requisite for Adoption,* 1966 Duke L.J. 392. See also Binavince, *Adoption and the Law of Descent and Distribution,* 51 Cornell, L.Q. 152 (1966); Wadlington, *Adoption of Adults in Louisiana,* 40 Tulane L. Rev. 1 (1965).

76. Cal. Stats. 1965, Ch. 1173.

77. Alaska Laws 1966, Ch. 34.

78. Cal. Stats. 1965, Ch. 1065; Okla. Laws 1965, Ch. 166; S.C. Laws 1966, Res. 1238.

79. Cal. Stats. 1965, Ch. 1824; Ind. Acts of 1965, Ch. 427; Texas Laws of 1965, Ch. 634.

80. Cal. Stats. 1965, Ch. 1530; Ga. Acts 1965, 651; Mich. Laws 1966, Act 80; Nev. Laws 1965, Ch. 36; Texas Laws 1965, Ch. 151.

81. Okla. Laws of 1965, Ch. 507; Nev. Laws 1965, Ch. 497.

82. Neb. Laws 1965, Ch. 233, 234; N.Y. Laws 1966, Ch. 792; W. Va. Laws 1965, Ch. 54. For a comprehensive compilation of recent adoption laws, see Infausto & Shanley, *Annual Review of Decisions and Statutory Revisions Affecting Adoption (1965-66),* 1 J. Fam. L.Q. 10, 21-24 (1967).

case was decided in Illinois,[83] there has been speculation over whether or not a tort action may lie for "wrongful life." The Illinois court, confronted with a suit by an adulterine bastard against his natural father, recognized that there had been a wrong but relegated the obstetrical function of delivering a remedy to the legislature.

Both New York and New Jersey have recently decided variations of the "wrongful life" problem and have held there was neither wrong nor remedy. In *Williams* v. *New York,*[84] the Court of Appeals held that the illegitimate offspring of a female patient at a state mental hospital had no cause of action against the state under the tort claims act for the institution's negligence in permitting her conception and birth out of wedlock. As damages, it was claimed that the plaintiff was "deprived of property rights; deprived of normal childhood and home life; deprived of proper parental care, support and rearing; caused to bear the stigma of illegitimacy."[85] New Jersey, in a four-to-three decision,[86] dismissed a malpractice suit against two doctors for allowing the birth of a blind, deaf, dumb and mentally retarded child whose mother sought and was denied an abortion after she had contracted German measles during the critical period of her pregnancy.

The New York court disavowed a "hardening of the categories" policy as to tort actions, but unlike the Illinois court, did not pass the buck to the legislature. Its decision is disturbing. The court relied heavily on "the absence from our legal concepts of any such idea as a wrong to a later-born child caused by permitting a woman to be violated and to bear the out-of-wedlock infant."[87] It was concluded that "being born under one set of circumstances rather than another or to one pair of parents rather than another is not a suable wrong that is cognizable in court."[88] A concurring opinion added that damages, if any, were impossible of ascertainment.

The reasoning of the majority tends to beg the question and perhaps is overly legalistic. The concurring opinion points to one of the difficult problems because damages suffered by a stigmatic status may

83. Zepeda v. Zepeda, 41 Ill. App. 2d 240, 190 N.E.2d 849 (1963).

84. 18 N.Y.2d 481, 223 N.E.2d 343 (1966), affirming 25 App. Div. 2d 206, 269 N.Y.S.2d 786 (3d Dep't 1966), reversing 46 Misc. 2d 324, 260 N.Y.S.2d 953.

85. *Id.* at 482, 223 N.E. at 343.

86. See N.Y. Times, Mar. 7, 1967, p. 1, col. 6.

87. 18 N.Y.2d at 482, 223 N.E. at 344.

88. *Id.* at 484, 223 N.E. at 344.

be more than offset by *joie de vivre* or may be too speculative for judicial determination. Granted that the Williams child was not in existence at the time the hospital negligently permitted the mother to be violated, and perhaps under the rationale of the *Palsgraf* case[89] was not a foreseeable plaintiff, nonetheless it is clear that the hospital's breach of duty owed to the mother created the very risk which was realized. If the mother had brought the action, under the reasoning of the majority, recovery should be permitted. Damages might include at least some of the items claimed in the actual case.

But why should the theory of the action be so crucial under the facts of the *Williams* case? Granted, slogans such as "wrongful life" are not helpful, but what is a sensible remedy in this case? The desirable solution would be to allow reparation for the wrong done to the mother and to establish a nest egg for the child. There is no need to indulge in fictions as to "transferred intent" nor to become entangled in privity concepts if attention is focused on the foreseeable consequences that flow from the hospital's failure to adequately protect its female mental patients. If the dynamic realism of Cardozo in *MacPherson* v. *Buick*[90] could cut through the legalisms which emanated from *Winterbottom* v. *Wright*.[91] surely our current court could with incisiveness lay bare the social and economic issues in the *Williams* case. In short, even if we agree there should be no damages for "wrongful life," it does not follow that recovery should not be allowed in order to provide for the child's care, maintenance and education. There may be no statutory remedy, it is true, but then there was none for *MacPherson*. Common law tort principles are viable enough to make a wrongdoer responsible for the foreseeable consequences of his negligence.

It is interesting to compare the New Jersey case with the *Williams* decision. The proper party, the mother, was the plaintiff, and although it is not clear that any wrong was committed, she came within one vote of recovering for what more appropriately might be called "wrongful birth." The opinions in the case contribute more to the current controversy over abortion laws reform than to an understanding of the evolution of tort law. The majority, however, does proclaim that the child's right to live is greater than and precludes the parental

89. Palsgraf v. Long Island R.R., 248 N.Y. 349, 162 N.E. 99 (1928).
90. 217 N.Y. 382, 111 N.E. 1050 (1916).
91. 10 M. & W. 109 (1842), 11 L.J. Ex. 415, 62 Rev. Rpts. 535.

right not to endure emotional and financial injury. Thus the tables are turned. Instead of the child having an action for "wrongful life," judicial recognition is given to a right to life, even though it be on terrible terms.

In addition to a renewal of the "wrongful life" controversy, the past year produced important articles on the legal status of illegitimate children,[92] including a proposed uniform act on legitimacy.[93] Finally, in New York, Judge Justine Wise Polier advanced the rights of children in two significant decisions which ordered the transfer of a child from a fondling home and placement with a private agency so that she more readily might be placed for adoption.[94]

V

Delinquency, Dependency and Neglect

As of this writing, the Supreme Court has not handed down its decision in the *Gault* case.[95] It is anticipated that the Court's deicision will either spell out in detail those requirements of due process that are applicable to juvenile court proceedings or may merely determine which, if any, due process requirements were abridged in the particular case. The case itself, however, involves a fairly complete catalogue of due process issues inasmuch as the Arizona Juvenile Code and the proceedings in question raise issues as to (1) the right to notice of the alleged acts of delinquency charged, (2) the right to counsel, (3) the right to confront and cross examine witnesses, (4) the privilege against self-incrimination, and (5) the right to a transcript of the proceedings. Certiorari was granted from the Arizona decision holding that in juvenile court proceedings there was neither a constitutional privilege against self-incrimination, nor a right to counsel; that it was sufficient if notice of the charges be given prior to adjudication; and that a

92. Krause, *Equal Protection for the Illegitimate,* 65 MICH. L. REV. 477 (1967); Note, *Liability of Possible Fathers: A Support Remedy for Illegitimate Children,* 18 STAN. L. REV. 859 (1966).

93. Krause, *Bringing the Bastard Into the Great Society—A Proposed Uniform Act on Legitimacy,* 44 TEXAS L. REV. 829 (1966).

94. In re Bonez, 48 Misc. 2d 200, 266 N.Y.S.2d 756, and 50 Misc. 2d 1080, 272 N.Y.S.2d 587 (Family Ct. 1966).

95. Application of Gault, 99 Ariz. 181, 407 P.2d 760 (1965). rev'd and remanded with direction, 87 Sup. Ct. 1428 (1967). Since this article was set in type the case has been decided in favor of requiring constitutional due process in juvenile proceedings.

written recora of the proceedings was not required.[96]

The grant of certiorari in *Gault* and the decision in *Kent* v. *United States*[97] warrant the inference that the Supreme Court is prepared to scrutinize and evaluate the procedure employed in juvenile court in terms of due process. Although the *Kent* case merely held that a sixteen year old boy accused of rape was entitled to counsel as a matter of right and to a hearing on the issue of a juvenile court's waiver of its jurisdiction to the criminal court, Mr. Justice Fortas questioned the *parens patriae* premise underlying juvenile court procedure. The assumption that juveniles are accorded treatment rather than punishment has come under increasing attack.[98] It should be noted that the differences are almost as great as the similarities between juvenile courts. New York, as contrasted with Arizona, respects the delinquent's right to remain silent, to be represented by counsel of his own choosing, or if unable to pay a lawyer, to have a law guardian assigned to him.[99] Thus, application of due process standards to such proceedings will merely force some states to adopt the procedures already in effect in more progressive jurisdictions.

Child abuse or the "battered child" syndrome continues to be a popular subject for discussion and statutory reform.[100] As of 1966, all

---

96. *Ibid.* See Ketchem, *The Gault Case and Due Process,* 17 Juv. Ct. Judges J. 103 (1966); Polow, *The Juvenile Court,* 53 A.B.A.J. 31 (1967).

97. 383 U.S. 541 (1966). For an analysis of the problem in the Kent case, see *Transfer of Juveniles to Adult Correctional Institutions,* 1966 Wis. L. Rev. 866. See also State v. Owen, 101 Ariz. 156, 416 P.2d 289 (1966); and Dillenburg v. Maxwell, 413 P.2d 940 (Wash. 1966).

98. For recent significant decisions as to the due process rights of juveniles, see People v. Castro, 52 Cal. Rptr. 469 (Cal. App. 1966); In re Carlo, 48 N.J. 224, 225 A.2d 110 (1966); In re Winburn, 32 Wis. 2d 152, 145 N.W.2d 178 (1966). See also Paulsen, *The Juvenile Court and the Whole of the Law,* 1 Wayne L. Rev. 597 (1965); Note, *Juvenile Delinquents, The Police, State Courts and Individualized Justice,* 79 Harv. L. Rev. 775 (1966); Note, *The Parens Patriae Theory and Its Effect on the Constitutional Limits of Juvenile Court Powers,* 27 U. Pitt. L. Rev. 894 (1966).

99. See N.Y. Fam. Ct. Act §§ 249, 728.

100. Foster & Freed, *Battered Child Legislation and Professional Immunity,* 52 A.B.A.J. 1071 (1966); Foster & Freed, *The Battered Child,* 3 Trial 33 (1966-67); McCloid, *The Battered Child and Other Assaults Upon the Family,* 50 Minn. L. Rev. 1 (1965); Paulsen, *The Legal Framework for Child Protection,* 66 Colum. L. Rev. 663 (1966); Paulsen, Parker & Adelman, *Child Abuse Reporting Laws,* 34 Geo. Wash. L. Rev. 482 (1966); Comment, 45 Ore. L. Rev. 114 (1966); Note, 44 Texas L. Rev. 584 (1966).

American jurisdictions except the District of Columbia and Hawaii had enacted statutes to remedy the situation. Nonetheless, cases of terrible abuse continue to come to light. The reaction of Judge Polier to such a case was to remove the child from its home, to place him with the grandmother under the protection of the court, to make recommendations for the improvement of the New York "battered child" statute so as to broaden the obligation to report suspected cases and to establish a central clearing house for information about such cases.[101]

101. In re Francis, 49 Misc. 2d 372, 267 N.Y.S.2d 566 (Family Ct. 1966) See also In re J. L. L., 402 S.W.2d 629 (Mo. Ct. App. 1966); In re Young, 50 Misc. 2d 271, 270 N.Y.S.2d 250 (Family Ct. 1966). For a case involving neglect but no physical abuse, see State v. Winters, 413 P.2d 425 (Ore. 1966).

THE BALANCE OF POWER AMONG INFANTS, THEIR PARENTS AND THE STATE

Andrew Jay Kleinfeld

The Balance of Power Among Infants, their Parents and the State

The following chapters will appear in future issues of Family Law Quarterly.

The Balance of Power Among Infants, their Parents and the State

ANDREW JAY KLEINFELD*

Introduction

Political philosophers traditionally have regarded the details of raising children as issues of fundamental concern to society as a whole[1] and the pattern of family government as an important model for consideration in the structuring of civil government.[2] Contemporary legal scholarship, however, has not adverted often to the questions suggested by these propositions.[3] No general, accepted modern treatise on the American law of infants exists. Many law review articles are written on the estate and probate law of infants, and much has been written about juvenile delinquency, but little modern commentary exists on most other aspects of the law of infants.

This essay surveys and criticizes a few of the most fundamental devices and concepts in the structure of infants' law. The first chapter examines the issue of representation in court, on the premise that effective representation is a practical prerequisite to implementation of any legally protected interest. The second chapter explores the scope of parental power over

---

* Andrew Jay Kleinfeld, a graduate of the Harvard Law School, is a law clerk to Justice Rabinowitz of the Alaska Supreme Court. Mr. Kleinfeld, who makes his home in Fairbanks, Alaska, is a member of the Bar of Alaska.
The attached article is the first of three parts of an extraordinarily comprehensive and perceptive article which breaks new grounds with regard to the status and rights of children.

1. Plato, THE REPUBLIC 235–264 (Cornford ed., 1945).

2. J. Locke, TREATISE OF CIVIL GOVERNMENT 34–50 (Sherman ed. 1937).

3. The paucity of legal scholarship may reflect a broad decline in many fields of interest in children. Seligman, *The State of Social Science*, 46 COMMENTARY 76 (Oct. 1968) notes that while the Encyclopedia of the Social Sciences contained a 65 page article on children, its new edition, The INTERNATIONAL ENCYCLOPEDIA OF THE SOCIAL SCIENCES, has only scattered comments in 80 articles and no central article.

infants, and the third, aspects of state regulation of individual conduct peculiar to individuals under the age of majority. This organization has been selected to facilitate the sketching out of a kind of constitutional law of infancy, that is, a description and criticism of the way in which infants are governed insofar as the mode of government is peculiar to their special status. What kind of authority do parents have over children? Why do they have any authority? What limits may children by formal or informal checks put on the scope and mode of exercise of this authority? When and why does the state partially or totally divest parents of their authority? Why does the state have broader authority over infants than other people? What political checks exist to prevent abuse of this authority? On what grounds do or should courts limit its scope or mode of exercise? That these questions may meaningfully be asked indicates that infants have a peculiar status in our society, radically different both from that of other persons and from the position of animals or chattels. Comprehensively different treatment of infants must, implicitly or explicitly, presuppose some philosophy justifying this treatment. The broader purpose of this essay is to discover the philosophy or competing philosophies underlying the status of infants, so that the coherence and rationality of this area of law may be properly analyzed and evaluated.

I. The Representational Context

A. The Value of Representation

A distinction may be drawn between the rights of a person to make various choices and the rights of a person to be protected from the choices or other initiatives of others. The first class includes such rights as voting, freedom to travel, free expression, free exercise of religion, and freedom to marry. The second class includes rights not to be imprisoned without due process, not to have one's property taken without just compensation, and not to be assaulted. These classes might be characterized as freedom to choose or act, and freedom from being affected improperly by choices or actions of others.

Rights of the first class imply some degree of choice-making conduct on the part of an actor exercising them; persons barely capable of intelligent choice rarely are denied these rights, but they do presuppose some kind of rationality on the part of one endowed with them. An animal could not meaningfully exercise a right to vote because it could not understand what it was doing, even if it were trained to manipulate a voting machine in ways behavioristically similar to human techniques. But rights of the second class require no rationality of the being endowed with them. A cow can have a right not to be cruelly treated under a criminal statute prohibiting cruelty to animals, no matter how unintelligent or imprudent the cow may be. Insofar, then, as a right may be categorized in the second rather than the first class, presupposing no intelligence of the person endowed with it, the youth of a person would not by reason of his lesser intelligence, experience or prudence justify denying him that right. On the contrary, where a right is intended to protect persons from the unfair initiatives of others, weakness and incompetence suggest that the right for him ought to be especially broad and inalienable.

In the second class falls the right to counsel. For a civil or criminal proceeding, to satisfy the Due Process Clause, usually a person who may be affected by it must have some opportunity to be represented by counsel. In the criminal context, the Constitution explicitly provides that the accused shall enjoy a right "to have the assistance of counsel for his defense."[1] In *Powell v. Alabama,*[2] which held that the Sixth and Fourteenth Amendments required counsel to be appointed in capital cases for indigent defendents, the Court explained the fundamentality of the right in terms of the incompetence of the ordinary layman to vindicate his rights in court without a lawyer; the Court regarded counsel as so necessary to fairness that

> If in any case, civil or criminal, a state or federal court were arbitrarily

1. U.S. CONST. amend. 6.
2. 287 U.S. 45 (1932).

> to refuse to hear a party by counsel, employed by and appearing for him, it reasonably may not be doubted that such a refusal would be a denial of a hearing, and, therefore, of due process in the constitutional sense.[3]

In extending the right to appointed counsel to indigents accused of non-capital crimes, at least felonies, *Gideon v. Wainwright*[4] characterized lawyers for defendents in criminal actions as "necessities, not luxuries,"[5] quoting with approval the statement in *Powell* that the ordinary layman generally could not competently defend himself. Since the right to counsel of adults is founded upon the incompetence of the ordinary layman, the logic of the right would seem to compel an even broader right to counsel for infants because of their presumably greater incompetence. The theory of *Gideon* and *Powell* does not by its own logic confine itself to the criminal context. Without counsel, *Powell* and *Gideon* suggest, a higher proportion of adjudications of all sorts will be unjust or inaccurate than they would be had counsel participated.

Though the judicial decisions developing the right to counsel in civil and criminal cases generally speak in terms of its promoting the accurate and just determination of rights, it may reasonably be speculated that the presence of counsel has a more profound effect. Though this essay includes no statistical account, it appears that a very high proportion of statutes affecting infants have never or rarely been construed by state courts of last resort, and many judicial rules of infants' law have rarely been examined in contexts where infants have traditionally lacked counsel. Many cases which raise substantial questions of the rights of infants have been decided on other bases without adversion to those rights, as for example the compulsory school law cases,[6] apparently because a parent or some other party did battle with briefs arguing solely on the basis of

---

3. *Id.* at 69.
4. 372 U.S. 335 (1963).
5. *Id.* at 344.
6. These are discussed in Ch. II and Ch. III, *infra*.

their own interests. In the areas of law where infants traditionally have been unrepresented, many of the rules seem crude and careless with regard to their interests. Yet none of these observations have any validity for areas where infants generally have been represented, such as probate law, where substantive as well as procedural rules regarding infants have been elaborated in the most intricate detail, and statutes have been frequently and meticulously construed. These impressions, if they are correct, suggest that without counsel, rights not only fail to be vindicated; they fail also to be created. A lawyer does not merely present facts to a court in a favorable light; he argues that theories not obviously applicable ought to be used to interpret those facts, suggests previously undiscovered meanings in statutes, and he appeals from court to court for vindication of his theories. The effect of all this is often to create rights where before they lay undiscovered.[7] The right to counsel, then, is not merely one of a panoply of rights insuring fair individual adjudication; it creates a context in which rights stated in case or statute are implemented, and new rights are created.

B. Standing To Be Heard

Before the right to counsel may be asserted, there must be a right to be heard. If a court will not hear the argument some person wishes to put before it, he is in no better position with counsel than without. A right to be heard presupposes that the adjudication in issue will affect other rights of the petitioner, so ordinarily there can be no right to be heard without a showing that some substantive right may be affected.[8] In the area of

---

7. McConnell, *Magistrate Courts: Fish or Fowl*, 54 A.B.A.J. 1091 (1968) argues, quite suggestively for this issue, that lack of counsel in magistrate courts has caused a lack of appellate court interpretation of statutes so that the same statutes are interpreted different ways in practice; the inequality produced is exacerbated by the generality of most American statutes, because legislatures depend on courts to fill them in, as compared with the self-sufficiency of European statutes. In addition, because unrepresented parties rarely can present a case with decorum and skill, the courts become inquisitorial and informal, creating ill will in the parties.

8. FED. RULES CIV. P. 24(a)(2) (intervention as of right); *id.*, 19(a) (joinder necessary parties).

infants' law, courts developed the notion, apparently simultaneously with the rise of the juvenile court system,[9] that children had no right to liberty, and therefore no right to be heard on the question of whether their liberty should be taken. *Ex parte Crouse*[10] said "we know of no natural right to exemption from restraints which conduce to an infant's welfare."[11] Citing *Crouse, Rule v. Geddes*[12] held that a child committed to a reform school by her father under a stubborn child law was not denied due process by the absence of a hearing, because

> The child herself, having no right to control her own action or to select her own course of life, had no legal right to be heard in these proceedings.[13]

The principle that a child was entitled to no liberty and therefore to no hearing in juvenile delinquency commitments has been reversed in most modern juvenile court acts,[14] and would appear to violate the Due Process Clause.[15] But in some areas, most notably divorces of parents, the courts generally have not yet categorized the interests of children affected as cognizable rights, so these interests have not been represented.

Under the Federal Rules of Civil Procedure, similar to most state rules, persons who must be joined as parties to an action if feasible as a prerequisite to a just adjudication include one who

> . . . claims an interest relating to the subject of the action and is so situated that the disposition of the action in his absence may (i) as a practical matter impair or impede his ability to protect that interest . . .[16]

To the extent that a judgment in the absence of one so interested might prejudice him, the prejudice cannot be avoided by a shaping of the relief as between the other parties, the judgment will be inadequate, or the plaintiff will have an ade-

---

9. The philosophy of the juveniic court system is discussed in ch. III, *infra*.
10. 4 Whart. 9 (Pa. 1838).
11. *Id.*, at 11.
12. 23 App. D.C. 31 (1904).
13. *Id.* at 50.
14. *E.g.*, Calif. Welf. & Inst. Code § 679.
15. *In re* Gault, 387 U.S. 1 (1966); Kent v. United States, 383 U.S. 544 (1966).
16. FED. R. CIV. P. 19(a)(2).

quate remedy if the action is dismissed by non-joinder, the court ought in equity and good conscience to lean toward treating the absent person as indispensable, therefore dismissing the action for non-joinder.[17] Where an action may properly proceed without participation of a party without depriving him of Due Process as his rights under necessary party rules, he may still have a right to participate in the action if he so wishes. A person may typically intervene as of right if he

> . . . claims an interest relating to the property or transaction which is the subject of the action and he is so situated that the disposition of the action may as a practical matter impair or impede his ability to protect that interest, unless the applicants' interest is adequately represented by existing parties.[18]

This right to intervene belongs to anyone who "would be substantially affected in a practical sense by the determination made in an action," not merely those with rights in a fund to be distributed or those whom the proceeding might bind as a matter of *res judicata,* and representation is inadequate under the rule even though a party has a legal duty to represent the would-be intervenor where it probably will be inadequate as a practical matter.[19]

Infants generally are bound by the same procedural rules as adults,[20] except that a representative, next friend or guardian at litem must sue or defend on the infant's behalf.[21] Where an action will likely affect the interests of infants, so that, were they adults, they would be necessary parties, they must be treated as necessary parties just as though they were adults.[22] For example, an infant is a necessary party to a proceeding to determine his parentage because of its practical impact on his future psychological and financial welfare,[23] an action regarding

17. *Id.,* 19(b).
18. FED. R. CIV. P. 24(a)(2).
19. *Id.,* Notes of Advisory Committee on Rules, 1966 Amendment to Rule 24.
20. Pintek v. Superior Court, 78 Ariz. 179, 277 P. 2nd 265, 268 (1954) (dictum).
21. FED. R. CIV. P. 17(c).
22. P. v. Dept. of Health, 200 Misc. 1090, 107 N.Y.S.2d 586 (1951).
23. P. v. Dept. of Health, 200 Misc. 1090, 107 N.Y.S.2d 586 (1951).

property put in trust for him as part of a divorce settlement,[24] a bill in equity for a sale of land for division among tenants in common where infants allegedly have an interest in the land,[25] a suit to set aside a conveyance where the infant is a judgment creditor of the grantor,[26] a lien priority contest as to land in which the infant owns an interest,[27] or a suit to construe a will under which the infant may be a beneficiary.[28] No case has been found suggesting any distinction between infants' and adults' rights to intervene.

Despite the clarity of those principles, they have not been universally applied where the interests of infants were materially affected. Most notably, infants have generally not been made participants in the divorce and custody proceedings of their parents. An infant ought to be considered a necessary and usually indispensable party to his parents' divorce proceedings if he has an "interest" in the marriage or in the financial and custody aspects of the decree which may, as a practical matter, be impaired if he is not represented as a separate party.[29] Similar criteria apply to determine whether the infant may intervene as of right, if he is not a necessary or indispensable party.[30] The concept of "interest" used in rules about necessary and indispensable parties and intervention as of right appears not to be congruent with formal concepts of legal interests. Rather, courts read the rules to mean that joinder should be required or intervention permitted where, considering the prac-

---

24. Workmen v. Workmen, 174 Neb. 471, 118 N.W.2d 764 (1962); Mabry v. Scott, 51 Cal. App. 2d 245, 124 P. 2d 659 (1942), cert. den. Title Ins. & Trust Co. v. Mabry, 317 U.S. 670 (1942) (all beneficiaries of a trust are indispensable parties including children, except that unborn and unascertained remaindermen may be virtually represented by living persons who have no interests hostile to theirs).

25. Amann v. Burke, 237 Ala. 380, 186 So. 769 (1939) (necessary and indispensable).

26. Hays v. McCarty, 239 Ala. 400, 195 So. 241 (1940).

27. Hickman Co. Bd. of Comm'rs v. Union Stock Land Bank, 259 Ky. 823, 83 S.W. 2d 511 (1935).

28. *In re* Cordes' Estate, 116 S.W. 2d 207 (Mo. App. 1938).

29. FED. R. CIV. P. 19(a)(2).

30. FED. R. CIV. P. 24(a)(2), and Notes of Advisory Committee on Rules, 1966 Amendment to Rule 24.

ticalities of the situation, participation is necessary to put "the controversy in such a posture that its final termination will be consistent with good conscience."[31] A child in a proceeding to determine parentage has been treated as having enough of an "interest" to be a necessary party because of remote and somewhat speculative effects which the decree might have on his future emotional and financial welfare.[32] Such an informal concept of interest may be required as a matter of logic, because until a proceeding has been completed the nature of an interest in the subject matter of the action cannot be ascertained, so courts must either base their decisions on the probably practical effects of their decisions in order to achieve justice, or else rely on allegations of legal interest which insofar as they do not coincide with practical effects will do unjust harm to the original parties where the third party has a legal but no substantial practical interest and to the third party where he has a practical interest, but cannot allege a traditionally recognized legal interest. More practically, it is doubtful whether interest ought to be limited to formal legal interests, because that would restrict the growth of the law through recognition of new legal interests in accord with practical concerns.

Children whose parents seek to be divorced certainly have interests in the practical sense, and may have formal legal interests in the divorce decree. Aside from the custody award and child support payments, the divorce itself probably is harmful to children in a large number of cases. While sometimes the divorce decree may merely ratify a family break-up consumated long before, and sometimes parents may be so bitter in their warfare before divorce that their separation by divorce may relieve the child of continual injury,[33] these propositions de-

---

31. Standard Oil Co. of Texas v. Marshall, 265 F.2d 46, 56 (1959) (Wisdom, J.). Usually the cases holding that interests for party rules are not legal interest and no others do so in the context of excluding some would-be party with a technical interest, but many cases admit parties without recognized technical interests.

32. P.V. Dept. of Health, 200 Misc. 1090, 107 N.Y.S. 2d 586 (1951).

33. J. L. Despert, CHILDREN OF DIVORCE 9–10 (1953); Plant, *The Psychiatrist Views Children of Divorced Parents*, 10 LAW & CONTEMP. PROB. 807, 813 (1944).

scribe only a fraction of divorce situations. Some spouses part without legal ratification of the termination of their marital status, but many do not, especially where they have property or income large enough to be worth the cost of litigating their disposition. Some parents undoubtedly inflict serious harm on their children by continual battling before divorce but many of them continue to attack each other viciously after their divorce, often using their children to an increased extent as weapons by telling them that the other parent left or sends little money because he did not love them and using them as spies to find out about the other and courriers to carry venomous messages.[34] The psychological and sociological literature on divorce seems fairly united behind the propositions that divorce tends to reduce children's self-esteem[35] in inverse proportion to the children's ages. That this effect is more pronounced with Jewish and Catholic than with Protestant children[36] suggests that it may be attributable to internalization of reference-group attitudes toward divorce and some sense that the sins of parents are attributable to their children. Some of the relation between the effect on self-esteem and age of the children has been explained as meaning that a child during his Oedipal period more than at other developmental stages interprets the divorce as punishment for his hostility toward his parents or as fulfillment of fantasy wishes which are more pronounced at that time, and so he feels guilty.[37]

Children of divorce often suffer slights because of the re-

---

34. Plant, *The Psychiatrist Views Children of Divorced Parents,* 10 LAW & CONTEMP. PROB. 807, 815 (1944); M. Hunt, THE WORLD OF THE FORMERLY MARRIED 179 (1966).

35. M. Rosenberg, SOCIETY AND THE ADOLESCENT SELF-IMAGE 85-106 (1965). The reduction in self-esteem is not associated with break-up of the family by death of one parent.

36. *Id.*

37. A. Freud & D. Burlingham, WAR AND CHILDREN 58 (1943). Anna Freud maintains that this guilt contributes to emotional disturbance. The explanation seems hard to reconcile with the findings of no drop in self-esteem when one parent dies, but perhaps death is more obviously attributable to some cause other than the child. It would appear that this explanation applies mostly to boys where the mother gets custody, and perhaps girls where the father gets custody.

duced status of their parents among their neighbors,[38] develop nightmares, crying spells, stammering, bed-wetting, and other problems,[39] and tend to have less successful marriages.[40] Divorce almost always harms children financially where the family is not very poor or very rich before the divorce, by dividing the same total assets and earning power over two households instead of one. This financial harm is accentuated by the tendency of courts to award custody to the mother since her assets and earning power generally are less than the father's, and the father may feel disinclined to contribute more than his legally required share of child support because his lack of daily contact with his child may reduce his awareness of its needs and his feelings of obligation.[41]

The custody award may also injure the child's interests substantially in non-pecuniary ways. If the parent with less affection for the child wins custody, the child's loss is obvious; this result is not avoided by only awarding custody to those who seek it, because some mothers seek custody even of children they dislike in order to maintain a hold on their husbands through visitation,[42] and fathers often seek custody not because they want the children but in order to drive their wives' alimony and child support demands down in exchange for dropping the custody contest,[43] or fail to seek custody not because they do not want it but because the fact that mothers get custody in over 90% of the cases[44] persuades them that they cannot get it or leads them to infer erroneously from the apparent judicial belief that fathers are generally less fit custodians than mothers that they personally would be less fit than their wives. When, as

---

38. M. Hunt, The World of the Formerly Married 207 (1966).

39. *Id.* at 229–230.

40. Barker, *The Child and Divorce* 73 Case & Com. 36 (1968).

41. Weinman, *The Trial Judge Awards Custody,* 10 Law & Contemp. Prob. 731, 726 (1944).

42. Plant, *The Psychiatrist Views Children of Divorced Parents,* 10 Law & Contemp. Prob. 807, 815–816 (1944).

43. Pokorney, *Observations by a "Friend of the Court",* 10 Law & Contemp. Prob. 778, 781 (1944); Weinman, *The Trial Judge Awards Custody,* 10 Law & Contemp. Prob. 721, 724 (1944).

44. Oster, *Custody Proceeding: A Study of Vague and Indefinite Standards,* 5 J. Fam. L. 21, 26 (1965).

almost always happens when their parents are divorced, boys grow up without fathers, the incidence among them of undue aggressiveness,[45] juvenile delinquency,[46] and low school achievement[47] are higher than for boys with fathers, especially where the fatherlessness takes place between ages 6 and 12,[48] so probably many of the custody awards of boys are harmful to their interests.[49]

The interests of children in preserving their relationships with both their parents have been recognized by a number of courts which have sustained damage awards to children against deserting parents and their new companions for loss of society, love, companionship, and guidance.[50]

Despite these very substantial interests of children in their parents' divorce proceedings, they generally are not necessary or even proper parties to the proceeding, and they may not by reason of their relationship to the parties intervene. Generally, a third person claiming an interest in property involved in a divorce action is a proper party and may intervene,[51] and where the plaintiff seeks a judgment determining a third person's rights or property, that person is a necessary and indispensable party.[52] These rules have been applied to permit adult children of the spouses to intervene in order to have their claims to property alleged by the spouses to be community property adjudicated in the divorce action[53] so there would appear to be no exception to the rules where the third persons are children of the parties. In the absence of statute, the interest of one alleged to have committed adultery with an offending spouse has not in this

---

45. McCord, McCord & Thurber, *Some Effects of Paternal Absence on Children,* 64 J. ABNORMAL SOC. PSYCH. 36 (1962).

46. *Id.*

47. Wylie & Delpado, *A Pattern of Mother-Son Relationship Involving the Absence of the Father,* 29 AM. J. ORTHOPSYCHIATRY 644 (1959).

48. McCord, McCord & Thurber, *Some Effects of Paternal Absence of Children,* 64 J. ABNORMAL SOC. PSYCH. 36 (1962).

49. No study has been found of the effects of motherlessness on boys so this conclusion must be tentative.

50. Miller v. Monson, 228 Minn. 400, 37 N.W.2d 543 (1949) and *see* Foster, *Relational Interests of the Family,* 1962 U. ILL. L. F. 493, 510 (1962).

51. Annot., 102 A.L.R. 814 (1936).

52. *Id.* at 817–819.

53. Elms v. Elms, 4 Cal. 2d 681, 52 P. 2d 223 (1935).

country generally been deemed substantial enough to warrant permitting him to intervene to protect his reputation,[54] but there may be a contrary common law rule in England[55] and some jurisdictions have statutes making correspondents proper[56] or even necessary parties,[57] apparently reflecting a legislative judgment that their interest is substantial enough to warrant permitting or even requiring representation. Though the rule has been stated that no third person may be heard on the question of whether a divorce should be granted,[58] no case has been found declaring the rule where the third person had more than a pecuniary interest. Since a child's interest in preventing a divorce may be far more substantial than that of a stranger to the family, and since intervention generally is permitted and third persons may even be necessary parties to divorce proceedings where their alleged property interests may be affected, children ought, other things being equal, to be permitted to intervene to contest the granting of a divorce. Yet no case has been found contrary to *Baugh v. Baugh,*[59] which held against a right of children to oppose their parents' divorce though recognizing that "it is true that the interests of children are in some important respects more nearly affected by such proceedings than by those which merely concern rights of property."[60] *Baugh* reasons that courts cannot compel discordant spouses to live together, which suggests courts can never deny petitions for divorce with any practical effect and fails to explain why their children should not be represented in deciding the terms upon which they will live apart. *Baugh* holds that though children are affected practically their legal rights are not invaded, which explains neither why "legal" rights should be required for in-

---

54. Annot., 1 A.L.R. 1414 (1919).
55. Howell v. Herriff, 87 Kan. 389, 124 P. 168 (1912).
56. MASS. GEN. LAWS ch. 208 sec. 9; Annot., 1 A.L.R. 1414 (1919).
57. Annot., 170 A.L.R. 163 (1947).
58. Bernheimer v. Bernheimer, 87 Cal. App. 2d 813 (1948).
59. 37 Mich. 59 (1877).
60. *Id.* at 61.

tervention nor why the children's practical interests should not be treated as legally cognizable rights.[61]

The better rule would seem to be that under the general rules defining necessary and indispensable parties children so qualify for all purposes in proceedings between their parents for divorce. They may have a profound interest in the preservation of the marriage and be substantially and irreparably harmed by the granting of a divorce. Such a right to intervene or status as a necessary party would not imply that divorce could not be granted where there were children, for in every lawsuit some represented parties lose. It would mean that where the grounds for divorce permit or encourage courts to consider the presence of children in deciding, for example, whether sufficiently "cruel treatment" exists to justify a divorce,[62] that children through their counsel would be permitted to articulate their interests. Public policy does not favor divorce, so there can be no general objection to permitting the entrance of a party who may decrease the probability that it will take place. Perhaps in many cases it would not be in a child's interest to contest his parents' divorce, but that would seem an appropriate question for determination in each case rather than by a rule prohibiting opposition in all cases. Opposition could be used by the child as a tactic to extract higher child support payments, much as fathers often use it to force their wives to accept lower alimony and child support; probably there would also be cases where the child's opposition to a divorce could provide both parents with a face-saving reason for reconciliation. Where children are very young, they may not be capable of making a wise decision as to whether to oppose divorce, but probably they are about as wise and mature on this question as their parents at some age well

---

61. COMP. L. MICH. sec 552.45 discussed below at p. 26 may be a legislative overruling of *Baugh*. In substantially similar form, it was added to the code by PUB. ACT. no. 137 (1887).

62. Hefferman v. Hefferman, 27 Wis. 2d 307, 134 N.W. 2d 439 (1965), holds that the absence of children loosens the construction of "cruel," so impliedly holds that the presence of children tightens the construction.

below 21, and perhaps for very young children the sociological evidence on the effects of divorce would justify a presumption that their interests were opposed to it. Their lawyer may be able to make a prudent decision that a contest will increase child support. Treatment of children as parties would not eliminate divorce from the statutes even for parents whose children had very strong interest in opposition, as for example if the children had some special psychological problems requiring the presence of both parents, for children grow up and after a certain age their interests in opposing divorce decline as they grow older; therefore, a child's right to contest divorce probably never could impose more than a few years delay upon his parents.

In any jurisdiction not limiting parties to divorce proceedings by statute to husband and wife, with rules of civil procedure resembling the Federal Rules with respect to necessary parties or intervention, courts could reform divorce practice to make children parties with the right to contest the granting of a divorce without new legislation. In the occasional jurisdiction where statute or judicial precedent would obstruct a simple application of the rules of civil procedure in this way, perhaps Due Process would nevertheless require that children be permitted to participate in an adjudication affecting them so substantially, but statutory reform might remedy the injustice more efficiently. Michigan provides by statute that in every divorce action where the spouses have children under 17 process must be served upon the county prosecuting attorney or official friend of the court, who must appear,

> and when, in his judgment, the interest of the children or the public good so requires, he shall introduce evidence and appear at the hearing and oppose the granting of a decree of divorce.[63]

This statute clearly establishes the principle in Michigan that children are substantially affected and have standing through their official representative to contest a divorce solely on their own behalf, though it is not clear whether they can do so on

---

63. COMP. LAWS MICH. sec. 552.45.

their own initiative with a private lawyer. The defendent spouse may not waive the provisions of the statute, and failure of the prosecuting attorney to appear due to the plaintiff's failure to serve process upon him is grounds at least for reversal on appeal of a divorce decree.[64] A somewhat broader statute in effect making all infant children necessary parties to their parents' divorce action with the right to contest the granting of a divorce has been drafted by the Harvard Student Legislative Research Bureau,[65] and an act based upon the Legislative Research Bureau draft has been submitted to the legislature of New Hampshire.[66]

If children may intervene or must be joined in order that they may contest the divorce, than *a fortiori* they may do so to contest custody or child support arrangements. Even if children may not intervene to contest a divorce, they should be heard on the other aspects of the decree which concern them so directly and concretely. A custody decree in effect deprives the child of the freedom to associate with the non-custodial parent, so one issued without granting him a hearing could conceivably violate Due Process, and would seem unquestionably to affect him substantially enough to satisfy the interest criteria of necessary party and intervention rules of civil procedure. Children, especially boys, might with participation and representation be able often to demonstrate that custody ought to be with their father, judging from psychological literature affirming the propositions that boys who grow up without fathers, especially between 6 and 12,[67] tend to be more aggressive than boys with fathers,[68] to become juvenile delinquents more frequently,[69] and to achieve less in school.[70] Those problems of boys without fa-

64. McClellan v. McClellan, 290 Mich. 680, 288 N.W. 306 (1939).

65. Bureau Project, *A Divorce Reform Act*, 5 Harv. J. Legis. 563, sec. 201 at 582–585 (1968).

66. Letter from David H. Bradley to Andrew J. Kleinfeld, Feb. 3, 1969.

67. McCord, McCord & Thurber, *Some Effects of Paternal Absence on Children*, 64 J. Abnormal Soc. Psych. 36 (1962).

68. *Id.*

69. *Id.*

70. Wylie & Delgado, *A Pattern of Mother-Son Relationship Involving the Absence of the Father*, 29 Am. J. Orthopsychiatry 644 (1959).

thers have been explained as an over-masculinity reaction to identification with their mothers caused by the absence of alternative models[71] and as the result of transference by divorced mothers to their sons of their erotic and hostile feelings toward their husbands.[72] Girls apparently are not so substantially affected by fatherlessness, but do tend to become abnormally dependent on their mothers.[73] An inadequate child support decree affects a child perhaps less profoundly but more concretely. He becomes poorer than he was before the divorce, and poorer than he would have been had his father been ordered to pay more child support. His housing, clothes, food, education and medical bills must be satisfied out of a smaller fund. Since a child has a legal right to support, his interest in the part of a divorce decree dealing with child support payments seems quite as cognizable as the interest of one claiming an interest in land in a divorce proceeding likely to culminate in a decree substantially affecting his interest. The third person with a property interest could intervene and might be a necessary and indispensable party; no distinction exists to justify excluding the child.

Despite strong reasons to the contrary, most jurisdictions award custody without any representation of the child. Only a little authority can be found for the proposition that a child is not a necessary party,[74] or even a permissible intervenor,[75] but nearly all jurisdictions conduct custody proceedings as if that were so. This practice may be not so much a reasoned decision as an historical survival from the period where custody decisions were made upon the basis of parental right rather than

---

71. Burton & Whiting, *The Absent Father and Cross-Sex Identity*, in STUDIES IN ADOLESCENCE 107 (R. Grinder ed. 1965); Lyn & Sawrey, *The Effects of Father-Absence on Norwegian Boys and Girls*, 59 J. ABNORMAL SOC. PSYCH. 256 (1959).

72. Wylie & Delgado, *A Pattern of Mother-Son Relationship Involving the Absence of the Father*, 29 AM. J. ORTHOPSYCHIATRY 644 (1959).

73. Lyn & Sawrey, *The Effects of Father-Absence on Norwegian Boys and Girls*, 59 J. ABNORMAL SOC. PSYCH. 256 (1959).

74. Weber v. Weber, 10 Alas. 214 (Dist. Ct. 1942).

75. Kenner v. Kenner, 139 Tenn. 211, 201 S.W. 779; Thomasson v. Angel, 74 So. 2d 295 (Fla. 1954).

best interests of the child, so the child had no recognized interest to be represented.[76] Some judges may believe that following a custody agreement between the spouses provides best for the welfare of the child .because it sheds light on which parent has the greater affection for the child,[77] or represents judgment meriting deference by the parent ceding custody that the other parent is fit to exercise it.[78] But since, as was discussed above, parents may seek custody for reasons other than love for the child or cede it for reasons other than lack of affection for the child or confidence in the other spouse as a parent these arguments rest on questionable factual premises.

> Unfortunately, experience has shown that the question of custody, so vital to a child's happiness and well-being, frequently cannot be left to the discretion of the parents. This is particularly true where, as here, the estrangement of husband and wife beclouds parental judgment with emotion and prejudice.[79]

Several jurisdictions have recognized that failure to make the child a party to the custody proceeding and provide him with representation eliminates in practice the distinction between advancing the child's best interests and treating him as a chattel.[80] The Milwaukee Family Court has relied on its inherent power to implement the welfare of children under the parents patriae doctrine for its practice of treating children as parties and appointing guardians ad litem for them where their custody is disputed or there is reason for grave concern as to their welfare.[81] The prosecuting attorney or friend of the court required to appear on behalf of children in Michigan[82] apparently is authorized to investigate and to argue on their behalf as to

---

76. Note, *Alternatives to "Parental Right" in Child Custody Disputes Involving Third Parties*, 73 YALE L.J. 151, 156 n. 24 (1963).

77. Weinman, *The Trial Judge Awards Custody*, 10 LAW & CONTEMP. PROB. 721, 730 (1944).

78. Dorsey v. Dorsey, 52 Utah 73, 172 p. 722 (1918).

79. Ford v. Ford, 371 U.S. 187, 193 (1962).

80. Hansen, *The Role and Rights of Children in Divorce Actions*, 6 FAMILY L.J. 1 (1966); Drinan, *Guardians Ad Litem In Divorce And Custody Cases: Protection of Child's Interest*, 4 J. FAMILY L. 181 (1964).

81. *Id.*

82. COMP. LAWS MICH. 552.45.

custody.[83] Massachusetts apparently permits third persons to intervene with respect to custody of children and provides representation to facilitate their participation.[84] The New Hampshire legislature is considering a provision for treatment of infant children as necessary parties and appointment of guardians ad litem to represent them on the question of custody[85] based upon a model act proposed by the Harvard Student Legislative Research Bureau.[86]

As to support orders, the child's legally recognized interest in his support makes the argument for necessary party status particularly strong. While the custodial parent has some interest in obtaining a high child support award, she cannot be depended upon to represent the child's interest because often she bargains for custody by accepting a low level of child support;[87] ordinarily courts do not permit parents to represent children as next friends where they may have interests contrary to the children's financial interests,[88] nor does the probate doctrine of "virtual representation" extend so far,[89] so courts should not find an adequate decree of representation to bar intervention or too little possibility of prejudice to require necessary party status. But it has been held that the child is not a necessary party,[90] and Georgia, at least, might even bar intervention on the ground that a child may not bring a support action because the custodian is the real party in interest.[91] These cases do not make sense, and should not be followed; the better rule at least permits a child to intervene,[92] and courts or legislatures ought

83. Geark v. Geark, 318 Mich. 614, 29 N.W. 2d 89 (1947).

84. MASS. GEN. LAWS ch. 208 sec. 28, ch. 208 sec. 16, ch. 215 sec. 56 A.

85. Letter from David H. Bradley to Andrew J. Kleinfeld, Feb. 3, 1969.

86. Bureau Project, *A Divorce Reform Act*, 5 HARV. J. LEGIS. 563, 582-585, sec. 201 (1968).

87. Pilpel & Zavin, *Separation Agreements: Their Function and Future*, 18 L. & CONTEMP. PROB. 33, 35 (1953).

88. White v. Osborne, 251 N.C. 56, 110 S.E. 449 (1959).

89. Looker, *Virtual Representation*, 34 BROOKLYN L. REV. 395 (1968).

90. Slattery v. Hatmaker, 255 S.W. 2d 334 (Tes. Civ. App. 1953).

91. Hooten v. Hooten, 168 Ga. 86, 147 S.E. 373 (1929).

92. Barry v. Sparks, 306 Mass. 80, 27 N.E. 2d 728 (1940).

to make children necessary parties and provide them with representation in proceedings where child support is at issue.[93]

C. *Provision of Next Friends and Legal Counsel*

Conceptually, standing is a prerequisite to representation; no lawyer can argue for one not permitted to be heard. Where infants have strong interests but no standing, provision of lawyers for them cannot vindicate their interests, because their opponents can successfully have them excluded from the proceeding. In practice, however, the converse of this conceptual argument probably makes more sense. An interested person, even with party status awaiting him there does not know how to approach the court without a lawyer. But with a lawyer, anyone, interested or not, may seek to intervene in a proceeding, or may attack a completed proceeding on the ground that he was a necessary and indispensable party not served with process. If his interests are significant, his chances of victory are substantial at the trial level, and if he loses there, he may appeal. Where the would-be party is an infant neither he nor his opponent will find many cases in point except in a few areas like probate where infants have had attorneys to create the cases, so both sides must argue by generalization and analogy about whether the infant has an interest of the sort which must or may be represented and whether it is adequately represented by another. In the absence of authority to the contrary, arguments of this sort tend to favor the infant, for in many contexts the courts have been liberal about what constitutes an interest meriting representation and skeptical about representation of interests by persons other than those seeking to be heard. The implications of all this are that given standing but no lawyers, infants will rarely be represented, but given lawyers but no standing, they will be represented in many battles for party status, a significant number of which will likely succeed, so that they will be represented generally.

---

93. Bureau Project, *A Divorce Reform Act*, 5 HARV. J. LEGIS. 563, 582–585, sec. 201 (1968).

In some areas of law, infants probably are as frequently represented by counsel as adults. When infants are defendents in tort actions where they are covered by liability insurance, for example, defense lawyers retained by insurance companies undoubtedly hasten to assert infants' interests as vigorously as they would were the insureds adults.[94] As potential beneficiaries under wills or takers under intestacy laws, infants traditionally have been represented by attorneys appointed by the probate court or their guardians and paid out of the estate. Indeed, those concerned with infants' welfare have complained that infants in probate have been over-represented, in the sense that so many people are hired to do so much to protect them that excessively large portions of the estate go to the representatives rather than to the infants.[95] Probate courts' provisions for representation of infants frequently arouse newspaper headlines like "Survey Shows Patronage Widespread in Probate Court" and "Judges Choose Friends for Routine Tasks Carrying High Fees."[96]

In other contexts, however, infants generally have not enjoyed representation by lawyers as frequently as adults. Doubtless a great many torts are committed against young children by their parents upon which no actions are brought even where parental immunity does not apply,[97] and much neglect goes on unhindered because the children have no lawyers to press their rights. Parents often have their children involuntarily committed to mental hospitals by proceedings in which no lawyer represents the child and not the parents, or induce them as they could not if the children were represented by misrepresenting their rights and the difficulty of getting out to commit themselves voluntarily.[98] Many young men are drafted because they

---

94. Where there is a conflict of interests between the infant insured and the insurance company, as where the choice is between a settlement just below the policy limit and litigation which may result in a damage award higher than the policy limit, other problems obviously arise.

95. C. Dickens, BLEAK HOUSE (1852, 1853).

96. Boston Globe, Oct. 7, 1968, at 1, 2.

97. Paulsen, *The Legal Framework for Child Protection*, 66 COLUM L. REV. 679 (1966).

98. Harris, *Mental Illness, Due Process and Lawyers*, 55 A.B.A.J. 65, 67 (1969).

do not know of their rights to exemptions and deferments or to appeals,[99] ignorance which lawyers could protect against. Infants proceeded against under juvenile delinquency acts have suffered gross deficiencies of Due Process because of the widespread absence of lawyers representing them.[100]

As comparison of areas in which children have been represented with those in which they have not suggests, the reasons for non-representation have been financial at least as often as doctrinal. Where money has been available, as in insurance defense work or probate practice, representation of children has been more than adequate. Where money generally has not been available, either because of poverty of the child's family or because his parents were proceeding against him and he had no money of his own, as in juvenile delinquency cases, representation has been thoroughly inadequate. Much non-representation in juvenile delinquency, neglect and child abuse cases may also be explained by ignorance of the potential value of a lawyer.

The prevalence of nonrepresentation has both ancient and recent historical roots. The ancient common law provided guardians almost exclusively for infant heirs, and those guardianships were not so broad as to give the guardians duties to litigate on behalf of their wards. Feudal interests overpowered even family ties, so that orphans were treated as adjuncts of their fathers' lands, but the lord's guardianship was a bundle of economic rights over the infant such as the right to charage the infant for the privilege of marrying one other than the lord's choice rather than a set of duties. The common law "looked at guardianship and parental power merely as profitable rights, and had only sanctioned them where they could be made profitable."[101] Because the concept of a general guardian with duties toward as well as powers over an infant had not been developed by the early common law, it sought fairness by special procedures where infants were parties. Infant plaintiffs lacked the

---

99. Washburn, The Draft Counselor, Boston Globe, Feb. 27, 1969, at 19.

100. *In re* Gault, 387 U.S. 1, 34-42 (1966), and materials cited therein.

101. 2 F. Pollock & F. Maitland, THE HISTORY OF ENGLISH LAW 444 (1898). *See also* T. Plucknett, A CONCISE HISTORY OF THE COMMON LAW 544-545 (5th ed. 1956).

capacity to appoint attorneys, but could sue *in propria persona* or with the help of some adult who would file a writ in the infant's name and could obtain legal counsel. Any adult could act as such a "next friend," regardless of his lack of kinship to the infant, and actions might thus be brought against parents and lords with various rights of guardianship over the infant. Courts sought to protect infants from incompetent or bad faith next friends by supervision of the next friends' conduct of the suit and relaxation of formalities such as precise recitation of formulae upon which children might stumble. Infants could be sued in their own name, and might appear without guardians of any sort, but courts would take upon themselves some burden of care for the infants' interests. A special principle prevailed in actions of ejectment, other actions relating to rights to land, and possibly debt, to preserve any possessory status quo with respect to land during infancy. If an infant inherited from one who died seised of land, a person with better title would suffer a demurrer of the parole if he brought an action, which meant that the action would remain in suspense during the infant's minority. Likewise, an infant's parole would demur if he brought an action to eject one seised when the infant's devisor or ancestor died.[102]

> So distant from our law has been any idea of representation of an infant by a guardian, that it will hand up a suit for many years rather than suffer it to proceed while an infant is interested in it.[103]

The demurrer of the parole died away, probably because of its impracticality, but the practice of next friends under the supervision of the court has continued and been institutionalized into a requirement of next friends or guardians ad litem[104] in most actions to which infants are parties. An infant party to an action is a ward of the court whom the court

---

102. F. Pollock & F. Maitland, The History of English Law 440–443 (1898).
103. *Id.* at 443.
104. Different jurisdictions use these terms differently, sometimes distinguishing between them and sometimes not. This essay uses them interchangeably.

has a broad duty and power to protect.[105] This duty requires the court to appoint[106] and supervise[107] a guardian ad litem for an infant party not so represented, and the infant lacks capacity to waive appointment of a guardian ad litem.[108] The guardian ad litem need not be an attorney and may be anyone not having interests in the case contrary to the infant's.[109] Where infants are plaintiffs, next friends are often relatives who obtain attorneys, make themselves responsible for court costs, and control the litigation under supervision of the court. Where infants are defendants, sometimes relatives are the next friends, but often the courts appoint attorneys to serve both as next friend and as counsel. If an infant attempts to bring an action without a next friend, the defendent may temporarily halt the action by a plea in abatement, but waives his objection if he pleads to the merits without raising the issue of a next friend.[110] Since one purpose of the next friend requirement is protection of the infant, it seems anomolous to permit the opposite party to waive it, and the minority rule requiring a next friend for jurisdiction[111] seems more consistent with the purposes of the requirement and the usual rule that the infant cannot himself waive a next friend.

No explicit authority has been found affirming or denying that the court's duty to supervise next friends requires it to compel them to retain attorneys on the infant's behalf where necessary. If the next friend need not retain an attorney though failure to retain one affects the infant adversely, then he is not performing the protective role for which the law requires him. In practice, next friends often do not retain attorneys, lower

---

105. Kingsbury v. Buckner, 134 U.S. 650, 680 (1890); Sangster v. Toledo Mfg Co., 193 Ga. 685, 19 S.E. 2d 723 (1942).

106. Eaton v. Eaton, 112 Me. 106, 90 A. 977 (1914).

107. *In re* Beghtel's Estate, 236 Iowa 953, 20 N.W. 2d 421 (1945); Lovett v. Stone, 239 N.C. 206, 79 S.E. 2d 479 (1954); Bertinelli v. Galoni, 331 Pa. 73, 200 A. 58 (1938).

108. *In re* Dobson, 125 Vt. 165, 212 A. 2d 620 (1965).

109. Annot. 118 A.L.R. 401, 408–409 (1939).

110. Canterbury v. Pennsylvania R. Co., 158 Ohio St. 68, 107 N.E. 2d 115 (1952).

111. Prudential Ins. Co. v. Gleason, 185 Miss. 243, 187 So. 229 (1939).

courts do not act to remedy the defect, and no appeal is taken on this point, perhaps partly because the infant has no lawyer to perceive the possibility of taking an appeal and partly because of the absence of favorable authority. This probably occurs frequently where the infant has no assets which can be tapped for an attorney's fee, and no device such as a public fund or requirement that attorneys serve without charge has been developed to protect indigent infants in the particular context. This practice can be questioned on several grounds. Since the court makes the next friend responsible for court costs, it would seem to have the power to make him responsible for other necessary litigation expenses on behalf of the infant. If no attorney is retained despite necessity, then the next friend requirement becomes one of form rather than substance; presumably the requirement was intended to have substantial effect. If an infant cannot sue or be sued with a next friend, and the next friend does not perform his duties nor does the court perform its duty of supervision, then it is as though the infant had had no next friend, and the adjudication ought not to affect him. If a public interest in avoiding delay of litigation until all parties attain majority requires a procedure for litigating with infants, then the public ought to provide by a fund or a requirement that attorneys accept uncompensated appointments for protection by legal counsel of infants' interests, just as it does when indigent adults are criminally prosecuted.

Depending upon how carefully judges supervise next friends and guardians ad litem, how carefully they appoint them, and whether they require them to retain attorneys where necessary, these doctrines can promote representation as adequately as possible where infants are brought before courts by others. Some judges will supervise and make appointments to line the pockets of their fellow politicians rather than to protect infants, but corrupt judges can pervert any system so this problem can better be handled by changing methods of judicial appointment than by cutting down court power over representation. The next friend system obviously cannot provide infants, especially very very young infants, with all the benefits that representation provides adults. Even assuming close judicial supervision to prevent conflicts of interest and imprudent decisions by the next friend, inevitably he will make some decisions about the conduct of the litigation contrary to what the infant would make were he in control, and some of these, though not imprudent, will be wrong decisions. It may also be doubted whether any person in any capacity can be trusted always to exert as much care and effort on behalf of someone without power to dismiss him or reduce his compensation as he would for one to whom he was more accountable in practical terms. The system does not generally create money where none existed before, though it can approach something functionally similar by requiring attorneys to appear without charge for infants or directing them to bill a public fund. But the options available for infants are next friends, treatment as adults, or incapacity to sue and be sued by any procedure. Treatment as adults, merely leaving it to the infant whether to obtain representation, would doubtless lead to gross exploitation of young children who would often fail to obtain representation, and often less adequate representation for infants where persons with conflicting interests retained their lawyers for them or their own lawyers acted less carefully on their behalf than they would for more sophisticated clients. Incapacity to sue and be sued even by next friends would revivify the demurrer of the parole. Where the aphorism "justice delayed is justice denied" would apply, such an innovation would be undesirable, but in a few areas such as divorce a delay until children reached majority would not be an inconceivable balancing of interests.

The next friend system has failed to yield representational equality to infants in several fundamental respects. Where an infant has a cause of action in which no sophisticated adult shares an interest, the system provides no means for calling judicial attention to the need to appoint representation. The younger the infant, the less likely it is that he will be sophisticated enough to seek representation for himself. Where compensation would be necessary from the infant, counsel will usually be impossible of attainment even by sophisticated infants, both because they usually lack assets and because complications may arise as to the capacity of infants with money to bind themselves to pay attorney's fees.[112]

A second problem has been that while the infant has a highly favorable set of legal rules to protect him from next friends with interests adverse to his and other problems likely to develop with the quality of his representation, he depends upon counsel retained by his next friend or the court to assert his rights under these rules. The judge's sense of his own duty to be and appear impartial and his inability to participate in lawyer-client conferences, investigate, and otherwise learn more than he might be told in court restrict his ability to function as an effective protector of one before his court; this principle has repeatedly been recognized in the criminal area,[113] and seems applicable also in civil cases. While an ethical lawyer may be sensitive to the impropriety of his being retained by a next friend with interests adverse to the infant, lay next friends are likely either not to perceive the problem or not to let it restrain them. Quite often, parents retain counsel both on their own behalf and as next friends for their children in proceedings in which their interests are opposed. This has often been the case in juvenile delinquency proceedings under disobedient child provisions where the parent was complainant.[114] A lawyer so retained could hardly move for substitution of a neglect proceeding against the parents, which might be the best defense, without violating his duty to the parents. Lawyers retained by parents as next friends may decide the child should have new custodians, but be unable to seek them because the parents wish to keep custody. They may be disabled from serving either side by

---

112. The safe procedure is for a next friend of the infant to apply to the court for permission to retain an attorney and authority to spend up to some amount. Richardson v. Tyson, 110 Wis. 572, 86 N.W. 250 (1901).

113. Powell v. Alabama, 277 U.S. 45, 61 (1932); *In re Gault*, 387 U.S. 1, 36 (1966).

114. Skoler & Tenney, *Attorney Representation in Juvenile Court*, 4 J. FAMILY L. 77, 83 (1964).

having learned the confidences of each.[115] Such joint representation of conflicting interests appears also to be prevalent when parents seek to have their children committed to mental hospitals.[116] The law clearly prohibits persons with conflicting interests in the litigation from serving as next friends, even where they are parents,[117] and the Canons of Ethics clearly prohibit lawyers from representing interests so fundamentally at odds, especially where one party is incompetent to understand and waive his right to independent representation.[118] Appellate courts have held, when the problem has been presented to them, that infants are entitled to independent representation when their parents seek to commit them to mental hospitals involuntarily,[119] or to have them punished by the state under disobedient child laws.[120] But the lower courts to whom these shocking situations are presented seem often not to be shocked. Because of the special nature of legal representation as a practical prerequisite to the implementation of rights, this most fundamental right tends not to be asserted where it is not already effective. Thus, a great deal of imporoper denial of independent representation of infants doubtless goes on because judges fail to stop it and the unrepresented have no lawyer to bring it to the judges' attention or to appeal. This problem can be solved in great part by firm rules requiring separate representation of infants and excluding parents as next friends in all cases, civil or criminal, in which parents and children are adverse parties or have adverse interests, but the entire burden of perceiving and correcting infractions of such rules must be borne with little assistance by judges of family, juvenile, and trial courts because until this rule is followed, infants lack counsel to obtain enforcement of any rules.

---

115. Welch, *Delinquency Proceedings—Fundamental Fairness for the Accused in a Quasi-Criminal Forum*, 50 MINN. L. REV. 653, 679–683 (1966).

116. Harris, *Mental Illness, Due Process and Lawyers*, 55 A.B.A.J. 65, 67 (1969).

117. White v. Osborne, 251 N.C. 56, 110 S.E. 2d 449 (1959).

118. CAN. PROF. ETHICS 6, 15.

119. *In re* Sippy, 97 A. 2d 455 (D.C. Mun. Ct. App. 1953) (Commitment under disobedient child law, not ordinary civil commitment).

120. Marsden v. Commonwealth, 352 Mass. 564, 227 N.E. 2d 1 (1967).

A number of jurisdictions have held that no distinction exists with regard to representation where infants are charged with crimes. In some states, the rule has been that guardians ad litem must be appointed in the criminal context, as elsewhere, where infants and defendents,[121] and this requirement has been carried over into the juvenile court system.[122] Presumably the usual rules as to supervision of the guardian ad litem would give the infant a right to have legal representation, selected by the guardian[123] where necessary if the guardian were not a lawyer, and to have guardians with conflicting interests replaced. But there has been a line of authority in several jurisdictions to the effect that where an infant is the defendent in a criminal prosecution, the rules requiring appointment of guardians ad litem do not apply.[124] The Illinois and Georgia cases cited for this proposition involved infants represented by lawyers, and the Texas case is silent on whether the infant had a lawyer, so it may be that guardians were dispensable only where the infants had attorneys because

> Such representation is much more efficient and valuable than that by an unprofessional guardian ad litem, which is often perfunctory. Whenever attorneys at law are appointed by the court to represent minor defendents who are charged with crime, and such minors are so represented, such appointments are in effect and to all intents and purposes of guardians ad litem.[125]

The juvenile court system, however, did not generally require representation for infants charged with delinquency comparable to the representation afforded infants in probate practice and other civil areas.

Sometimes the theory has been that the proceeding involved

---

121. *In re* Dobson, 125 Vt. 165, 212 A. 2d 620 (1965); Fahay v. State, 25 Conn. 205 (1856).

122. *Ex parte* State *ex rel*, Echols, 245 Ala. 353, 17 So. 2d 449 (1944).

123. No authority has been found either way on this proposition, perhaps because when no lawyer is appointed, there is no one to argue for it, and where one is appointed, no one need argue for it.

124. People v. Crooks, 326 Ill. 266, 157 N.E. 218 (1927); *Ex parte White*, 50 Tex. Cr.R. 473, 98 S.W. 850 (1906); Summerour v. Fortson, 174 Ga. 862, 164 S.E. 809 (1932).

125. Summerour v. Fortson, 174 Ga. 862, 164 S.E. 809, 814 (1932).

a mere change of custody from the parents to a reform school, so since the child had no right to choose his own custody or right to liberty, there was neither necessity nor occassion for appointment of counsel.[126] This theory amounts to the surprising proposition that an infant is not a proper party to his own juvenile delinquency proceeding. Even after *Powell v. Alabama*[127] and *Gideon v. Wainwright*[128] made appointment of counsel for indigents charged with felonies mandatory, infants were often denied counsel in juvenile delinquency proceedings on the theory that they were non-criminal interventions by the state to rehabilitate rather than punish. An enormous literature developed describing and debunking this theory.[129] The debunking literature reasoned that regardless of how its founders envisioned it, the juvenile court took liberty and created a stigma when it adjudicated that an infant was a juvenile delinquent, so Due Process required advice as to rights to counsel and appointment of counsel for indigent infants. This attack generally included debunking of the *parens patriae* theory under which infants were regarded as wards of the court, so not needing separate counsel.[130] No commentator seems to have argued for counsel in delinquency proceedings on the ground that the court's duty to protect the infant's rights required it here as in probate and elsewhere. This is surprising, since that argument is usually the one advanced for counsel for children when their parents obtain divorces. The commentators do not explain why such a theory does not suggest itself. The commentators' almost[131] unanimous attack succeeded com-

---

126. *Ex parte* McDermott, 77 Cal. App. 109, 246 P. 89 (1926). This theory is discussed more fully in ch. III, secs. A, C, *infra*.

127. 287 U.S. 45 (1932).

128. 372 U.S. 335 (1963).

129. Paulsen, *Fairness to the Juvenile Offender*, 41 MINN. L. REV. 547 (1957); Handler, *The Juvenile Court and the Adversary System: Problems of Form and Function*, 1965 WISC. L. REV. 7 (1965) are particularly important in the extensive literature describing and debunking this theory.

130. The *parens patriae* theory is discussed at ch. 3, secs. 1, 3 *infra*.

131. Shears, *Legal Problems Peculiar to Children's Courts*, 48 A.B.A.J. 719 (1962) is among the last important articles accepting uncritically the non-libertarian position.

pletely in 1966, when *In re Gault*[132] held, citing much of the attacking commentary and adopting its theory, that

> the Due Process Clause of the Fourteenth Amendment requires that in respect of proceedings to determine delinquency which may result in commitment to an institution in which the juvenile's freedom is curtailed, the child and his parents must be notified of the child's right to be represented by counsel retained by them, or if they are unable to afford counsel, that counsel will be appointed to represent the child.[133]

---

132. 387 U.S. 1 (1966).
133. *Id.*, at 41.

THE BALANCE OF POWER AMONG INFANTS, THEIR PARENTS AND THE STATE
Part II

Andrew Jay Kleinfeld

The Balance of Power Among Infants, Their Parents and The State

ANDREW JAY KLEINFELD*

II. Parental Power

Adults, so far as the law is concerned, generally may act as they wish, except where the state itself has through some duly authorized body imposed on them a duty to conduct themselves in some special way or refrain from a particular kind of conduct. If an adult must conduct himself as another private person directs, this subordinate position generally will be limited to some distinct area of his conduct and will be based upon his own consent. Though these generalizations have never been perfectly descriptive, they probably are reasonably accurate in the United States since the Thirteenth Amendment and the emancipation of women. At least in theory, an adult American is subordinate in a broad range of his activities and without his consent only to the state, and his subordination there is tempered by his freedom to vote and to emigrate.

Infants, however, experience general nonconsensual subordination to their parents. Their consent is unnecessary to parental power, and in general they may not without parental consent emigrate from home as an adult may emigrate from the state. Parental control is not limited to some narrow area of conduct, but extends to almost any area. Indeed, the limitations on state control of private conduct are transformed into parental control in a kind of mirror image; to the extent that the state may not

* Andrew Jay Kleinfeld, a graduate of the Harvard Law School, is a law clerk to Justice Rabinowitz of the Alaska Supreme Court. Mr. Kleinfeld, who makes his home in Fairbanks, Alaska, is a member of the Bar of Alaska.

interfere in some sort of conduct, it often may not interfere with parental regulation of that sort of conduct in children.

Perhaps when married women lived under the nearly unfettered authority of their husbands and black men under the control of their owners, the status of children seemed but one more expression, less questionable than many others, of a society in which liberty was restricted to a privileged class. In America after the Civil War, perhaps pointing to the lack of liberty for some special class when the franchise at least formally extended to all male adults rather than the limited classes elsewhere, would have seemed like calling a pitcher partly empty instead of nearly full. But today liberty has been extended so far as the law alone may extend it to all adults, white or black, male or female, rich or poor, intelligent or stupid; subordinate relations to private persons must be consensual relations and probably cannot, under the Thirteenth Amendment and common law limitations on the freedom to contract, be total.

As our society has extended its democracy to include nearly all adults in the class of free men, bound only to the state, the special position of infants in relation to their parents has become anomolous. What are the philosophical foundations of this relationship? What is the scope of parental power? What sanctions does the state provide to parents or forbid them to use?

A. Philosophical Foundations of Parental Power

Aristotle theorized that (1) children require the care and authority of another because they are incapable of wise and effective self-government; (2) their deficiencies can be remedied only if their governor is mature; (3) the government of children will be more acceptable to them if they know it is temporary and if they bear natural affection toward their governor; therefore, the governor ought to be the father, because of his greater maturity and the natural affection of children for their father, and his government should terminate when the child reaches maturity.[1]

1. Aristotle, Politics 32–33, 316 (E. Barker transl. 1962).

The purpose of parental control, in Aristotle's theory, seems to be the welfare of the child rather than the welfare of others in the society or benefit to the parent. This purpose suggests that the state ought to regulate parental supervision to prevent it from disserving the welfare of children. It may suggest also that children ought to be free to disobey parental commands not conducive either separately or as part of a general scheme to their welfare. Liberty at an age of maturity is integral to the theory, and the age would seem to be a function of two variables (1) the development of children's intellectual, judgmental and physical abilities, and (2) the minimum levels of these abilities required in the particular society for prudent and effective management of one's own affairs.

The idea that parents ought to have a great deal of control over their children has not been accepted in all times and at all places. The Soviet regime, especially in earlier years, intentionally weakened parental authority in order to strengthen state influence over children's political and religious beliefs and general conduct.[2] Nor has the notion that parental power ought to be regulated in the interests of the child always been accepted. Before the Conquest, the English father had some power to sell into slavery his child less than seven years old and may have been free to kill his child "who had not yet tasted food."[3] Under the Twelve Tables, it is said that the Roman father was free to kill his child.[4] But the idea of regulated parental control dominates contemporary American law in every state. Much of the Aristotelian theory seems reflected in the statement of policy of the Massachusetts laws on the protection and care of children:

> It is hereby declared to be the policy of this commonwealth to direct its efforts, first, to the strengthening and encouragement of family life for the protection and care of children; . . . and to provide substitute care of children only when the family itself or the resources available to the

---

2. H. K. Geiger, The Family in Soviet Russia, 292–320 (1968).

3. F. Pollock & F. Maitland, The History of English Law, 436–437 (2d ed. 1898).

4. People *ex rel.* O'Connell v. Turner, 55 Ill. 280, 285 (1870).

> family are unable to provide the necessary care and protection to insure the rights of any child to sound health and normal physical, mental, spiritual and moral development.
>
> The purpose of this chapter is to insure that the children of the commonwealth are protected against the harmful effects resulting from the absence, inability, inadequacy or destructive behavior of parents or parent substitutes, and to insure good substitute parental care in the event of the absence, temporary or permanent inability or unfitness of parents to provide care and protection for their children.[5]

B. The Scope of Parental Power

Parental power probably cannot be defined except as a residue of all power not lodged elsewhere by the law.

> Save as mediated by the Legislature, in domestic affairs the family has remained a self-governing entity, under the discipline and direction of the father as its head.[6]

Much authority of this sort supports the general proposition that except where there is some authoritatively expressed public policy to the contrary, parental power extends to all areas of a child's life.

Some traditional categories of this broad parental power are rights to name the child, to custody and society, to services and earnings, to control of religion and education, and to discipline the child. Categories traditionally viewed as parental duties toward children imply powers necessary to carry out those duties. For example, the duty of support implies a power to make decisions about where the child will live, what he will eat, and how he will dress. The duty to provide a favorable moral environment probably implies a power to censor the books read and movies seen by the child. A list of categories such as this cannot logically exhaust the universe of parental power, because since that power is limited only by a finite set of prohibitions and regulations, its potential scope is infinite. The scope of effective parental power in a particular household probably is restrained more by the imagination of the parents and the efficiency of the available sanctions than by law.

---

5. MASS. GEN. LAWS ch. 119, sec. 1.
6. Matarese v. Matarese, 47 R.I. 131, 131 A. 198, 199 (1925).

In the context of education, parental power has achieved a degree of constitutional protection from state intervention. Before public education became widespread, education was owed the child by the parent as a part of the duty of support, but

> Education is a duty of imperfect obligation, for the reason that it is not capable of practical enforcement. The amount and kind and mode of furnishing education, moral or intellectual, must therefore be left largely to the decision of the parent in each case.[7]

Probably there was little state impingement on parental control in those days, provided that the education was not training for crime or inculcation of vice.[8]

As education became a matter largely of state action, the scope of parental direction was narrowed. The courts did not resist legislative provisions for compulsory education. Against arguments that compulsory school laws invaded "the natural right of a man to govern and control his own children," *State v. Bailey* held that the parent owed a duty to educate his child to the state as well as the child, and the state could properly regulate the discharge of this duty by making schooling compulsory.[9] The *Bailey* case relies on the propositions that the state may regulate conduct affecting the state generally and that education of children is such conduct. This theory was explained more thoroughly in an earlier case upholding the state's right to commit a child to reform school against her father's will:

> It is to be remembered that the public has a paramount interest in the virtue and knowledge of its members, and that, of strict right, the business of education belongs to it. That parents are ordinarily entrusted with it is because it can seldom be put in better hands; but where they are incompetent or corrupt, what is there to prevent the public from withdrawing their faculties, held, as they obviously are, at its sufference? The right of parental control is a natural, but not an inalienable one.[10]

---

7. Com. v. Stewart, 12 Pa. Co. Ct. 151, 2 Pa. Dist. R. 43 (1879), as quoted in annot. 36 A.L.R. 866, 869 (1925).
8. *Ex parte* Crouse, 4 Whart. 9 (Pa. 1838).
9. 157 Ind. 324, 61 N.E. 730 (1901).
10. *Ex parte* Crouse, 4 Whart. 9 (Pa. 1838).

A New Hampshire case recognized a natural, inalienable right of a parent to prevent his child from attending school where attendance would threaten her life because she was ill, but said that the legislature could compel school attendance against the parent's mere whim or pleasure because "education of the citizen is essential to the stability of the state."[11] An oft-quoted characterization of the parent's duty is

> One of the most important natural duties of the parent is the obligation to educate his child; and this duty he owes not to the child only, but to the commonwealth. If he neglects to perform it or willfully refuses to do so, he may be coerced by the law to execute such civil obligation.[12]

The theory variously expressed in these cases may be summarized as (1) education benefits the state, not just the child; (2) this benefit is essential to the state's stability and prosperity; (3) the benefit may be assured only by giving the state standing on its own behalf to compel parents to obtain education for their child (to be contrasted with merely permitting the state to act as representative of the child to enforce the education aspect of their very flexible support duty). A general assumption implicit in this theory is that parental power should be regulated by the state in areas where it affects persons other than the child and the parent. The argument does not, however, assume that effects on the child alone justify state intervention. The latter assumption is not inconsistent with the argument, but the courts apparently did not feel that it would be adequate justification for overriding the "natural rights" of the parent. Apparently the courts have felt that what economists call "neighborhood effects" were necessary to justify state intervention in parental control of education.

During and after the First World War, many states sought to restrict the teaching of foreign languages to young children, partly in order to repress German-American culture and partly in order to foster cultural homogeneity against the pressures of

---

11. State v. Jackson, 71 N.H. 552, 53 A. 1021, 60 LRA 739, 740 (1902).
12. Annot. 39 A.L.R. 477 (1925).

the many nationalities which had recently become large segments of the population. Nebraska promulgated a statute in 1919 prohibiting the teaching in private or public schools of foreign languages to children not yet graduated into the ninth grade. The Nebraska supreme court affirmed a conviction of one who taught German in a private school to a ten-year-old, holding that the statute was a valid exercise of the police power because teaching children a foreign language would "naturally inculcate in them the ideas and sentiments foreign to the best interests of this country," and as to native-born parents who presumably could have their children schooled in foreign languages without undermining American interests, the legislature could decide that children below ninth grade would be better off studying other subjects or playing than learning foreign languages.[13] A passionate dissent claimed that the statute interfered with the " 'God-given and constitutional right' " of a parent over his child's education.[14] *Meyer v. Nebraska*[15] held that the statute violated the Due Process Clause because since it did not restrict generally the burden school could place on a child's mental activities it could not be justified as a health measure, and the state could not interfere with parental right where the demonstrated danger to the state from foreign language teaching was not more substantial. The court quoted a passage from Plato's Republic advocating completely socialized education of Guardians' children and alluded to the socialized education of Spartan boys, then said,

> Although such measures have been deliberately approved by men of great genius, their ideas touching the relations between individual and state were wholly different from those upon which our institutions rest; and it hardly will be affirmed that any legislature could impose such restrictions upon the people of a state without doing violence to both letter and spirit of the Constitution.[16]

During the 1920's, the Oregon Ku Klux Klan grew increasingly disturbed at the proliferation of private schools for

---

13. Meyer v. State. 107 Neb. 657, 187 N.W. 100, 102 (1922).
14. *Id.*, at 104.
15. 262 U.S. 390 (1923).
16. *Id.*, at 402.

Catholics, Jews, and wealthy white Protestants. Fearing that the failure of these schools to impart a common culture to the children in their charge would lead to fragmentation of society by preventing the sharing of fundamental mores, the Klan obtained passage of legislation prohibiting parents from sending their children to schools other than the public schools. Under this legislation, not only was education compulsory, but it had to take place in the public schools through the eighth grade or until age sixteen.[17] *Pierce v. Society of Sisters*[18] held that the statute unreasonably restricted the liberty of parents to direct the education of their children, in violation of the Due Process Clause. The court sharply criticized the theory that effects of education on persons other than the student and his parents justified state regulation of parental action:

> The fundamental theory of liberty upon which all governments in this Union repose excludes any general power of the state to standardize its children by forcing them to accept instruction from public teachers only. The child is not the mere creature of the state; those who nurture him and direct his destiny have the right, coupled with the high duty, to recognize and prepare him for additional obligations.[19]

The states could not evade *Meyer* and *Pierce* by permitting parents to send their children to private foreign language schools but so regulating the schools as to drive them out of business or reduce them to the status of after-school activities for children; this would

> . . . deprive parents of fair opportunity to procure for their children instruction which they think important and we cannot say is harmful. The . . . parent has the right to direct the education of his own child without unreasonable restrictions . . .[20]

Meyer, Pierce, and their progeny did not prohibit compulsory school laws or regulation of private schools in order to assure the high moral character and patriotism of their teachers and to require

---

17. Tyack, *The Perils of Pluralism: The Background of the Pierce Case*, 74 Am. Hist. Rev. 74 (1968). The various qualifications on the legislation are not relevant to this discussion.

18. 268 U.S. 510 (1925).

19. *Id.*, at 535.

20. Farrington v. Tokushige, 273 U.S. 284, 298 (1927).

> that certain studies plainly essential to good citizenship must be taught, and that nothing be taught which is manifestly inimical to the public welfare.[21]

Their effect was to require state regulation of private schooling to meet a test of substantial reasonableness, and to assure parents the right to send their children exclusively to private schools. These cases never mention rights or interests of the children involved. Since they rest instead entirely on a doctrine of parental right, the question of whether the parent may not be loyal to the interests of his child is not discussed. The arguments for the invalidated state laws generally were cast in terms only of a public interest in fostering homogeneity; they did not argue that the states sought to protect the child's interest in an Americanizing education which would facilitate his own career advancement against his parents' interest in molding the child to resemble and be loyal to them and their culture.[22] Therefore, the effect of the cases on the scope of parental control of children cannot be confidently stated. On the one hand, the language of the decisions suggests broad parental discretion to provide children with non-conforming education, restricted only where the state could show a substantial interest in protecting society from totally ineffective or highly dangerous education. On the other hand, in none of the cases were the children aligned against their parents nor did the state claim to represent their interests against their interests against their parents; therefore, the broad judicial approval of parental discretion cannot confidently be regarded as holding with respect to a potential action by a child to restrain his parents from imposing on him an education contrary to his best interests, or an action by the state claiming to represent such a child. The historic source of parental discretion in parental duty to support might tend to support the child's claim against his parents, but the language of the cases would not.

---

21. Pierce v. Society of Sisters, 268 U.S. 510, 534 (1925).

22. The state argued in Meyer that it sought to protect the child's health from over-zealous teachers by preventing excessive studying being imposed on him, but the Supreme Court treated this as patently specious, since the law contained no general restrictions on subjects to be studied or hours of study which could be imposed.

Several years ago, Milton Friedman pointed out that while education had neighborhood effects (i.e., contributed to the welfare of persons whom the student could not in a voluntary setting persuade to contribute toward its cost), these justified only publicly subsidized compulsory education, not free public schools. He advocated abolition of the free public school system and substitution of a system whereby parents would be required to obtain education for their children and would be given subsidies with which to purchase it in the private market. This would widen the range of choice open to all parents, for a parent could obtain a better education for his child merely by paying the incremental cost of the superior school, without the added expense required by the existing system of moving to a more expensive neighborhood. A parent could use a minimum educational expenditure to purchase a different kind of education by sending his child to a different school, without having to persuade the entire community to adopt the kind of education he preferred, as the parent of a child in the public school system must do. The antipluralistic tendency of the present system's requirement that a parent seeking a private school education for his child must pay the private school tuition on top of, rather than instead of, the public school tax would be eliminated.[23] John Stuart Mill long ago proposed nearly the same plan on the grounds that a state educational system tended to reduce diversity to an undesirable degree and produced too many disputes about what to teach.[24]

To avoid integrating its schools after *Brown v. Bd. of Educ.*,[25] Virginia instituted a local option system under which counties were free to abolish public schools and compulsory schooling and offer tuition grants to students attending private schools. Prince Edward County did so. *Griffin v. Prince Edward Co. School Bd.* held the program unconstitutional and ordered that the District Court frame a decree which would guarantee that the petitioners would receive education com-

23. M. Friedman, Capitalism and Freedom 86-94 (1962).
24. J. S. Mill, On Liberty 156-160 (Kirk ed., 1955).
25. 347 U.S. 483 (1954), 349 U.S. 294 (1955).

parable to that given by Virginia public schools, ordering the reopening of public schools if necessary. The decision rested on several grounds: black children did not in fact have a school until several years after the plan was adopted; the plan was county-wide rather than statewide; all the schools operating under the plan were segregated in fact; the motives of the state legislature and county officials in creating the system were improper.[26] One cannot predict from *Griffin* whether the Court would distinguish a state-wide Friedman plan, or a Friedman plan adopted without segregationist motives, or one not resulting in segregated schools. Cases on "freedom-of-choice" plans, however, suggest a broad interpretation of *Griffin,* at least in Southern states where parental discretion results in segregation. Under freedom-of-choice plans, a child is assigned to the school he has attended in the past, but his parents may freely transfer him to any school within a district containing both predominantly white and predominantly black schools. The Supreme Court has struck down several of these plans, presented as techniques for complying with *Brown v. Board of Education,*[27] on the ground that the particular plans have in fact not substantially reduced school segregation.[28] While holding that "freedom-of-choice" was neither constitutional nor unconstitutional in itself, the Court found it an inadequate means to achieve integration, apparently because the choice of parents was not really free, but influenced by white harassment.[29]

> Rather than further the dismantling of the dual system, the plan has operated simply to burden children and their parents with a responsibility which *Brown II* placed squarely on the School Board.[30]

These decisions do not speak directly to parents about the scope of their discretion with respect to their children's education; they are directed against states. But the content of the

26. Griffin v. Prince Edward County School Board, 377 U.S. 218 (1964).

27. 347 U.S. 483 (1954); 349 U.S. 294 (1955).

28. *E.g.,* Green v. County School Board, 391 U.S. 430 (1968); Monroe v. Bd. of Commissioners, 391 U.S. 450 (1968).

29. Green v. County School Bd., 391 U.S. 430, 440 n. 5 (1968) cites without approval or disapproval Civil Rights Commission views to this effect, but seems to rely on them.

30. *Id.,* at 441–442.

messages to states amounts to a restriction on parental discretion. In effect, the Court tells states, "you may not permit parental discretion where it results in no education or segregated education for black children." Perhaps the cases should be viewed narrowly as affecting only school segregation; they are cast as stages in the implementation of *Brown*. But the logic of the decisions requires propositions which cannot easily be limited to the school segregation context. Both in *Griffin* and in the freedom-of-choice cases, the parents of the black children could have chosen alternatives other than those they did choose. In *Griffin*, they could have seen to it that their children went to some school, albeit a private one which white students most probably would not have attended. In *Green*, black parents could have chosen to transfer their children to predominantly white schools in order to obtain for them the benefits of integration. The parental decisions in *Griffin* may have been based on a motive of building an appealing case for anticipated litigation.[31]

The *Green* parental decision was probably based on fear of white hostility and retaliation against themselves and their children, embarassment at sending their children to school with poorer clothing than their peers, and improvements in black schools reducing or eliminating the superiority of white schools.[32] The purpose of the *Griffin-Green* rule, states may not

---

31. The private school attended by the white children was supported mostly by tuition furnished by state and county tuition grants to the students (Griffin v. Prince Edward County School Bd., 377 U.S. 218, 223 (1964)), so probably black parents did not choose to send their children to private school because of economic inability. The Court sees a special burden on black children in that Prince Edward County for several years had a white private school but no black public school (Griffin at 230), but since the white private school was not established until after the tuition grant plan went into effect and a black private school was established five years later and before the case reached the Supreme Court, the special burden on black children may possibly be explained, not by economic or organizational inadequacies of black parents, but by the court's observation that (when the tuition grant plan went into effect)

> An offer to set up private schools for colored children in the county was rejected, the Negros of Prince Edward preferring to continue the legal battle for desegregated public schools. . . . (Griffin at 223).

32. This is a summary of the views of the U.S. Civil Rights Commission which the Court cited (Green v. County School Bd., 391 U.S. 430, 440 n. 5), saying "we neither adopt nor refuse to adopt" them (*Id.*) but seems to rely on as an explanation of the conduct of the parents of the black children involved.

permit parental discretion where it results in no school or segregated school for black children, is to improve the education of black children generally in order to create equality with white children.[33] Assuming that the rule is a reasonable means to achieve this purpose, the cases framing the rule must assume that parental discretion would result in inferior education for black children. This result may flow from a conflict of interests between black parents and their children, or the structural impossibility in *Griffin* of a black parent choosing integration where all white parents choose segregation, or the true or mistaken belief of a black parent in the *Green* situation that the lavishly financed black school may be better for his child than the ordinary white school regardless of the general effects of segregation. Not only may a state deprive parents of the liberty to make these decisions leading to segregation; apparently a state must in some contexts not permit parental discretion in this area.[34]

The *Griffin-Green* rule may limit *Meyer*[35] and *Pierce*.[36] Those cases held, under the Due Process Clause, that the states could not prohibit parents from sending their children to private schools, even private schools teaching subjects regarded (unreasonably) by the state legislature as having substantial subversive effects. But after *Griffin*, a state cannot permit parents to send their children to private schools where this discretion predictably will lead to segregation. Nor, under *Green*, may a state permit parents to choose between public schools for their children, where parental discretion will lead to substantial seg-

---

33. The decisions are cast as attempts to implement Brown v. Bd. of Educ., 347 U.S. 483 (1954), 349 U.S. 294 (1955).

34. Note that the Griffin-Green rule has the effect of limiting parental discretion more than Prince v. Massachusetts, 321 U.S. 158 (1944), holding that the Free Exercise Clause of the First Amendment did not prevent enforcement of a state child labor law against a Jehovah's Witness who permitted her nine-year-old niece to distribute pamphlets with her. In Prince, the court was saying only that a state *may* prohibit parents from making their children martyrs to their beliefs. In Griffin-Green, the court holds that states *must*, in some circumstances, prohibit parents from exercising discretion over their children's education where the exercise will lead to segregation.

35. Meyer v. Nebraska, 262 U.S. 390 (1923).

36. Pierce v. Society of Sisters. 268 U.S. 510 (1925).

regation. The discretion of parents must be limited, under *Green* and *Griffin,* because the parents may have interests in conflict with their children's interests and will probably make choices which subvert an important public policy. *Meyer* and *Pierce* did not consider children's interests, and required weighty justification for state interference with parental discretion over education. *Griffin* and *Green* may mean that parental discretion cannot be permitted where the interest of parents and children conflict and parental discretion will have the effect of subverting an important public policy. The conflict of interests seems no more prominent in *Griffin* and *Green* than in *Meyer* and *Pierce.* The public policy at stake in *Griffin* and *Green,* integration, certainly is more important than the cultural homogenization policy behind the invalidated laws in *Meyer* and *Pierce.* But the choices denied the parents by *Griffin* and *Green* are, viewed individually, not obviously as subversive of public policy as the parental decisions permitted by *Meyer* and *Pierce.* If a state today were to prohibit parents from sending their children to private school because its public schools had become overwhelmingly black and nearly all white parents were sending their children to private schools, the Court might hold that under *Griffin,* the prohibition was not only permissible but required.[37] If this evaluation is correct, then *Pierce* is sharply limited.

During the days when compulsory school laws were being litigated, the courts developed the principle that parental discretion may be limited in order that some general social interest may better be served. Then when restrictions on immigrant parents were tested, the Supreme Court developed a contrary principle that parental discretion is itself of great value, and ought not to be superseded except for the weightiest reasons. Most recently in cases involving segregated schools, the Court

---

37. Hobson v. Hansen, 269 F.Supp. 401 (D.D.C. 1967) holds that educational policies must be subjected to a thorough search for justification when they adversely affect a disadvantaged minority, regardless of their non-discriminatory intent. Note, *Hobson v. Hansen: Judicial Supervision of the Color-Blind School Board,* 81 HARV. L. REV. 1511 (1968).

has apparently qualified the second principle in favor of the first. But this history may not be entirely cyclic. The courts in the compulsory school cases usually did not mention any conflict of interests between parents and children as a reason for limiting parental discretion; they relied on the public interest in an educated citizenry. The segregation cases do not offer parent-child conflicts of interests as grounds for decision, but despite their reliance on other public policy grounds, they do suggest in their statements of fact that such conflicts may exist, and use them as partial explanations of why public policy is disserved by parental discretion. The Supreme Court may be moving toward a doctrine permitting and sometimes requiring limits on the scope of parental discretion over education where parents and children have conflicting interests, as well as where parents may otherwise subvert important public policies.

C. Sanctions for Enforcing Parental Power

Within the scope of permitted parental discretion, the effectiveness of parental decision-making must depend upon the ability of parents to obtain compliance by their children with their decisions. Most of the means used to obtain compliance do not directly involve public law. A very small child can be physically compelled to comply with most parental desires without the commission of an act approaching legally prohibited child abuse. For example, his wandering can be prevented by putting him in crib or play-pen. A great proportion of the decisions made by parents for children cannot meet with resistance because the child is too ignorant and unsophisticated to understand the ramifications of the decision and question it, or even to realize that legitimate alternatives were open and a decision was made. For example, a small child may not realize that he could have a religion different from that in which his parents are raising him. Much compliance is undoubtedly obtained because of the manifest wisdom of particular parental decisions, the affection of children for their parents and eagerness to please them, and the superior ability of the parents to argue in support of a decision, though Aristotle undoubtedly overstated his case when he said,

> Youth never résents being governed, or thinks itself better than its governors . . .[38]

Much compliance can be obtained by manipulation of economic rewards and punishments without interference from the child support laws. For example, a parent can undoubtedly send a misbehaving child to bed without dinner, offer money if the child will spend more time on his homework, and require of a young person that he attend the college of the parents' choice if the parents are to pay tuition; these sanctions depend for their effectiveness on the limited earning power and assets of most infants. A substantial amount of brute force may be used to obtain compliance without interference from the child abuse laws. There is no law against an ordinary spanking.

Public law affects parental sanctions in two ways. First, it limits them. At some point, the harshness of discipline amounts to criminal conduct. Second, it offers the parents an additional sanction which can be afforded only by the state. Infants who disobey their parents or leave home may be guilty of criminal conduct.

1. PARENTAL ABUSE OF AUTHORITY

When parents enforce their commands to children by the use of force, there arises a risk that they will not judiciously confine the force applied within limits of safety to the child's health or appropriateness to his conduct. Though judicial opinions sometimes seem colored by a belief that parents because of their natural love for their children and wisdom are constitutionally incapable of abusing their power, publicity about gross instances of child abuse has recently impelled legislatures to pass new legislation to curb it.[39] As an army may lay seige to a town instead of attacking it, so may a parent enforce a child's com-

---

38. ARISTOTLE, *supra,* note 1 at 316.

39. Paulsen, *Child Abuse Reporting Laws: The Shape of the Legislation.* 67 COLUM. L. REV. 1 (1967).

pliance by deprivation instead of physical aggression. Deprivation can range from subtle expressions of emotional coldness to expelling a child from the home without money or adequate clothing. At some point, deprivation becomes a violation of laws respecting child support. As to physical aggression, parents have long had a privilege to batter for discipline, provided the amount and form of force applied was reasonable considering the nature of the child's offense, the child's sex, age, and strength. A number of older cases have said that where the force applied is without malice and results in no serious injury, parental judgment controls its reasonableness, but modern cases apply an external standard, "it would seem more properly for the protection of the helpless at the mercy of the merciless."[40]

Though parents have traditionally not been free to impose unreasonably harsh corporal punishment, both doctrinal and practical problems have impeded enforcement of the restriction. Infants have always been free to bring actions against their parents in matters affecting property, and though the matter is not perfectly clear, it appears that at common law an infant was long free to sue his parent in tort.[41] But beginning with a Mississippi case in 1891,[42] the courts created an immunity for parents from actions by their children, basing the immunity mainly on a public policy in favor of tranquility in the home and parental discipline.[43] The immunity covered intentional torts quite as fully as negligence,[44] even protecting a father from an action by his daughter for rape.[45]

Commentators have long criticized the parental immunity

---

40. W. Prosser, The Law of Torts 139–140 (3d ed, 1964).

41. Dunlap v. Dunlap, 84 N.H. 352, 150 A. 905 (1930); W. Prosser, Law of Torts 886 (3d. ed. 1964). *cf.*, 1 F. Harper & F. James, The Law of Torts 648 (1956).

42. Hewlett v. George, 68 Miss. 703, 9 So. 885 (1891), (malicious false imprisonment in a mental hospital) cited as the first case supporting parental immunity in W. Prosser, The Law of Torts 886 (3d ed. 1964) and 1 F. Harper & F. James, 648 (1956).

43. Wick v. Wick, 192 Wis. 260, 262, 212 N.W. 787 (1927).

44. W. Prosser, Law of Torts 886 (3d ed. 1964).

45. Roller v. Roller, 37 Wash. 242, 79 P. 788 (1905).

doctrine, pointing out its irrationality in distinguishing between actions on property matters and those for personal injuries, since either kind of lawsuit is about equally likely to disturb the tranquility of the home, and doubting that

> an uncompensated tort makes for peace in the family and respect for the parent, even though it be rape or a brutal beating and even though the relation itself has been terminated by death before the suit.[46]

Though parental immunity did not disappear simultaneously with a husband's immunity for torts to his wife, the courts have in the past few years created numerous exceptions to it, as where the child is emancipated,[47] serious personal injuries are inflicted,[48] the parent is dead,[49] or the injury is inflicted in the course of a business activity carried on by the parent as master with the child as a servant.[50] Alaska has abolished the doctrine where the parent inflicts the injury by negligent driving, and possibly on a much broader basis.[51] Wisconsin has abolished the immunity except "where the alleged negligent act involves an exercise of parental authority over the child" or "ordinary parental discretion with respect to the provision of food, clothing, housing, medical and dental services, and other care;"[52] these exceptions to the abolition of immunity are dicta, and it is not clear whether the use of the word "negligent" in the first exception implies that a child can bring an action for an intentional tort against a parent who exceeds the permissible bounds of disciplinary action. The course of the law in this area has not been an unbroken ascent toward greater humanitarianism, but presently the trend away from parental immunity seems fairly dependably to be leading toward total abolition of the doctrine.[53] Insofar as parental immunity obstructs civil en-

46. W. Prosser, Law of Torts 887 (3d ed. 1964)
47. Wurth v. Wurth, 322 S.W. 2d 745 (Mo. 1959).
48. Gillett v. Gillett, 168 Cal. App. 2d 102, 335 P.2d 736 (1959).
49. Hale v. Hale, 312 Ky. 867, 230 S.W. 2d 610 (1950).
50. Trevarton v. Trevarton, 378 P.2d 640 (Colo. 1963).
51. Hebel v. Hebel, 435 P.2d 8 (1967). The court notes that family tranquility is unlikely to suffer where the liability is of a sort generally insured against.
52. Goller v. White, 20 Wis. 2d 402, 122 N.W. 2d 193, 198 (1963).
53. Hinkle, *Intra-Family Litigation-Parent and Child,* Ins. L.J. 133 (March, 1968).

forcement of the limits of permissible parental discipline, the obstruction is being removed by the developing line of cases holding the doctrine inapplicable to cases of excessive punishment.[54]

The demise of the parental immunity doctrine hardly can suffice, however, to reduce substantially the level of child abuse, at least with young children. An older child, beaten almost to death, might conceivably be sophisticated enough to realize that he could obtain revenge, compensation, and deterrence by retaining a lawyer on contingent fee, though this does not seem likely. But a young child most probably would not know of his available remedies, and even if his wounds were severe enough and obviously enough his parents' fault to enable him to convince teachers or neighbors of his story as to how he received them, they might refrain from helping the child to obtain a lawyer because of fear of legal liability for stimulating the litigation. The inadequacy of the child's civil remedy as a deterrent has stimulated continuing attempts to deter excessive punishment by various criminal law techniques and to rescue the child from dangerous parents by state intervention.

During most of the nineteenth century, such regulations as the law placed on parental cruelty toward children short of murder went unenforced, but in 1822 in England, and in 1866 in New York, societies were organized to prevent cruelty to animals. Though legislatures continued to ignore cruelty to children, these animal protection societies were able to obtain legislation against cruelty to animals and authority to prosecute violators in criminal actions. In 1874, a church social worker in New York City learned of a child who was seriously ill from being chained to her bed, fed only bread and water, and beaten daily. Though no public authority would act, the church lady persuaded the American Society for the Prevention of Cruelty to Animals to prosecute the parents, and the Society won on the ground that children were members of the animal kingdom.

---

54. *E.g.* Gillett v. Gillett, 168 Cal. App. 2d, 102, 335 P.2d 736 (1959).

Responding to this cause celebre, the New York legislature passed child abuse legislation and authorized creation of societies for prevention of cruelty to children to enforce them. Many animal protective societies across the country obtained modification of their charters to include children, and eventually independent child protective societies were formed.[55]

The cruelty to children statutes generally enacted around the turn of the century overlap with criminal assault and battery and also provide for punishment of acts involving neglect and false imprisonment.[56] These criminal provisions do not prohibit the reasonable use of force by parents for discipline,[57] and occasionally excuse even homicide when committed accidentally in the course of discipline.[58] While criticism of criminal law to solve social problems has become quite fashionable, much of the criticism of the cruelty to children laws seems to be of dubious merit. They are typically criticized on the ground that a criminal prosecution will engender parental hostility against the child,[59] but it seems likely that where parents beat their children to the point where they may be prosecuted, they are already hostile. It is said that "a conviction carries with it no social services,"[60] but this overlooks the value of a conviction against a parent as a deterrent, to a potential foster parent or social agency seeking custody, and to a child needing a defense to a charge of delinquency as a "stubborn" child or "runaway." Criticized in terms of how well they operate to deter child abuse and to punish parents who commit it, the curelty to children statutes are most vulnerable on the ground

---

55. This history is taken from V. De Francis, The Fundamentals of Child Protection 3–5 (1955), and is widely known among social workers as the Mary Ellen affair. The historic connection between child and animal protection has never been severed and appears even in Int. Rev. Code sec. 501 (c) (3), "as for the prevention of cruelty to children or animals."

56. Cal Pen. Code sec. 273 (a); N.Y. Pen. L. sec. 483.

57. N.Y. Pen. Law sec. 246.

58. Cal. Pen. Code sec. 195.

59. Paulsen, *The Legal Framework for Child Protection*, 66 Colum. L. Rev. 679, 692 (1966).

60. *Id.*, at 692.

that most child abuse goes undetected and the burden of proof in a criminal case is heavy, so a cruel parent can predict with a high degree of accuracy that unless he kills his child or leaves very conspicuous marks of unambiguous import, he will not be caught.[61]

Cruelty legislation has in many states been bolstered by juvenile court acts permitting emergency action on behalf of an abused child by a court without a criminal conviction of the parent. The court may be empowered to act without a hearing,[62] or even without a neglect petition having been filed.[63] Under such legislation, a judge typically may order a child temporarily removed from parental custody and given medical care if necessary.[64] Such legislation fails to solve the reporting problem and creates dangers of error based on hasty actions without procedural safeguards, but permits emergency action for the child where a criminal conviction would be difficult to obtain[65] or delay would be dangerous to the child. By sharply distinguishing temporary from permanent removals of children from parental custody, the acts offer judges a middle road out of the dilemma of destroying permanently a family or sending a child back into a household in which he may be killed. In a number of states, the reporting problem is mitigated by child protective associations which send social workers to investigate homes on slighter bases than would justify court action.[66]

The legal machinery for protecting children from cruelty requires information to set it in operation. Children cannot adequately provide this information, for they will often lack credibility when contradicted by parents alleging a need for

61. *Id.*, at 692, cites the difficulty of proof, and, at 710, the reporting problem.

62. UTAH CODE ANN. sec. 55-10-87 (supp. 1965).

63. N.Y. Family Ct. Act sec. 322.

64. UTAH CODE ANN. sec. 55-10-86 (supp. 1965).

65. Most juvenile court acts require only a preponderance of evidence. Paulsen, *The Legal Framework for Child Protection*, 66 COLUM. L. REV. 679, 697 (1966).

66. *Id.*, at 708, discusses the problems created by authorizing these social workers to intrude into a family's privacy and often compel cooperation under threat of initiating court action. Though these agencies may develop regularized channels of information through teachers, traunt officers, doctors, and talkative neighbors, they too are faced necessarily with a reporting problem.

discipline; also, if they are very young or very badly injured, as is often the case, they may be physically incapable of telling their story. Neighbors, doctors, and teachers who suspect child abuse may be silent because they fear liability of some sort if they are wrong, do not wish to be considered officious intermeddlers, in the case of physicians sense an impropriety in revealing what they learned through a medical relationship, and because they do not know of some agency to whom they can report with a reasonable assurance of intelligent, speedy action on behalf of the child. In order to solve the reporting problem by stimulating those most able to diagnose accurately child abuse, nearly all the states have passed statutes in the last few years requiring doctors to report suspected child abuse, removing any possibility of liability for reporting, and facilitating admission into evidence of reporting doctors' testimony in court.[67] A considerable number of reports have come into the designated agencies as a result of these statutes and the publicity and community concern often surrounding them,[68] and reporting statutes receives strong support from commentators, the Children's Bureau of the Department of Health, Education, and Welfare, and the Council of State Governments.[69]

Mandatory reporting statutes seem unlikely to be a panacea, however, and could conceivably produce a more dangerous situation for many battered children. Since cases are reported under them only when a parent takes his battered child to a doctor, their effect should be predicted on the basis of what sorts of parents take their battered children to doctors, and how they are likely to react to reporting legislation. It may be specu-

---

67. *See, e.g.*, ALASKA STAT. secs. 11.67.010-11.67.070 (Supp. 1965); CAL. PEN. CODE sec. 11161.5 (supp. 1965); MASS. GEN. LAWS ch. 119 sec. 39 A (1965); N.Y. PEN. LAW sec. 483-d; WIS. STAT. ANN. sec. 325.21 (f) (supp. 1965) protects only against civil liability. As of 1966, 42 states made reporting mandatory, 6 had statutes protecting doctors who reported from liability but leaving them discretion not to report, and only the District of Columbia, Hawaii, and Mississippi were without reporting laws. Paulsen, *The Legal Framework for Child Protection*, 66 COLUM. L. REV. 678, 711-712 (1966).

68. Paulsen, *The Legal Framework for Child Protection*, 66 COLUM. L. REV. 678, 715-716 (1966).

69. *Id.*, at 710, 716-717.

lated that three classes of parents take the children to doctors: (1) spouses of the cruel parents, concerned with their children's welfare; (2) parents who abuse their children in fits of temper (3) cold-blooded parents without concern for their children's welfare but fearing imminent death of their abused children with attendant investigation by police if medical aid is not obtained. The third class might be undeterred by reporting laws, since cruelty to children carries lighter penalties than murder or manslaughter, but the first and second classes might be restrained by fear of prosecution of their spouses or themselves from going to doctors who would have to report. If these predictions are accurate, then reporting will only work where the parents fear death of the child, care more about the child's welfare than their own or their spouse's freedom (not very likely among brutal child abusers), or are ignorant of their doctor's duty to report (not likely after the first beating and doctor's visit, and many child abusers are repeaters).[70]

The reporting problem probably declines in importance for children old enough to go to school. Teachers may detect the marks of beatings, and mention their suspicions to school social workers. Truant officers investigating unexcused absences from school sometimes discover the reason for absence is parental neglect or abuse.[71] Older children can tell their stories themselves, though they undoubtedly have trouble finding police or other officials who will believe them, and may fear that the police will act against them under disobedient child laws, rather than their parents.

Even if the reporting problem were solved, child abuse would

70. The American Medical Association supports legislation such as has been enacted in fourteen states to permit doctors to treat infants for venereal disease without parental consent, because many infants continue to suffer from and spread venereal disease rather than have their parents informed. Keifitz, "Every Two Minutes." New York Times, March 9, 1969 (Magazine) at 85, 87, 90. If fear of reporting causes sufferers from venereal disease to bear its pain and risk without treatment, probably it will stimulate parents not themselves in pain to even greater reluctance to obtain medical service for their children.

71. Fairbanks Daily News-Miner, February 8, 1969, at 6.

still present thorny problems of remedy. Social agencies[72] and courts[73] are reluctant to seek or order permanent termination of parental custody, perhaps partly out of misplaced tenderness for the interests of vicious parents and gullibility toward the parents' promises not to repeat their conduct, but also because the foster care alternatives may present risks of their own to the child's welfare.[74] Many courts order supervision of the home to prevent repetition of the abuse,[75] but supervision may be inadequate to protect the child from parents too hateful or stupid to heed the danger that their viciousness creates for themselves when they are under surveillance. Some jurisdictions lack emergency foster care facilities, creating the spectacle of three-year olds in jail because their parents beat them.[76] At least one state has recently increased the barriers to removing children from homes where they are maltreated; to the old requirements of proof of neglect has been added a requirement of an express finding that parents are unfit.[77] One must infer from the cases on parental tort immunity and the literature and statutes on child abuse that parents very often go beyond the permissible limits supposedly imposed by law on disciplinary violence with impunity.

2. INFANTS' INSUBORDINATION

The preceding material in this section suggests that formal legal techniques for restraining parents who act beyond the scope of

---

72. Polier, *Problems Involving Family and Child,* 66 COLUM. L. REV. 305–310 (1966).

73. Paulsen, *The Legal Framework for Child Protection,* 66 COLUM. L. REV. 679, 702–703 (1966).

74. One frequently sees news stories on orphanages which suggest that they have not changed greatly since Dickens wrote about Oliver Twist's birth,

> Oliver cried loudly. If he could have known that he was an orphan, left to the tender mercies of churchwardens and overseers, perhaps he would have cried the louder. C. DICKENS, OLIVER TWIST 4 (1839, Collier ed. 1911).

75. *See, e.g.,* N.Y. Family Ct. Act. secs. 353, 354(a), 356.

76. A Senate panel was told that this is the practice in Baltimore. Boston Globe, March 8, 1969, at 3.

77. KAN. STAT. ANN. sec. 38–824 (1964), enacted in 1957. *See* note, *Infants-Termination of Parental Rights,* 14 KAN. L. REV. 117 (1965).

their authority or go beyond the reasonable limits of discipline lack effectiveness in many contexts. Dean Pound suggested that the failure of the courts to enforce parental duties and limits on parental rights in favor of children could be attributed partly to judicial commitment to maintaining family unity even by depriving children of bargaining power and partly to an historical quirk that family law became fixed relatively early when the law was more concerned with family than with individual interests.[78] In effect if not in law, the limits on parental authority and discipline are largely precatory rather than mandatory.[79] Since formal sanctions against parents lack effectiveness, one would expect a rational legal system to show tolerance for informal techniques of confining parents within reasonable bounds. When Congress fears over-zealousness by administrative agencies, it often permits those regulated by them to disobey their orders without serious consequences, giving the agency no direct enforcement power but only the authority to seek injunctions from courts. Analogously, courts and legislatures might view disobedience by children, not always as a sign of their vicious disposition, but as a possible indicator of parental error, and either refuse to participate at all in the parental discipline process except to prevent child abuse or else participate impartially. Yet the course of the law has been in the opposite direction, toward increasing state support of parental authority with little evaluation of the particular case. Parents have been given criminal sanctions to have imposed on children who disobey or flee the home, and little control has been placed on application of the sanctions.

Though history is shadowy in this area, it appears that in the past the law was far more reluctant to intervene in family life to support the parent against the disobedient or runaway child. Massachusetts provided for the commitment of "runaways"

---

78. Pound, *Individual Interests in the Domestic Relations,* 14 MICH. L. REV. 177, 186-187 (1916).

79. Lord Eldon said, "The courts of law can enforce the rights of the father, but they are not equal to the office of enforcing the duties of the father." Wellesley v. Duke of Beaufort, 2 Russ. 1, 33.

and "stubborn children" to workhouses where they could be shackled, whipped up to "ten stripes" at once, and "set to labour" at least as early as 1699.[80] England provided at least as early as 1866 for a parent of a child under fourteen to have him sent to an "industrial school" by representing to two justices or a magistrate that he was unable to control the child.[81] But many commentators view disobedient child statutes as novelties, coming into the law at the turn of this century along with the juvenile court system, as part of the wide net designed to discover children who needed help.[82] Perhaps the commentators are wrong, but possibly the ancient Massachusetts statute was a quirk peculiar to Puritan society, and the English statute cited represented the beginning of the juvenile court movement which crossed the ocean a few years later. In any case, judging from the frequency of cases, the doctrine of implied emancipation was far more often applied before the twentieth century to free children from the duty to obey their parents. A child is emancipated by operation of law if his parent is guilty of desertion, nonsupport, or other censurable conduct toward him, and is free to leave home and do as he wishes with his earnings.[83] Also, until recent years, the courts seem to have interpreted the disobedient child statutes strictly in favor of the children. Older cases hold that a child does not "absent" himself from his home within the meaning of the statute unless he leaves home intending never to return,[84] and that a child is not a "delinquent" if he has run away only once, because a "child is not incorrigible who disobeys but once."[85]

---

80. 1 ACTS & RESOLVES OF THE PROVINCE OF MASSACHUSETTS BAY ch. 8 secs. 2, 3 (1692-1714). But parents had to pay for the support of children whom they had committed (*id.*, sec. 5), which may have deterred parents from taking advantage of the statute.

81. Industrial Schools Act of 1866, sec. 16 (29 & 30 VICT. ch. 118).

82. The President's Commission on Law Enforcement and the Administration of Justice, Task Force Report: Juvenile Delinquency and Youth Crime 22 (1967).

83. Annot. 165 A.L.R. 723, 727 (1946).

84. People v. Day, 321 Ill. 552, 152 N.E. 495 (1926). Here a girl took an automobile trip with some boys leaving home about 8 P.M. one evening and not returning until that time the next evening, yet the court held that she did not "absent" herself.

85. *In re* Hook, 95 Vt. 497, 115 Atl. 730, 733 (1922).

Today courts and legislatures cooperate to punish summarily children who disobey their parents, with little more restraint than landlord-tenant courts display in evicting tenants who fail to pay their rent. Massachusetts includes in its penal code a provision against "stubborn children" and "runaways."[86] California provides that

> Any person under the age of 21 years who persistently and habitually refuses to obey the reasonable and proper orders or directions of his parents, guardian, custodian, or school authorities, or who is beyond the control of such persons, or any person who is a habitual truant from school within the meaning of any law of this State, or who from any cause is in danger of leading an idle, dissolute, lewd, or immoral life, is within the jurisdiction of the juvenile court which may adjudge such person to be a ward of the court . . .[87]

Under the California statute and others like it, parents usually are the complainants, scope of apellate review is very narrow,[88] and, until recently, children have rarely had lawyers.[89] The quantum of proof necessary for a finding of delinquency has been diluted from beyond a reasonable doubt to a mere preponderance of the evidence.[90] Most of the statutes do not go into the detail of the California statute in defining the kind of disobedience covered; the Massachusetts statute is not unusual in merely stating that "stubborn children" and "runaways" are criminals. Perhaps because of the generality of most of the statutes, and the lack of legal representation for children, no body of case law seems to have developed to make unreasonableness of the parental command or general impropriety of

---

86. MASS. GEN. LAWS ch. 272 sec. 53.

87. CAL. WELFARE & INST. CODE sec. 601.

88. *In re* Schubert, 153 Cal. App.2d 138, 313 P.2d 968 (1957). Case law under these statutes is extremely scarce, partly because children adjudicated delinquent under them have in the past rarely had lawyers, and partly because even if they had lawyers, the lawyers had little to appeal on, since appellate courts routinely affirm the lower court decisions as to fact and usually no written record of proceedings is kept in which the lawyer can show improprieties justifying a new hearing.

89. California did not provide by statute for appointment of counsel for indigent children, or children whose parents are the complainants, until 1961. CAL. STATS. 1961, ch. 1616, p. 3475, sec. 2, now CAL. WELF. & INST. CODE sec. 634. Many states provided no counsel when *In re* Gault, 387 U.S. 1 (1966) came down and are only now coping with the problem.

90. *In re* J.F., 242 N.E. 2d 604, 605 (Ohio Juv. Ct. 1968) (dictum).

parental conduct defenses against disobedient child proceedings. Such defenses could be created as applications of general definitions of insubordination, which require that an order be reasonable and emanate from proper authority.[91] Or they could proceed by the argument that improper conduct of the parent had emancipated the child, so his duty to obey had been destroyed.[92] Both these theories would bring parental behavior before the court so as to expose unfit parents. Yet scanty authority, none quite in point, can be found for them in this context.

The effect of the mistakes undoubtedly made on the side of parents in enforcing disobedient child law probably is very substantial. A very high proportion of those adjudicated juvenile delinquents, especially among girls, are so adjudicated under disobedient child laws.[93] One purpose of making criminal such behavior as disobeying parents is to cast a wide net in order that the juvenile court may rehabilitate youths before they become habituated to criminal behavior.[94] But even putting aside the constitutional questionability of extremely vague crimes of which status as a child is a prerequisite, it is doubtful whether the goal of rehabilitation is served by casting so wide a net. The juvenile court and reform school system has a notoriously poor rehabilitative record for all sorts of criminal conduct.[95] The reading of a large number of court cases involving juvenile delinquency can lead one to believe that juvenile court

---

91. MacIntosh v. Abbott, 231 Mass. 180, 120 N.E. 383 (1918); Garvin v. Chambers, 195 Cal. 212, 231 P. 696, 701 (1924).

92. In some juvenile courts lawyers for children obtain dismissals of charges against their clients by moving for substitution of neglect proceedings against their parents. Skoler & Tenney, *Attorney Representation in Juvenile Court, 4* J. FAM. L. 77, 83 (1964).

93. Over half the girls referred to juvenile courts in the United States in 1965 were referred for conduct not criminal if committed by an adult, mostly running away and ungovernable behavior. President's Commission on Law Enforcement & the Administration of Justice, The Challenge of Crime in a Free Society. (Avon ed. 1968).

94. Handler, *The Juvenile Court and the Adversary System: Problems of Function and Form,* 1965 WISC. L. REV. 7, 15 (1965).

95. Even such staunch advocates of the juvenile court system as the Gluecks have long been disturbed by this. S. GLUECK & E. GLUECK, ONE THOUSAND JUVENILE DELINQUENTS 233-234 (1934).

judges, perhaps because their roles require a peculiarly high degree of confidence in normative propositions and unverified empirical propositions, lack the ability to ever improve their performance as rehabilitative social workers, because they are not inclined to seek empirical confirmation of the sociological propositions about institutions and individuals on which they base their judgments.[96] Less charitable commentators suggest that part of the failure of juvenile court rehabilitation may be attributed to a less esoteric form of judicial incompetence; in many court systems, the juvenile court attracts the least qualified persons; juvenile court judges are often not lawyers and rarely good lawyers.[97] Disobedient child laws may tend to cause children spotted and "rehabilitated" under them to participate in more conduct criminal for adults than they otherwise would have; by labeling these somewhat rebellious children as delinquents, the system confirms their alienation, thereby weakening their inhibitions against serious anti-social conduct.[98]

A fundamental purpose of runaway statutes is to keep families together; indeed, this purpose underlies most family law.[99] An old child support case suggests by implication the way in which the runaway statutes attempt to accomplish this:

> The delicate parental duty which requires of a child submission to reasonable restraints, and demands habits of propriety, obedience, and conformity to domestic discipline, may induce a minor to abandon his father's home rather than submit to what may seem to the parents proper discipline and necessary restraints of the household. It would be intolerable if any one who should choose to furnish a minor necessaries,

---

96. A superb example of the kind of remark obnoxious to the sociological mind which judges are wont to make came in a recent case where parents placed their child elsewhere than the institution recommended but not required by the judge. The judge seems to have seen no problem in saying of the juvenile, J. F.:

> We have no knowledge of his present situation; whatever it may be we are confident that if the Court's plan for placement at Hawthorne Cedar Knolls had been effected J.F. would have had a happier, healthier life. *In re* J.F. 242 N.E. 2d 604, 608 (Ohio Juv. Ct. 1968).

97. Polier, *Problems Involving Family and Child*, 66 COLUM. L. REV. 305, 306 (1966).

98. President's Commission on Law Enforcement and the Administration of Justice, The Challenge of Crime in a Free Society, 218, 220 (Avon ed. 1968).

99. Not only do cases express this purpose, but statutes occassionally express it in the strongest terms. MASS. GEN. LAW ch. 119 sec. 1.

> under all circumstances could compel a father to answer to a court or jury concerning the propriety of the family discipline. If this were allowed, a child impatient of parental authority might be incited to set at naught all reasonable domestic control by holding over his father's head the alternative of allowing him his way at home, or of paying for his support abroad.[100]

This passage suggests that (1) often parental commands are at least questionable (2) children would often like to leave home rather than obey these and other parental commands (3) if children could obtain support away from home when the commands they fled were unreasonable, they would often leave home or compel parents by the economic threat of leaving home to compromise their own demands with the child's. The passage concludes that the consequence in (3) should be avoided, but this conclusion is not inevitable. The court sees the family as a political unit in which an authority issues many commands, some reasonable, some not, and obtains compliance by threatening its subjects with violence if they stay without complying and the most abysmal poverty if they leave; the court seeks to preserve these sanctions because otherwise the authority would have to compromise with his subjects. Such a policy invites emigration even at the cost of poverty, or revolution.

Looked at more concretely from the point of view of the runaway child, he has left home because he found it so intolerable that he was willing to face substantial problems of taking care of himself on the street in order to escape it.[101] If his parents love him or are embarrassed by the public display of dissatisfaction with their régime, the child's act gives him bargaining power with which he can negotiate a compromise with his parents that he can live with. Before his flight, his parents would not concede enough to him so that he could live under

---

100. Ramsey v. Ramsey, 121 Ind. 215, 217, 23 N.E. 69 (1889) (no duty upon father to pay for support voluntarily furnished to his child by his divorced wife while she maintains custody).

101. Often, "running away seems to be a healthy mode of response to an intolerable situation." Shellow, Schamp, Liebrow, & Unger, *Suburban Runaways of the 1960's*, 32 SOC'Y FOR RESEARCH IN CHILD DEVELOPMENT 4 (1967).

their authority without sacrifices of intolerable amounts of dignity, autonomy, privacy and other values; therefore he left fully intending to return shortly after registering a protest and bolstering his ability to negotiate a livable arrangement. If the police intervene, forcibly returning him to his home (runaways are usually booked, detained a few hours or days, then sent home instead of to an institution, with or without a trial), then his return is not based on a negotiated compromise, and the conditions which caused his runaway usually cause him to flee again. Sometimes the child invites police intervention when negotiations have failed in order to return home while saving face. But usually police intervention not only heightens the youth's resentment but also amounts to termination of negotiations before they have proceeded as far as they otherwise would, and by precluding modification of the home government to make it tolerable to the youth, the police intervention increases the likelihood of repeated running away. This theory explains the statistic that runaways brought home by police tend to run away again more frequently than those who return home voluntarily.[102] If correct, this theory implies that runaway laws tend to defeat their own purpose of keeping children with their families.[103]

Runaway and disobedient child laws are not inevitable. The Soviet Union provides free or heavily subsidized dormitories for youths above a certain age in order to strengthen their bargaining power within the home so as to accelerate the replacement of pre-Revolutionary with Communist mores.[104] State law often does permit infants to leave home against paren-

---

102. This view of running away as a bargaining strategem is persuasively argued with supporting statistics by a minister who has operated a runaway shelter in San Francisco. L. Beggs, Huckleberry's for Runaways 14–15, 22, 30, 35–37 (1969).

103. This is not to say that there would be fewer runaways without runaway laws. Possibly the spectre of a police record deters more runaway behavior than the higher level of resentment and disruption of bargaining by police intervention causes. But the theory at least suggests that runaway laws are to some extent self-defeating, and an efficient way to accomplish their purpose.

104. H.K. Geiger, The Family in Soviet Russia 307 (1968).

tal commands by permitting girls over eighteen to marry against parental opposition.[105] This exception to anti-runaway policy probably reflects a legislative belief that at some point youths will break the law rather than remain at home, and laws certain to be broken should not be promulgated, combined with some respect for the wisdom of youthful decisions. But the exception seems queer in view of the rigor with which runaway law is otherwise maintained, since it encourages youths to make a momentous decision for a bad reason, the desire to leave home. If youthful marriages cannot be prevented, then at least the incentive provided by the runaway laws to marriage for the wrong reasons ought to be eliminated by reducing the runaway age to the age at which marriage is permitted.[106]

Where the alternatives open for a child are custody with one parent or with the other, as in divorce cases, many states and many other nations accord considerable respect to the wishes of a youth over fourteen or so. A number of countries make the choice of a post-puberty youth binding.[107] Georgia, Illinois, Utah, Arizona, California and Oklahoma make the preference of children over ages between ten and fourteen binding or extremely strong factors in custody awards between parents.[108]

---

105. ALAS. STAT. sec. 25.05.011; Cal. Civ. Code sec. 56. A California girl of 16 can marry with one parent's consent against the other parent's opposition. These ages have in many states risen over the years. The predecessor to the present California statute enacted in 1872 permitted a girl of 15 to marry against the opposition of both parents; the age was raised in 1921.

106. The California law covers runaways of both sexes up to age 21, but the San Francisco police rarely look for or arrest runaways over 18. Such an age reduction, then, might amount to no more than formal recognition of actual enforcement policy. Its effect would them be to eliminate application of the runaway laws in a discriminatory way or for ulterior purposes among those over 18, and to eliminate an incentive to marry merely in order to escape parental authority among girls over 18 not aware of actual enforcement policy or fearing that their parents would obtain an extension of usual enforcement policy in their zeal to maintain control.

107. Lemkin, *Orphans of Living Parents: A Comparative Sociological View*, 10 LAW & CONTEMP. PROB. 834, p. 841–842 (1944) cites England, Ontario, Canada, and Ecuador.

108. Annot. 4 A.L.R. 3d 1396 (1965) surveys all the law as to children's wishes in custody decisions. *See* Ga. Acts of 1962, pp. 713, 714, amending GA. CODE sec. 30-127 to give infants over 14 an absolute right of choice between fit parents; CAL. CIV. CODE sec. 138; UTAH CODE sec. 30-3-5.

Some courts have, without such statutes, developed case law to the effect that a youth's wishes as to custody ought to weigh heavily in custody decisions, basing it on statutes giving children over the age of twelve or so the right to choose guardians.[109] Most states require the written consent of a child over twelve or so to adoption.[110] These statutes and cases rest on an implicit proposition that youths over twelve or so have sufficient judgment to make wise decisions about their own custody, compared with the decisions that their parents might make by settlement or that third parties including judges might make. They may also imply a recognition that the best interests of the child, the goal custody law claims to seek, cannot be served by placing him in the custody of a parent whose domination he vehemently opposes. They may also suggest a notion that a youth has certain inherent rights to free association, extending to the custodial relationships to which he is subject. These propositions underlying much law of child's preference in custody decisions cannot be reconciled with the propositions affirming unquestioned parental domination underlying disobedient child laws.

The scope of parental authority has not been carefully limited to protect the interests of children, though the law may be moving in this direction. The formal legal sanctions designed to enforce the limits on scope of parental authority and techniques used by parents to obtain compliance are not very effective, and probably never can be fully effective. This problem of ineffective formal sanctions could be partially solved by greater permissiveness toward informal techniques for keeping parents within proper bounds. Yet the disobedient child statutes, by providing one-sided state intervention against children who disobey or flee parental authority no matter how justified their action, drastically reduce the availability of informal sanctions and fail even to serve their own goals of preserving the unity of

---

109. Annot., 4 A.L.R. 3d 1396, 1424 (1965).
110. *E.g.*, MASS. GEN. LAWS ch. 210 sec. 2.

families. These statutes ought to be abolished. The informal sanctions available to parents for obtaining obedience and the economic disincentives to running away are so strong that when children do engage in chronic disobedience or flight, quite likely their conduct is justified, or if it is not, state intervention will not deter it or prevent repetition.

THE BALANCE OF POWER AMONG INFANTS, THEIR PARENTS AND THE STATE
Part III

Andrew Jay Kleinfeld

The Balance of Power Among Infants, Their Parents and The State

ANDREW JAY KLEINFELD*

III. The Relation to The State

The relationship between citizen and state in the United States has been developed, from pre-Revolutionary informal controls through constitution-making days and centuries of constitutional interpretation, into a structure of checks on the power of government. By his power to vote, the citizen may obtain compliance with his preferences by legislators and executives (and even some state judges) because of his power, when a substantial number of persons agree with him, to hire and fire them without cause. Even where he can find only a small minority who share his preferences, he may obtain compliance from elected officials to the extent that the minority preference is intense enough to make those who hold it one-issue voters, while the majority with the conflicting preference care at least as much about other issues, so will not reject the politician for going along with the minority on the issue in question.[1] When his elected government seeks to regulate his activities, the citizen can often obtain a court ordered halt to the regulatory activity if it is unreasonable, unfair, or otherwise improper, and to the extent that the regulation proceeds by a suspect classification or inhibits an activity of fundamental importance, the courts will tend to sympathize with his claim.[2] The citizen's liberty to come and go where he pleases, to occupy himself as he likes, and to prohibit touchings of his body, can rarely be

---

* Andrew Jay Kleinfeld, a graduate of the Harvard Law School, is a law clerk to Justice Rabinowitz of the Alaska Supreme Court. Mr. Kleinfeld, who makes his home in Fairbanks, Alaska, is a member of the Bar of Alaska.

1. R. DAHL, A PREFACE TO DEMOCRATIC THEORY 90–123 (1956).

2. *See Developments in The Law Equal Protection*, 82 HARV. L. REV. 1065 (1969) for a description of judicial restrictions on unfair and unreasonable regulation.

restricted except in very limited respects, or for short periods, or for the commission of a crime.[3]

Infants do not generally share in this liberty against the government to replace those who make and execute the laws and to control their persons. Though the franchise has gradually been extended to include black man,[4] women,[5] and some persons who cannot read and write English,[6] few states permit persons under 21 to vote. An infant is compelled to yield up his body to school for much of the time until age 16, and his activities in school are controlled by persons over whom he has little formal control. The scope of the control exercised by the school over his body has extended not only to where he must be, what he must do there, and what he must talk about and when, but also to such intimate matters as how he must dress, how he may wear his hair, whether he may smoke, and even when he may go to the bathroom.

This chapter explores the peculiarities of the relationship between the infant and the state. Because it is so fundamental to the securing and maintenance of the recognition of all other interests, the franchise is separately discussed. Most of the other discussion focuses on the power of schools over children, because nearly all children participate in this relationship, and it raises most of the issues pertinent to infancy which arise in other contexts. The discussion of infancy and criminal law is limited partly because much of the special law for infants was discussed in the previous chapter and partly because excellent commentary abounds on this subject.[7]

---

3. A striking exception to this generalization is the citizen judged to be mentally ill. Of course, there are others, such as the Internal Security Act, 50 U.S.C. sec. 811 ff. (1959), and if it is still good law, the imprisonment of suspect ethnic groups during wartime. Hirobayashi v. United States, 320 U.S. 81 (1943); Korematsu v. United States, 323 U.S. 214 (1944).

4. U.S. CONST. amend. 15.

5. U.S. CONST. amend. 19.

6. 42 U.S.C. § 1973(b) (e) (Supp. III, 1968), the section of the Voting Rights Act of 1965 which prohibits states from denying the franchise for illiteracy in English to persons who have completed the 6th grade in an American-flag school teaching a language other than English.

7. Paulsen, *Fairness to the Juvenile Offender,* 41 MINN. L. REV. 547 (1957); Handler, *The Juvenile Court and the Adversary System: Problems of Function and Form,* 1965 WISC. L. REV. 7 (1965); Mack, *The Juvenile Court,* 23 HARV. L. REV. 104 (1909); and see the mountain of commentary cited by *In re* Gault, 387 U.S. 1 (1967).

What philosophical notions underlie the peculiarly non-libertarian condition which is imposed upon infants? Is denial of the franchise to persons under 21 just? What limits are there to the scope of state discretion to regulate the activities and seize the bodies of infants? Are the restrictions upon infants' liberty likely to serve their purposes, insofar as the purposes are legitimate?

A. Philosophical Foundations of the Special Relationship Between Infants and The State

Direct state management of infants' affairs traditionally has been explained by the doctrine of *parens patriae* ("father of his country"). One of the earliest applications of the doctrine to children, *Eyre v. Countess of Shaftsbury,*[8] reasons that the king has a duty to protect lunatics because they can not take care of themselves, and this reason applies to children as well, so the king has a duty to protect children. *Eyre* seems to found the general duty to protect those incapable of protecting themselves on a duty to protect all citizens so far as necessary. The doctrine was elaborated in the famous custody case of *Wellesley v. Wellesley,*[9] denying the petition of a father against his deceased wife's sisters for custody of his minor children because he was living in adultery and was otherwise a poor moral exemplar.[10] Lord Rosedale assumed that parents had rights to their children only by grace of the state, and explained the usual delegation of control over children to parents as a trust, with which parents were endowed because usually they would discharge it faithfully on behalf of the child. Where the trust was not faithfully discharged, as where the father was cruel to his child, or failed to maintain him, the state traditionally intervened on the child's behalf. Analogously, Chancery for 150 years had regulated testamentary guardians as trustees on infants' behalf. Lord Rosedale cited also the anology to lunatics drawn in *Eyre*. He

8. 24 Eng. Rep. 659 (Ch. 1722).
9. 4 Eng. Rep. 1078 (H.L. 1828).
10. Mr. Wellesley, while living with a Mrs. Bligh in Paris, to which he had gone to escape his creditors, had sent letters to his son with such moral advice as "study hard, but as soon as you have completed your tasks. go out, in all weathers, and play hell and Tommy, etc, chase cats, dogs, and women, old and young, but spare my game." *Id.*, at 1079.

cited also the ancient practice of the City of London, which must have been based on a grant of power from the Crown, to care for orphans.[11]

The *Wellesley* theory of *parens patriae* has not changed a great deal during its passage through time or across the Atlantic. *Ex parte Crouse*[12] justified the defeasibility of the trust to parents on the ground that "the public has a paramount interest in the virtue of its members."[13] Most cases have not offered this argument, that child rearing affects persons other than the parents and children; usually the theory is put forward solely as a protective device for children against their parents.[14] Sometimes the trust envisioned by *parens patriae* is defeasible only if the parents are unfit,[15] but other cases say that whatever rights parents enjoy in their children are granted at the grace of the state, and may be removed without a showing of parental unfitness.[16] The analogy to treatment of the insane frequently appears; sometimes the reasoning goes in the opposite direction from *Eyre v. Countess of Shaftsbury*,[17] which deduced *parens patriae* over children from *parens patriae* over lunatics, and instead deduces control over lunatics from control over children.[18]

Though an occasional commentator and many courts still reiterate the doctrine uncritically,[19] most commentators now seem less than respectful of it.[20] Invocation of *parens patriae*,

11. *Id.*, at 1080-1081.

12. 4 Whart. 9 (Pa. 1839) (denying a father's habeus corpus petition to have his daughter returned from reform school to which she had been committed because of her mother's disobedient child complaint.)

13. *Id.*, at 11.

14. *In re* Ferrier, 103 Ill. 387 (1882).

15. *Id.* at 372 ("whenever . . . the parents is grossly unfit").

16. *Ex parte* Crouse, 4 Whart. 9 (Pa. 1839) makes parental unworthiness or incompetence for the particular function enough without general unfitness. State v. Bailey, 157 Ind. 324, 61 N.E. 730 (1901), a compulsory school case, permits state intervention into any area of child rearing affecting society generally, without any requirement of parental inadequacy.

17. 24 Eng. Rep. 659 (Ch. 1722).

18. *In re* Huekelekian, 24 N.J. Sup. 407 (1953), (Bigelow, J.A.D., dissenting).

19. Shears, *Legal Problems Peculiar to Children's Courts*, 48 A.B.A.J. 719, 720 (1962).

20. History has not been an uninterrupted progress here. 2 F. POLLOCK & F. MAITLAND, THE HISTORY OF ENGLISH LAW 445 (1898) seems to regard the doctrine as an arrogant assertion of the king's justices in an over-governed country. The great ascent of the doctrine came with the juvenile court movement; *see* Mack, *The Juvenile Court*, 23 HARV. L. REV. 104 (1909). Only very recently have courts and commentators moved toward the nineteenth century attitude of skepticism of the doctrine.

at least as a talisman to justify denial of due process to infants, should decline, now that the Supreme Court has said "its meaning is murky and its historic credentials are of dubious relevance."[21] But the idea behind the doctrine of a right of the state to interfere in child-rearing on behalf of the child or society generally has more recently been reaffirmed as a justification for variable obscenity legislation,[22] so probably the courts will continue to apply theory though perhaps eschewing the words *parens patriae* when they do so.

The *parens patriae* theory conflicts radically with the oft-expressed notion that parental rights are natural, sacred,[23] and inalienable.[24] Both ideas have been relied upon by high authority for many years, and neither has fallen into disuse. The justifications offered for it in *Wellesley* are subject to attack on the grounds that testamentary guardians can be distinguished because they are the creature of the state while procreation could occur without any state, and the analogies to lunatics and London orphans beg the question of why the state ought to protect anyone not a criminal or dangerous to the extent of taking him into custody. The suggestion in *In re Crouse*[25] that state control over infants rests on the effects on society generally of child rearing suggests another justification of the theory. Aristotle founded his argument for compulsory education in state schools on the proposition that political stability required indoctrination of all citizens during their youth with the constitutional principles of their particular state.[26] John Stuart Mill relies on the principle that effects on others justify state intervention for his proposal that the state require parents to limit the number of children they have when overpopulation threat-

21. *In re* Gault, 387 U.S. 1, 16 (1967).

22. Ginsberg v. New York, 390 U.S. 629 (1968).

23. *In re* Agar-Ellis, 10 Ch.D. 49, 71-72 (1878) (upholding the father against the mother on control of their children's religious education, but saying *in dictum* at 72 that the state may never interfere with parental control except where the father's conduct is so grossly improper as to amount to an abdication of his authority). The case holds that more is required to induce a court to interfere with a father than with a testamentary guardian; this undermines one analogy on which Wellesley based the theory of *parens patriae*. *Accord*, *In re* Agar-Ellis, 24 Ch.D. 317 (1883).

24. Sayre, *Awarding Custody of Children*, 9 U. CHI. L. REV. 672 (1942).

25. 4 Whart. 9 (Pa. 1839).

26. ARISTOTLE, POLITICS 332 (Barker ed. 1962).

ens substantial unemployment.[27] The argument of effects on others justifies state intervention insofar as parents contest it. If a child has no right to liberty, but only to custody,[28] then state substitutions for the parent as custodian can be justified by the harm that parental custody does to third persons. But this argument leaves unexplained its premise that infants have rights only to custody, not liberty. The *parens patriae* doctrine was originated to deny liberty to parents, but has sometimes been applied, as in the juvenile court movement, to take liberty from infants. Where the infant is a very young child, the argument may be made that (1) liberty implies a process of making choices for one's self, (2) a young child cannot comprehend most of the decisions which he would have to make, were he treated as an adult, (3) therefore, the young child cannot because of his incapacity to perform the activities of liberty enjoy liberty in more than name. But this argument cannot be applied to youths who have attained most or all of their intellectual and judgmental maturity, and persons generally reach their adult levels of abstract intelligence and moral development long before the termination of infancy, at around puberty.[29] For the last eight years or so of infancy, a person has about as much capacity to exercise choice as an adult, yet is denied adult liberty.

---

27. J. MILL, ON LIBERTY 160 (Kirk ed. 1955).

28. Shears, *Legal Problems Peculiar to Children's Courts,* 48 A.B.A.J. 719, 720 (1962).

29. Piaget's extensive research on cognitive development suggests that adolescents have attained the adult capacity for logical thought and are capable of envisioning future consequences of present action. J. FLAVELL, THE DEVELOPMENTAL PSYCHOLOGY OF JEAN PIAGET 202-225 (1963). E. HILGARD, INTRODUCTION TO PSYCHOLOGY 411 (1953) summarizes generally accepted views of psychometricians that persons reach average adult level of performance on intelligence tests at about age 13. Query, *The Influence of Group Pressures on the Judgements of Children and Adolescents—A Comparative Study,* 3 ADOLESCENCE 10 (1968) finds that the tendency to yield to group pressure against one's own better judgment declines to adult levels around age 16. Infants' judgments about attribution of moral responsibility resemble those of adults by age 12 or so, according to Shaw, Briscoe, Garci, & Esteve, 2 *A Cross-Cultural Study of Attribution of Responsibility,* INT'L J. PSYCHOLOGY (forthcoming). MASS. GEN. LAWS ch. 10 sec. 2 requires the consent of a child over 12 to adoption. GA. CODE ANN. 30-127, as amended in 1962, gives infants over 14 an absolute right to choose between fit parents in custody disputes. F. POLLOCK & F. MAITLAND, 2 THE HISTORY OF ENGLISH LAW 438-439 (1898) says that infancy terminated for burgesses when they could count money and measure cloth, and for sokemen at 15, and only the tenant by knight's service remained an infant until 21. They explain the prolongation of infancy by increasing amounts of knowledge necessary and say it was hastened by the introduction of heavy armor requiring greater strength.

If it is conceded that infants mature well before majority, then insofar as *parens patriae* justifies more state incursions on the liberty of infants than of adults, it must rest on a political theory otherwise in accord with the American libertarian position but containing some rationale for denying liberty to newly mature persons. John Stuart Mill seems to suggest such an exception to his own libertarian argument:

> But I cannot consent to argue the point as if society had no means of bringing its weaker members up to its ordinary standard of rational conduct, except waiting till they do something irrational, and then punishing them, legally or morally, for it. Society has had absolute power over them during all the early portion of their existence: it has had the whole period of childhood and nonage in which to try whether it could then make them capable of rational conduct in life. . . If society lets any considerable numbers grow up mere children incapable of being acted on by rational consideration of distant motives, society has itself to blame for the consequences.[30]

Since Mill distinguishes in this passage and others[31] between childhood and nonage or youth, he must intend to posit "absolute power" of the state even over relatively mature persons. The passage suggests as a theory in support of this "absolute power" that (1) society should seek as libertarian a state as practicable, (2) a highly libertarian state requires a highly competent citizenry, (3) therefore, liberty ought to be denied to young persons for so long as the state needs to educate them efficiently to make them fit to exercise it wisely. Under this theory, competence to take care of one's self does not limit the scope of legitimate state control. The limit is the age at which, given a particular level of competence thought necessary to sustain a libertarian system and the available means of instilling this competence, the state has had a fair chance to raise the average person to the minimum standard. The age of majority varies proportionally with the level of competence thought necessary and inversely with the effectiveness of available educational techniques. If the former were high, or the latter low, the age would rise with no obvious maximum. At some point, the society will appear more gerontocratic than democratic; per-

---

30. J. Mill, On Liberty 120-121 (Kirk ed. 1955).
31. *Id.*, *e.g.*, at 13, distinguishes children from young persons under the age of majority.

haps Mill's democratic principles would provide an additional parameter limiting the rise of the age of majority.[32]

B. The Franchise

English Dissenters of the seventeenth century believed that because of man's natural tendency to be selfish, those in positions of governmental authority would tend to benefit themselves at the expense of the subjects of the government. This phenomenon could be prevented only by separating power so that those in positions of authority would tend to restrain each other, and by structuring government so that persons in power could be compelled by their subjects to bear any oppressive burden which they as authorities imposed. This intellectual tradition informed the thought of the American colonists during the eighteenth century, and helps to explain the importance to them of representation in Parliament. When they drafted the Constitution, the American revolutionaries believed that governmental oppression could be avoided only by actual representation of all interests, with periodic reelection of representatives.[33]

> Through the power of re-election the people could bring oppressive laws to bear upon all by reducing the authors of these laws to the condition of subjects at the next election. Faced with the sustained threat of being made to feel the consequences of their own actions, no representative could contemplate the enslavement of his constituents while the franchise was still effective.[34]

This Dissenter tradition gives meaning to the proposition that the vote is a fundamental political right, because it is pre-

---

32. This interpretation of Mill is somewhat problematic. Since he opposed public schools, favoring tuition grants to poor parents and compulsory education with a private school system (*Id.*, at 156-160), because he feared the loss of diversity of views that a state system would entail, he cannot be characterized as favoring indoctrination in institutional norms as Aristotle did. *See* Ten, *Mill and Liberty*, 30 J. Hist. Ideas 47, 53 (1969). But his libertarian proposition may have been the refutable one that liberty is good because each is the best judge and guardian of his own interest, rather than the irrefutable one that it is good in itself, and he was highly skeptical of the competence as judges for themselves of most adults, so he cannot clearly be regarded as more democratic than meritocratic. West, *Liberty and Education: John Stuart Mill's Dilemma*, 40 Philosophy 129 (1965).

33. Buel, *Democracy and the American Revolution: A Frame of Reference*, 21 Wm. & Mary Q. (3d ser.) 165 (1964).

34. *Id.*, at 186.

servative of all rights.[35] The fundamentality consists in the power of the vote, and only the vote, to prevent governmental oppression. Where the Constitution or a statute creates a right, and government refuses to honor it, courts can remedy the oppression. But where the Constitution is silent, so that there is no right but only an interest, then courts must be restrained, and oppressive but arguably rational governmental treatment of persons and interests often cannot be defeated by then. Since human nature, in the view of those who made voting a fundamental right in our polity, is self-centered, and persons have many conflicts of interest, non-voters will tend to be oppressed.

But it is fairly clear that the law today countenances withholding the franchise from infants. *Gray v. Sanders* classified minors together with felons as groups properly excludable.[36] *Lassiter v. Northampton Co. Bd. of Elections* said *in dictum* that age was an "obvious" factor which the state could take into account.[37] A state case may have held that the franchise may be denied young men who otherwise have attained majority.[38] Most states by statute require that one must be 21 to vote, and make voting the last incident of full age to be obtained, but at least four states give persons under 21 the franchise.[39] Election laws are one of very few areas of the law of infants where, instead of conferring gradually increased rights upon infants as they approach majority, the law draws a sharp line distinguishing persons over 21 from all others, and treats persons of 20 identically with new born babies.

Because of the fundamental character of the suffrage as a

35. Reynolds v. Sims, 377 U.S. 533, 562 (1964), says "preservative of other basic civil and political rights."

36. 372 U.S. 368, 380 (1963) (*dictum;* the holding was that the Georgia county unit system denied equal protection).

37. 360 U.S. 45, 51 (1959) (literacy tests held not a *per se* denial of Equal Protection).

38. Riley v. Homer, 100 Fla. 938, 131 So. 330 (1930). A statute removed all disabilities of no age from males who were married, but this did not override a constitutional provision limiting the franchise to those over 21 despite another constitutional provision authorizing the legislature to relieve minors from disabilities.

39. ALAS. STAT. 15.05.010(2) requires that voters have passed their 19th birthday, but under ALAS. STAT. 25.20.010 and 25.20.020 males arrive at majority for all purposes at 19 and females at 19 or upon marriage, whichever comes first. GA. CONST. 2-702 makes persons 18 or over qualified to vote, though GA. STAT. 74-104 makes 21 the age of majority. REV. LAWS HAWAII 330-1 makes 20 the age of majority. KY. CONST. § 145 gives the franchise to persons 18 or over, though minority for some purposes lasts till 21, *e.g.*, KY. REV. STAT. § 337.010(3) (b).

preservative of all other rights, restrictions upon the right to vote are subject to the closest scrutiny for violations of the Equal Protection Clause and other Constitutional provisions, and are carefully confined to the boundaries implied by their own rationales when they are permissible.[40] This principle implies that age restrictions on voting must be examined critically for rationality, and the particular age set must be no higher than that justified by the rationale supporting age restrictions. The justification for age qualifications cannot be that infants have less of an interest in governmental activities than adults; indeed, few groups in society can claim so substantial an interest in foreign affairs as this group which bears so large a part of the burden of conscription for the military, or in state and local government as students who spend so large a portion of their time under the broad authority of public schools. The justification must argue for the exclusion of highly interested persons on the sole ground of age.

Lassister v. Bd. of Elections upheld the constitutionality of a state literacy test on the ground that the ability to read and write "has some relation to standards designed to promote intelligent use of the ballot"[41] and was neutral with respect to race, creed, color and sex.[42] *Harper v. Virginia Bd. of Elections,* in striking down a poll tax, reaffirmed the criterion that a restriction on voting must be related to the ability to vote intelligently.[43] This criterion would seem to imply that a state must have justification for the proposition that persons below its minimum voting age are substantially less capable of "intelligent use of the ballot" than citizens above that age. Up to now, most cases rejecting voting qualifications for denials of equal protection have held that the criterion used by the state lacked sufficient relevance to legitimate purposes. But the strict standard of review applied justifies the proposition that the criterion must not only be relevant in a general sense, but must be limited to exclude only those for whom it is relevant.[44] An

40. Reynolds v. Sims, 377 U.S. 533, 562 (1964); Harper v. Virginia Bd. of Elections, 383 U.S. 663, 670 (1966).

41. 360 U.S. 45, 51 (1959).

42. *Id.*, at 51.

43. 383 U.S. 663, 666 (1966).

44. Carrington v. Rash, 380 U.S. 89 (1965).

alternative statement of this proposition would be that the criterion must be relevant in all its particularity, and not merely in a general sense. Over-inclusiveness or under-inclusiveness will not be tolerated. The legislative judgment as to what age ought to be used as a qualification deserves the extraordinarily critical scrutiny generally given a distinction which disadvantages a politically unrepresented or impotent class.[45]

When requirements that voters be over 21 are viewed this critically, they do not relate sufficiently to the ability to make "intelligent use of the ballot" to satisfy the Equal Protection Clause. Conceding the propriety of the "intelligent use of the ballot" criterion, a voting age requirement of 21 cannot be reconciled with lower age limits for marrying without parental consent,[46] choosing whether to consent to adoption[47] or between parents in a custody proceeding,[48] and entering into burdensome contracts.[49] If the importance and difficulty of intelligent choice for those permitted activities are greater than for voting, then a state permitting lower age limits for such other activities concedes that its voting age is set higher than the "intelligent use of the ballot" criterion permits. An age requirement for voting higher than for many other activities requiring intelligent choice, seems also to be inconsistent with the very minimal level of ability required for votes at the other end of the age continuum. Though lunatics and idiots generally may not vote, the uncontradicted rule appears to be that admittedly feeble and mentally deteriorated old people are not dis-

---

45. United States v. Carolene Prod. Co., 304 U.S. 144, 153 n.4 (1938); South Carolina Hwy. Dept. v. Barnwell Bros., 303 U.S. 177, 184-185 n.2 (1938).

46. CAL. CIV. CODE § 56 permits females to marry without parental consent at 18; most states are at least this liberal.

47. MASS. GEN. LAWS ch. 210 § .2 requires the consent of a child over 12 to adoption.

48. UTAH CODE § 30-3-5 provides that children 10 or over of sound mind may select between parents.

49. Alaska permits females to enter into contracts without restriction and exercise all the prerogatives of majority upon marriage. ALAS. STAT. § 25.20.020, though not permitting them to vote until 19 under ALAS. STAT. § 15.05.010(2). A proposal by the Latey Committee in England to reduce the age of majority to 18 for all purposes except voting is criticized in Downey, *Report of the Committee on the Age of Majority*, 31 MOD. L. REV. 429, 432 (1968) on the ground that a person old enough to own and manage property, marry, raise children, and enter into burdensome contracts, is old enough to vote.

qualified unless demonstrably *non compos mentis.*[50] If the standard for "intelligent use of the ballot" were as high as the average adult's level of political knowledge and voting skill, and higher than that of many or most adults, a far lower age than 21 would fulfill it; children are settled into their life-long party identifications, which account for an overwhelming preponderance of adult voting behavior,[51] by about age 10,[52] and are about as well-informed as most adults about the major political institutions by about age 14,[53] though issue orientations develop later if at all.[54]

The "intelligent use of the ballot" criterion makes sense if it means only that voting should be at least faintly comprehensible as a decision-making situation to the voter, but it probably cannot require much more than that. The Constitution does not seem to intend to create a meritocracy of the intelligent, in which only a minority of persons with superior intelligence may vote, so the level of intelligence required probably is well below the median. In a two-party system, where the parties serve most voters as easily used guides to self-interested voting, little intelligence is necessary for intelligent use of the ballot. Even if it were conceded that were the voting age much lower than 21 many infants would not make "intelligent use of the ballot," the consequences would not be serious. The data cited above on political development suggest that many young voters with retarded political development would merely show greater party loyalty than mature voters so that the vote might swell somewhat for the party whose adult adherents had had a higher birth rate several years before.[55]

This consequence does not seem detrimental enough to the

---

50. Welsh v. Shumway, 232 Ill. 54, 75-76, 83 N.E. 549 (1907); Sinks v. Reese, 19 Ohio St. 306, 320 (1869).

51. F. GREENSTEIN, THE AMERICAN PARTY SYSTEM AND THE AMERICAN PEOPLE 30-36 (1963) states the finding, generally accepted by political scientists since V.O. Key's work, that party identification predicts voting behavior far more accurately than a voter's issue orientations or candidate preferences.

52. F. GREENSTEIN, CHILDREN AND POLITICS 71-72 (1965).

53. *Id.*, at 55.

54. *Id.*, at 67-71.

55. If birth rates did not vary substantially by party, probably neither party would benefit. Downey, *Report of the Committee on the Age of Majority*, 31 Mod. L. Rev. 429, 432 (1968) suggests that among politicians opposition to reducing the voting age is attributable to fear of aiding the party whose adherents have more children, not evaluation of the fitness of young persons to vote intelligently.

political system to merit retaining an age qualification excluding a class of which a large proportion could vote intelligently.

Two arguments not based upon the proposition that persons under 21 could not vote wisely are often made against the proposition that young persons are unfairly oppressed by denial of the franchise to them. Some argue that young persons should not fear oppression because their parents will protect their interests. This argument resembles the "virtual representation" theory with which the British replied to American colonists' complaints about taxation without representation.

> If Philadelphia sent no actually elected deputies to the Commons, so this argument ran, neither did Manchester in England, yet both places enjoyed a "virtual representation," since members of the Commons did not in any case speak for local constituencies, but made themselves responsible for imperial interests as a whole.[56]

The Stamp Act and the century of commercial regulation preceding it refuted this argument in the eighteenth century,[57] and the American Revolution may be viewed as a kind of popular determination of the inevitable inadequacy of "virtual representation." In the context of extending the franchise to young persons, the argument breaks down on the conflicts of interests between youths and their elders. Since they tend to be in lower tax brackets than adults, young persons have an interest in larger allocations of money for schools than even their own parents, who will not suffer directly from poor schools but will from higher taxes. Where the law strengthens parental power over infants with little regard for infants' legitimate interests, as disobedient and runaway child statutes do, the child-parent conflict is clear. When the polity must choose whether to go to war and conscription is the means used to raise an army, the conflict between parents and children may resemble that between two people in a lifeboat when the weaker one is thrown overboard by the stronger.

The other argument is that a discrimination against youth lacks the invidiousness of a discrimination against black people or women because youth is temporary while those other status

---

56. R. PALMER & J. COLTON, A HISTORY OF THE MODERN WORLD 325 (1962).

57. Buel, *Democracy and the American Revolution: A Frame of Reference*, 21 WM. & MARY Q. (3d ser.) 165, 280 (1964).

classifications are permanent. This argument falters on the problem of conscription of infants, since many of those conscripted die before reaching the age of majority. More seriously, it misconceives an important function of representation. It is not enough that the subject may become master; the master must be in constant peril of being compelled by his subjects to return to their status.[58] This non-invidiousness argument would support an upper limit on age, but not a lower limit. Persons over 80 might be denied the vote on the ground that so high a proportion of them have deteriorated mentally that a person over 80 would not be able to make "intelligent use of the ballot." The old persons affected by such a qualification could be confident of some check on oppression by younger people, because every younger person voting on a provision or candidate threatening to harm persons over 80 would risk the same harm to himself if he survived long enough to join that class. If the upper limit were set somewhat lower, the disenfranchised old people would have still more protection because the young people would have a higher probability of joining the disenfranchised class. But no person over 21 ever grows younger. An adult may vote for candidates or laws oppressive to infants perfectly secure in the belief that he will never suffer from the oppression. When an infant graduates into the adult class, he may have some desire for revenge on his oppressors, but countering it is a strong interest in perpetuating a system oppressive to infants now that he is its beneficiary rather than its victim. In the sense that it contributes to oppression, disqualification of infants is invidious indeed.

Mill's argument for denying liberty to young persons long enough so that society may make them competent citizens does not justify denial of the vote. One kind of competence society needs to impart consists of adherence to the norms and processes of democratic government and an experience of colonialism will in this respect be a poor teacher.[59] The kind of liberty

---

58. See the discussion of the Dissenter tradition and the American Revolution at the beginning of this section.

59. West Va. State Bd. of Educ. v. Barnette, 319 U.S. 624, 637 (1943); (that Boards of Education "are educating the young for citizenship is reason for scrupulous protection of Constitutional freedoms of the individual, if we are not to strangle the free mind at its source and teach youth to discount important principles of our government as

which Mill's argument justifies denying to infants would seem to be the liberty not to be educated, not the liberty to protect one's self by voting.[60]

One response to the argument of this section, that an age qualification for voting of 21 denies Equal Protection to many persons below that age, could obviously be state legislative action to lower the age. A second could be a federal statute requiring all the states to set their age minimum at or below some maximum, say 18. *Katzenback v. Morgan*[61] holds that despite the constitutionality *in vacuo* of state literacy tests in English, Congress has the power to make a conclusive finding that persons who have completed the 6th grade in American flag schools teaching in non-English languages are denied Equal Protection by state literacy tests in English. Under *Katzenbach v. Morgan,* Congress can probably make a conclusive finding under the 14th and 15th amendments that denial of the vote to persons over 18 is an invidious discrimination in violation of the Equal Protection Clause.[62]

Judicial intervention is not inconceivable. The endorsements of age qualifications in *Gray v. Sanders*[63] and *Lassister v. Northampton Co. Bd. of Elections*[64] are mere *dicta,* and say only that age is a proper criterion, not that age 21 is proper. Since these cases, the constitutional rights of infants have been radically expanded by *In re Gault,*[65] holding *inter alia* that the Equal Protection Clause bars taking the liberty of infants without the same fundamentals of due process as apply to adults,[66] and *Tinker v. Des Moines School Dist.*[67] holding that students

---

mere platitudes. E. FRIEDENBERG, COMING OF AGE IN AMERICA 27–50 (1963); L BEGGS, HUCKLEBERRY'S FOR RUNAWAYS 259–260 (1969) ("The crowning insult to the young person today is a society which withholds the vote from him, while compelling him to face death for democracy!").

60. The justification cannot be that young persons would use the vote to relieve themselves of restrictions thought by older persons to be good for them for " 'Fencing out' from the franchise a section of the population because of the way they may vote is constitutionally impermissible." Carrington v. Rash, 380 U.S. 89, 94 (1965).

61. 384 U.S. 641 (1966).

62. Claude, *Nationalization of the Electoral Process,* 6 HARV. J. LEGIS. 139, 160 (1969).

63. 372 U.S. 368, 380 (1963).

64. 360 U.S. 45,51 (1959).

65. 387 U.S. 1 (1966).

66. *Id.*, at 61.

67. ——— U.S. ———, 21 L.Ed. 2d 731 (1969).

in school are "persons" under the Constitution possessed of fundamental rights including free speech with only such regulation as the First Amendment permits. Some Justices suggest that the validity of high age qualifications for voting is less obvious after *Gault* and *Tinker.* Dissenting in *Tinker,* Justice Black suggested in hostility rather than approval that "the next logical step, it appears to me, would be to hold unconstitutional laws that bar pupils under 21 or 18 from voting. . . ."[68] Justice Stewart said:

> I think that a State may permissibly determine that, at least in some precisely delineated areas, a child-like someone in a captive audience-is not possessed of that full capacity for individual choice which is the presupposition of First Amendment guarantees. It is only upon such a premise, I should suppose, that a State may deprive children of other rights-the right to marry, for example, or the right to vote-deprivations that would be constitutionally intolerable for adults.[69]

Justice Stewart's test of a voting qualification would apparently be whether it rationally distinguished age groups on the basis of "full capacity for individual choice," and depriving a class possessing this capacity of the vote would be "constitutionally intolerable."

Judicial intervention could probably not be avoided by a demonstration that age was a valid criterion for denying the suffrage. *Harper v. Virginia Bd. of Elections* says that restrictions on voting not only must be "closely scrutinized," but also "carefully confirmed."[70] The latter standard means that over-inclusion in a class denied the vote cannot be tolerated. Such a reading is compelled by *Carrington v. Rash*[71] which holds that, though non-residents may be disqualified from voting, all members of the military may not be classified as non-residents because such a classification is over-inclusive in its impingement on the right to vote. Age may be a valid criterion, but the age qualification cannot be set so high as to be over-inclusive.

The Court would face a substantial problem of fashioning a remedy for infants if it regarded denial of the vote as unconstitutional. Once having found that a state had not supported an

68. *Id.*, at 744.
69. Ginsberg v. New York, 390 U.S. 629, 649-650 (1968) (*concurring*).
70. 383 U.S. 663, 670 (1966).
71. 380 U.S. 89 (1965).

age qualification of 21 with substantial rather than merely tenable justification, it would have to decide what order should issue. One approach could be to say "age is a permissible criterion, but 21 is too high, so this election statute is invalid"; the state could then be left temporarily without any age qualification, but would have an implicit invitation to write a new statute for submission to the federal courts. Eventually the Court would approve a statute, and the states would set their voter qualification statutes at ages equal to or lower than the age in the approved statute. If a state set a higher age, a federal District Court or Court of Appeals might order election officials to operate on the basis of the age approved by the Supreme Court until the legislature passed a statute with an equal or lower age requirement.

A second approach could be an order voiding an age qualification of 21, and suggesting some particular lower age or substitute for an age qualification. If a state terminated other disabilities of infancy at some lower age, the court might order that the state treat as qualified to vote persons not under other disabilities of infancy. Or, focusing on the value of the vote to young persons, the Court might suggest the age at which some heavy burden is imposed on young people by the state as a time after which their interest was so substantial and the chance of unintelligent use of the ballot so small relative to adults that persons over that age could not be disqualified; the age of conscription, 18, suggests itself here.

A third approach could be for the Court to suggest a scheme whereby very young persons, say children under 13, would be excluded, and persons between 13 and 21 would be permitted to qualify themselves by passing a standard, non-discriminatory literacy test applied to all voters. A variation on this approach would be to set no lower age limit, and let the literacy test perform the function of excluding those unable to make "intelligent use of the ballot." Voting is so important that the administrative burden of operating a fair system of voter qualification cannot suffice to justify an unfair system.[72] Problems

72. Carrington v. Rash, 380 U.S. 89, 96 (1965).

with this remedy might develop if the literacy test were made so difficult as to exclude a large proportion of persons under 21.

Though remedy would pose a problem, the problem seems no more difficult than the one which the Court decided was surmountable in *Baker v. Carr.*[73] Where the disadvantaged class cannot seek redress in the legislature effectively, the Court goes further than it otherwise would in shaping remedies in difficult areas. If a state set a voting qualification requiring that persons be over the age of 50 to vote, it is inconceivable that the Supreme Court would refuse to act. The data supporting the proposition that 21 is over-inclusive in terms of its function of excluding those who could make "intelligent use of the ballot" is the same kind of data upon which the Court relied in *Brown v. Bd. of Educ.*[74] The importance of the vote to infants should outweigh the difficulty of shaping a remedy.

C. Special Legislation for Infants

"The Equal Protection Clause prevents States from arbitrarily treating people differently under their laws."[75] The meaning of equality and the willingness of courts to treat distinctions as arbitrary depend upon a number of variables, such as whether the distinction is automatically suspect, whether fundamental interests are affected, and whether the class discriminated against can obtain redress in the legislature.[76] Though once regarded as "the last resort of constitutional arguments,"[77] the Equal Protection Clause has in the last few years expanded prodigiously in the scope of its application, performing many of the functions for which the Due Process Clause was once used, as well as its traditional narrower role.[78] Though substantive Due Process review of economic regulations has fallen into disrepute, the Due Process Clause too has been expanded in

---

73. 369 U.S. 186 (1962).

74. 347 U.S. 483 (1954).

75. Harper v. Virginia Bd. of Elections, 383 U.S. 663, 681 (1966) (Harlan, J., dissenting).

76. *Developments in the Law-Equal Protection,* 82 HARV. L. REV. 1065 (1969).

77. Buck v. Bell, 274 U.S. 200, 208 (1927) (Holmes, J.).

78. *Developments in the Law-Equal Protection,* 82 HARV. L. REV. 1065, 1131-2 (1969).

some areas of "human rights," notably in criminal procedure. Today the meanings of Due Process and Equal Protection for infants are changing rapidly in the direction of greater conformity with these standards for adults.[79] This section discusses a few of the ways in which the state has treated infants differently from adults.

Much of the special legislation for infants concerns fundamental rights, such as the right not to be compelled to yield one's body to the state without due process and rights of speech and religion under the First Amendment. Where distinctions affect the exercise of fundamental rights, they are subject to a stricter standard of review under the Equal Protection Clause and other constitutional provisions than are regulations of less important interests.[80] So long as infants cannot vote, however, strict review ought not to be limited to fundamental rights. Voting is regarded as a fundamental right because it is "preservative of other basic civil and political rights";[81] that is, exclusion of a class from the suffrage substantially increases the risk that the excluded class will be oppressed in many other ways by the state. Justice Jackson commented that there

> is no more effective practical guarantee against arbitrary and unreasonable government than to require that the principles of law which government would impose on a minority must be imposed generally.[82]

The need for such a guarantee grows very strong when the group specially imposed upon has no vote with which to protect itself in the legislature. Justice Stone's famous *dictum* on state regulation of interstate commerce applies as well to discriminations against non-voting infants:

> . . . when the regulation is of such a character that its burden falls principally upon those without the state, legislative action is not likely to be subjected to those political restraints which are normally exerted on legislation, where it affects adversely some interests within the state.[83]

---

79. *In re* Gault, 387 U.S. 1 (1966); Tinker v. Des Moines School Dist., ————U.S.————21 L.Ed. 2d 732 (1969); *cf.*, Ginsberg v. New York, 390 U.S. 629 (1968).

80. Harper v. Virginia Bd. of Elections, 383 U.S. 663, 670 (1966) (voting); *Developments in the Law-Equal Protection.* 82 HARV. L. REV. 1065, 1120-1124, 1127-1131 (1969).

81. Reynolds v. Sims, 377 U.S. 533,561-562 (1964).

82. Railway Express Agency v. New York, 336 U.S. 106 (1949).

83. South Carolina Hwy. Dept. v. Barnwell Bros., 303 U.S. 177,185 n.2 (1938).

Justice Stone offered the quoted dictum to explain why the Court treated state regulations as impinging on the Commerce Clause even where Congress had not acted when the effect was to benefit those within the state at the expense of those without; an analogous differential standard of review ought to apply where non-economic interests of persons denied the vote are at stake.

For several purposes, the state takes the bodies of young persons without proof that they have committed any act which would be criminal for an adult or that they could otherwise be seized were they adults. Three of the most frequent occasions are for conscription, for education and for moral rehabilitation.

1. CONSCRIPTION

Conscription amounts to a taking of liberty, and falls disproportionally upon the young, though it extends to young men over 21 as well as infants. Its constitutionality with regard to the Thirteenth Amendment, of which it would seem to be a *prima facie* violation, has long been upheld on the authority of the proposition in the *Selective Draft Law Cases*[84] that

> Finally, as we are unable to conceive upon what theory the execution by government from the citizen of the performance of his supreme and noble duty of contributing to the defense of the rights and honor of the nation, as the result of a war declared by the great representative body of the people, can be said to the imposition of involuntary servitude in violation of the prohibitions of the Thirteenth Amendment, we are constrained to the conclusion that the contention to that effect is refuted by its mere statement.[85]

If this summary proposition rests upon any foundation, it must be the assumption stated earlier in the opinion that

> It may not be doubted that the very conception of a just government and its duty to the citizen includes the reciprocal obligation of the citizen to render military service in case of need and the right to compel it.[86]

The statute under review in this case drafted only persons above the age of 21,[87] so the opinion may not apply to a system of conscripting persons under 21. This distinction is supported

84. 245 U.S. 366 (1918).
85. *Id.*, at 390.
86. *Id.*, at 378.
87. *Id.*, at 375.

by the proposition quoted about the reciprocal duties of government and "citizen"; since an infant does not enjoy all the rights and benefits of a "citizen," he ought not to be charged with duties reciprocal to those rights and privileges. The question[88] of whether conscription, though valid for adults, violates the constitutional rights of infants was settled in favor of the government by *United States v. Williams.*[89] *Williams* does not discuss the problem in terms of infants' exclusion from the franchise; the action was brought by a dead soldier's mother to recover war risk insurance, and the opinion seems to be based on a questionable application of *parens patriae,* here meaning the superiority of the state's over the parent's right to control an infant. *Williams,* therefore, is distinguishable from a defense against conscription by an infant on his own behalf.[90] Such a defense might proceed on the theory that if the duty to serve in the armed forces is a corollary of citizenship, as the *Selective Draft Law Cases* hold, then no duty to serve could exist without citizenship. This theory implies that the duty of infants would be no greater than the duty of aliens. Some old state cases suggest that while all aliens are not exempted from conscription, only those showing an intent to become permanent residents or those granted the right to vote may be drafted.[91] But modern federal cases have held that aliens are as liable to conscription as citizens, except as otherwise provided by statute.[92] Infants could be distinguished from aliens on the ground that aliens by coming here have indicated an intent to take on

---

88. Argument has tended to focus on the question of whether conscription is valid without a congressional declaration of war, United States v. O'Brien, 391 U.S. 367, 389-391 (1968) (Douglas, J., *dissenting, In re* Holmes 391 U.S. 936, 936-949 (1968) (Douglas, J., *dissenting*) or whether it is valid at all. Bernstein, *Conscription and the Constitution: The Amazing Case of Kneedler v. Lane,* 53 A.B.A.J. 708 (1967), not on the problem of conscription of minors.

89. 302 U.S. 46 (1937).

90. But a court might refuse to draw such a distinction on the ground that *parens patriae* also justifies state takings of custody as against the infant. This argument relies on an interpretation of *parens patriae* justifying a taking of custody for any purpose, and not solely for the benefit of the infant.

91. *E.g., In re* Wehlitz, 16 Wis. 468 (1863) holds that under a law drafting citizens, an alien for federal purposes to whom the state had extended the right to vote became, by virtue of the right to vote and his residence, enough of a citizen so that he was subject to conscription.

92. Leonhard v. Eley, 151 F.2d 409 (1945).

such burdens as the government might impose, but infants have exercised no choice; moreover, in most of the alien cases, some intent to reside here permanently exists. But even if infants have a stronger case for exemption than aliens, a court probably would not act on it, because of the vigor with which the political question doctrine is asserted in this area. As to aliens,

> The question of whether or not aliens should be conscripted is a matter of public policy—a political question which is for the executive and legislative branches of Government to solve. Such questions are entirely outside the realm of the judicial branch.[93]

The Supreme Court has recently characterized Congress' power to raise and support armies as "broad and sweeping,"[94] and probably would be very reluctant to restrict that power to adults. Thus while the argument in the *Selective Draft Law Cases* for excluding conscription from the prohibition of the Thirteenth Amendment would seem to imply an exception to the exclusion for infants, the federal judiciary very probably would defer to the judgment of the other two branches as to whether such an exception ought to be created. An argument to the other two branches would be directed toward persons elected solely by non-infants and perhaps more concerned with the ability as soldiers of 18–21 year old boys than the injustice of depriving them of liberty and sometimes life by a process in which they are not represented.

2. THE JUVENILE COURT SYSTEM

One special feature of the juvenile court system is the application of substantive quasi-criminal laws applying only to infants. Prominent among these have been disobedient child and runaway laws, discussed above in the chapter on parental authority. Typically, states provide many grounds applicable only to infants besides disobedience to parents, however, upon which they may be placed in the custody of the state. The California scheme, like many, casts its standards for involuntary takings of infants into custody not as crimes, but as

---

93. United States v. Rumsa, 212 F.2d 927, 936 (7th Cir., 1954), *cert. den.* 348 U.S. 838 (1954).

94. United States v. O'Brien, 391 U.S. 367 (1968).

grounds for juvenile court jurisdiction. An infant may be adjudged a "ward of the court" for violating any federal, state or local statute or ordinance,[95] or for persistently disobeying his parents or being beyond their control.[96] He is also within the juvenile court's jurisdiction if he is destitute,[97] not properly cared for and controlled by a parent or guardian,[98] or

> from any cause is in danger of leading an idel, dissolute, lewd, or immoral life.[99]

"Dissolute," "idle," and "immoral" have been held to meet constitutional standards of definiteness.[100] Under the quoted section, as "idle" has been construed, an infant may be made a ward of the court if from any cause he is in danger of being unemployed or a loafer.[101] "Immoral" does not refer only to sexual matters, but to anything inimical to good order, against the welfare of the general public, and contrary to good morals.[102] "Dissolute" means "lewd."[103]

Such statutory schemes are intended as nets to catch any young persons who might for any reason need some sort of help not provided by their home environments toward leading law-abiding and otherwise successful lives.[104] The effect of such broad grants of jurisdiction is to enable the juvenile court to take custody of almost any active youth on some pretext if it so wishes,[105] and they are under attack by most commentators because

> the system allows intervention by the government into the affairs of people without their consent and without standards and controls. Experience has taught us that this is objectionable even if it may be characterized as "disinterested benevolence."[106]

---

95. CAL. WELF. & INST. CODE § 602.
96. *Id.*, at § 601.
97. *Id.*, at § 600.
98. *Id.*
99. *Id.*, at § 601.
100. People v. Deibert, 117 Cal. App. 2d 410, 256 P.2d 355 (1953) (conviction for contributing to the delinquency of a minor affirmed for selling liquor to three boys.)
101. *Id.*, at 359.
102. *Id.*, at 360-361.
103. *Id.*, at 360.
104. Handler, *The Juvenile Court and the Adversary System: Problems of Function and Form*, 1965 WISC. L. REV. 7, 15 (1965).
105. *Id.*, at 14.
106. *Id.*, at 19.

This special system was created, not to do justice in a retributive sense, but to rehabilitate. A much-quoted explanation of this extension of *parens patriae* argues,

> Why is it not just and proper to treat these juvenile offenders as we deal with neglected children, as a wise and merciful father handles his own child whose errors are not discovered by the authorities? Why is it not the duty of the state, instead of asking merely whether a boy or a girl has committed a specific offense, to find out what he is, physically, mentally, morally, and then if it learns that he is treading the path that leads to criminality, to take him in charge, not so much to punish as to reform, not to degrade but to uplift, not to crush but to develop, not to make him a criminal but a worthy citizen.[107]

Noble as its idea may have been, the juenile court system as it has operated has given

> grounds for concern that the child receives the worse of both worlds: that he gets neither the protections accorded to adults nor the solicitous care and regenerative treatment postulated for children.[108]

Kent v. United States,[109] which expressed this concern, held[110] only that the discretion of a juvenile court to waive jurisdiction and remit a juvenile for trial to a criminal court "assumes procedural regularity sufficient in the particular circumstances to satisfy the basic requirements of due process and fairness,"[111] not satisfied where the juvenile's lawyer is denied the access to records afforded him by statute, no hearing is provided despite counsel's motion, and no ruling on the motion or reasons are given. *In re Gault*[112] went beyond *Kent,* holding that juvenile court proceedings which might lead to involuntary commitment to an "industrial school" were required to meet constitutional standards of Due Process as to notice, right to counsel, the privilege against self-incrimination, and the right to confront and cross-examine witnesses. Though Justice Fortas' majority opinion rested on a Due Process notion, Justice Black's concurring opinion reasoned that the state could not deny to children charged with crimes the same procedural

---

107. Mack, *The Juvenile Court,* 23 HARV. L. REV. 104, 107 (1909).

108. Kent v. United States, 383 U.S. 541, 555 (1966).

109. *Id.*

110. *Id.,* at 556 explicitly refuses the invitation to hold more broadly that juveniles are entitled to the constitutional protections of adults.

111. *Id.,* at 553.

112. 387 U.S. 1 (1966).

safeguards which it afforded adults within the confines of the Equal Protection Clause.[113] The court indicated dissatisfaction with the *parens patriae* theory[114] and with the rehabilitative performance of the juvenile court experiment;[115] by its comments that "neither the Fourteenth Amendment nor the Bill of Rights is for adults alone"[116] and "under our Constitution, the condition of being a boy does not justify a kangaroo court,"[117] it seemed to express sympathy with the Equal Protection argument advanced by Justice Black.

Gault's dissatisfaction with the juvenile court system appears so deep that the spirit of the decision may not stay within the scope of its holdings.[118] State courts seem not to have developed a concensus on whether to interpret *Gault* broadly or narrowly. The Alaska Supreme Court, since *Gault,* held a statute permitting peremptory disqualification of judges in "civil or criminal" actions if a party fears unfairness or partiality, inapplicable to juvenile delinquency proceedings;[119] this holding seems inconsistent with the Equal Protection spirit if not the Due Process letter of *Gault.* Illinois, on the other hand, has interpreted the spirit of *Gault* to require replacement of its preponderance of the evidence standard in juvenile delinquency proceedings with a standard of proof beyond a reasonable doubt.[120] Some of *Gault* suggests that distinctions between juvenile delinquency proceedings and criminal proceedings may continue, but must be functionally related to the special purposes of the juvenile court system.[121] But *Gault* also suggested that the theoretical foundation of the juvenile court system, replacement of the adversary process with an inquisitorial, be-

---

113. *Id.,* at 61.

114. *Id.,* at 16

115. *Id.,* at 21-27.

116. *Id.,* at 13.

117. *Id.,* at 28.

118. People v. Allen, 22 N.Y.2d 465, 293 N.Y.S.2d 280 (1968) reads Gault as imposing all criminal due process standards on juvenile delinquency proceedings.

119. *In re* White, 445 P.2d 813 (Alas. 1968).

120. *In re* Urbasek, 38 Ill. 2d 535, 232 N.E.2d 716 (1967); People v. Archie, 245 N.E.2d 59 (App. Ct. Ill. 1969).

121. Justice Harlan takes a view somewhat like this in his opinion, concurring in part and dissenting in part, at *In re* Gault, 387 U.S. 1, 65 (1966). The opinion of Justice Fortas appears sympathetic to this position, but neither endorses nor rejects it. If the Court in Gault were prepared to reject all distinctions, the opinion could have been more appropriately structured as an Equal Protection argument and a reference to criminal Due Process decisions.

nevolent system, was untenable. This position could lead to the conclusion that no differences may properly exist between juvenile courts and criminal courts beyond physical separateness, unless the juvenile courts grant greater rather than lesser procedural safeguards because of the greater weakness and gullibility of those before them.

Gault says nothing explicitly about the propriety of treating much conduct as justifying confinement of infants which would not justify confinements of adults. Some of the substantive provisions such as being "in danger of leading an idle, dissolute, lewd, or immoral life"[122] could be invalidated for vagueness were a court so inclined. Some, such as provisions making it criminal for children to run away from home,[123] would probably satisfy vagueness tests and other procedural challenges, and would require some sort of Equal Protection invalidation. Equal Protection arguments for invalidation of disobedient child statutes would be difficult to formulate, since the need for care and protection of infants, or at least young children, affords substantial justification for provisions facilitating police intervention, though they may be unwise. Some applications of the vaguer juvenile delinquency provisions, such as court-ordered sterilization or insertion of intra-uterine contraceptive devices in unmarried mothers,[124] could be ruled violations of Due Process because they "shock the conscience"[125] or invasions of a constitutionally protected penumbra of privacy.[126] Such juvenile court jurisdiction as is founded upon parental neglect or unfitness rather than juvenile misconduct must be confined by some Due Process standard, but since its grounds bear considerably less resemblance to criminal proceedings than juvenile misconduct cases, its conclusion in incarceration or institutionalization may not suffice to import criminal Due Process standards.[127]

---

122. CALIF. WELF. & INST. CODE § 601.

123. MASS. GEN. LAWS ch. 272 § 53.

124. Young, Alverson & Young, *Court-Ordered Contraception,* 55 A.B.A.J. 223 (1969) argues that both would be permissible under most juvenile court statutes and advocates the latter.

125. Rochin v. California, 342 U.S. 165 (1952).

126. Griswold v. Connecticut, 381 U.S. 479 (1965).

127. *In re* Gault, 387 U.S. 1, 76-77 (1966) (Harlan, J., *concurring in part and dissenting in part).*

The New York Court of Appeals has said in *People v. Allen,*[128]

> It seems fair to read *Gault* as Justice Stewart described it in dissent, that it tended to impose on juvenile courts the "restrictions that the Constitution made applicable to adversary criminal trials" (387 U.S. p.78, 87 S.Ct. p.1470),
>
> To be consistent, this procedural requirement should apply as well to the substantive definition of acts committed by juveniles which are made the subject of corrective or penal discipline.[129]

In vacuo, the second paragraph of this statement could mean either that substantive definitions of juvenile delinquency ought to be strictly construed, or that they must meet criminal Due Process vagueness standards. If the latter interpretation is correct, then the statement is *dictum,* since *Allen* refused to overrule *People v. Salisbury*[130] which upheld against a vagueness attack the statute in question in *Allen* deeming persons between 16 and 21 to be wayward minors if they were willfully disobedient to parents' or guardians' reasonable commands and morally depraved or in danger of becoming morally depraved. *Allen* appears to follow the former meaning, interpreting *Gault* to require an otherwise unjustifiably narrow meaning of "morally depraved or in danger of becoming morally depraved."[131] The court held that the facts did not justify findings of depravity or danger of depravity in the three cases consolidated for appeal: a girl of 18 was seeing a man of 30, had a key to his apartment, and stayed away from home two nights; a boy between 17 and 19 sometimes stayed out all night; a boy of 20 wrongfully took fifteen cents from his mother, and was a narcotics addict. If even a narcotics addict is not depraved or in danger of being depraved, probably few infants can be.[132] Thus, the holding of *Allen* probably is that juvenile delinquency statutes will be strictly construed. But *Allen* goes beyond this holding in its *dictum* that

---

128. 22 N.Y.2d 465, 239 N.E.2d 879, 293 N.Y.S.2d 280 (1968).

129. *Id.*, at 239 N.E.2d 879, 880.

130. 18 N.Y.2d 899, 223 N.E.2d 43, 276 N.Y.S.2d 634 (1966).

131. N.Y. CODE CRIM. PRO. § 913(a) (5, 6).

132. People v. Allen, 22 N.Y.2d 465, 239 N.E.2d 879, 881, 22 N.Y.S.2d 465 (1968) says that the characteristics of depraved persons as defined in a dictionary "are undoubtedly rare in young people."

> It is true, of course, as the People argue, that the protection of the young permits some variation in statutory and other legal arrangements affecting them. Obscenity in its impact on children is one example. But, as the court held in *People v. Munoz,* an act made an offense for a juvenile and not for an adult is open to attack as discriminatory.[133]

This *dictum* suggests that juvenile delinquency statutes which are criminal in nature, as opposed to sumptuary and other legislation to protect infants from themselves or others, perhaps cannot differ from the provisions of the criminal code for adults; at least the court must mean that a difference raises an Equal Protection issue requiring the state to bear a burden of going forward with substantial justification.

3. COMPULSORY EDUCATION

Most states require that every infant between about 6 and 16 be "committed to an institution where he may be restrained of liberty"[134] during the better part of every weekday. Compulsory school laws are often complicated in order to provide for children in remote locations, specially handicapped children, suspended and expelled children, Indians, and others, but basically they command the parent to send his child to school[135] or the infant to attend school.[136] Many of the statutes permit infants to quit attending school at substantially younger ages if employed.[137] Compulsory education has ancient Jewish and Spartan predecessors, the former intended for inculcating religion and the latter for developing patriotism. These purposes have since motivated most compulsory education legislation, in the Reformation to teach Protestantism, and in the French Revolution, on the theory that the "child belongs to the state," to teach Revolutionary ideals, to create a happier and more useful citizenry by enlightenment, and to provide equality of opportunity to develop ability. The American compulsory edu-

---

133. *Id.,* 239 N.E.2d 880–881 (citations omitted). People v. Munoz, 9 N.Y.2d 51, 172 N.E.2d 535, 211 N.Y.S.2d 146 (1961) held void for vagueness a city ordinance prohibiting persons under 21 from possessing in public places knives or sharply pointed or edged instruments, but refused to hold that no anti-weapon ordinance could validly distinguish between infants and adults, so it is not strong authority for Allen.

134. *In re* Gault 387 U.S. 1, 27 (1966).

135. *E.g.,* CALIF. EDUC. CODE § 12101.

136. *E.g.,* ATLAS. STAT. § 14.30.010.

137. *E.g.,* MASS. GEN. LAWS ch. 76 § 1.

cation movement was based in the eighteenth century on ideas of the French philosophers, but although Massachusetts provided for it, in the seventeenth century[138] compulsory education did not generally reestablish itself in law after the American Revolution until the last half of the nineteenth century, and was not effective because of minimal attendance requirements and exemptions for working children until well into the twentieth century.[139] Though some Southern states have recently partially or totally repealed compulsory education to avoid school integration,[140] most infants in the United States fall at some time under a compulsory school law.

No case has been found in which a court held either for or against a child claiming on his own behalf a right not to attend school. All the cases found on the constitutionality of compulsory schools involve disputes between parents and officials, and the defense that no child may constitutionally be compelled to attend school appears not to have been raised in truancy cases. This lack of judicial consideration of a taking of liberty of so many persons may be due partly to disabilities of infants to bring actions on their own behalf or to their lack of counsel; partly, the old notion that "the basic right of a juvenile is not to liberty but to custody"[141] may have led lawyers arguing against compulsory schools to rely on the "sacred"[142] parental custo-

---

138. The Massachusetts school statute of 1647 is voluntary as to attendance, but compulsory on townships to hire teachers "to teach all such children as shall resort to him to write and read" or to set up schools if over 100 families. The statute states as its purpose, "It being one chief project of that old deluder, Satan, to keep man from the knowledge of the Scriptures, as in former times keeping them in an unknown tongue, so in these later times by persuading from the use of Tongues, that so at least the true sense and meaning of the Originall might not be clouded with false glosses of Saint-seeming deceivers: and that Learning may not be buried in the graves of our fore-fathers in Church and Commonwealth, the Lord assisting our endeavors . . ." THE LAWS AND LIBERTIES OF MASSACHUSETTS, "Schools" p. 47 (1648, 1929 ed). Another provision required parents to "endeavor to teach by themselves or others their children & apprentices so much learning as may enable them perfectly to read the English tongue & knowledge of the Capital laws," *Id.*, "Children," p. 11, which may have made the public system compulsory in effect.

139. This history is taken from Kandel, *Public Education,* 3 ENCYC. SOCIAL SCIENCES 414. (1931, 1937 ed.). His view of the intellectual origins of the American compulsory education movement may be generally correct, but cannot be reconciled with the preamble to the Massachusetts statute quoted in the previous footnote.

140. *E.g.,* Miss. Laws 1956, ch. 288.

141. Shears, *Legal Problems Peculiar to Children's Courts,* 48 A.B.A.J. 719, 720 (1962).

142. *In re* Agar-Ellis, 10 Ch.D. 49, 71-72 (1878).

dial rights which were established in other areas rather than children's rights. The French Revolutionary notion that the child belonged to the state could not stand as a rationale against the statement in *Meyer v. Nebraska*[143] that Platonic-Spartan educational

> ideas touching the relation between individual and State were wholly foreign from those upon which our institutions rest; and it hardly will be affirmed that any legislature could impose such restrictions upon the People of a State without doing violence to both letter and spirit of the Constitution.

The French Revolutionary notion is rejected explicitly by the comment in *Pierce v. Society of Sisters*[144] that

> the child is not the mere creature of the State; those who nurture him and direct his destiny have the right, coupled with the high duty, to recognize and prepare him for additional obligations.

The obvious theory being unacceptable, the courts appear to have developed two more subtle theories to justify the state compulsion of the infant, though neither theory seems to have been tested in a confrontation of child against state. One is that parents owe a child a duty to educate him, and the state as protector of infants' interests may compel them to perform their duty; this is the classical narrower application of *parens patriae*.[145] The second is that parents owe a duty to the state to educate their children, which the state may compel them to perform; here the state exercises compulsion on its own behalf, but justifies its taking of infants into custody on the ground that it is stepping into the parental shoes, and parents clearly may compel their child to educate himself.[146] Both these theories generally are expressed together; perhaps the conjunction results from a felt contradiction in the second taken alone, at the point where the state steps into the parent's shoes while opposing the parent on its own behalf, or from a sensed inadequacy in the first, where the state carries its protective duty out so much

143. 262 U.S. 390, 401-402 (1923).

144. 268 U.S. 510, 535 (1925).

145. This theory, along with the other, is used in State v. Bailey, 157 Ind. 324, 61 N.E. 730 (1901); a famous expression in a somewhat different context, committing a disobedient child to reform school on her mother's complaint but against her father's wish, is in *Ex parte* Crouse, 4 Whart. 9 (Pa. 1839).

146. State v. Bailey, 157 Ind. 324, 61 N.E. 730 (1901).

more forcefully and broadly for education than for other needs of the infant. Only one case has been found suggesting a duty running directly from the infant to the state:

> The primary purpose of the maintenance of the common school system is the promotion of the general intelligence of the people constituting the body politic and thereby to increase the usefulness and efficiency of the citizens, upon which the government of society depends. Free schooling furnished by the state is not so much a right granted to the pupils as a duty imposed upon them for the public good. If they do not voluntarily attend the school provided for them, they may be compelled to do so.[147]

This notion finds much support in philosophy, Mill as well as the Greeks, but may be somewhat questionable after *Meyer* and *Pierce*.

Though no ferment has developed about the states' rights to compel children to attend school, the courts have often been called upon to adjudicate questions of what students may do in school. The rules which students must obey in school rarely are statutory, nor are they generally in writing as formal regulations issued in advance by any authority. Where statutes exist, they often prescribe a few grounds for suspensions or expulsions of students, including disobedience, and do not limit the scope of commands, disobedience of which may result in expulsion.[148] Discipline less severe than expulsion, though it may be limited as to form by statutes against corporal punishment, rarely or never is limited by statute as to reason. Public school students typically live in a regime where a few commands are statutory, a few are in regulations, addressed often to teachers or administrators rather than to pupils and not posted or otherwise generally available, and a great number are unarticulated regulations by numerous teachers and administrators.

Public schools have generally had very broad discretion to regulate many phases of student life in and out of class for the

---

147. Fogg v. Board of Educ., 76 N.H. 296, 82 Atl. 173, 174-175 (1912) (dictum). The case held that the school board had a duty to provide transportation for a child living too far from the school (4 miles) to walk.

148. *E.g.*, CALIF. EDUC. CODE § 10602. The California limit on scope is that the conduct be "related" to school activity or attendance. Leonard v. School Committee, 349 Mass. 704, 212 N.E.2d 468 (1965) holds that where a statute authorizes a school committee to "make regulations," this does not require formal adoption and publication of regulations by the committee, and does not restrict the manner in which school administrators or teachers maintain discipline and decorum.

purpose of maintaining a disciplined environment conducive to learning.[149] Rules prohibiting the wearing of immodest clothes or cosmetics,[150] long haircuts,[151] and metal heelplates on shoes,[152] or requiring the wearing of uniforms[153] have been sustained, generally on the ground that they were reasonably related to school disicpline. *Leonard v. School Committee*[154] a long hair case, holds that the scope of review of school regulations is very narrow; the court will not examine the wisdom or desirability of the regulation, even where the rule affects out-of-school conduct or personal life or the penalty for violation is exclusion from school, but will sustain any rule unless convinced that it could have no reasonable connection with successful operation of a public school. This narrow scope of review has been justified on the grounds that courts have more important duties than considering students' complaints, school officials are elected by the "patrons" (parents?) of the school, school officials know the conditions with which they must deal, and that judicial reversal of school rules would present to students a poor lesson by instilling in them a critical attitude toward authority.[155]

School regulations obviously have gone so far toward controlling every aspect of life at school, and so many out-of-school aspects of life that might be considered quite private and personal, that clash between school rules and strongly-felt values of students and parents has been endemic to our school systems. In many states, parents have fought and lost legal battles against compulsory schools on various religious grounds.[156] But performance of religious exercises in school has been ruled unconstitutional under the Establishment Clause,[157] and both

149. Waugh v. Board of Trustees, 237 U.S. 589 (1915) (ban on joining fraternities). The court did not rely on the notion, later often applied to state college as opposed to compulsory school cases, that attendance was a privilege and could be conditioned upon the giving up of a right. Counsel appears not to have argued on Free Association grounds.

150. Pugsley v. Sellmeyer, 158 Ark. 247, 250 S.W. 538 (1923).

151. Leonard v. School Committee, 349 Mass. 704, 212 N.E.2d 468 (1965).

152. Stomberg v. French, 60 N.D. 750, 236 N.W. 477 (1931).

153. Jones v. Day, 127 Miss. 136, 89 So. 896 (1921).

154. 349 Mass. 704, 212 N.E.2d 468 (1965).

155. Pugsley v. Sellmeyer, 158 Ark. 247, 250 S.W. 538 (1923) makes all these arguements, and is often cited.

156. *E.g.*, Commonwealth v. Beiler, 168 Pa. Super. 462, 79 A.2d 134 (1951).

157. School Dist. v. Schempp, 374 U.S. 203 (1963).

parents and students have standing to complain.[158] In *West Virginia Bd. of Educ. v. Barnette*[159] students and their parents who were Jehovah's Witnesses challenged the constitutionality of a requirement that school children recite the pledge of allegiance though *Minersville School Dist. v. Gobitis*[160] had upheld a similar flag salute law against a Free Exercise Clause challenge by Jehovah's Witnesses only three years before. The Court overruled *Gobitis* and held that children could not be required to recite the Pledge, but its grounds seem broader than Free Exercise. Justice Jackson's majority opinion held that where a refusal to declare a belief takes place in a school which children are compelled to attend, the refusal is protected as freedom of expression, because no other person's rights are interfered with by the refusal and no clear and present danger is created; no religious views are necessary to justify the refusal. The opinion rejects the narrow scope of review of state education law affirmed by Justice Frankfurter's majority opinion in *Gobitis* on the ground that it invited oppression of minorities, and rejects the *Gobitis* notion that schools may properly be used for compulsory measures to bring about national unity.

> That they (school boards) are educating the young for citizenship is reason for scrupulous protection of constitutional freedoms of the individual, if we are not to strangle the free mind at its source and teach youth to discount important principles of our government as mere platitudes.[161]

The implications of *Barnette* for infants' liberty in the schools in other contexts was obscured by the disunity of the court. Justices Frankfurter, Roberts and Reed dissented, adhering to *Gobitis*. Justices Black, Douglas, and Murphy concurred; while their opinions nowhere explicitly reject the secular free expression argument of Justice Jackson, neither do they follow it, relying instead on Free Exercise arguments. It would appear, then, that three Justices would permit required flag salutes, three would not on Free Exercise grounds, and three would not on secular free expression grounds.

158. *Id.*, at 224 n.9.
159. 319 U.S. 624 (1943).
160. 310 U.S. 586 (1940).
161. West Virginia Bd. of Educ. v. Barnette, 319 U.S. 624, 637 (1943).

During the recent period of dissension over the rights of young people, civil rights and the war in Vietnam, the secular free expression questions left unanswered by most of the Court in *Barnette* have frequently been litigated. Prohibition of long hair on boys was held in *Davis v. Firment*[162] not to interfere with "symbolic expression" or to constitute an invasion of constitutionally protected privacy or cruel and unusual punishment, and to be justified by the need to foster an environment conducive to discipline and learning. But *Breen v. Kahl*[163] held that a long hair regulation violated substantive Due Process, because hair is within the penumbra of privacy described in *Griswold v. Connecticut*[164] and the regulation violates human dignity, a basic value "implicit in the concept of ordered liberty." Though *Breen* stretches *Griswold* and *Palko*[165] very far, it seems a wise balancing of the interests involved. The disruptive effect of long hair on school discipline cannot be much greater than the disruptive effect of suspensions for what many students view as unjust cause, and the interest of male students in long hair may be more than whimsical, for social responses to long hair cause the issue to resolve itself for youths into the broad and fundamental question of whether one is to be a self-directing individual.[166]

In 1966, the Fifth Circuit faced two cases of suspensions of students from school for violating regulations against "freedom buttons," advocating equal rights for black people. It held in *Burnside v. Byars*[167] that the regulation was unconstitutional as an infringement upon the students' protected rights of free expression, but held in *Blackwell v. Issaquena Bd. of Educ.*[168] that the regulation was reasonable. The court distinguished the cases on the ground that in *Burnside,* the buttons caused only mild curiosity among non-wearers though the principal promulgating the regulation had predicted that they would cause com-

---

162. 269 F.Supp. 524 (D.C. La. 1067).
163. 37 U.S.L.W. 2506 (D.C.W. Wis. Feb. 20, 1969).
164. 381 U.S. 479 (1965).
165. Palko v. Connecticut, 302 U.S. 319 (1937).
166. L. Beggs, Huckleberry's For Runaways 67 (1969).
167. 363 F.2d 744 (1966).
168. 363 F.2d 749 (1966).

motion and difficulty in calling classes to order, while in *Blackwell,* button-wearers tried to pin buttons on to non-wearers against their will, were boisterous, disrespectful of teachers, and disruptive in class, and threw buttons through windows into classrooms when asked to leave. The pair of cases unequivocally assumes a right of free expression in students, independent of any religious issue, following Justice Jackson's theory in *Barnette.* They also clearly reject the traditional narrow scope of review, under which courts have sustained any school regulation unless convinced that it could have no reasonable connection with successful operation of the school.[169]

> It is not for us to consider whether such rules are wise or expedient but merely whether they are a reasonable exercise of the power and discretion of school authorities.
>
> Regulations which are essential in maintaining order and discipline on school property are reasonable.[170]

Under this test, the court apparently decides whether, as things turned out, the regulation was reasonable. *Burnside* appears to employ hindsight, for the principal's prediction of commotion was not groundless and would, if respected by the court, require an opposite conclusion. That a regulation must be "essential" and not merely "related" to preserving order is required by recognition of a constitutionally protected right of free expression in students; school officials

> cannot infringe on their students' rights to free and unrestricted expression as guaranteed to them under the First Amendment to the Constitution, where the exercise of such rights in the school buildings and schoolrooms do not materially and substantially interfere with the requirement of appropriate dicipline in the operation of the school.[171]

The *Burnside* reading of *Barnette* was tested in *Tinker v. Des Moines School Dist.*[172] School district officials, alerted to the plans of some students to wear black arm bands to school to protest the Vietnam war, issued a regulation prohibiting the wearing of arm bands on school facilities. The Tinker children wore black armbands though they knew of the regulation and were suspended. Some students made hostile remarks to the Tinkers outside class, but no threats, violence, or disruption

169. Leonard v. School Committee, 349 Mass. 704, 212 N.E.2d 468 (1965).
170. Burnside v. Byars, 363 F.2d 744, 748 (1966).
171. *Id.*, at 749.
172. _____U.S._____, 89 S.Ct. 733 (1969).

occurred.[173] The district court refused to enjoin enforcement of the regulation, on the ground that the school officials could reasonably predict that armbands would cause classroom disturbance, and rejected the *Burnside* rule against interfering with free expression by students unless there is material and substantial interference with discipline, in favor of a rule upholding school officials' actions reasonably calculated to prevent reasonably foreseeable disruption.[174] The Eighth Circuit divided equally, so affirmed without opinion.[175] The Supreme Court reversed, holding that the regulation unconstitutionally interfered with the students' right to free expression, because

> undifferentiated fear or apprehension of disturbance is not enough to overcome the right to freedom of expression.[176]

To prohibit pure speech, the school must at least satisfy the *Burnside* requirement of showing that the expression would " 'materially and substantially interfere with the requirements of appropriate discipline in the operation of the school.' "[177] The Court found this prohibition particularly suspect because the school officials had permitted students to wear political campaign buttons and the Iron Cross, so appeared to be singling out a particular opinion for exclusion from the school rather than attempting to avoid importation of all controversial opinion.[178]

Speaking more broadly, the Court held that students are "persons" under the Constitution, possessed of fundamental rights which the state must respect, so "state-operated schools may not be enclaves of totalitarianism."[179] The state may not conduct its schools so as to foster a homogeneous people,[180] and therefore it may not prohibit student expressions of opinion except where they materially disrupt classwork or involve substantial disorder or invasion of the rights of others.[181] Apparently, slight disruption does not justify intereference.

173. Justice Black's dissent disagrees with this statement of fact by the majority opinion.

174. Tinker v. Des Moines School Dist., 258 F.Supp. 971 (1966).

175. Tinker v. Des Moines School Dist. 383 F.2d 988 (1967).

176. Tinker v. Des Moines School Dist., ——— U.S. ———, ———, 89 S.Ct.733, 737 (1969) (Fortas, J.).

177. *Id.*, at 738.

178. *Id.*

179. *Id.*, at 738.

180. *Id.*, at 739.

181. *Id.*, at 740.

Justice Stewart concurred, but read the opinion as treating the first Amendment rights of children as coextensive with those of adults, inconsistently with other cases upholding differential First Amendment rights on the ground that children lack a full capacity for individual choice.[182] Justice White concurred, refusing to subscribe to all that *Burnside* held. Justice Black dissented vehemently, on the grounds that while loud and boisterous disruption did not occur, the armbands were shown to have diverted students' minds from school work to the Vietnam War, the right of free expression did not apply on school property, students' free expression rights were not so broad as adults, the Court's scope of review was overly broad, and the Court's opinion would tend to promote student insubordination and disorder.[183] Justice Harlan dissented on the narrower ground that school officials should have "the widest authority in maintaining discipline and good order," so complaints ought to be required to show that a regulation was issued for other than legitimate school concerns, such as a desire to prevent expression only of a particular point of view; he did not find the good faith of the school officials impugned by their failure to exclude political campaign buttons or Iron Crosses.[184]

Tinker may not bar regulation of all student conduct except where material interference with discipline would result; it distinguishes regulation of hair styles, clothes and deportment,[185] apparently on the theory that only specially protected constitutional rights and not all kinds of liberty are protected by the *Burnside* test from regulation. But where a student interest can claim constitutional protection, *Tinker* applies a broad scope of review and a stringent substantive test of the regulation. Though the Court purports to infer its conclusion largely from *Meyer v. Nebraska,*[186] that case struck down a restriction on the speech of teachers in a private school, not students in public schools. Other cases cited by the court, with the exception of *Barnette,* involve restrictions on the rights of parents, teachers,

182. *Id.,* at 741.
183. *Id.,* at 741-746.
184. *Id.,* at 747.
185. *Id.,* at 737.
186. 262 U.S.390 (1923).

or college students, or the Establishment Clause (not the Free Exercise Clause), rather than the rights of young students. Only *West Virginia v. Barnette*[187] is squarely in point, but in that case only three Justices relied on students' rights to secular free expression.

Though local school authorities may be expert, this does not justify the traditional narrow scope of review of their decisions rejected by *Tinker* because

> small and local authority may feel less sense of responsibility to the Constitution, and agencies of publicity may be less vigilant in calling it to accounts. . . . There are village tyrants as well as village Hampdens, but none who acts under the color of law is beyond reach of the Constitution.[188]

Tinker rejects the philosophical position that liberty for adults requires and justifies totalitarian control over children so that they may be socialized in norms and trained in skills which will contribute to political stability. This rejection appears to be educationally sound, for it is doubtful whether students can absorb and believe the libertarian ideas underlying our polity when they themselves are denied fundamental liberty during the very process of learning; the conduct of totalitarian schools speaks louder than the words of lecturers therein.[189]

4. INSULATION FROM DETRIMENTAL STIMULI

The scope of *Tinker* outside the context of schools remains unclear. The state has for many years sought to protect children from various kinds of environmental conditions to which adults have been free to subject themselves. In most states, a child may be removed from his parents if a court judges that they constitute a poor moral environment,[190] or if any stimuli in his environment create a danger that he will become "idle, dissolute, lewd, or immoral."[191] Such statutes apparently have their roots in English Poor Laws enabling churchwardens and overseers to seize and control children of the poor.[192] Unlike

---

187. 319 U.S. 624 (1943).

188. West Virginia Bd. of Educ. v. Barnette, 319 U.S. 624, 637-638 (1943) (Jackson, J.).

189. E. FRIEDENBERG, COMING OF AGE IN AMERICA 27-50 (1963).

190. *E.g.*, CAL. WELF. & INST. CODE § 600(b).

191. *E.g.*, CAL. WELF. & INST. CODE § 601.

192. Ten Broek, *California's Dual System of Family Law: Its Origin, Development, and Present Status*, 16 STAN. L. REV. 257, 279-80 (1964).

juvenile delinquency statutes, they do not relate to the conduct of the infant, so even if *Gault* strikes down the former where they do not apply also to adults, under the Equal Protection Clause,[193] it may not affect these neglect and poor moral environment statutes.[194] But such statutes may be void for vagueness or otherwise violative of Due Process because unreasonable.[195] A second common kind of statute controls the stimuli reaching infants by prohibiting the sale to them or purchase by persons under some age of alcohol,[196] cigarettes,[197] or pornography obtainable by adults.[198] One variety of the second kind of statute, a variable obscenity law, recently survived a constitutional challenge in *Ginsberg v. New York.*[199]

Ginsberg was found guilty of violating a criminal statute prohibiting the sale to persons under 17 of magazines depicting a prohibited degree of female nudity appealing to the prurient interest of minors, offensive to community standards of suitable literature for minors, and utterly without redeeming social importance for minors. The "girlie" magazines sold were not obscene by adult standards. The New York Supreme Court affirmed the conviction, and defendent was denied leave to appeal to the New York Court of Appeals.[200] He appealed to the Supreme Court of the United States on various grounds including the argument that the First Amendment right to read material concerned with sex could not depend on whether the reader was an adult or an infant, so the variable obscenity law, insofar as it deprived young persons of the opportunity to read materials available to older persons, unconstitutionally deprived

193. People v. Allen, 22 N.Y.2d 465, 293 N.Y.S.2d 280, N.E.2d 879, 880–881 attached (1968) (dictum).

194. *In re* Gault, 387 U.S. 1, 76–77 (1966) (Harlan, J., *concurring in part and dissenting in part*).

195. People *ex rel.* O'Connell v. Turner, 55 Ill. 280 (1870) holds unconstitutional a statute authorizing institutionalization of a child who is "destitute of proper parental care, and is growing up in mendicancy, ignorance, idleness and vice," partly on the ground that it interfered unconstitutionally with the child's own right to liberty in that it was vague and also that it unreasonably interfered with parental control.

196. ALAS. STAT. § 04.15.060, 04.15.080 (age 19).

197. ALAS. STAT. § 11.60.080 (age 18).

198. Ginsberg v. New York, 390 U.S. 629, 647-648 (1968) lists 36 state "variable obscenity" laws.

199. 390 U.S. 629 (1968).

200. *Id.*, at 633.

them of protected liberty.[201] The Court held that the statute under which defendant had been convicted did not interfere with infants' First Amendment rights because the Court could "say that it was not irrational for the legislature to find that exposure to material condemned by the statute is harmful to minors,"[202] and could not say that the variable obscenity statute "has no rational relation to the objective of safeguarding such minors from harm."[203] The Court held that state power to control children exceeds the scope of its authority with respect to adults because it has an independent interest in protecting children from whatever might prevent their growth into " 'free and independent well-developed men and citizens.' "[204] Alternatively, the Court justified variable obscenity laws on the grounds that

> The legislature could properly conclude that parents and others, teachers, for example, who have this primary responsibility for children's well-being are entitled to the support of laws designed to aid discharge of that responsibility.[205]

Justice Stewart concurred in the result, saying

> I think a state may permissibly determine that, at least in some precisely delineated areas, a child – like someone in a captive audience – is not possessed of that full capacity for individual choice which is the presupposition of First Amendment guarantees.[206]

Justices Black and Douglas dissented on the grounds that the First Amendment protected obscenity as well as other forms of speech, so that the substantive Due Process "reasonableness" standard of review could not properly be applied.[207] Justice Fortas dissented on the grounds that, while the state could differentiate between literature saleable to adults and literature saleable to children, this power could not be used arbitarily, and obscenity had to be determined by a more particularized analysis of the publication than had been applied, especially where there was no pandering in the sale.[208] He criticized the

---

201. *Id.*, at 636.
202. *Id.*, at 641.
203. *Id.*, at 643.
204. *Id.*, at 638-641.
205. *Id.*, at 639.
206. *Id.*, at 649-650.
207. *Id.*, at 650-656.
208. *Id.*, at 671-675.

length to which the court had carried the state's independent interest in the welfare of the child for giving

> the State a role in the rearing of children which is contrary to our traditions and to our conception of family responsibility.[209]

The *Ginsberg* case relies upon *Prince v. Massachusettes*[210] for the propositions that the state may control the conduct of children beyond the scope of permissible control upon adults, and that any rational control upon children is constitutionally permissible. *Prince* upheld the conviction of a Jehovah's Witness under a child labor act for permitting a child in her custody to sell religious literature with her, and said that society had an independent interest in protecting children so that they would become fit citizens, and therefore had broader authority over children's activities than adults.[211] But *Prince* explicitly refused to go so far as to countenance any limitation upon children in the name of their welfare. It is distinguishable from *Ginsberg* on the grounds that the infant involved in *Prince,* a girl of 9, was less able to choose for herself than the 16 year old boy involved in *Ginsberg,* and therefore the Free Exercise argument on behalf of the little girl was rejected more on the facts, her inability to participate in meaningful Free Exercise, than on a theory that infants were not entitled to Free Exercise. *Prince* may be better explained as a limitation upon parental rights to harm their children than as a restriction on children's rights. This reading of *Prince* finds support in its famous lines:

> Parents may be free to become martyrs themselves. But it does not follow that they are free, in identical circumstances, to make martyrs of their children before they have reached the age of full and legal discretion when they can make that choice for themselves.[212]

Ginsberg's reliance on *Prince* also seems dubious because *Prince* relies for its theory of an independent state interest in making children good citizens upon the broad doctrine of *parens patriae*[213] since rejected by *Gault;* at least, the Court ought in *Ginsberg* to have explained how much of *parens*

---

209. *Id.*, at 674.
210. 321 U.S. 158 (1944).
211. *Id.*, at 171.
212. *Id.*, at 170.
213. *Id.*, at 166-167.

patriae was consistent with the rejection of one traditional application of it in *Gault*.

Ginsberg does not explain why it applies so narrow a scope of review as rationality for variable obscenity legislation. The objection to this standard on the ground that expression was at stake by Justices Black and Douglas, seems more consistent with the traditional scope of review in obscenity cases. Nor does the court explain how it can find that the statute validly prohibited sale of the magazines without looking at them to see whether they satisfied the statutory and constitutional standards required even for censorship of children's reading. The narrow scope of review also fails to square with the usual broader review where the burden of a regulation falls mainly on a group not permitted to participate in the political process. Variable obscenity laws may be good policy, but the proposition that children's reading may or should be censored more than adults' reading hardly implies that any censorship not patently unreasonable should be permitted, which is what *Ginsberg* seems to hold.

Ginsberg appears to be sharply limited by *Tinker*. The majority opinion in *Tinker* by Justice Fortas, who dissented in *Ginsberg*, does not cite *Ginsberg* and does not distinguish its proposition that the state may regulate the First Amendment rights of infants more than those of adults; rather, it applies a broad scope of review to a limitation upon students' free expression in school, requiring considerably more justification for a regulation than that it not be unreasonable. Justice Stewart read the *Tinker* majority opinion as treating childrens' and adults' First Amendment rights as coextensive, and found this assumption inconsistent with *Ginsberg*.[214] Distinctions between the cases cut both ways. On the one hand, the *Tinker* restriction was a mere administrative regulation while the *Ginsberg* restriction was a state statute; obscenity may merit less protection than political speech; and the right to buy may be less important than the right to speak.[215] On the other hand, the restriction struck down

214. Tinker v. Des Moines School Dist., ———— U.S. ————, 89 S.Ct. 733, 741 (1969) (Stewart J., concurring).

215. The right to buy literature perhaps is of lesser importance now that the right to read it has been distinguished and given greater protection in Stanley v. Georgia, ———— U.S. ————, 37 U.S.L.W. 4315 (April 7, 1969).

in *Tinker* applied only to the infants' hours in school, where the state presumably could properly compel them to go primarily to study prescribed curricula rather than to express their political views, while the restriction upheld in *Ginsberg* applied at all hours of the day to prohibit young persons from buying "girlie" magazines, for no ultimate purpose except to keep them from seeing what was in them.

Conclusion

Infants have lacked adequate representation both in the legislative and in the adjudicative processes. These denials of representation have not been the product of doctrine. While the theory of *parens patriae* has been blamed for the failure of the juvenile court system to appoint lawyers for infants charged with delinquency, a broader survey of infants' law shows that *parens patriae* has in many contexts improved representation. Exclusion of infants from the representation by which adults secure and protect their rights appears to have no coherent philosophical foundation. Deferral of the right to vote until long after the age of political maturity may rest partly on the evolution of 21 as the age of majority centuries before contemporary democratic norms developed, partly upon questionable empirical propositions about the age of political maturity, and partly upon the reluctance of persons over 21 to share power with youths whose interests conflict with theirs. Inadequacy of legal representation of infants appears to be attributable to their lack of money, the insensitivity of the bar and trial court judges to conflicts of interest where parents proceed against infants and the same lawyer serves both sides, and infants' ignorance of their need for or the avaliability of legal assistance.

English and American courts and legislatures have shared a common philosophy of the status of infants for centuries. Though accretion and erosion have at various times changed this stream of thought, its content has always flowed from very ancient ideas most discoverable in the works of Aristotle. Below some age it has always been thought that persons lack the competence to care for themselves, so others ought to protect and nurture them. This duty has generally been lodged primarily in their parents because of the natural affection between children and parents, a belief that parents have some natural right to the control of their children, and perhaps a tendency long in the past to minimize the number and scope of governmental activities.

But society has rarely or never left parents entirely on their own in the matter of child rearing. The state has intervened, sometimes to protect children from undesirable parental conduct, sometimes to compel obedience to parents, and sometimes to compel submission by the infant to some duty imposed upon him by the state. Intervention has been explained by the doctrine of *parens patriae,* which includes two distinguishable ideas: the state ought to protect all who cannot protect themselves, and this duty requires protection of infants from their parents and others who may harm them; the state may compel infants and their parents to act in ways most beneficial to society. These ideas cannot be reconciled where the aggressor against the infant is the state, and *Gault* and *Tinker* suggest that in such conflicts, the law may compel more respect for the former notion than it has received during the past few decades.

The original doctrine of *parens patriae,* a duty upon the state to protect infants from all who would harm them, suggests many reforms in the law of infants, some of which have been advocated in the previous chapters. But some injustice to infants probably can survive any reform. Infants, especially young children, are weak, ignorant, and incompetent. These qualities are why the law treats infants as a special class. Characteristically, when the weak, ignorant and incompetent clash with the strong, clever and able, the former lose. The law can handicap the strong and gird the weak, but it cannot change their natures. The clever find ways to untie ropes that bind them, and the incompetent use their weapons inefficiently. The clash cannot be replaced by a neutral process of judgment by a third party; the history of the juvenile court system illustrates that where the interests of infants and others clash, attempts to reconcile the interests merely paper over the clash, so tend to become mere pretenses for oppressing infants. While much reform ought to be made, no reform should eliminate the unease which a powerful legal system ought to feel when it operates upon the weak.

CHILDREN AND YOUTH
Social Problems and Social Policy

An Arno Press Collection

Abt, Henry Edward. **The Care, Cure and Education of the Crippled Child.** 1924

Addams, Jane. **My Friend, Julia Lathrop.** 1935

American Academy of Pediatrics. **Child Health Services and Pediatric Education:** Report of the Committee for the Study of Child Health Services. 1949

American Association for the Study and Prevention of Infant Mortality. **Transactions of the First Annual Meeting of the American Association for the Study and Prevention of Infant Mortality.** 1910

Baker, S. Josephine. **Fighting For Life.** 1939

Bell, Howard M. **Youth Tell Their Story:** A Study of the Conditions and Attitudes of Young People in Maryland Between the Ages of 16 and 24. 1938

Bossard, James H. S. and Eleanor S. Boll, editors. **Adolescents in Wartime.** 1944

Bossard, James H. S., editor. **Children in a Depression Decade.** 1940

Brunner, Edmund DeS. **Working With Rural Youth.** 1942

Burns, Eveline M., editor. **Children's Allowances and the Economic Welfare of Children:** The Report of a Conference. 1968

Care of Dependent Children in the Late Nineteenth and Early Twentieth Centuries. Introduction by Robert H. Bremner. 1974

Care of Handicapped Children. Introduction by Robert H. Bremner. 1974

[Chenery, William L. and Ella A. Merritt, editors]. **Standards of Child Welfare:** A Report of the Children's Bureau Conferences, May and June, 1919. 1919

The Child Labor Bulletin, 1912, 1913. 1974

Children In Confinement. Introduction by Robert M. Mennel. 1974

Children's Bureau Studies. Introduction by William M. Schmidt. 1974

Clopper, Edward N. **Child Labor in City Streets.** 1912

David, Paul T. **Barriers To Youth Employment.** 1942

Deutsch, Albert. **Our Rejected Children.** 1950

Drucker, Saul and Maurice Beck Hexter. **Children Astray.** 1923

Duffus, R[obert] L[uther] and L. Emmett Holt, Jr. **L. Emmett Holt:** Pioneer of a Children's Century. 1940

Fuller, Raymond G. **Child Labor and the Constitution.** 1923

Holland, Kenneth and Frank Ernest Hill. **Youth in the CCC.** 1942

Jacoby, George Paul. **Catholic Child Care in Nineteenth Century New York:** With a Correlated Summary of Public and Protestant Child Welfare. 1941

Johnson, Palmer O. and Oswald L. Harvey. **The National Youth Administration.** 1938

The Juvenile Court. Introduction by Robert M. Mennel. 1974

Klein, Earl E. **Work Accidents to Minors in Illinois.** 1938

Lane, Francis E. **American Charities and the Child of the Immigrant:** A Study of Typical Child Caring Institutions in New York and Massachusetts Between the Years 1845 and 1880. 1932

The Legal Rights of Children. Introduction by Sanford N. Katz. 1974

Letchworth, William P[ryor]. **Homes of Homeless Children:** A Report on Orphan Asylums and Other Institutions for the Care of Children. [1903]

Lorwin, Lewis. **Youth Work Programs:** Problems and Policies. 1941

Lundberg, Emma O[ctavia] and Katharine F. Lenroot. **Illegitimacy As A Child-Welfare Problem, Parts 1 and 2.** 1920/1921

New York State Commission on Relief for Widowed Mothers. **Report of the New York State Commission on Relief for Widowed Mothers.** 1914

Otey, Elizabeth Lewis. **The Beginnings of Child Labor Legislation in Certain States;** A Comparative Study. 1910

Phillips, Wilbur C. **Adventuring For Democracy.** 1940

Polier, Justine Wise. **Everyone's Children, Nobody's Child:** A Judge Looks At Underprivileged Children in the United States. 1941

Proceedings of the Annual Meeting of the National Child Labor Committee, 1905, 1906. 1974

Rainey, Homer P. **How Fare American Youth?** 1940

Reeder, Rudolph R. **How Two Hundred Children Live and Learn.** 1910

Security and Services For Children. 1974

Sinai, Nathan and Odin W. Anderson. **EMIC (Emergency Maternity and Infant Care):** A Study of Administrative Experience. 1948

Slingerland, W. H. **Child-Placing in Families:** A Manual For Students and Social Workers. 1919

[Solenberger], Edith Reeves. **Care and Education of Crippled Children in the United States.** 1914

Spencer, Anna Garlin and Charles Wesley Birtwell, editors. **The Care of Dependent, Neglected and Wayward Children:** Being a Report of the Second Section of the International Congress of Charities, Correction and Philanthropy, Chicago, June, 1893. 1894

Theis, Sophie Van Senden. **How Foster Children Turn Out.** 1924

Thurston, Henry W. **The Dependent Child:** A Story of Changing Aims and Methods in the Care of Dependent Children. 1930

U.S. Advisory Committee on Education. **Report of the Committee, February, 1938.** 1938

The United States Children's Bureau, 1912-1972. 1974

White House Conference on Child Health and Protection. **Dependent and Neglected Children:** Report of the Committee on Socially Handicapped — Dependency and Neglect. 1933

White House Conference on Child Health and Protection. **Organization for the Care of Handicapped Children, National, State, Local.** 1932

White House Conference on Children in a Democracy. **Final Report of the White House Conference on Children in A Democracy.** [1942]

Wilson, Otto. **Fifty Years' Work With Girls, 1883-1933:** A Story of the Florence Crittenton Homes. 1933

Wrenn, C. Gilbert and D. L. Harley. **Time On Their Hands:** A Report on Leisure, Recreation, and Young People. 1941